# Springer Series in Behavior Modification
## THEORY / RESEARCH / APPLICATION

Cyril M. Franks / Series Editor

Volume 1
## Multimodal Behavior Therapy
Arnold A. Lazarus

Volume 2
## Behavior-Therapy Assessment
Eric J. Mash and Leif G. Terdal, editors

**Eric J. Mash** is associate professor in the Psychology Department of the University of Calgary, in Canada. A graduate of the City University of New York who received his Ph.D. from Florida State University, Dr. Mash was a USPHS-sponsored research fellow and is currently a Canada Council Leave Fellow and Visiting Associate Professor of Medical Psychology at the University of Oregon Health Sciences Center. He also draws on a varied background of psychological service in the United States and Canada. His publications include numerous articles and books, among them *Behavior Change: Methodology, Concepts, Practice; Behavior Modification and Families;* and *Behavior Modification Approaches to Parenting.*

**Leif G. Terdal** is on the faculty of the University of Oregon Health Sciences Center, where he is associate professor of medical psychology in the Crippled Children's Division. As part of an interdisciplinary team, he is also currently engaged in providing internship training as well as providing psychological service and consultation in a university-affiliated mental retardation center. Dr. Terdal received his Ph.D. from Michigan State University and is a frequent contributor to professional periodicals and books, particularly in connection with handicapped children.

# Behavior-Therapy Assessment

## Diagnosis, Design, and Evaluation

*Edited by*

*ERIC J. MASH*
*and*
*LEIF G. TERDAL*

SPRINGER PUBLISHING COMPANY, New York

Springer Publishing Company, Inc.
200 Park Avenue South
New York, N.Y. 10003

76 77 78 79 80 / 10 9 8 7 6 5 4 3 2 1

**Library of Congress Cataloging in Publication Data**

Main entry under title:

Behavior-therapy assessment.

    (Springer series in behavior modification)
    Includes bibliographical references and index.
    1. Behavior modification.  2. Personality
assessment. I. Mash, Eric J.  II. Terdal, Leif, G.,
1937—   [DNLM: 1. Behavior therapy.  WM420 B4175]
BF637.B4B445         616.8'914         76-15618
ISBN 0-8261-1930-1

Printed in the United States of America

*To*

*Abe and Mary Mash     Alf and Harriet Terdal*

# Contents

# Foreword

Since behavior therapy and behavioral assessment are part of one and the same process, we might expect that the direct treatment of maladaptive behavior by techniques derived specifically from social learning theory, or more generally from experimental psychology and psychiatry, would of necessity have engendered correspondingly new approaches to diagnosis and assessment. Regrettably, despite all the creative innovations that have marked the development of behavior therapy in recent years, the assessment of its outcomes remains relatively neglected. The conceptual sophistication and scientific rigor characterizing behavior therapy are lacking in behavioral assessment; as late as 1970, some behavior therapists were writing books and articles seriously advocating projective techniques as appropriate pretherapy assessment procedures.

A suitable model of behavioral assessment would have to discard prevailing psychiatric classification systems, rooted as they are in the psychodynamic symptoms-disease model and its futile attempts to categorize patients according to different and questionable psychopathological entities. As we now know, assigning patients to traditional diagnostic categories is neither reliable nor predictive with respect to response or treatment, or to the form treatment should take.

Traditionally, personality assessment has engaged in making remote inferences about putative underlying processes, to the neglect of behavior, cognition, and affect themselves. Behavior is interpreted symbolically in terms of deep-seated, general traits, even though the assumption that people possess enduring and general personality traits has been seriously questioned. (It is, of course, possible to work within a factor-analytic trait theory framework firmly anchored to operationally defined variables without recourse to speculative and mentalistic underlying processes.)

Assessment and continuous monitoring of the process of change are essential to the behavior-therapy model; hence, behavior therapists need to develop strategies of assessment capable of identifying the environmental variables—internal as well as external, self-imposed as well as imposed by others—that are currently maintaining the individual's maladaptive thoughts, feelings, and behavior. This requires analyzing both the specific environmental events controlling the maladaptive response repertoire and the broader social learning and biological histories that are mediating or otherwise influencing the ways in which the environment modifies the behavior.

Clearly, then, traditional methods of assessment—the clinical interview, the case history, psychological testing—have to be supplanted or, at the very least, drastically adapted if they are to answer the sort of questions the behavior therapist asks about antecedent stimuli and response consequences. Unfortunately, remarkably few behavioral clinicians have concerned themselves with developing the necessary techniques; only within the past few years has the literature even begun to reflect a concern with such issues.

To think in these terms, the clinical psychologist must radically alter both concepts and role. First, he must replace an isolated and rigid set of procedures, derived from an invariant system or school of psychotherapy, with an open-minded, flexible set of guiding principles. A priori clinical assumptions have to be replaced by empirically validated relationships of demonstrable predictive utility. Second, he must come to view assessment not merely as a precursor to therapy—the customary role of traditional testing—but as an ongoing process interwoven with the process of therapy itself. Third, the clinical psychologist must come to see himself not as a team member performing circumscribed tasks, first testing and then therapy, but rather as a professional for whom assessment and intervention are intrinsically integrated.

Within this context, Mash and Terdal have performed a signal service, assembling under one cover the best that modern behavioral assessment has to offer. They cast their net wide, covering a variety of clinical and other settings, a diversity of problems, and a broad range of populations.

In addition to the admirable choice of papers, the editors' own input is considerable, and it is this that makes their work uniquely valuable. Eric J. Mash and Leif G. Terdal provide a scholarly and far-reaching introduction and conceptual framework that set the stage for what follows. Astute comments precede the various sections, neatly complementing the Introduction and placing the various papers squarely in context.

Unlike much of the literature presently available, *Behavior-Therapy Assessment* is not a rehash of hackneyed procedures, a book to be put on the shelf and forgotten. More than a compendium of techniques, it is a comprehensive reference work in behavior therapy and a source of guidance to assessment. For the professional whose theoretical identification is not primarily behavioral, this book offers a rich source of new clinical and research tactics. It will reassure him that behavioral assessment involves much more than the naive evaluation of overt motor behavior. Increasingly, behavior therapists talk to their patients. They are concerned with what their patients say they have done or would have done in a particular situation, and not exclusively with what they actually do. Similarly, the patient's beliefs, values, and feelings are viewed as important sets of data that cannot be ignored. It remains the responsibility of the behavior therapist to resolve the many conceptual and technical problems of validation and reliablity which, as far as behavioral assessment is concerned, are still with us.

This volume will help greatly to resolve such problems, because it suggests how a vast array of techniques and fresh approaches may be integrated into the armamentaria of the behavioral clinician and research investigator alike. Professors Mash and Terdal are to be congratulated for their foresight and for the systematic way they have contributed to this goal.

·Cyril M. Franks

# Preface

During the past decade there has been a clear and persistent acceleration in the use of behavior-therapy procedures. At the same time, traditional psychiatric and psychological assessment approaches have come under severe attack from many quarters. In this context of rapid change in both theory and therapeutic approaches, a number of significant developments and contributions have been made in the area of behavior-therapy assessment. A wide range of assessment procedures now employ a functional analysis of behavior.

There have been few systematic attempts to integrate and bring together some of these newer assessment approaches. Our goal in compiling this book is to provide a systematic organization and framework for current and future developments in the area of behavior-therapy assessment. We have attempted to present both theoretical concerns related to a range of assessment issues and examples of assessment procedures that should be of value to researchers and practitioners.

We hope that this book will prove appropriate for use in assessment and behavior-modification courses at both the undergraduate and graduate levels, in areas such as psychology, education, counseling, social welfare, and medicine, and, in addition, that it will satisfy a need in applied settings and training programs for those who wish to introduce new assessment procedures.

The assessment procedures described in this book have demonstrated their utility across a range of clinical settings including schools, outpatient clinics, medical schools, hospitals, and other institutional settings. In addition, the procedures have applicability to a range of populations including children and adults and to a range of problems including alcoholism, assertiveness, fears, delinquent behaviors, parent-child conflicts, marital relations, depressions, anxieties, and social competencies.

We would like to extend our thanks to the many colleagues and students who have served as a source of stimulation and encouragement for our work. Among these, two individuals stand out as deserving our special gratitude: Ann Garner, whose clear conceptual thinking, together with her continuing willingness to discuss, share, and elaborate ideas has been a continuing source of support for us both; and Charles Costello, for his valuable feedback during the preparation of this volume and for his constant encouragement as a colleague and friend.

We would like to thank others who in different ways have contributed to our work: Russell Jackson, Constance Hanf, Beth Baker, and John McElwee, and Drs. Victor Menashe and LeRoy Carlson for their administrative assistance. Much of the preparation for this volume was supported by Canada Council Grants S72-0461 and S70-1567 to Eric Mash, who gratefully acknowledges this research support. The secretarial help of Elfrieda Koch and Vi Biden have been instrumental in the completion of this volume. We express our thanks to the contributors of this volume for permission to reproduce their work.

Finally, we thank our families, Heather, Marge, Erik, and Paul, and the bar at Garibaldi—which never got crossed.

# Contributors

Kathryn A. Anderson
*City Hospital Mental Health Center*
*Meadville, Pennsylvania*

Donald M. Baer
*University of Kansas*

Sheila Bastien
*West Virginia University*

Donald N. Bersoff
*University of Georgia*

Joseph R. Cautela
*Boston College*

Paul W. Clement
*Fuller Theological Seminary*
*Pasadena, California*

Joseph A. Cobb
*(1933-1972)*

Marvin F. Daley
*Plymouth State Home and Training*
*School, Plymouth, Michigan*

James S. DeLo
*West Virginia University*

Ronald Friend
*University of Toronto, Canada*

John P. Galassi
*University of North Carolina*

Merna D. Galassi
*West Virginia University*

James H. Geer
*State University of New York*
*Stony Brook*

Marvin R. Goldfried
*State University of New York*
*Stony Brook*

Jesse W. Hawk, Jr.
*Georgia Regional Hospital*
*Augusta, Georgia*

Cornelius J. Holland
*University of Windsor, Canada*

Frederick H. Kanfer
*University of Illinois*

Robert J. Kastenbaum
*University of Massachusetts*

Alan E. Kazdin
*Pennsylvania State University*

Ronald N. Kent
*State University of New York
Stony Brook*

Edward S. Kubany
*University of Hawaii*

Peter M. Lewinsohn
*University of Oregon*

Marian MacDonald
*State University of New York
Stony Brook*

G. Alan Marlatt
*University of Washington*

Eric J. Mash
*University of Calgary, Canada*

John D. McElwee
*University of Calgary, Canada*

Jesse B. Milby, Jr.
*University of Alabama School of
Medicine*

Dale Moyer
*University of Georgia*

Roberta S. Ray
*University of Wisconsin*

Robert C. Richard
*Walnut Creek, California*

Todd R. Risley
*University of Kansas*

George Saslow
*Sepulveda Veterans Administration
Hospital, Sepulveda, California*

Barbara B. Sloggett
*University of Hawaii*

Freida Stuart
*New York, New York*

Richard B. Stuart
*Weight Watchers International
New York, New York*

Leif G. Terdal
*University of Oregon Health Sciences
Center*

David Watson
*University of Hawaii*

Kathy Whitfield
*University of Alabama*

Herman C. Willcutt
*University of Alabama School of
Medicine*

Montrose M. Wolf
*University of Kansas*

Joseph Wolpe
*Temple University School of Medicine*

# INTRODUCTION

The recent and rapid development and application of behavior-modification procedures has been extensively described and documented (Bandura, 1969, 1974; Franks, 1969; Franks & Wilson, 1973, 1974, 1975; Kanfer & Phillips, 1970; Lazarus, 1971; O'Leary & Wilson, 1975; Rimm & Masters, 1974; Wolpe, 1973; Yates, 1970). These developments have resulted in an increasing use of behavior-modification techniques by individuals with an increasingly wide range of training and backgrounds, in an increasing number of situations, for a greater variety of problems, and with a greater range of populations (Goldiamond, 1974). While some form of assessment has been an integral part of these applications, the nature of the assessment procedures used has been highly diverse and idiosyncratic. In fact, as the heterogeneity of procedures and techniques encompassed under a behavior-therapy rubric has increased, so has the heterogeneity of assessment efforts. The lack of consistency in the assessment approaches taken by behavioral practitioners and researchers was clearly evident in a report by Kanfer (1972) in which a survey of leading behavior modifiers revealed a remarkable absence of consistency or standardization in the types of assessment procedures that were being employed.

In spite of the fact that behaviorally oriented individuals have placed assessment issues in a central role (Johnson & Bolstad, 1973), the emphasis given to treatment issues in the literature seems much greater and quite disproportionate when compared to the amount of information available on questions related to assessment. That this imbalance has been recognized is shown by the fact that recent projections of future developments in the behavior-therapy area have frequently indicated the importance of assessment and issues relating to taxonomy and diagnosis (Kanfer & Grimm, 1975). This relative lack of attention to systematic treatments of behavioral assessment, as well as the idiosyncratic approach described above, has served as a primary impetus for this book.

There are also a number of commonalities that would support the elaboration and development of the area of behavioral assessment as a unitary one, which is both related to, yet distinct from, other approaches to clinical assessment. Unquestionably, several assessment themes have been evident at both a conceptual and pragmatic level.

The major conceptual focus (to be discussed in Part I) has been provided by those theories of personality that have taken as their major unit of analysis the behavior of individuals in relation to specific situational variables (Mischel, 1968, 1973; Wallace, 1966, 1967). Another related conceptual focus has been supplied by the approaches to abnormal behavior that have viewed deviancy in terms of quantitative variations of behavior and context rather than in terms of absolute qualitative categories (Bandura, 1969). These social learning views have emphasized the notion that deviancy represents a social labeling process following from behavioral occurrences that are either deficient, excessive, or situationally inappropriate, in contrast to behavioral occurrences that are qualitatively different from individual to individual (Kanfer & Saslow, 1965, 1969). These conceptualizations of personality and abnormality have provided specific directions for the type of assessment information that is viewed as most relevant for treatment.

Pragmatic issues stemming from changes in the role of the clinical psychologist have provided another recurrent theme. For the most part, behavior therapists have shared a common view regarding the role definition of what a clinical psychologist is, which is quite different from, and at times even impatient with, previous role models. One major difference has been the outright rejection of the psychometrician role, which designated the psychologist as an assessment specialist who might function quite separately from the treatment process. The outcome of this role was to create a lacuna between clinical assessment and treatment. Dissatisfaction with this role has served to foster the viewpoint of assessment as being an integral and integrated component of treatment. A behavioral position, then, sees assessment not as a static process resulting in a typological or nosological outcome (Peterson, 1968) but rather as a process having as its major goal the generation of information that can be utilized in the development of behavior-change programs. The sine qua non of behavior-therapy assessment is that it be functional.

These conceptual and pragmatic foci have begged the question in terms of the need for clear statements and organization of behavior-therapy assessment assumptions, principles, and procedures. Such initial and tentative statements are beginning to appear (Bersoff, 1971, 1973; Bijou & Peterson, 1971; Cautela, 1968; Ellett & Bersoff, 1973; Goldfried & Kent, 1972; Goldfried & Pomeranz, 1968; Goldfried &

Sprafkin, 1974; Jenkins, 1971; Kanfer, 1972; Krasner, 1969; Mash & Terdal, 1974; Wolff & Merrens, 1974). Nowhere has this need for organization become more evident than in the context of undergraduate, graduate, and postgraduate behavioral training programs that attempt to provide an assessment focus that rejects traditional formal testing as the major assessment alternative and in turn offers a curriculum based upon the conceptual and pragmatic consistencies described above (Evans & Nelson, 1974; Ross, 1974).

Given the above considerations, our purposes in this book are as follows:

1. To provide a consistent conceptual framework for behavior-therapy assessment, based upon the three interrelated processes of problem diagnosis, treatment design, and outcome evaluation. This categorization stems from the unitary and functional view of the assessment process as purposive, and attempts to designate varying but related purposes within the assessment-treatment enterprise. It is hoped that such a framework may serve as a basis for development of taxonomies of assessment principles and procedures that have grown out of assessment approaches having similar ends or objectives.

2. Within this framework to bring together a variety of representative behavior-therapy assessment instruments that reflect the current development of the field. We make clear at the outset that the procedures presented in this volume are intended to be illustrative rather than inclusive. This decision is dictated both by practical limitations and by our view of behavior-therapy assessment as a developing field currently in greater need of conceptual and procedural clarification and development than of a final statement or definition. Our hope, then, is that the procedures we have selected will point out some of the strengths and deficits in the area and provide an impetus for the development of more sophisticated behavioral measures. Such sophistication presumably would include traditional assessment concerns dealing with reliability, validity, objectivity, normative data, and utility (Kanfer, 1972).

## ORGANIZATION OF THE BOOK

The book is broadly organized into two major sections. The first, consisting of Part I, presents a selection of papers dealing with some of the broader conceptual issues and assumptions for behavior-therapy assessment. The second section, consisting of Parts II–V, is oriented toward application and includes descriptions of a number of specific behavior-therapy assessment techniques and procedures. It is intended that Part I give added meaning to the rest of the book, which in turn should serve as a source of feedback to aid in evaluating some of the conceptualizations provided by the papers in Part I.

The papers in Part I are presented to illustrate a number of points. Initially, the conceptualization of behavior-therapy assessment as involving diagnosis, design, and evaluation receives elaboration and a broad definition of the field is given (Mash & Terdal, paper 1). Assessment is related to the social learning conceptualization of personality, as well as to a reconceptualization that has come to include a greater consideration of the role of cognitive mediating variables (Mischel, 1973). Some of the major assumptions underlying behavioral assessment procedures are then presented, and these are contrasted with the differing assumptions characteristic of the more traditional approaches to psychological assessment (Goldfried & Kent, paper 2). Behavior-therapy assessment is then placed within the broader treatment context of applied behavior analysis (Baer, Wolf, & Risley, paper 3), the emphasis here being on the interrelationship between assessment information and the implementation and evaluation of behavior-change programs. As such, the "dimensions," goals, and strategies of behavioral treatment have direct implications for issues relating to assessment. Finally, there is additional recognition of the view that a major defining characteristic of behavior modification is its stress on careful and systematic procedural specification and evaluation of treatment outcome (Kazdin, paper 4). As such, evaluative behavior-therapy assessment, including both measurement and design considerations, is viewed as being of primary importance. It should be noted that such a view is quite consistent with definitions of behavior modification that emphasize the application of experimentally based findings to clinical problems and situations (Davison & Taffel, 1972; Mahoney, Kazdin, & Lesswing, 1974).

The remainder of the book, which deals with the techniques of behavior-therapy assessment, includes four parts: (II) behavioral interviewing, (III) self-report measures, (IV) assessment for potential reinforcers, and (V) observational assessment. The sequence of topics and selections within these parts is intended to reflect a differing emphasis on different types of procedures as one goes through the successive stages of problem diagnosis, treatment design, and outcome evaluation. So, for example, early stages of the assessment process likely will rely upon interview-verbal report information, whereas later assessments concerned with evaluation of treatment outcome, while remaining concerned with verbal report measures, will also be likely to involve some attempts at direct observational assessment. Intermediate stages of assessment concerned with the development of treatment programs may have a greater emphasis on assessments for identifying potential reinforcers. It should be recognized that these stages are not intended to be mutually exclusive or independent. While recognizing the dynamic properties of this triadic categorization, it is believed that it is also conceptually and practically useful to examine the assessment process from a sequential perspective.

It should also be noted that the sequential arrangement of papers reflects a general trend toward the use of more highly structured assessment instruments as one moves through the successive phases of assessment. So, for example, we go from some loosely defined guidelines for behavioral interviewing during the diagnosis phase to some highly structured direct observational procedures during the evaluation phase. Again, however, it should be recognized that the assessment process is dynamic rather than sequential and that there are several exceptions to this general trend.

The dynamic view of behavior-therapy assessment is clearly evident in the approaches that have attempted to use multiple outcome measures in evaluating treatment effectiveness (Brady, 1971; Johnson & Bolstad, 1973; Tavormina, 1975). In this regard, we note that several different types of measures (e.g., verbal report and observation) are being employed within the same treatment phase. Nevertheless, it does appear that certain types of assessment procedures tend to be *more* characteristic of a particular phase.

Within each part, an attempt is also made to present procedures that are applicable across a wide range of assessment and treatment situations and populations. Instruments are presented for assessing both child and adult problems, and for assessing behavior in a wide range of settings including clinic, classroom, and home.

# Part I

A Framework for Behavior-Therapy Assessment: Theory, Assumptions, and Strategies

The papers in Part I are intended to provide an overview of some of the major assumptions underlying the use of behavior-therapy assessment procedures. These assumptions fall into two broad categories: those relating to a social-learning conceptualization of human behavior and those relating to the central position given to an empirical approach to behavior-modification practice. It is believed that the elaboration of assumptions provided in these papers offers a consistent and heuristic base from which to consider the procedural developments described in subsequent parts.

The first paper, by the editors, serves as a general introduction to behavior-therapy assessment and offers a tentative definition of the area by delineating some of the features that have generally characterized this approach to clinical and personality assessment (Bersoff, 1971, 1973, 1974; Bijou & Peterson, 1971; Golfried & Pomeranz, 1968; Goldfried & Sprafkin, 1974; Kanfer, 1972; Mischel, 1968; O'Leary, 1973; Peterson, 1968), in contrast to some of the more "traditional" alternatives (Allport, 1937; Bem & Allen, 1974; Bowers, 1973; Goldberg, 1971; Goodenough, 1949).

This paper by Mash and Terdal emphasizes the importance of considering the functional properties or utility of behavior-therapy assessments and considers the major purposes of problem diagnosis, treatment design, and outcome evaluation as outlined in the introduction. In addition, a major point concerns the need for consideration of reliability and validity questions in relation to these prescribed purposes. Most behavioral studies dealing with such questions (e.g., Johnson & Bolstad, 1973) have posed them primarily in terms of the quality of data —for example, with respect to the reliability of data collected through the use of direct observational procedures (e.g., see Part V), or in terms of correlations between information obtained through differing measures such as verbal report and direct observation (e.g., convergent validity). It is suggested in this first paper that while these types of reliability and validity information are both necessary and important, it is also necessary to examine more generally the reliability of behavioral assessment as a way of describing and identifying some of the more specific process variables involved. Hence, it becomes important to examine the degree to which similar assessment information consistently results in similar decisions relating to the selection of treatment targets, design of treatment programs, and development of schemes for evaluating treatment outcomes.

Behavioral assessment represents an extension of the social-learning reconceptualization of personality, as presented by Walter Mischel (1968, 1973). Mischel has developed and elaborated the implications of this approach to personality for clinical assessment, emphasizing the importance of examining behavior in relation to the conditions under which it occurs. A major assessment challenge that has emerged from the ideas presented by Mischel (1973) relates to the way in which one conceptualizes these contextual events for behavior.

There are several levels at which one may consider situational determinants from an assessment perspective. Mischel (1973) points out that at the most primitive level of assessment there is no regard for contextual events. The fact that this has often been the rule rather than the exception in personality and clinical assessment is evidenced by the existence of a large number of tests designed to measure dispositions and a relative absence of measures for describing situations. Even those investigators and clinicians who have rejected a dispositional approach to behavior have tended to treat situation variables in a relatively unsophisticated way.

Consequently, many behavioral studies have described behavior in relation to situational variables that are often globally and sometimes naively formulated. An example here would be to describe a situation as "home" or "classroom," without any systematic attempt to elaborate on the specific features and stimulus-controlling properties within these environments. These studies have ignored the real possibility that some classroom environments may be more similar to other home environments than to other classroom environments. While this possibility focuses on the need to consider the "effective stimulus environment" which will be discussed below, it also points to the more direct question of measuring situations, even when situations are described in absolute rather than effective terms.

Numerous writers (Craik, 1973; Willems, 1973, 1974) have discussed the importance of considering the interface between behavior and situations, yet the methodology for categorizing and conceptualizing situations has been slow in developing. Even when we restrict our comments to consideration of physical situations that have been shown to exert strong control over behavior (LeLaurin & Risley, 1972), the number of studies that deal with such behavior-situation relationships is small.

The next level of behavior-situation relationships involves situational events describing the social behavior of another individual. While the assessment task under such circumstances makes behavioral and situational assessment quite congruent, a major consideration here is the reciprocal interplay between the two sets of events. It becomes evident under these conditions that situational assessment cannot be considered as having static properties, since the behavior in the situation can drastically alter the situation. Such an interplay points to the general importance of idiosyncratic assessments in clinical practice.

The next level in considering situations, which relates to both physical and social situations, is the critical role of considering not the absolute but rather the effective situation. As pointed out by Mischel (1973), the way in which we assess the acquired meaning of stimuli is at the heart of social-behavior assessment. At this point, it is important to note that the social-learning foundation for behavior-therapy assessment is somewhat at odds with a more traditional Skinnerian model, in relation to the importance of considering such mediational variables (Mahoney, 1974). Behavioral assessment that relies totally upon observable environmental stimuli has much utility, but it is believed that this approach does not typify some of the more current assessment strategies which attempt to assess more directly the role of covert events in the determination of behavior. It would, however, be possible to consider the "meaning" of stimulus events totally in terms of their functional properties. For example, the conditional probability analyses of sequential observation data done by Patterson (1974) highlight the fact that the same objective stimulus may have different controlling properties across individuals, across time, and across situations. So while there is the feasibility of looking at the functional properties of stimuli as a way of establishing their meaning, it is also believed that such meanings may often be better obtained through verbal reports that directly involve the individual in the assessment process (see Part III).

Attempts to do this have tended to focus heavily on the role of cognitive variables in mediating behavior. The role of cognitive factors was considered by Mischel (1973) and has recently been discussed in a number of places; therefore, no attempt will be made to discuss these rather complex issues at this point. However, it should be pointed out that the assessment of such cognitive variables is one of the major challenges currently facing behavioral assessment. It should also be noted that the need for these types of assessments is especially evident when one considers the recent work that has attempted to influence directly a person's cognitions in order to produce behavior change, including those programs relying on covert conditioning (Homme, 1965; Mahoney, 1974).

This approach is also reflected in the recent work of Meichenbaum

(1971, 1972, 1974). It is interesting to note that Meichenbaum points out a number of the assessment implications that follow from such a "cognitive behavior modification" approach and describes a number of assessment procedures that have been useful in getting such information. These include: (1) having the client close his eyes and mentally run a "movie" of a recent incident involving his problem, while reporting in detail the sequence of *thoughts* and behaviors that caused disturbance; and (2) having the client perform his maladaptive behavior while it is videotaped: after the taping, the therapist and client look at the behavior and attempt to reconstruct the thoughts that were being experienced on the tape. These techniques reflect useful additions to some of the more typically used procedures for assessing cognitive events, such as having the person self-record thoughts and impulses. Imagery and videotape procedures have the advantage of directly reproducing the situation and therefore decrease the excessive reliance on retrospective information. It is clear that the cognitive social-learning position (Mischel, 1973) has a number of strong implications for clinical assessment.

In the next paper in Part I, Goldfried and Kent consider behavioral personality assessment in contrast to assessment approaches within the more traditional personality frameworks. The emphasis in their article is not on a differentiation at the pragmatic level (e.g., in terms of relevance to treatment), a point made in a number of places in this volume, but rather at the level of underlying *assumptions* for the different assessment approaches. Differences in underlying assumptions involving such things as the conceptualization of personality and the selection and interpretation of test items are discussed. Implicit in the consideration of these different underlying notions is the idea that a behavioral approach (including a social-learning conceptualization of personality, conditioning principles, empirical emphasis, etc.) may provide a general orientation for the development of assessment procedures, in the same way that such an approach has led to the development of effective treatment procedures. Also emphasized are the points that assessments based upon a behavioral orientation involve fewer inferences and are more amenable to empirical test. As such, they may serve as more effective predictors of behavior than assessments involving nonbehavioral assumptions.

A recurrent theme in this volume is that behavioral assessment is a purposive activity and that a major purpose involves relevance to treatment. In the now classic paper by Baer, Wolf, and Risley, several of the important "dimensions" of behavioral treatment are presented and discussed (paper 3). It is believed that it is not only important for behavioral assessment to be consistent with the aims of behavioral intervention as outlined in this paper but also that in many instances the dimensions of "applied behavior analysis" are the same as the dimensions of "applied behavior assessment." In fact, a significant aspect of the definition of applied behavior analysis involves its unique emphasis on the importance of assessment-related activities, with respect to both explicit procedural specification and the objective description of treatment outcome. A major emphasis in this paper is on the "analytic" approach to treatment, characterized by the incorporation of single subject experimental designs into treatment endeavors. Such an analytic approach is most closely related to the evaluative function of behavioral assessment as presented in this volume.

In order to stress the primary importance of the evaluative aspects of behavior-therapy assessment, the fourth paper, by Kazdin, deals with methodological and assessment considerations in evaluating applied programs. In this paper, Kazdin examines the logic of within-subject designs in applied programs and considers some of the conceptual and methodological problems involved in their application. The importance of employing control-group designs is also discussed. It is believed that this article provides a strong base from which evaluative assessments may be developed and incorporated into applied programs.

In summary, the articles in Part I provide a general conceptual, pragmatic, and methodological basis for behavior-therapy assessments. As such, the reader is encouraged to consider the procedural developments presented in later sections from this general perspective. It is believed that such considerations should provide a strong impetus for the continued development of more sophisticated behavior-therapy assessment procedures.

# 1

---

## Behavior-Therapy Assessment:
## Diagnosis, Design, and Evaluation

*Eric J. Mash*
*Leif G. Terdal*

The behavioral assessment issues presented in this paper are the direct outcome of recent and parallel developments in the areas of both personality theory and clinical treatment. With regard to personality theory, changing assessment needs may be attributed to accounts of personality encompassed under the rubric of social learning. A number of theorists (Bandura, 1969; Mischel, 1968, 1973; Peterson, 1968; Wallace, 1966, 1967) have elaborated on this position, and although there are minor differences among them, the basic tenet of assessment, derived from these theories, is that people should be assessed in terms of what they do (referring both to behavioral and cognitive events) *in relation* to those circumstances under which they do it. These circumstances may be defined both in terms of their absolute stimulus properties as well as their functional value in controlling behavior. So, for example, comparing social learning and trait approaches to personality, Mischel (1973) states that with the social-learning position, "the focus shifts from describing situation-free people with broad trait adjectives to analyzing the specific interactions between conditions and the cognitions and behaviors of interest" (p. 265). The various terms used to describe assessment procedures derived from the basic social-

Reprinted with permission of publisher: Mash, E. J., & Terdal, L. G. Behavior therapy assessment: Diagnosis, design and evaluation. *Psychological Reports*, 1974, *35*, 587-601.

During the preparation of this paper the first author was supported by Canada Council Grants S72-061 and S70-1567.

learning position, for example, Behavioral Personality Assessment (Goldfried & Sprafkin, 1974) and Psychosituational Assessment (Bersoff, 1973) clearly reflect this shifting emphasis toward assessment of what a person does with regard to the situation or context in which he does it.

In the area of clinical treatment, the behavior modification approaches (i.e., Bandura, 1969; Franks, 1969; Kanfer & Phillips, 1970; Schwitzgebel & Kolb, 1974) which have developed rapidly over the past 10 years are, for the most part, consistent with the general social-learning personality theories and have associated with them similar assessment needs. Although many of the behavior-modification treatment procedures may not be direct derivatives of learning theory (London, 1972), the general assumption underlying all such treatment is that the behaviors of interest are maintained by contemporaneous stimulus events surrounding their occurrence (both antecedent and consequent), and it is through the alteration of these stimulus events that behavioral change is accomplished (Patterson, 1973). While behavior modification programs have typically emphasized the alteration of external stimulus events in producing behavioral change, that is, contingency management and stimulus control, a consideration of internal stimulus events, that is, self-control, as providing a context for the occurrence and maintenance of behavior is also consistent with the basic underlying assumption and is receiving an increasingly greater amount of attention (Goldfried & Merbaum, 1973; Mahoney & Thoresen, 1974; Mischel, 1973). It becomes evident that, if behavioral change is dependent upon the alteration of significant maintaining stimuli, any assessment prior to treatment must provide a description of behavior in relation to those conditions under which it occurs. This approach to assessment which includes a description of antecedent and consequent stimulus events surrounding the occurrence of a behavior has been referred to as "functional analysis" (Bijou & Peterson, 1969). Within this framework, the *raison d'etre* of diagnosis, or assessment, is to obtain information which can be utilized in the planning and implementation of behavioral change programs (Peterson, 1968).

### Assessment Purposes

Assessment occurs for a reason. Implicit in the notion of assessment is that it is a purposeful process directed at some goal rather than an end in and of itself. In spite of the fact that these goals have been different across different theoretical positions, leading sometimes to nosological or typological outcomes, sometimes to dimensional outcomes, sometimes to explanatory or dynamic outcomes, and sometimes to outcomes regarding treatment decisions (Peterson, 1968), it is always the way in which assessment information is utilized that gives significance to the process. In discussing assessment tools, Goldberg (1971) has explicated two typical viewpoints regarding their use, the "basic" science and "applied" science positions. With the former, assessment is viewed primarily in terms of the development of psychological theories, whereas the latter approach emphasizes the prediction of outcomes viewed by society as having importance. While recognizing a disparity between the two approaches, Goldberg states that "today most psychologists make at least an implicit assumption that theoretically meaningful variables, when reliably measured, can be used to predict important societal criteria and, conversely, that those individual differences which turn out empirically to be the most useful in the prediction of significant human outcomes are the variables that an eventual theory of individual differences will have to include" (pp. 1–2). Consequently, the disparity between the two viewpoints may not be as large as once imagined. Given that assessment procedures are likely to develop in both a theoretical and applied context, it is useful to consider whether the questions raised within particular theoretical frameworks are more-or-less consistent with the types of questions being posed and the kinds of decisions characteristic of clinical situations.

## Inter- versus Intra-Individual Differences

Clinical assessment is primarily concerned with decision making about individuals and has typically involved the collection of information that can be relied upon to implement judgments concerning these individuals. At times, assessment may be directed at groups, but in this context the group is treated as an individual entity and takes on the characteristics of a distinct unit. In such a decision-making process, the primary concern is with intra-individual differences. That is, we wish to ascertain, or account for, individual variability over time in the same situation, or differences in the same individual's behavior across different situations. So, for example, with a business executive who suddenly finds himself unable to function effectively in a situation in which he had formerly been able to, assessment questions would relate to why this difference in the behavior, given "apparently" the same set of circumstances. Although information about his performance relative to some other business executive may be of some use, such information about inter-individual differences would not be of paramount importance in providing help to this person. In the same vein, if we were assessing a female college student who exhibited extreme anxiety in a test situation but was otherwise relaxed, information regarding how anxious other college students were in test situations, again, might be interesting, but not particularly useful for decision making about how to help this co-ed through her difficulties. These examples should serve to illustrate the point that, for the most part, assessments used to answer applied questions are primarily concerned with the description of within-person variability.

In contrast to the intra-person information obtained in clinical practice, assessments designed to obtain information to be utilized in the construction of global personality theories have traditionally been concerned with the collection of information regarding inter-person differences. Most of the major personality theories have been trait-oriented, and the major goal in assessment has been that of determining the way in which one individual differs from another on some specifiable characteristic or dimension (Guilford, 1959; Goldberg, 1971). Assessment procedures have typically taken the form of standardized tests possessing group norms with which an individual's responses could be compared. The question being asked was "how much of a trait does one person have, when compared to how much of the trait other people had?" This focus on inter-individual differences would appear to create a lacuna between basic and applied assessment needs, with a concomitant failure to provide an adequate bridge between the two.

Social-learning theories of personality are certainly not incompatible with an interest in the identification of important inter-individual differences (Bijou & Peterson, 1969). Reliable differences in the manner in which different people respond to similar situations are important in the formulation of general principles of behavior as are behavioral norms for particular reference groups (Delfini, Bernal, & Rosen, 1974). However, the fact that social-learning approaches tend to focus on the same individual's response in relation to various situational factors means that intra-individual differences are usually of primary concern. Given this, in contrast to development of trait theory, the types of assessment needs associated with development of social-learning theory seem to be more consistent with the types of assessment needs involved in practice. It should be noted that trait notions of personality do not ignore situational influences, which may affect the amount of a particular characteristic manifested in a particular situation, without altering the rank ordering of individuals on that characteristic, which should remain relatively constant across situations. In spite of this recognition, the within-individual variation from situation to situation tends to be viewed as unimportant when compared with the between-individual stability. Consequently, for trait approaches it appears that assessment procedures used for development of theory are not as consistent with the assessment purposes of clinical practice, as are the assessment procedures for the theories grouped under the social-learning rubric.

## What Is Assessment in Behavior Therapy?

Given the rapid developments that have taken place, both within social-learning theory formulation and behavior-modification practice, a clear definition(s) of behavior-therapy assessment has been relatively slow in forthcoming. Most definitions have been put forth in relation to previous assessment approaches, and comparisons have been made with respect to the different underlying assumptions regarding personality, test construction, interpretation, and use (Goldfried & Kent, 1972).

For example, in discussing ''behavioral personality assessment,'' Goldfried and Sprafkin (1974) state:

. . . the point of divergence between traditional and behavioral approaches lies in the assumptions underlying the construction and interpretation of these assessment methods. A delineation of the contrasting assumptions should provide . . . the general principles of behavioral personality assessment. As indicated by Goldfried and Kent (1972) a comprehensive distinction between traditional and behavioral personality assessment must involve the assumptions underlying (a) what is basically involved in the definition of ''personality,'' (b) the selection of the items to be included within the test, and (c) the approach taken to the interpretation of the individual's responses (p. 3).

The differential assumptions relating to each of these areas are elaborated by Goldfried and Kent (1972). Bersoff (1971) in discussing ''psychosituational assessment'' states:

. . . to obtain a better sample of typical functioning, it may be necessary to pursue techniques more appropriate to that end. These techniques can be considered within the framework of what the author calls a ''psychosituational assessment'' —defined as an assessment designed to measure and interpret behavior as it is elicited through interaction with specific stimulus situations. A number of specific methods have been constructed to accomplish such a goal (p. 392).

Bersoff outlines these methods as including primarily the systematic observation of behavior in its usual context and the design of assessment situations which resemble the more natural settings in which behaviors occur. These methods attempt to minimize the amount of inference necessary in generalizing assessment information to an individual's usual life circumstances.

In presenting some of the problems in developing assessment procedures for behavior modification, Kanfer (1971) makes the following points:

A distinguishing feature of behavior-modification techniques is the belief that the target of treatment must be a specific observable class of behaviors rather than a change in the personality structure of the patient. From this basic belief follows the rejection of traditional broad-gauge test instruments which purport to assign a person to a psychiatric diagnosis, or to reveal essential personality mechanisms, or the intra-personal organization of personality components. The behavior modifier is interested in intra-personal organization only when it is relevant for his choice of treatment strategies. In behavior therapy the treatment goal is to produce changes in a person's life situation either by altering the patient's response repertoire, or by changing the patient's social environment, or by altering the motivational variables that maintain the deviant behaviors. In more recent approaches, behavior therapists have also included in their work efforts to modify . . . the patient's behavior toward himself. As a consequence of the assumptions about the task of behavior therapy, most of the traditional assessment instruments have either been used in rather untraditional ways or have been bypassed altogether. What the behavior therapist asks of his assessment instruments then is primarily that they help to develop his treatment strategy and to assess the progress in treatment. Pre-treatment assessment has the following specific three purposes:

(1) To help pinpoint some specific target behaviors that would alter the patient's discomforts or social inefficiences, and which are potentially changeable by the means at the therapist's and patient's disposal.

(2) That the assessment instruments reveal the biological and psychological resources of the patient, and of the patient's environment that could be utilized for bringing about behavioral change.

(3) That they offer some clues concerning the appropriateness of different therapeutic techniques for the individual case, be it on the basis of the patient's past history, or his current potentials. These tasks require sampling of particular behaviors and of the environmental context in which the patient lives (pp. 1-2).

Several key generalizations may be extracted from the above statements as characteristic of behavior-therapy assessment.

1. Behavior-therapy assessment is usually predicated on the assumption that intra-individual variability in behavior across time and situations (and perhaps response topography) is the rule rather than the exception.

2. A less emphasized, but equally important point is that given the "same" situation, defined in either absolute or effective terms or both, *stability* in an individual's behavior should be expected.

3. It follows from the first two points that all behavior-therapy assessments must include some measure of the context in which the behavior being assessed occurs. Ideally, any instrument for assessment of behavior therapy should measure behavior *in relation to* those stimuli which are present (either directly or symbolically) while the behavior is occurring.

4. Given this central importance of situational variables, the development of instruments to describe and measure situations, environments, contexts, etc., is as important as the refinement of behavioral measures and is always an integral part of behavior-therapy assessment (Moos & Insel, 1974).

5. The primary focus of assessments in behavior therapy is on pro-

viding information that can be utilized in the design, implementation, and evaluation of programs of behavioral change.

6. An important underlying assumption for assessment in behavior therapy is that most behaviors are learned and maintained by naturally occurring stimulus events (both internal and external) in the person's environment. Therefore, the appropriate arena for assessment is the individual's natural environment (Tharp & Wetzel, 1969).

7. Recognizing that assessment in the natural environment may not always be feasible, for both pragmatic and methodological reasons, behavior therapy may also include assessments conducted outside of the individual's immediate social and physical environment. However, these types of assessments should attempt to replicate naturally occurring conditions to as great an extent as is possible and, by doing so, attempt to minimize questions regarding the generalizability of the assessment information (Martin, 1974).

8. Assessment in behavior therapy is both ongoing and self-corrective. In contrast to more traditional approaches in which the end point of assessment may be the designation of a ''diagnosis'' or label prior to treatment, assessment in behavior therapy is a continuous and interactive process which precedes, is concomitant with, and follows the introduction of behavior-change programs. While part of the behavioral assessment may be used to evaluate the effectiveness of treatment, since a primary goal of assessment is to identify resources for change, the effectiveness of treatment may also be used to evaluate the inadequacies or strengths of the initial behavioral assessment. If the procedures for change suggested by the initial assessments are not effective in producing behavioral change, additional assessment becomes necessary, and the original assessment must be revised. Consequently, assessment in behavior therapy is a highly empirical activity which may be directly supported or refuted depending upon whether or not its specified objectives are met.

9. Assessment in behavior therapy is not oriented toward pathology. In identifying resources for change it is as important to specify individual and contextual strengths and assets as it is to identify deficiencies (Kanfer & Saslow, 1969).

These generalizations about assessment in behavior therapy indicate that the term has come to refer to a complex set of heterogeneous activities rather than a singular or monolithic scheme. A number of different types of procedures have come to be included under the label of behavioral assessment, some having to do with the identification of problematic areas, others with the design of programs for behavioral change, and still others with the evaluation of treatment outcomes. Recognizing that assessment in behavior therapy is an ongoing and continuous process, these different activities are in part related to the point in time at which the assessment occurs. It may be useful to consider such assessment as it relates to the different goals which may be reflected at different times in the assessment sequence. It should be recognized that the framework given below to accomplish this is an arbitrary categorization with much overlap between categories.

## A FRAMEWORK FOR ASSESSMENT IN BEHAVIOR THERAPY: DIAGNOSIS, DESIGN, AND EVALUATION

### Diagnosis

The fact that the term ''diagnosis'' has been predominantly associated with medical-psychiatric formulations of psychopathology, in which it often refers to the process of identifying some underlying disease through the study of symptoms, has led to an eschewal of the term in the literature of behavior therapy. Although some authors (e.g., Kanfer & Saslow, 1969) have used the term ''behavioral diagnosis,'' the extraneous and often misleading meanings carried by the term diagnosis have led most to shy away from its use. In spite of this eschewal any initial analysis of the problem situation is ultimately concerned with the basic diagnostic questions of ''what, if anything, is the problem?'' Physicians may look at physical symptoms, and identify the problem as an underlying and identi-fiable disease process, such as a viral infection. Dynamically oriented psychiatrists may look at behavioral symptoms and identify the problem as an unobservable and theoretically designated underlying conflict asso-ciated with sexual and aggressive themes. Behavior therapists may look at behavioral symptoms and identify the problem as the reaction of the environment or the individual to those responses being emitted. Regard-less of the direction in which problem identification is being sought, one must face the initial question of diagnosis phrased in terms of whether or not there is a problem, what it is, and its extent. Assessment in behavior therapy is not exempt from these types of broad diagnostic questions.

Several authors (e.g., Bandura, 1969) have pointed out how the determination of whether or not there is a problem ultimately includes some type of evaluative social judgment. For example, Bandura (1969) states:

The designation of behavior as pathological thus involves social judgments that are influenced by, among other factors, the normative standards of persons making the judgments, the social context in which the behavior is exhibited, cer-tain attributes of the behavior, and numerous characteristics of the deviator himself. An adequate theory of deviant behavior must therefore be concerned with the factors determining evaluative judgments. Unfortunately, in spite of widespread use of diagnostic classifications and the potentially serious consequences of labeling persons as mentally disturbed there has been surprisingly little systematic study of the factors governing such judgmental behavior (p. 3).

The identification of factors which may be involved in making social judgments regarding the appropriateness or inappropriateness of behavior has continued to be a major area of neglect. The questions raised by, and procedures involved in, preliminary definition of a problem and diagnosis have probably been the most passed over by behavioral practitioners and theorists alike. The decision-making rules and assessment procedures for deciding what behavior or behaviors are selected as targets for change have either been ignored or not made explicit. If anything, there has been an oversimplified and implicit rule which might be stated as, "if the individual, or a significant other, reports a behavior as a problem —then the problem is defined—it is that behavior." While this general rule may apply to a number of situations it is the many exceptions to its applicability which suggest that other more implicit decision-making rules may be involved.

Consider the following example. The parents of a 13-year-old girl reported concern over their daughter's school performance. The parents were elderly, in their 60s, and had adopted the girl when she was an infant. Their primary concern was that, although she was a B student, they felt she could do much better if she studied more. Other reported problems were that she did not practice the piano as often as she was supposed to and did not take enough responsibility around the house. During an interview, the parents reported that their daughter usually was up at six-thirty in the morning, was dressed, had breakfast, cleaned her room, made her bed, and helped with the breakfast dishes by eight o'clock. From eight to eight-forty-five she was to practice her piano. Following this she would leave for school. Coming home at three-thirty p.m., she was to study for two hours before dinner, have dinner, help with the dinner dishes, continue with her homework until finished, and practice the piano. Some TV was permitted if all work was completed (although, not surprisingly, this rarely happened). The schedule for weekends was similar, with the addition of a few more general household chores.

Obviously, the behaviors being reported as problematic could not be accepted at face value given the information above. To accept the parents' verbal report of the problem at face value with a subsequent identification of studying, piano practicing, and doing household chores as behavioral deficits which needed to be increased would have been a gross and possibly dangerous oversimplification of the problem. Rather in this instance the targets identified were less study, piano practice, and household chores and a concomitant effort to identify and increase alternative responses for which the child could receive parental approval.

The validity of this initial assessment is secondary at this point. What is emphasized here is the lack of any explicit statement of the assessment procedures used in defining this treatment target(s). The focus of treatment was likely based upon a set of implicit behavioral norms of the therapist and of the society in which these norms have developed and in which the therapist functions.

The point here is that a major part of assessment in behavior therapy involves some initial diagnostic decision regarding whether or not treatment should be instituted, that is, the behavior is a problem, and if so, what behavior(s) should be the target of change (Hawkins, 1974). This process has been referred to as "static assessment" by Ferster (1965). Given this to be the case, behavioral practitioners have, for the most part, neglected to make explicit the assessment procedures being used to arrive at this definition. In most reported behavioral applications the initial diagnosis is omitted. So, for example, countless studies begin with a baseline(s) on some targeted behavior(s), without any description of how and why that, and not some other, behavior was selected as the focus for treatment.

This raises an important question regarding the reliability of behavioral diagnosis. Traditionally, the reliability of diagnosis has involved a comparison of the judgments of independent raters making a decision regarding the appropriateness of one nosological category over another, given information about the same individual (Zigler & Phillips, 1961). Such inter-rater reliabilities for nosological classificatory systems have typically been low. Clearly, behavioral diagnosis is not concerned with agreement about some typological outcome. But the purpose of an initial behavioral diagnosis *is* to identify target behaviors for treatment, and to this extent the reliability of behavioral diagnosis is an unanswered question. Not only is it an unanswered question, but in spite of its importance, it is a question which seems to have gone unasked. For example, there do not appear to be any studies which have presented similar assessment information to behavioral practitioners and compared their level of agreement regarding which behaviors are selected as treatment targets. This same reliability question will apply when the question of "what treatment procedures are suggested by the assessment in behavior therapy?" is raised in a later section. It is believed that such reliability information should serve to make more explicit those decision-making rules which are being applied in the initial diagnosis of problematic behavior.

### Design

In this category we refer to that part of the assessment sequence in behavior therapy which is concerned with the collection of information which can be directly utilized in the design of a program for behavioral change. This has been one of the most frequently emphasized characteristics of assessment in behavior therapy in contrast to other assessment approaches—its relevance to treatment. Traditional approaches to assessment have been criticized for the lack of continuity between assessment procedures and treatment action. Often the treatment of choice has been based more on the theoretical predilections of the therapist than upon the information obtained during assessment. Clearly, treatment programs following assessment in behavior therapy are not excluded from this type of theoretical biasing; however, it is more often the case that treatment procedures following behavioral assessment are directly related to assessment information.

It should be noted that the design phase of assessment in behavior therapy is not distinct from the diagnostic phase. Certainly, it is necessary to both describe and define the behavior(s) of interest prior to and concomitant with the design of any program for behavioral change. However, it is possible to make the distinction in that initial diagnosis is concerned with a selection and a description of a target behavior in conjunction with its *general* evaluation by the immediate social environment and the individual himself. Often these preliminary general evaluations are represented by subjective verbal report measures. Assessment for treatment design includes a continued description and definition of the behavior but also attempts to get much more specific information regarding the physical and social context in which the behavior occurs. While the design phase of assessment may also be concerned with the evaluation of behavior by the social environment, relative to initial diagnosis, this evaluation is assessed more in terms of direct behavioral reactions and outcomes than through verbal report.

The amount of information from assessment obtained during the design phase is likely to exceed information collected during the initial diagnosis and evaluative phases. This phase of assessment is an ongoing process in which information is either utilized or discarded depending upon its *apparent relevance to treatment.* Apparent relevance to treatment is a critical concept here in that there is no way of knowing on an a priori basis which of the variables assessed will be important for behavior change. Fortunately, however, the relevance of information from assessment in the design of any change program can be supported or refuted by the outcome of that program.

The focus of the design phase of assessment in behavior therapy is on the identification of those antecedent and consequent stimulus events which may be contributing to the maintenance of inappropriate behavior or limiting the occurrence of appropriate behaviors. Not only is it important to identify these variables, but it is also important to assess the feasibility of attempting to modify some factors as opposed to others. This involves an assessment of a client's resources for change. A major assumption underlying assessment is that behavior is maintained by events occurring in the natural environment. Consequently, there has been an emphasis on utilizing persons and situations in the natural environment in mediating behavioral change, and most assessments for treatment design have been carried out in the natural environment. In assessing the specific parameters to be used in developing a treatment program, it is crucial to assess also the likelihood that any changes produced by these procedures will be maintained by naturally occurring events in the person's environment.

Behavior therapy is not a monolithic system (Patterson, 1974). Given similar behavioral problems, it would be possible to accomplish change through a variety of procedures. This would apply to both similar behaviors across individuals as well as for the individual case. However, for the individual case it is not unreasonable to expect our behavior-therapy assessment procedures to designate a particular treatment strategy as being most appropriate, that is, efficient. Here again, we are faced with an important reliability question. If assessment in behavior therapy provides information relevant to treatment, then given the same information should we not expect similar programs for behavioral change to be designed? If this is not the case, we can only assume that the treatment choice is based more upon implicit personal preference and theoretical bias than information from assessment, and the claim that assessment in behavior therapy provides information for treatment is closer to illusion than reality. There is little information pertinent to this question of reliability. In part, this may be related to the fact that there have been few standardized assessments employed in behavior therapy. Consequently, the likelihood that different practitioners would be required to make decisions regarding similar treatment designs, based upon almost identical information from assessment, has been quite low.

### Evaluation

An ongoing evaluation of behavior concomitant with and following the introduction of procedures for behavioral change has been one of the major defining characteristics and strengths of assessment in behavior therapy. There are at least two aspects to such evaluative assessment. The first relates to whether or not the objectives for behavioral change specified during the diagnosis and design phases are being met. In its most rudimentary form this is simply a question of measurement which asks if the behavior(s) change in frequency, intensity, duration, time, or location of occurrence as specified in the initial objectives for behavior change. To answer this question all that is required is an ongoing, accurate, and reliable measure of the targeted behavior(s).

The second aspect of evaluative assessment in behavior therapy includes careful measurement, but in addition requires some considerations of design as well. Here, the question is whether or not any observed changes in behavior may be attributed to the specific procedures for behavioral change which have been introduced (Baer, Wolf, & Risley, 1968). If programs of behavior modification are to have any generality across treatment, persons, and situations, such evaluative assessment is critical. In addition, assessment of this sort is necessary for the development of more efficient procedures for behavioral change.

Typically, assessments in behavior therapy directed at the evaluation of effectiveness of treatment have been carried out using a within-subject experimental design. These involve, first, reversal designs in which stimulus control is demonstrated through intra-behavior replications involving successive introductions and withdrawals of treatment procedures accompanied by successive and concomitant changes in behavior. A second type of within-subject design has been the multiple-baseline, or multiple-element baseline, design in which effectiveness of treatment (stimulus-control) is demonstrated through either inter-behavioral, inter-situational, or inter-individual replications involving successive introductions of procedures in treatment accompanied by temporally concomitant behavioral change. Extensive discussions of these designs are presented by Baer, Wolf, and Risley (1968), Barlow and Hersen (1973), Chassen (1967), Leitenberg (1973), Sidman (1960), and Kazdin (1973).

In contrast to the diagnosis and design phases of assessment in behavior therapy, evaluative assessment may not require as much information. Given that there has been some selectivity following initial assessments, the evaluation phase may involve measurement of only one or two variables of interest. Also, evaluations of treatment outcomes may sometimes require only baserate information designed to get at actuarial questions (Baer, 1971). It is important to note that, while assessments made for problem diagnosis and treatment design must always involve the measurement and analysis of behavior in relation to specific and ongoing situational events, for some types of evaluative behavioral assessment this may not be as important. This is often the case if we are measuring change in the same situation over time. However, if the evaluative assessment is to include a design attempting to demonstrate change as a function of a particular treatment condition, then it is necessary to measure both the behavior and the specific treatment variables being introduced.

A critical aspect of evaluative assessment in behavior therapy involves obtaining information regarding the generalizability of behavioral change across response classes, situations, and time periods (Conway & Bucher, 1974). The efficacy of any change procedure must be evaluated in relation to both the permanence and generality of change, and it is essential to obtain estimates of this in order to answer questions regarding the efficiency of a program for change. Questions of generalizability require that assessment in behavior therapy continue after treatment is discontinued (follow-up) and that some measures of behavior(s) and situation(s) besides those targeted for change be obtained. It is only through such additional information that generality of effects may be assessed.

The development of treatment programs in behavior modification seems to have taken place much more rapidly than developments in the area of behavioral assessment and analysis. This discrepancy is probably related to some of the exigencies involved in clinical practice. In any event, there would, at the present time, appear to be a much more sophisticated technology for behavior change than for assessment in behavior therapy. Thus far there has been little standardization or consistency in the types of assessments in behavior therapy that have been employed. This is especially so for the diagnostic and design aspects of assessments. Evaluative assessments have probably shown some degree of uniformity in terms of a general concern for reliable measurement of a behavior throughout the course of treatment and a consistent use of single-subject experimental designs. This lack of standardized instruments for assessment in behavior therapy was reflected in the results of a study conducted by Kanfer (1971) in which a survey of a number of active behavioral practitioners showed little similarity in the types of procedures being employed. This lack of uniformity may be attributable to the operation of a number of factors.

First, the fact that traditionally used standardized procedures for assessment do not provide information necessary for a functional analysis of behavior has probably led to their outright rejection by many behavior therapists. This rejection may have resulted in a temporary situation during which time alternative, but still standardized, instruments for assessment that are more consistent with a functional analysis would be developed. Alternatively, since assessment in behavior therapy is both intra-personal and individualized, it may be argued that there is little need for standardized assessment instruments given the lack of a primary interest in making inter-individual comparisons. Both positions would probably find supporters among behavioral practitioners.

As indicated earlier, a behavioral approach is not at all incompatible with attempts to identify important inter-individual differences in response to the same situation or treatment. This can only be achieved through some degree of standardization of measures across individuals. The development of some uniformity in procedures for assessment in behavior therapy will likely be necessary if our theories of behavior are to obtain some degree of generality, and if comparative studies of treatment effectiveness (Bachrach & Quigley, 1966) are to be carried out.

## REFERENCES

Bachrach, A. J., & Quigley, W. A. Direct methods of treatment. In I. A. Berg & L. A. Pennington (Eds.), *Introduction to clinical psychology.* New York: Ronald, 1966. Pp. 482-560.

Baer, D. M. Behavior modification: you shouldn't. In E. A. Ramp & B. L. Hopkins (Eds.), *A new direction for education: behavior analysis 1971.* Lawrence: University of Kansas, Department of Human Development, 1971. Pp. 358-369.

Baer, D. M., Wolf, M., & Risley, T. R. Some current dimensions of applied behavior analysis. *Journal of Applied Behavior Analysis, 1968, 1,* 91-97.

Bandura, A. *Principles of behavior modification.* New York: Holt, Rinehart & Winston, 1969.

Barlow, D. H., & Hersen, M. Single-case experimental designs. *Archives of General Psychiatry, 1973, 29,* 319-325.

Bersoff, D. N. Current functioning "myth": an overlooked fallacy in psychological assessment. *Journal of Consulting and Clinical Psychology, 1971, 37,* 391-393.

Bersoff, D. N. Silk purses into sow's ears: the decline of psychological testing and a suggestion for its redemption. *American Psychologist, 1973, 28,* 892-899.

Bijou, S. W., & Peterson, R. F. The psychological assessment of children: a functional analysis. In P. McReynolds (Ed.), *Advances in psychological assessment.* Vol. 2. Palo Alto, Calif.: Science and Behavior Books, 1971. Pp. 63-78.

Chassen, J. B. *Research designs in clinical psychology and psychiatry.* New York: Appleton-Century-Crofts, 1967.

Conway, J. B., & Bucher, B. D. Transfer and maintenance of behavior change in children: a review and suggestions. In Mash, E. J., Hamerlynck, L. A., & Handy, L. C. (Eds.), *Behavior modification and families.* New York: Brunner/Mazel, 1976. Pp. 119-159.

Delfini, L. F., Bernal, M. E., & Rosen, P. M. A comparison of normal and deviant boys in their homes. Paper presented at the Sixth Banff International Conference on Behavior Modification, Banff, Alberta, Canada, 1974.

Ferster, C. B. Classification of behavioral pathology. In L. Krasner & L. P. Ullmann (Eds.), *Research in behavior modification: new developments and implications.* New York: Holt, Rinehart & Winston, 1965. Pp. 6-26.

Franks, C. M. (Ed.) *Behavior therapy: appraisal and status.* New York: McGraw-Hill, 1969.

Goldberg, L. R. Some recent trends in personality assessment. Invited lecture presented at the meeting of the American Psychological Association, Washington, D.C., September, 1971.

Goldfried, M. R., & Kent, R. N. Traditional versus behavioral personality assessment: a comparison of methodological and theoretical assumptions. *Psychological Bulletin, 1972, 77,* 409-420.

Goldfried, M. R., & Merbaum, N. (Eds.), *Behavior change through self-control.* New York: Holt, Rinehart & Winston, 1973.

Goldfried, M. R., & Sprafkin, J. *Behavioral personality assessment.* Morristown, N. J.: General Learning Press, 1974.

Guilford, J. P. *Personality.* New York: McGraw-Hill, 1959.

Hawkins, R. P. Who decided *that* was the problem?: two stages of responsibility for applied behavior analysts. Invited paper presented at the First Drake Conference on Professional Issues in Behavior Analysis, Drake University, Des Moines, Iowa, March, 1974.

Kanfer, F. H. Assessment for behavior modification. Paper presented at the Symposium on Newer Approaches to Personality assessment to the American Psychological Association Convention, Washington, D.C., September, 1971.

Kanfer, F. H., & Phillips, J. S. *Learning foundations of behavior therapy.* New York: Wiley, 1970.

Kanfer, F. H., & Saslow, G. Behavioral diagnosis. In C. M. Franks (Ed.), *Behavior therapy: appraisal and status.* New York: McGraw-Hill, 1969. Pp. 417-444.

Kazdin, A. E. Methodological and assessment considerations in evaluating reinforcement programs in applied settings. *Journal of Applied Behavior Analysis*, 1973, *6*, 517-531.

Leitenberg, H. The use of single-case methodology in psychotherapy research. *Journal of Abnormal Psychology*, 1973, *82*, 87-101.

London, P. The end of ideology in behavior modification. *American Psychologist*, 1972, *27*, 913-920.

Mahoney, M. J., & Thoresen, C. E. *Self-control: power to the person.* Monterey, Calif.: Brooks/Cole, 1974.

Martin, S. The comparability of behavioral data in laboratory and natural settings. Paper presented at the Sixth Banff International Conference on Behavior Modification, Banff, Alberta, Canada, 1974.

Mischel, W. *Personality and assessment.* New York: Wiley, 1968.

Mischel, W. Toward a cognitive, social learning reconceptualization of personality. *Psychological Review*, 1973, *80*, 252-283.

Patterson, G. R. Changes in status of family members as controlling stimuli: a basis for describing treatment process. In L. A. Hamerlynck, L. C. Handy, & E. J. Mash (Eds.), *Behavior change: methodology, concepts and practice.* Champaign, Ill.: Research Press, 1973. Pp. 169-191.

Patterson, G. R. Follow-up evaluations of a program for parents retraining their agressive boys. In F. Lowey (Ed.), *Symposium on the seriously disturbed pre-school child.* Canadian Psychiatric Association Journal, 1974, in press.

Peterson, D. R. *The clinical study of social behavior.* New York: Appleton-Century-Crofts, 1968.

Schwitzgebel, R. K., & Kolb, D. A. *Changing human behavior: principles of planned intervention.* New York: McGraw-Hill, 1974.

Sidman, M. *The tactics of scientific research: evaluating experimental data in psychology.* New York: Basic Books, 1960.

Tharp, R. G., & Wetzel, R. J. *Behavior modification in the natural environment.* New York: Academic Press, 1969.

Wallace, J. An abilities conception of personality: some implications for personality measurement. *American Psychologist,* 1966, *21,* 132-138.

Wallace, J. What units shall we employ?: Allport's question revisited. *Journal of Consulting Psychology,* 1967, *31,* 56-64.

Zigler, E., & Phillips, L. Psychiatric diagnosis: a critique. *Journal of Abnormal and Social Psychology,* 1961, *63,* 607-618.

# 2

Traditional Versus Behavioral
Personality Assessment:
A Comparison of Methodological and
Theoretical Assumptions

*Marvin R. Goldfried*
*Ronald N. Kent*

Among the many changes that have occurred within clinical psychology
in recent years, the very sharp increase in the popularity of behavior-
modification procedures represents one of the most exciting trends. As a
treatment approach based upon the application of experimentally derived
psychological principles to the clinical setting, behavior modification en-
compasses a number of different procedures that have been found to be
successful in alleviating a variety of different behavioral problems.

Because the successful implementation of behavior-modification
techniques depends directly upon an adequate assessment of the specific
behaviors in need of change and those variables maintaining these
behaviors, this approach to treatment has also stimulated a renewed interest in clinical assessment (Goldfried & Pomeranz, 1968; Kanfer &
Saslow, 1969; Mischel, 1968; Peterson, 1968). Greenspoon and Gersten (1967) have noted the importance of clinical assessment for the effective application of behavior-modification procedures and argued for the

Reprinted from *Psychological Bulletin,* 1972, 77, 409–420. Copyright © 1972 by
the American Psychological Association. Reprinted by permission.

The preparation of this paper was supported by Research Grant MH15044 from the
National Institute of Mental Health.

The authors are grateful to James H. Geer, Anita P. Goldfried, Kathleen Kent, and
P. Scott Lawrence for their many helpful comments on an earlier draft of this paper.

possible utility of currently available tests of personality. Close examination reveals, however, that there are certain basic assumptions associated with traditional personality tests which make this approach to assessment less appropriate from a behavioral viewpoint. Just as the behavioral framework has been used to generate new therapeutic procedures, it would seem advantageous to use this orientation for the construction of new assessment techniques as well.

Before proceeding further, we would like to note briefly what we mean by "traditional" and "behavioral" approaches to assessment. Although the ultimate goal of both procedures may be essentially the same (e.g., the prediction of human behavior), the general approach that has been employed in the pursuit of this goal has differed. The traditional approach to personality assessment has been directed primarily toward an understanding of the individual's underlying personality characteristics or traits as a means of predicting behavior. This general approach to assessment is reflected in most of our currently available personality tests—both projective techniques (Rorschach, Thematic Apperception Test, Draw-A-Person, etc.) as well as objective personality inventories (Minnesota Multiphasic Personality Inventory [MMPI], California Psychological Inventory, etc.). The behavioral approach to personality assessment, by contrast, involves more of a direct measurement of the individual's response to various life situations. The techniques associated with behavioral assessment include the observation of individuals in naturalistic situations, the creation of an experimental analogue of real-life situations via role playing, and the utilization of the individual's self-reported responses to given situations.

These two general approaches to personality assessment may be differentiated on a pragmatic level as well. In the case of the traditional procedures, the focus has been on the accuracy with which they might be used to predict behavior, with relatively little emphasis being placed on their utility for selecting therapeutic procedures (cf. Meehl, 1960). The therapeutic approach employed in any given case is usually more a function of the therapist's particular orientation than it is of psychological test findings (Goldfried & Pomeranz, 1968; London, 1964). By contrast, the interest in behavioral assessment has been generated by its utility for providing the information essential to the selection and implementation of appropriate behavior-modification procedures. Some of the possible reasons underlying the differential clinical utility of the two approaches have been discussed in greater detail elsewhere (Goldfried & Pomeranz, 1968) and are not dealt with here. Instead, the primary point of comparison on which we focus involves those assumptions underlying each approach, as well as the potential use each has for accurately predicting human behavior.

Although traditional personality tests and behavioral tests share many of the same methodological assumptions (e.g., reliability of scoring, adequacy of standardization) the primary purpose of this article is to compare the *differing* assumptions involved in these two approaches. The basic conception of personality and those assumptions associated with the selection of test items and the interpretation of test responses are first described and evaluated for both traditional and behavioral approaches to assessment, after which a comparison is drawn between these two approaches for predicting human behavior.

## ASSUMPTIONS INVOLVED IN THE TRADITIONAL APPROACH TO ASSESSMENT

### Conception of Personality

Most of our currently available personality tests are based on a common conceptualization of human functioning and have been directed toward obtaining information relevant to the underlying "personality structure" of the individual. Depending upon one's specific theoretical orientation, these inferred characteristics may consist of "motives," "needs," "drives," "defenses," "traits," or other similar psychodynamic constructs.

For the most part, the various psychodynamic or trait theories are based on the notion of psychic determinism, whereby a person's actions are assumed to be motivated by certain underlying dynamics. According to this conception of personality, the most appropriate way in which to predict human behavior should be based on a thorough assessment of those inferred characteristics of which the overt actions are believed to be a function.

Basic to the traditional conception of personality functioning is the assumption that consistencies in behavior (i.e., traits) exist independent of situational variations. Data from several studies, however, have failed to support this assumption. The effect of varying stimulus conditions on behavior has been demonstrated by Hartshorne and May's (1928) classic study on honesty, in which children were provided with opportunities to cheat, lie, and steal in a diversity of settings (e.g., home, party games, athletics). Hartshorne and May found a lack of a generalized code of morals, and concluded that "as we progressively change the situation we progressively lower the correlations between the tests [p. 384]." More recently, Endler and Hunt (1966, 1969) have similarly demonstrated the importance of situational effects in their S-R Inventory of Anxiousness, where they found that the interactions between situations and subjects contributed more to the total variance than did the variance associated with individual differences alone. On the basis of both questionnaire data and direct observations, Moos (1969) similarly found a substantial proportion of the variance resulting from Subject × Setting interactions. Although Mischel and Ebbesen (1970) have reported individual differences among children in the ability to delay gratification, it was possible to substantially modify the period of delay by creating variations in the particular situation. Mischel (1968) has reviewed a number of other studies dealing with this issue, the results of which have failed to confirm the conception of human functioning which does not take into account the importance of environmental influences on behavior.

### Selection of Test Items

An important consequence of the view that consistencies in behavior exist independently of situational variables has been the fact that relatively little emphasis has been placed on specifying the procedures to be used in selecting the pool of stimulus items for traditional tests of personality (Loevinger, 1957). Although test constructors often employ rigorous selection procedures to obtain a final set of items, the procedures for defining the original pool are rarely discussed. This original item pool is obviously not determined on a random basis, but is presumably related to the test constructor's assumptions regarding the nature of the personality variables in question.

Loevinger (1957) and Jessor and Hammond (1957) have criticized this poorly defined approach to selecting the initial set of items and suggested instead the use of a specific theoretical orientation as an alternate guide in selecting the item pool. In using personality theory to select test items, one assumes that the theory in question has some "validity." Although certain constructs associated with specific theoretical orientations have received some research support, there does not appear to be any one personality theory which, as yet, has achieved adequate enough empirical confirmation to justify such an approach to item selection (cf. Pervin, 1970).

### Interpretation of Test Responses

While variations in the stimulus aspects of the test situation have been considered to be relatively unimportant, the interpretation of responses has been the subject of extensive and detailed consideration. The interpretive significance of any particular test response may be determined by either *intuitive* or *empirical* means (Hase & Goldberg, 1967; Loevinger, 1957). The intuitive approach may be based on an informal rationale with few explicit theoretical assumptions, or it may involve more formal deductions from theory. In using the empirical approach, on the other hand, the interpretive significance of test responses is derived solely from the empirically established relationship between test and external criteria.

Even in those instances where the intuitive approach is used initially to specify the interpretive significance of various signs, empirical checks on the accuracy of those interpretations are clearly needed. However, logical or theoretical assumptions underlying the meaning of test signs are often so firmly held that failure to obtain empirical confirmation often has little effect on changing clinicians' interpretations. Thus, despite evidence indicating that Hutt and Briskin's (1960) proposed interpretation of various signs lacks empirical confirmation (Goldfried & Ingling, 1964), the revised edition of the manual (Hutt, 1968) continues to recommend the use of invalid interpretations.

The tendency for clinicians to retain certain interpretive hypotheses about test scores is directly illustrated in a study by Chapman and Chapman (1969), where they asked experienced psychodiagnosticians to determine which of several Rorschach signs reflected male homosexuality. The signs presented to the clinicians were selected from Wheeler's (1949) initial list of 20 possible Rorschach indicators of homosexuality, only some of which have held up under empirical test. The results indicated that clinicians tended to select those signs which they believed to be most indicative of male homosexuality on a rational-intuitive basis (e.g., "buttocks")—despite the fact that research findings failed to confirm the empirical validity of these signs—and almost never selected those indices that were, in fact, empirically valid. As noted by the authors, these "illusory correlations" between sign and inferred characteristics are likely to be a source of considerable error in predicting criterion behaviors.

Although such illusory correlations are only a problem for intuitively derived tests, other potential sources of error exist with empirically derived measures. For example, despite the fact that the clinical scales on the MMPI were originally derived to assist in diagnostic classification, the test is currently being used for more complex decisions (Dahlstrom & Welsh, 1960; Little & Shneidman, 1954; Rychlak, 1968). Rather than simply using an MMPI protocol to determine diagnostic category, the clinician more typically carries out a profile analysis, in which both the absolute and relative scores on the various scales are used to construct a personality description. Any such interpretation must assume a high correspondence between the diagnostic categories associated with the scales and the inferred personality traits. Such an assumption, however, has failed to receive empirical support, in that considerable overlap in behavioral characteristics has been found to exist among the various diagnostic classifications (Mischel, 1968; Zigler & Phillips, 1961).

Another assumption basic to the interpretation of test responses is that the protocol provides a sufficient sampling of the individual's personality characteristics (MacFarlane & Tuddenham, 1951; Murstein, 1961). In the case of projective techniques, Murstein acknowledged that since this ''sampling'' is determined by the subject's own response to the test situation—which differs from individual to individual—one cannot always be certain that sufficient data have, in fact, been obtained. In the case of objective tests, guidelines for determining the adequacy of the sample are virtually nonexistent, with the exception of Loevinger's (1957) suggestion that theory serve as the background for test construction.

## ASSUMPTIONS INVOLVED IN THE BEHAVIORAL APPROACH TO ASSESSMENT

### Conception of Personality

In contrast to the psychodynamic orientation, which focuses on the characteristics an individual ''has,'' the behavioral view of human functioning places greater emphasis on what a person ''does'' in various situations (Mischel, 1968). That is, rather than hypothesizing certain underlying constructs (e.g., ''instincts'' or ''needs'') which are believed to function as motivational determinants of behavior, the basic unit for consideration involves the individual's response to specific aspects of his environment. Human behavior is viewed as being determined not only by the person's previous social-learning history but also by current environmental antecedents and/or consequences of the behavior in question.

The behavioral orientation to personality is well represented by Wallace's (1966, 1967) ''abilities'' conception. Wallace used the concept *response capability* as referring to the individual's behavioral repertoire or potential, which is determined primarily by earlier learning experiences. This closely parallels what is typically referred to when one speaks of an acquired skill, such as the ability to drive a car, ride a bicycle, or other learned proficiencies. The likelihood that an individual will actually *perform* in a given way, however, will depend on the extent to which certain situational factors elicit and/or reinforce this particular response. From this point of view, then, personality may be construed as an intervening variable that is defined according to the likelihood of an individual manifesting certain behavioral tendencies in the variety of situations that comprise his day-to-day living.

As noted in conjunction with our discussion of the traditional conception of personality, the available research evidence does, in fact, indicate that the likelihood of an individual responding in a certain way depends not only on his own response capability but also on the nature of the situation as well (cf. Endler & Hunt, 1966, 1969; Hartshorne & May, 1928; Mischel & Ebbesen, 1970; Moos, 1969). After reviewing the experimental literature regarding the consistency of personality variables, Mischel (1968) has concluded that ''behaviors which are often construed as stable personality trait indicators actually are highly specific and depend on the details of the evoking situations and the response mode employed to measure them (p. 37).''

## Selection of Test Items

Consistent with a conception of personality which emphasizes the individual's specific response to specific situations, a crucial assumption of behavioral tests is that stimulus situations are adequately represented. Adequate representation of situations requires not only careful simulation during the measurement process (e.g., movies, slides, written descriptions) but also rigorous definition of the appropriate pool of situations. For example, in surveying fear behavior (Geer, 1965; Wolpe & Lang, 1964), it is necessary to obtain measures of fear in situations which sample, in a representative manner, the population of potentially anxiety-producing situations. In selecting the stimulus items, then, the concept of content validity, as it has been traditionally applied to proficiency tests, becomes highly relevant for behavioral assessment.

Goldfried and D'Zurilla (1969) have followed this line of thinking and developed a ''behavioral analytic'' method for test construction. For example, Goldfried and D'Zurilla have applied the behavioral analytic model in the study of college freshman effectiveness by identifying those responses which are differentially rewarded by significant individuals in situations which define the college environment. The initial step in selecting a pool of test items consisted of a ''situational analysis,'' in order to obtain a sample of problematic situations that were likely to be encountered by freshmen during their first semester. The situational analysis was accomplished by means of written daily records of problematic situations obtained from freshmen themselves, as well as through interviews with staff members having frequent contact with freshmen. The large pool of situations resulting from these procedures was then presented to a new sample of freshmen during the second semester, who were asked to indicate which of these situations they had ever encountered. Only those instances that had a high likelihood of occurrence were retained in the item pool. The following is an example of one such situation (Goldfried & D'Zurilla, 1969):

A lengthy composition is due in your English class this Friday. It was assigned a week before and is on a rather difficult topic, which you really don't understand.

On Wednesday afternoon when you sit down to work, you find that you have absolutely no idea about what to include in the paper. You realize, however, that you must start writing the composition soon in order to have it in on time.

This approach to the selection of an item pool carries with it the assumption that the informants have provided an accurate account of the problematic situations associated with the college environment, as well as the assumption that the particular situations selected will continue to have a high probability of occurrence over the period of time during which the assessment is to take place. These assumptions are capable of direct empirical confirmation by utilizing a different group of informants, and by surveying the frequency of occurrence of these situations at a later point in time.

## Interpretation of Test Responses

In discussing the assumptions underlying the interpretation of behavioral tests, we may note the basic distinction drawn by Goodenough (1949) between the ''sign'' and the ''sample'' approaches to the interpretation of test responses. The sign approach assumes that the response may best be constructed as an indirect manifestation of some underlying personality characteristic. The sample approach, on the other hand, assumes that the test behavior constitutes a subset of the actual behaviors of interest. Whereas traditional personality tests have typically taken the sign approach to interpretation, behavioral procedures approach test interpretation with the sample orientation.

The assumption that behavioral test responses constitute a sample of certain response tendencies is closely tied to the assumption that the test items themselves consist of a representative sample of situations relevant to the behaviors of interest. In the assessment of assertiveness toward authority, for example, a sampling interpretation of the individual's test reponses would rest on the assumption that the test items represent an adequate sample of interpersonal situations involving authority figures.

Another issue related to the interpretation of test behavior as a sample of criterion behavior is that of the *method* employed in allowing for the expression of the response. The ideal approach to response expression would constitute the individual's actual response in a real-life situation, in that this represents the most direct approach to behavioral sampling. Within certain settings, such as hospitals and classrooms, this approach can be readily implemented. Unless these observations are unobtrusive, the assumption that the behavior remains unaffected by the assessment procedures may turn out to be faulty. For example, a study by Patterson and Harris[1] suggests that such considerations as deciding to have an outside observer, rather than the mother herself, make observations of her child's behavior in the home may produce differences in the data obtained. Moos (1968) similarly found a tendency for hospitalized patients to respond differently when they were aware that their behavior was being observed.

In instances where unobtrusive direct observation procedures are not feasible, other approaches to response expression must be employed. A potentially useful alternative consists of role-playing procedures, where the individual is required to act out his response as if he were actually in the situation in question. The available research on the use of role playing for assessment offers some support for the assumption that the role-played response parallels the behavior in the real-life setting. For example, in an attempt to predict competent behavior under conditions of interpersonal stress, Stanton and Litwak (1955) found that subjects' responses to role-playing situations involving such stress correlated .82 with independent ratings by informants who were familiar with the subjects' behavior in this type of situation. Further support for the value of role playing as an assessment procedure comes from the work of Weiss (1968) on the prediction of "reinforcing skill" in interpersonal situations. This assessment technique consists of placing the subject in a role-playing situation where he is asked to listen to a speaker and do whatever he can to "maintain rapport" with this individual. The frequency of the subject's reinforcing behaviors as recorded in the role-playing assessment has been found to be predictive of peer ratings for social behavior (e.g., "fun at a party"), and of independent ratings of the competence and reinforcing skill among therapists.

Still another approach in assessing an individual's response is through self-reports of behavior. The assumption associated with the use of self-report is that the individual can accurately observe and communicate his reaction to certain situations. The most extensive use of self-report procedures has been in conjunction with the assessment of anxiety. In the use of fear survey schedules, for example, a list of potentially frightening objects (e.g., blood, spiders) and situations (e.g., being criticized, being alone) is presented to the subject, who must indicate the extent to which he subjectively finds each of these to be frightening. Findings by Geer (1965) indicate that subjects' responses to specific items on the fear survey schedule (i.e., dogs, rats) were predictive (e.g., rho correlation ranging from .52 to .92) of their fear reaction when

---

[1] G. R. Patterson & A. Harris. Some methodological considerations for observation procedures. Paper presented at the meeting of the American Psychological Association, San Francisco, September 1968.

placed in an actual situation where they had to approach these objects. Paul's (1966) successful use of the S-R Inventory of Anxiousness to predict anxiety in a public speaking situation ($r = .50$ and $.72$ for two separate samples) similarly adds credibility to the assumption that verbal self-prediction bears a good correspondence to behavior in real-life situations.

The use of direct observation, role playing, or self-report procedures for behavioral assessment is based on the assumption that the particular method selected contributes little variance to the responses that are sampled. Although it is possible that the results obtained by using each of these different methods will differ, there currently exists no research evidence bearing on this question. Using Campbell and Fiske's (1959) suggested approach to studying method variance, however, the degree of correspondence among responses obtained through these different procedures can readily be subjected to direct empirical test.

In addition to the question of the particular method employed in the assessment procedures, there is also the issue of how to *categorize* or *score* this response. Rather than attempting to develop scoring keys based on either intuitive or empirical grounds, the behavioral approach to assessment utilizes information about the actual criterion behaviors—that is, those behaviors which are the target of the prediction. In the case of the S-R Inventory of Anxiousness (Endler & Hunt, 1966, 1969), for example, 14 "modes of response" were selected to assess the individual's "anxiety" reaction to any given situation. These several modes of response (e.g., heart beating faster, getting an uneasy feeling, wanting to avoid a situation, perspiring) were chosen to represent the multidimensional character that has been found to typify the actual fear response (cf. Lang, 1968).

In their description of the behavioral analytic approach to assessing effectiveness, Goldfried and D'Zurilla (1969) have suggested guidelines for conducting a criterion analysis to be used in establishing standards for scoring behavioral measures. This behaviorally oriented criterion analysis consists of (1) a *situational analysis*, in which the relevant environmental events are sampled; (2) a *response enumeration*, where a pool of responses for each of these several situations is obtained; and (3) the *response evaluation*, which entails the categorization of each potential course of action in a situation according to its degree of effectiveness. So as to parallel the "actual" effectiveness of these several behaviors in the real-life setting, it is recommended that the judgments of effectiveness be made by "significant others"—that is, individuals who are respected by those people toward whom the assessment is being directed, and who have the role of labeling behavior as being effective in that particular environment.

The basic assumption underlying this approach to establishing scoring criteria is that there exist common standards or behavioral norms for effectiveness within the particular life setting in question, and that these standards are relatively stable over the period of time during which the assessment is to take place. In light of the rapidly changing value system associated with many aspects of our society, this assumption may prove to be faulty in the assessment of certain behaviors (e.g., students' interactions with authority). It should be emphasized, however, that failure to confirm empirically the existence of a stable set of behavioral norms would have implications not only for the establishment of scoring criteria but also for the selection of criterion behaviors against which any validation could take place. However, this would pose a problem for any attempt at predicting human behavior, whether it be behavioral or traditional.

## COMPARISON OF TRADITIONAL AND BEHAVIORAL ASSESSMENT

At this point, a more direct comparison may be drawn between traditional and behavioral approaches to assessment, taking into account the levels of inference associated with each, and the available data on comparative predictive ability.

### Comparative Levels of Inference

In order to compare more systematically the nature of the assumptions involved in traditional and behavioral assessment, the inferences associated with the prediction of behavior from each of these approaches have been depicted graphically in Figure 1. The arrows in the figure pointing upward refer to those assessment inferences or inductions associated with the interpretation of the test scores themselves, whereas the arrows pointing downward reflect validation inferences—that is, deductions from the interpretation of the test which are associated with the prediction of the criterion. The three levels of inference associated with both the induction and deduction include: (1) Those inferences that allow one to conclude that the *recorded observation* accurately reflects the occurrence of some specific *event,* namely, the ''true'' test response, or the ''true'' criterion behavior. This is clearly the most basic of all inferences and carries with it such assumptions as the reliability with which the test response and criterion behavior is recorded and scored, as well as the absence of variance which might be attributed to the specific method employed in assessing the event in question (cf. Campbell & Fiske, 1959). (2) The second level of inference, in which one concludes that the event being measured is a sample of some *larger population,* is based on the assumption that the responses obtained by the test—or the criterion behaviors selected for observation—are representative of the relevant aspects of the entire population of true responses (or criterion behaviors) in question. (3) Following the assumption that the population of responses has been adequately sampled, it may additionally be inferred that the test performance has been indicative of some unobservable *construct* and, in turn, that this construct may be reflected by certain criterion behaviors. This third level of inference requires theoretical assumptions that describe the relation between the construct in question, and both the population of responses and the population of criterion behaviors.

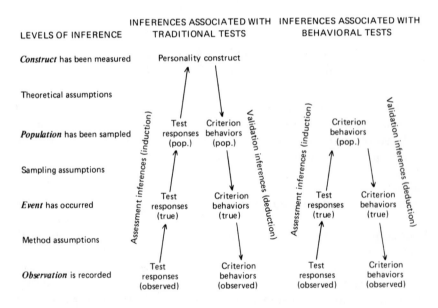

*Fig. 1.   Levels of inference in traditional and behavioral tests*

Using this schematic outline of levels of inference, we may compare the prediction process from two approaches to assessment. As an example, consider the prediction of anxiety in relationships with same-sex peers, first from the traditional point of view and then from a behavioral approach.

Using a traditional test of personality, the most basic of all assumptions would be that the relevant test responses as observed (e.g., presence of inanimate movement on the Rorschach or high social introversion on the MMPI) are only negligibly affected by scoring error or any artifacts associated with the measurement process itself. These "true" test responses, in turn, are assumed to constitute an adequate sample of some hypothetical population of potential anxiety-related test responses which the particular examinee might give if, for example, the measure were administered at another time or the length of the test had been extended. Once the adequacy of this sample has been assumed, additional assumptions are required to relate this population of signs to an underlying personality construct believed to be related to anxiety in same-sex peer relations. The construct selected would vary from theory to theory, and might include such inferred characteristics as basic insecurity, conflicts over underlying homosexual tendencies, incongruence between self- and ideal-concept, or other similarly hypothesized variables. In using this information deductively to predict behavior, additional theoretical assumptions are required to relate the inferred personality construct to a population of criterion behaviors which might reflect various anxiety-laden interactions with same-sex peers. Depending upon the particular theory of personality employed at this stage of the prediction process, the behavioral definition is apt to vary. From this hypothetical population of behaviors, specific behavioral interactions are then sampled (e.g., conversational ability in specific social situations), and procedures for measuring these criterion behaviors are selected (e.g., direct observation, peer ratings).

A behavioral test to predict anxiety in same-sex peer relationships, by contrast, would consist of placing the subject in a representative sample of situations requiring peer contact and eliciting his response. Inasmuch as this procedure might take any one of several forms (e.g., direct observations in actual situations, role-playing, self-report), it is assumed that the individual's "true" response contributes more variance than does the particular method selected. The next level of inference is based on the assumption that the elicited responses have provided an adequate sample of potential criterion behaviors which define anxiety in such relationships. In contrast with the traditional approaches to personality assessment, behavioral assessment views the responses given as consisting of samples of the criterion themselves. Further, these behaviors are derived directly from an empirically defined criterion analysis (e.g., sampling situations involving interactions with peers), thereby eliminating the need for either the inductive or deductive use of theoretical assumptions. Once these criterion behaviors to be used for the validation have been specified, essentially the same psychometric procedures employed by traditional personality measures would be used in testing for criterion-related validity.

This comparison between the two approaches to prediction, in fact, is oversimplified. Rarely would a traditional diagnostician predict to a criterion measure, such as anxiety in relations with members of the same sex, on the basis of one type of test response and the inference from one personality construct. Rather, several types of responses, elicted by a battery of different tests, would be evaluated, and several personality constructs inferred. Then, as a further inference involving additional theoretical assumptions, these constructs would be interrelated to provide a dynamic picture of the individual's personality functioning. This attempt to develop a "theory of a person" (cf. Sundberg & Tyler, 1962) involves inferences most removed from the data and most dependent upon the clinician's theoretical orientation and clinical experience.

Even in the more simplified form in which we have presented it, the comparison underlines a crucial difference in the construction of traditional and behavioral tests. To recapitulate, traditional personality tests have developed methods for eliciting behaviors that may serve as signs of underlying personality variables. The responses elicited by the tests serve as a basis for theoretical inferences regarding basic personality functioning, which is then related to criterion measures. By contrast, behavioral tests, such as those following the behavioral analytic model (Goldfried & D'Zurilla, 1969), may be developed by working backward from criterion measures. That is, a sampling of the criterion situation and behaviors is obtained first, after which an attempt is made to develop efficient measurement procedures for assessing these behavior-environment interactions.

### Comparative Predictive Ability

It is interesting to note that because of its greater predictive potential, there has been a general leaning over the years toward more direct, criterion-related measures within the realm of traditional personality testing. In conjunction with a review of the prognostic use of various personality measures, for example, Fulkerson and Barry (1961) have concluded that of all the possible ways to predict behavior, the most accurate predictor rémains the individual's previous behavior in similar situations.

After reviewing the research on the TAT, Murstein (1963) concluded that certain aspects of the subject's response to the testing situation itself may prove to be potentially useful in predicting overt behavior in the criterion situation. As he noted, however, these responses "are not really part of the stories, but represent miniature bits of overt behavior similar to the criterion overt behavior. It is small wonder, therefore, that caustic comments in the telling of a TAT story are related to overt aggression (pp. 318-319)." In a similar vein, Kagan (1956), rather than utilizing theoretical constructs to improve the relationship between TAT scores and overt aggression, was successful in improving predictive ability by using stimulus materials that more accurately sampled the actual criterion situation (rather than the typical ambiguous stimuli), and scored the protocols for only those aspects of aggression (e.g., tendency to fight) that were of interest in the criterion situation.

In the case of the Rorschach, the procedure that most closely approximates scoring and interpreting test responses as a sample of overt behavior has been developed by Friedman (1953). Using Werner's (1948) description of perceptual and cognitive development, Friedman has described a procedure for using each response as a sample of perceptual behavior. In comparison to many of the other approaches to scoring the Rorschach, Friedman's approach stays much closer to the data and involves considerably fewer assumptions and—perhaps as a result of this—has consistently resulted in favorable empirical validation (Goldfried, Stricker, & Weiner, 1971).

In addition to these indirect findings regarding the predictive potential of behavioral assessment, there have been some studies in which a direct comparison was made between the predictive ability of traditional and behavioral assessment procedures (e.g., Carroll, 1952; Hase & Goldberg, 1967; Paul 1966; Wallace & Sechrest, 1963).

In conjunction with a larger study on the effectiveness of systematic desensitization as a procedure for reducing anxiety in a public speaking situation, Paul (1966) administered a variety of personality measures prior to treatment (Institute for Personality and Ability Testing [IPAT] Anxiety Scale, Bendig's Emotionality Scale, Bendig's Extraversion-Introversion Scale, Anxiety Differential, and the S-R Inventory of Anxiousness). Using as a criterion the subjects' personal report of confidence when in a public speaking situation, Paul found that the correlations obtained with the S-R Inventory of Anxiousness item involving public speaking exceeded by far the correlations found with the more traditional tests. Thus, with data from two separate samples, the average correlation obtained between criterion and the S-R Inventory was .61, in comparison to correlations of .15 for IPAT anxiety, of −.24 for extraversion-introversion, .07 for emotionality, and .29 for the Anxiety Differential.

Wallace and Sechrest (1963) conducted a study in which they compared the predictive accuracy of several projective techniques with the subjects' own self-ratings in the assessment of achievement, hostility, somatic concern, and religious concern. The results of the study indicated that whereas the correlations between criterion (peer ratings on each of the variables) and self-ratings on these dimensions averaged .57, the average correlations for the other tests were .05 for the Rorschach, .08 for the TAT, and .14 for Rotter's Incomplete Sentences Blank.

The results of a study reported by Carroll (1952) similarly found simple self-ratings yielded higher correlations than did scores on the Guilford-Martin Personnel Inventory. In an analysis of method variance via a multitrait-method correlation matrix, Campbell and Fiske (1959) have noted that Carroll's findings also suggest that the self-ratings appeared to be less confounded by method variance.

Using the item pool of the California Psychological Inventory, Hase and Goldberg (1967) compared the predictive power of scales constructed by various means (e.g., theoretical, empirical, factor-analytic) with subjects' self-ratings. Against the criterion of peer ratings on such variables as dominance, sociability, responsibility, and other similar characteristics, Hase and Goldberg reported that "in almost every case, the subjects' self-ratings were more predictive. . .than *any* of the scales (p. 245)." Even when linear regression equations were used to capitalize on the optimal combination of scales, self-prediction proved to be more accurate.

Inasmuch as the growing interest in behavioral approaches to assessment is a recent phenomenon, relatively few studies have been carried out to compare their predictive ability with more traditional procedures. The limited data that are available, however, would seem to favor behavioral assessment.

## CONCLUSIONS

One of the basic characteristics of behavioral assessment is the attempt to maximize the similarity between test response and criterion measure. The desirability of approaching the prediction process in such a way so as to reduce the number of inferences has been argued by Cronbach (1956), who has observed:

Assessment encounters trouble because it involves hazardous inferences. Very little inference is involved when a test is a sample of the criterion or when an empirical key is developed. Simple test interpretations involve inference from test to construct to behavioral prediction. But assessors attempt a maximum inference from tests. As current writers describe the process. . .personality theory is applied to weave nomothetic constructs into a construct of the individual's personality structure; predictions are then derived by inferring how that structure will interact with the known or guessed properties of the situation. Assessors have been foolhardy to venture predictions of behavior in unanalyzed situations, using tests whose construct interpretations are dubious and personality theory which has more gaps than solid matter (pp. 173–174).

While the successfully validated test provides support for the numerous assumptions involved in predicting criterion behaviors from test behavior, the unsuccessful effort at validation provides no clue to the weak link in the inference process. The analysis presented in this article suggests that any breakdown of the predictive powers of a test may productively be viewed as due to one or more inferences based on faulty assumptions concerning the measurement process and the phenomena of interest.

In the case of traditional personality tests, some of the basic underlying assumptions—such as the existence of behavioral consistencies across a wide variety of stimulus situations—have been found to be unsupported by empirical evidence. Other assumptions, such as those involving theoretical relationships hypothesized between test responses and constructs, are often vaguely stated or poorly defined and consequently are difficult to test directly. The assessment of personality by means of behavioral tests, by contrast, is more consistent with the findings that human functioning is due to both the individual's behavioral repertoire and the demands of the specific stimulus situation. Further, relatively fewer assumptions are associated with this approach to test construction, and those that are involved can more readily be subjected to direct experimental investigation. By allowing for a more systematic elimination of erroneous inferences when validity coefficients are unsatisfactory, the behavioral approach to personality assessment would appear to have greater potential for the development of procedures that may enhance our ability to predict human behavior.

## REFERENCES

Campbell, D. T., & Fiske, D. W. Convergent and discriminant validation by the multitrait-multimethod matrix. *Psychological Bulletin,* 1959, *56,* 81-105.

Carroll, J. B. Ratings on traits measured by a factored personality inventory. *Journal of Abnormal and Social Psychology,* 1952, *47,* 626-632.

Chapman, L. J., & Chapman, J. P. Illusory correlations as an obstacle to the use of valid psychodiagnostic signs. *Journal of Abnormal Psychology,* 1969, *74,* 271-280.

Cronbach, L. J. Assessment of individual differences. *Annual Review of Psychology,* 1956, *7,* 173-196.

Dahlstrom, W. G., & Welsh, G. S. *An MMPI handbook.* Minneapolis: University of Minnesota Press, 1960.

Endler, N. S., & Hunt, J. McV. Sources of behavioral variance as measured by the S-R Inventory of Anxiousness. *Psychological Bulletin,* 1966, *65,* 336-346.

Endler, N. S., & Hunt, J. McV. Generalizability of contributions from sources of variance in the S-R Inventories of Anxiousness. *Journal of Personality,* 1969, *37,* 1-24.

Friedman, H. Perceptual regression in schizophrenia: An hypothesis suggested by use of the Rorschach test. *Journal of Projective Techniques,* 1953, *17,* 171-185.

Fulkerson, S. C., & Barry, J. R. Methodology and research on the prognostic use of psychological tests. *Psychological Bulletin,* 1961, *58,* 177-204.

Geer, J. H. The development of a scale to measure fear. *Behavior Research and Therapy,* 1965, *3,* 45-53.

Goldfried, M. R., & D'Zurilla, T. J. A behavioral-analytic model for assessing competence. In C. D. Spielberger (Ed.), *Current topics in clinical and community psychology.* Vol. 1. New York: Academic Press, 1969.

Goldfried, M. R., & Ingling, J. H. The connotative and symbolic meaning of the Bender-Gestalt. *Journal of Projective Techniques and Personality Assessment,* 1964, *28,* 185-191.

Goldfried, M. R., & Pomeranz, D. M. Role of assessment in behavior modification. *Psychological Reports,* 1968, *23,* 75-87.

Goldfried, M. R., Stricker, G., & Weiner, I. B. *Rorschach handbook of clinical and research applications.* Englewood Cliffs, N.J.: Prentice-Hall, 1971.

Goodenough, F. L. *Mental testing.* New York: Rinehart, 1949.

Greenspoon, J., & Gersten, C. D. A new look at psychological testing: Psychological testing from the standpoint of a behaviorist. *American Psychologist,* 1967, *22,* 848-853.

Hartshorne, H., & May, M. A. *Studies in the nature of character.* Vol. 1. *Studies in deceit.* New York: Macmillan, 1928.

Hase, H. D., & Goldberg, L. R. Comparative validity of different strategies of constructing personality inventory scales. *Psychological Bulletin,* 1967, *67,* 231-248.

Hutt, M. L. *The Hutt adaptation of the Bender-Gestalt test: Revised.* New York: Grune and Stratton, 1968.

Hutt, M. L., & Briskin, G. J. *The clinical use of the revised Bender-Gestalt test.* New York: Grune and Stratton, 1960.

Jessor, R., & Hammond, K. R. Construct validity and the Taylor anxiety scale. *Psychological Bulletin,* 1957, *54,* 161-170.

Kagan, J. The measurement of overt aggression from fantasy. *Journal of Abnormal and Social Psychology,* 1956, *52,* 390-393.

Kanfer, F. H., & Saslow, G. Behavioral diagnosis. In C. M. Franks (Ed.), *Behavior therapy: Appraisal and status.* New York: McGraw-Hill, 1969.

Lang, P. J. Fear reduction and fear behavior: Problems in treating a construct. In H. H. Strupp & L. Luborsky (Eds.), *Research in psychotherapy.* Washington, D.C.: American Psychological Association, 1968.

Little, K. B., & Shneidman, E. S. The validity of MMPI interpretations. *Journal of Consulting Psychology,* 1954, *18,* 425-428.

Loevinger, J. Objective tests as instruments of psychological theory. *Psychological Reports,* 1957, *3* (Monograph Supplement 9).

London, P. *The modes and morals of psychotherapy.* New York: Holt, Rinehart & Winston, 1964.

MacFarlane, J. W., & Tuddenham, R. D. Problems in the validation of projective techniques. In H. H. Anderson & G. L. Anderson (Eds.), *An introduction to projective techniques.* Englewood Cliffs, N.J.: Prentice-Hall, 1951.

Meehl, P. E. The cognitive activity of the clinician. *American Psychologist,* 1960, *15,* 19-27.

Mischel, W. *Personality and assessment.* New York: Wiley, 1968.

Mischel, W., & Ebbesen, E. B. Attention in delay of gratification. *Journal of Personality and Social Psychology,* 1970, *16,* 329-337.

Moos, R. H. Behavioral effects of being observed: Reactions to a wireless radio transmitter. *Journal of Consulting and Clinical Psychology,* 1968, *32,* 383-388.

Moos, R. H. Sources of variance in responses to questionnaires and in behavior. *Journal of Abnormal Psychology,* 1969, *74,* 405-412.

Murstein, B. I. Assumptions, adaptation level, and projective techniques. *Perceptual and Motor Skills,* 1961, *12,* 107-125.

Murstein, B. I. *Theory and research in projective techniques (emphasizing the TAT).* New York: Wiley, 1963.

Paul, G. *Insight vs. desensitization in psychotherapy.* Stanford, University Press, 1966.

Pervin, L. *Personality: Theory, assessment, and research.* New York: Wiley, 1970.

Peterson, D. R. *The clinical study of social behavior.* New York: Appleton-Century-Crofts, 1968.

Rychlak, J. F. *A philosophy of science for personality theory.* Boston: Houghton Mifflin, 1968.

Stanton, H. R., & Litwak, E. Toward the development of a short form Test of Interpersonal Competence. *American Sociological Review,* 1955, *20,* 668-674.

Sundberg, N. D., & Tyler, L. E. *Clinical psychology.* New York: Appleton-Century-Crofts, 1962.

Wallace, J. An abilities conception of personality: Some implications for personality measurement. *American Psychologist,* 1966, *21,* 132-138.

Wallace, J. What units shall we employ? Allport's question revisited. *Journal of Consulting Psychology,* 1967, *31,* 56-64.

Wallace, J., & Sechrest, L. Frequency hypothesis and content analysis of projective techniques. *Journal of Consulting Psychology,* 1963, *27,* 387-393.

Weiss, R. L. Operant conditioning techniques in psychological assessment. In P. McReynolds (Ed.), *Advances in psychological assessment.* Palo Alto, Calif.: Science and Behavior Books, 1968.

Werner, H. *Comparative psychology of mental development.* (Rev. ed.) Chicago: Follett, 1948.

Wheeler, W. M. An analysis of Rorschach indices of male homosexuality. *Rorschach Research Exchange,* 1949, *13,* 97-126.

Wolpe, J., & Lang, P. J. A fear survey schedule for use in behavior therapy. *Behaviour Research and Therapy,* 1964, *2,* 27-30.

Zigler, E., & Phillips, L. Psychiatric diagnosis: A critique. *Journal of Abnormal and Social Psychology,* 1961, *63,* 607-618.

# 3

## Some Current Dimensions of Applied Behavior Analysis

*Donald M. Baer*
*Montrose M. Wolf*
*Todd R. Risley*

The analysis of individual behavior is a problem in scientific demonstration, reasonably well understood (Skinner, 1953, Sec. 1), comprehensively described (Sidman, 1960), and quite thoroughly practiced (*Journal of the Experimental Analysis of Behavior*, 1957—). That analysis has been pursued in many settings over many years. Despite variable precision, elegance, and power, it has resulted in general descriptive statements of mechanisms that can produce many of the forms that individual behavior may take.

The statement of these mechanisms establishes the possibility of their application to problem behavior. A society willing to consider a technology of its own behavior apparently is likely to support that application when it deals with socially important behaviors, such as retardation, crime, mental illness, or education. Such applications have appeared in recent years. Their current number and the interest which they create apparently suffice to generate a journal for their display. That display may well lead to the widespread examination of these applications, their refinement, and eventually their replacement by better applications. Better applications, it is hoped, will lead to a better state of society, to

Reprinted from *Journal of Applied Behavior Analysis*, 1968, *1*, 91-97. Copyright © 1968 by the Society for the Experimental Analysis of Behavior, Inc. Reprinted by permission.

whatever extent the behavior of its members can contribute to the goodness of a society. Since the evaluation of what is a ''good'' society is in itself a behavior of its members, this hope turns on itself in a philosophically interesting manner. However, it is at least a fair presumption that behavioral applications, when effective, can sometimes lead to social approval and adoption.

Behavioral applications are hardly a new phenomenon. Analytic behavioral applications, it seems, are. Analytic behavioral application is the process of applying sometimes tentative principles of behavior to the improvement[1] of specific behaviors, and simultaneously evaluating whether or not any changes noted are indeed attributable to the process of application—and if so, to what parts of that process. In short, analytic behavioral application is a self-examining, self-evaluating, discovery-oriented research procedure for studying behavior. So is all experimental behavioral research (at least, according to the usual strictures of modern graduate training). The differences are matters of emphasis and of selection.

The differences between applied and basic research are not differences between that which ''discovers'' and that which merely ''applies'' what is already known. Both endeavors ask what controls the behavior under study. Non-applied research is likely to look at any behavior and at any variable which may conceivably relate to it. Applied research is constrained to look at variables that can be effective in improving the behavior under study. Thus it is equally a matter of research to discover that the behaviors typical of retardates can be related to oddities of their chromosome structure and to oddities of their reinforcement history. But (currently) the chromosome structure of the retardate does not lend itself to experimental manipulation in the interests of bettering that behavior, whereas his reinforcement input is always open to current redesign.

Similarly, applied research is constrained to examining behaviors which are socially important, rather than convenient for study. It also implies, very frequently, the study of those behaviors in their usual social settings, rather than in a ''laboratory'' setting. But a laboratory is simply

---

[1]If a behavior is socially important, the usual behavior analysis will aim at its improvement. The social value dictating this choice is obvious. However, it can be just as illuminating to demonstrate how a behavior may be worsened, and there will arise occasions when it will be socially important to do so. Disruptive classroom behavior may serve as an example. Certainly it is a frequent plague of the educational system. A demonstration of what teacher procedures produce more of this behavior is not necessarily the reverse of a demonstration of how to promote positive study behaviors. There may be classroom situations in which the teacher cannot readily establish high rates of study, yet still could avoid high rates of disruption, if she knew what in her own procedures leads to this disruption. The demonstration which showed her that would thus have its value.

a place so designed that experimental control of relevant variables is as, easy as possible. Unfortunately, the usual social setting for important behaviors is rarely such a place. Consequently, the analysis of socially important behaviors becomes experimental only with difficulty. As the terms are used here, a non-experimental analysis is a contradiction in terms. Thus, analytic behavioral applications by definition achieve experimental control of the processes they contain, but since they strive for this control against formidable difficulties, they achieve it less often per study than would a laboratory-based attempt. Consequently, the rate of displaying experimental control required of behavioral applications has become correspondingly less than the standards typical of laboratory research. This is not because the applier is an easy-going, liberal, or generous fellow, but because society rarely will allow its important behaviors, in their correspondingly important settings, to be manipulated repeatedly for the merely logical comfort of a scientifically sceptical audience.

Thus, the evaluation of a study which purports to be an applied behavior analysis is somewhat different than the evaluation of a similar laboratory analysis. Obviously, the study must be *applied, behavioral,* and *analytic;* in addition, it should be *technological, conceptually systematic,* and *effective,* and it should display some generality. These terms are explored below and compared to the criteria often stated for the evaluation of behavioral research which, though analytic, is not applied.

## APPLIED

The label applied is not determined by the research procedures used but by the interest which society shows in the problems being studied. In behavioral application, the behavior, stimuli, and/or organism under study are chosen because of their importance to man and society, rather than their importance to theory. The non-applied researcher may study eating behavior, for example, because it relates directly to metabolism, and there are hypotheses about the interaction between behavior and metabolism. The non-applied researcher also may study bar-pressing because it is a convenient response for study: easy for the subject, and simple to record and integrate with theoretically significant environmental events. By contrast, the applied researcher is likely to study eating because there are children who eat too little and adults who eat too much, and he will study eating in exactly those individuals rather than in more convenient ones. The applied researcher may also study bar-pressing if it is integrated with socially important stimuli. A program for a teaching machine may use bar-pressing behavior to indicate mastery of an arithmetic skill. It is the arithmetic stimuli which are important.

(However, some future applied study could show that bar-pressing is more practical in the the process of education than a pencil-writing response.[2])

In applied research, there is typically a close relationship between the behavior and stimuli under study and the subject in whom they are studied. Just as there seem to be few behaviors that are intrinsically the target of application, there are few subjects who automatically confer on their study the status of application. An investigation of visual signal detection in the retardate may have little immediate importance, but a similar study in radarscope watchers has considerable. A study of language development in the retardate may be aimed directly at an immediate social problem, while a similar study in the MIT sophomore may not. Enhancement of the reinforcing value of praise for the retardate alleviates an immediate deficit in his current environment, but enhancement of the reinforcing value of 400 Hz (cps) tone for the same subject probably does not. Thus, a primary question in the evaluation of applied research is: how immediately important is this behavior or these stimuli to this subject?

## BEHAVIORAL

Behaviorism and pragmatism seem often to go hand in hand. Applied research is eminently pragmatic; it asks how it is possible to get an individual to do something effectively. Thus it usually studies what subjects can be brought to do rather than what they can be brought to say; unless, of course, a verbal response is the behavior of interest. Accordingly a subject's verbal description of his own nonverbal behavior usually would not be accepted as a measure of his actual behavior unless it were independently substantiated. Hence there is little applied value in the demonstration that an impotent man can be made to say that he is no longer impotent. The relevant question is not what he can say, but what he can do. Application has not been achieved until this question has been answered satisfactorily. (This assumes, of course, that the total goal of the applied researcher is not simply to get his patient-subjects to stop complaining to him. Unless society agrees that this researcher should not be

---

[2]Research may use the most convenient behaviors and stimuli available, and yet exemplify an ambition in the researcher eventually to achieve application to socially important settings. For example, a study may seek ways to give a light flash a durable conditioned reinforcing function, because the experimenter wishes to know how to enhance school children's responsiveness to approval. Nevertheless, durable bar-pressing for that light flash is no guarantee that the obvious classroom analogue will produce durable reading behavior for teacher statements of "Good!" Until the analogue has been proven sound, application has not been achieved.

bothered, it will be difficult to defend that goal as socially important.)

Since the behavior of an individual is composed of physical events, its scientific study requires their precise measurement. As a result, the problem of reliable quantification arises immediately. The problem is the same for applied research as it is for non-applied research. However, non-applied research typically will choose a response easily quantified in a reliable manner, whereas applied research rarely will have that option. As a result, the applied researcher must try harder, rather than ignore this criterion of all trustworthy research. Current applied research often shows that thoroughly reliable quantification of behavior can be achieved, even in thoroughly difficult settings. However, it also suggests that instrumented recording with its typical reliability will not always be possible. The reliable use of human beings to quantify the behavior of other human beings is an area of psychological technology long since well developed, thoroughly relevant, and very often necessary to applied behavior analysis.

A useful tactic in evaluating the behavioral attributes of a study is to ask not merely, was *behavior* changed? but also, *whose* behavior? Ordinarily it would be assumed that it was the subject's behavior which was altered; yet careful reflection may suggest that this was not necessarily the case. If humans are observing and recording the behavior under study, then any change may represent a change only in their observing and recording responses, rather than in the subject's behavior. Explicit measurement of the reliability of human observers thus becomes not merely good technique, but a prime criterion of whether the study was appropriately behavioral. (A study merely of the behavior of observers is behavioral, of course, but probably irrelevant to the researcher's goal.) Alternatively, it may be that only the experimenter's behavior has changed. It may be reported, for example, that a certain patient rarely dressed himself upon awakening, and consequently would be dressed by his attendant. The experimental technique to be applied might consist of some penalty imposed unless the patient were dressed within half an hour after awakening. Recording of an increased probablity of self-dressing under these conditions might testify to the effectiveness of the penalty in changing the behavior; however, it might also testify to the fact that the patient would in fact probably dress himself within half an hour of arising, but previously was rarely left that long undressed before being clothed by his efficient attendant. (The attendant now is the penalty-imposing experimenter and therefore always gives the patient his full half-hour, in the interests of precise experimental technique, of course.) This error is an elementary one, perhaps. But it suggests that in general, when an experiment proceeds from its baseline to its first experimental phase, changes in what is measured need not always reflect the behavior of the subject.

## ANALYTIC

The analysis of a behavior, as the term is used here, requires a believable demonstration of the events that can be responsible for the occurrence or nonoccurrence of that behavior. An experimenter has achieved an analysis of a behavior when he can exercise control over it. By common laboratory standards, that has meant an ability of the experimenter to turn the behavior on and off, or up and down, at will. Laboratory standards have usually made this control clear by demonstrating it repeatedly, even reduntantly, over time. Applied research, as noted before, cannot often approach this arrogantly frequent clarity of being in control of important behaviors. Consequently, application, to be analytic, demonstrates control when it can, and thereby presents its audience with a problem of judgment. The problem, of course, is whether the experimenter has shown enough control, and often enough, for believability. Laboratory demonstrations, either by over-replication or an acceptable probability level derived from statistical tests of grouped data, make this judgment more implicit than explicit. As Sidman points out (1960), there is still a problem of judgment in any event, and it is probably better when explicit.

There are at least two designs commonly used to demonstrate reliable control of an important behavioral change. The first can be referred to as the ''reversal'' technique. Here a behavior is measured, and the measure is examined over time until its stability is clear. Then, the experimental variable is applied. The behavior continues to be measured, to see if the variable will produce a behavioral change. If it does, the experimental variable is discontinued or altered, to see if the behavioral change just brought about depends on it. If so, the behavioral change should be lost or diminished (thus the term ''reversal''). The experimental variable then is applied again, to see if the behavioral change can be recovered. If it can, it is pursued further, since this is applied research and the behavioral change sought is an important one. It may be reversed briefly again, and yet again, if the setting in which the behavior takes place allows further reversals. But that setting may be a school system or a family, and continued reversals may not be allowed. They may appear in themselves to be detrimental to the subject if pursued too often. (Whether they are in fact detrimental is likely to remain an unexamined question so long as the social setting in which the behavior is studied dictates against using them repeatedly. Indeed, it may be that repeated reversals in some applications have a positive effect on the subject, possibly contributing to the discrimination of relevant stimuli involved in the problem.)

In using the reversal technique, the experimenter is attempting to show that an analysis of the behavior is at hand: that whenever he applies a certain variable, the behavior is produced, and whenever he removes this variable, the behavior is lost. Yet applied behavior analysis is exactly the kind of research which can make this technique self-defeating in time. Application typically means producing valuable behavior; valuable behavior usually meets extra-experimental reinforcement in a social setting; thus, valuable behavior, once set up, may no longer be dependent upon the experimental technique which created it. Consequently, the number of reversals possible in applied studies may be limited by the nature of the social setting in which the behavior takes place, in more ways than one.

An alternative to the reversal technique may be called the "multiple baseline" technique. This alternative may be of particular value when a behavior appears to be irreversible or when reversing the behavior is undesirable. In the multiple-baseline technique, a number of responses are identified and measured over time to provide baselines against which changes can be evaluated. With these baselines established, the experimenter then applies an experimental variable to one of the behaviors, produces a change in it, and perhaps notes little or no change in the other baselines. If so, rather than reversing the just produced change, he instead applies the experimental variable to one of the other, as yet unchanged, responses. If it changes at that point, evidence is accruing that the experimental variable is indeed effective, and that the prior change was not simply a matter of coincidence. The variable then may be applied to still another response, and so on. The experimenter is attempting to show that he has a reliable experimental variable, in that each behavior changes maximally only when the experimental variable is applied to it.

How many reversals, or how many baselines, make for believability is a problem for the audience. If statistical analysis is applied, the audience must then judge the suitability of the inferential statistic chosen and the propriety of these data for that test. Alternatively, the audience may inspect the data directly and relate them to past experience with similar data and similar procedures. In either case, the judgments required are highly qualitative, and rules cannot always be stated profitably. However, either of the foregoing designs gathers data in ways that exemplify the concept of replication, and replication is the essence of believability. At the least, it would seem that an approach to replication is better than no approach at all. This should be especially true for so embryonic a field as behavioral application, the very possibility of which is still occasionally denied.

The preceding discussion has been aimed at the problem of *reliability:* whether or not a certain procedure was responsible for a corresponding behavioral change. The two general procedures described hardly exhaust the possibilities. Each of them has many variations now seen in practice; and current experience suggests that many more variations are badly needed if the technology of important behavioral change is to be consistently believable. Given some approach to reliability, there are further analyses of obvious value which can be built upon that base. For example, there is analysis in the sense of simplification and separation of component processes. Often enough, current behavioral procedures are complex, even "shotgun" in their application. When they succeed, they clearly need to be analyzed into their effective components. Thus, a teacher giving M & M's to a child may succeed in changing his behavior as planned. However, she has almost certainly confounded her attention and/or approval with each M & M. Further analysis may be approached by her use of attention alone, the effects of which can be compared to the effects of attention coupled with candies. Whether she will discontinue the M & M's, as in the reversal technique, or apply attention with M & M's to certain behaviors and attention alone to certain others, as in the multiple-baseline method, is again the problem in basic reliability discussed above. Another form of analysis is parametric: a demonstration of the effectiveness of different values of some variable in changing behavior. The problem again will be to make such an analysis reliable, and, as before, that might be approached by the repeated alternate use of different values on the same behavior (reversal), or by the application of different values to different groups of responses (multiple baseline). At this stage in the development of applied behavior analysis, primary concern is usually with reliability, rather than with parametric analysis or component analysis.


## TECHNOLOGICAL


"Technological" here means simply that the techniques making up a particular behavioral application are completely identified and described. In this sense, "play therapy" is not a technological description, nor is "social reinforcement." For purposes of application, all the salient ingredients of play therapy must be described as a set of contingencies between child response, therapist response, and play materials, before a statement of technique has been approached. Similarly, all the ingredients of social reinforcement must be specified (stimuli, contingency, and schedule) to qualify as a technological procedure.

   The best rule of thumb for evaluating a procedure description as technological is probably to ask whether a typically trained reader could replicate that procedure well enough to produce the same results, given only a reading of the description. This is very much the same criterion applied to procedure descriptions in non-applied research, of course. It needs emphasis, apparently in that there occasionally exists a less than precise stereotype of applied research. Where application is novel, and derived from principles produced through non-applied research, as in current applied behavior analysis, the reverse holds with great urgency.

Especially where the problem is application, procedural descriptions require considerable detail about all possible contingencies of procedure. It is not enough to say what is to be done when the subject makes response $R_1$; it is essential also whenever possible to say what is to be done if the subject makes the alternative responses, $R_2$, $R_3$, etc. For example, one may read that temper tantrums in children are often extinguished by closing the child in his room for the duration of the tantrums plus ten minutes. Unless that procedure description also states what should be done if the child tries to leave the room early, or kicks out the window, or smears feces on the walls, or begins to make strangling sounds, etc., it is not precise technological description.

## CONCEPTUAL SYSTEMS

The field of applied behavior analysis will probably advance best if the published descriptions of its procedures are not only precisely technological, but also strive for relevance to principle. To describe exactly how a preschool teacher will attend to jungle-gym climbing in a child frightened of heights is good technological description; but, further to call it a social-reinforcement procedure relates it to basic concepts of behavioral development. Similarly, to describe the exact sequence of color changes whereby a child is moved from a color discrimination to a form discrimination is good; to refer also to "fading" and "errorless discrimination" is better. In both cases, the total description is adequate for successful replication by the reader; and it also shows the reader how similar procedures may be derived from basic principles. This can have the effect of making a body of technology into a discipline rather than a collection of tricks. Collections of tricks historically have been difficult to expand systematically, and when they were extensive, difficult to learn and teach.

## EFFECTIVE

If the application of behavioral techniques does not produce large enough effects for practical value, then application has failed. Non-applied research often may be extremely valuable when it produces small but reliable effects, in that these effects testify to the operation of some variable which in itself has great theoretical importance. In application, the theoretical importance of a variable is usually not at issue. Its practical importance, specifically its power in altering behavior enough to be socially important, is the essential criterion. Thus, a study which shows that a new classroom technique can raise the grade level achievements of culturally deprived children from D− to D is not an obvious example of applied behavior analysis. That same study might conceivably revolutionize educational theory, but it clearly has not yet revolutionized education. This is of course a matter of degree: an increase in those children from D− to C might well be judged an important success by an audience which thinks that C work is a great deal different than D work, especially if C students are much less likely to become dropouts than D students.

In evaluating whether a given application has produced enough of a behavioral change to deserve the label, a pertinent question can be, how much did that behavior need to be changed? Obviously, that is not a scientific question, but a practical one. Its answer is likely to be supplied by people who must deal with the behavior. For example, ward personnel may be able to say that a hospitalized mute schizophrenic trained to use 10 verbal labels is not much better off in self-help skills than before, but that one with 50 such labels is a great deal more effective. In this case, the opinions of ward aides may be more relevant than the opinions of psycholinguists.


## GENERALITY

A behavioral change may be said to have generality if it proves durable over time, if it appears in a wide variety of possible environments, or if it spreads to a wide variety of related behaviors. Thus, the improvement of articulation in a clinic setting will prove to have generality if it endures into the future after the clinic visits stop; if the improved articulation is heard at home, at school, and on dates; or if the articulation of all words, not just the ones treated, improves. Application means practical improvement in important behaviors; thus, the more general that application, the better, in many cases. Therapists dealing with the development of heterosexual behavior may well point out there are socially appropriate limits to its generality, once developed; such limitations to generality are usually obvious. That generality is a valuable characteristic of applied behavior analysis which should be examined explicitly apparently is not quite that obvious and is stated here for emphasis.

That generality is not automatically accomplished whenever behavior is changed also needs occasional emphasis, especially in the evaluation of applied behavior analysis. It is sometimes assumed that application has failed when generalization does not take place in any widespread form. Such a conclusion has no generality itself. A procedure which is effective in changing behavior in one setting may perhaps be easily repeated in other settings, and thus accomplish the generalization sought. Furthermore, it may well prove the case that a given behavior change need be programmed in only a certain number of settings, one after another, perhaps, to accomplish eventually widespread generalization. A child may have 15 techniques for disrupting his parents, for example. The elimination of the most prevalent of these may still leave the remaining 14 intact and in force. The technique may still prove both valuable and fundamental, if when applied to the next four successfully, it also results in the "generalized" loss of the remaining 10. In general, generalization should be programmed, rather than expected or lamented.

Thus, in summary, an *applied* behavior analysis will make obvious the importance of the behavior changed, its quantitative characteristics, the experimental manipulations which analyze with clarity what was responsible for the change, the technologically exact description of all procedures contributing to that change, the effectiveness of those procedures in making sufficient change for value, and the generality of that change.

## REFERENCES

Journal of the Experimental Analysis of Behavior. Bloomington: Society for the Experimental Analysis of Behavior, 1957-.

Sidman, M. *Tactics of scientific research.* New York: Basic Books, 1960.

Skinner, B. F. *Science and human behavior.* New York: Macmillan, 1953.

# 4

Methodological and Assessment
Considerations in Evaluating Reinforcement
Programs in Applied Settings

*Alan E. Kazdin*

The application of reinforcement systems to various populations in treatment and educational settings has proliferated in recent years (Bandura, 1969; Kazdin & Bootzin, 1972; O'Leary & Drabman, 1971). In spite of the apparent success of programs applying contingent social and/or token reinforcement, the evaluation of such programs, in many instances, has revealed a failure to recognize certain methodological factors that may influence the results of experiments or their interpretation. The present paper attempts to discuss certain issues of experimental design that need to be considered in evaluating behavior-modification (operant conditioning) programs. The discussion is restricted in general to those studies specifically evaluating reinforcement programs because they usually employ a within-subject experimental design.

Studies have evaluated reinforcement programs in a variety of settings, including psychiatric hospitals (Ayllon & Azrin, 1965), classrooms (Wolf, Giles, & Hall, 1968), sheltered workshops (Zimmerman, Stuckey, Garlick, & Miller, 1969), institutions (Burchard, 1967), home-

Editor's note: This article has been abridged by the editors. The full article appeared in the *Journal of Applied Behavior Analysis,* 1973, 6, 517-531. The original article was published with Reviewer's comments (pp. 532-539) which are not included in this volume because of space limitations. However, the reader is referred to the original source for these excellent comments. Copyright © 1973 by the Society for the Experimental Analysis of Behavior, Inc. Reprinted and abridged by permission.

The author gratefully acknowledges K. Daniel O'Leary for his reading of the manuscript.

style treatment facilities (Phillips, 1968), the home (Wahler, 1969), and several others. The design employed in such studies is referred to as the intrasubject replication design (Sidman, 1960). . . .

Briefly, the basic logic of the design is to determine operations that relate functionally to the performance of behavior. The effect of a variable (e.g., contingent praise) on behavior is demonstrated by the consecutive presentation, removal, and representation of the variable to a subject. Control over a behavior is demonstrated if the behavior can be altered at will by altering the experimental operations. This research strategy is contrasted with the between-group approach, which seeks to demonstrate group differences after manipulation of the independent variable(s), usually in a single session. In this design, the data are subjected to statistical evaluation, and the focus is on mean differences instead of the behavior of individual subjects. . . .

## Specific Designs

The first design is frequently referred to as the ABAB design (where A refers to baseline conditions, and B refers to the experimental condition). . . . The design employs alternate presentations of the baseline and experimental conditions within a subject or group of subjects. Several variations may be used in this design. More than one experimental condition may be presented before the second baseline (or reversal) phase. . . . The reversal condition (usually a return to baseline) is an essential ingredient in this design. Only such a reversal can demonstrate that behavior changes only when the experimental condition is in effect. This design is quite powerful and rules out several alternative explanations that may account for behavior change.

In spite of the usefulness and power of the design, it makes a major presupposition, namely that behavior changes made under various experimental conditions are reversible when baseline conditions are reinstated. The demonstration of a functional relationship between the presence of the experimental condition and performance requires that the changes made be transient and therefore reversible. However, the changes made in reinforcement programs might not be reversible when the experimental condition is withdrawn (e.g., Surratt, Ulrich, & Hawkins, 1969). Indeed, we would hope that they are not always reversible, because this is tantamount to demonstrating only slight resistance to extinction.

If the effects of a reinforcement program are not reversible, the effect of the experimental condition(s) is not clear. . . .

Recently, other within-group designs have been discussed that are not susceptible to the reversibility problem outlined above. These designs are particularly useful in situations where: effecting a reversal would be undesirable because of exigencies of the situation; a reversal in responses would not be expected, as in training competence in academic skills; or where an experimental condition used is expected to inhibit a reversal of responses. The multiple-element baseline design (Sidman, 1960) or multiple-baseline design (Baer et al., 1968) provides a valuable alternative to the ABAB design. In this design there is no reversal of conditions required to demonstrate the efficacy of the contingencies. Instead, data are collected across behaviors, across individuals, or across situations.

In the multiple-baseline design across behaviors, two or more behaviors are observed for the subject(s). After the behaviors have reached stable rates, the experimental condition is implemented for only one of the behaviors while baseline conditions are continued for the other(s). The behavior exposed to the experimental condition should change while the other behavior remains at baseline levels. When rates are stable for both behaviors, the second behavior is brought into the contingency. This procedure is continued until all behaviors for which multiple-baseline data were gathered are sequentially brought into the contingency. Ideally, each behavior changes only as it is included in the experimental contingency and not before. This is a powerful demonstration that the experimental condition exerts control over the behavior. The strength of the demonstration stems from the consideration that events occurring in time other than the experimental condition cannot plausibly account for the specific changes in behavior. This is demonstrated without a reversal of experimental conditions.

A major area of concern in using this design is that one must be reasonably assured beforehand that the target behaviors used are not interdependent or interrelated highly with each other. In such a situation, implementing a contingency for the performance of one behavior may be expected to alter the behavior(s) for which continued baseline data are collected. For example, in a classroom situation it may not be the most appropriate design to gather multiple-baseline data across inappropriate motor behavior, inappropriate verbalizations, and inappropriate tasks as three separate target behaviors. Although these behaviors are used as distinct categories that can be reliably observed, they are also moderately intercorrelated in terms of frequency within individual children's repertoires (Kazdin, 1973c).[1] Change in one of these responses may

---

[1]This problem stems, in part, from the definition of an operant. As a response class, any operant may include responses or elements that are part of other operants. Skinner (1953, p. 94) noted this in stating that: "In reinforcing one operant we often produce a noticeable increase in the strength of another," and "The reinforcement of a response increases the probability of all responses containing the same elements." For a discussion of problems associated with defining operants, the reader is referred to Schick (1971).

result in other response changes. An even greater demonstration of this problem of response correlations is evident from the literature on generalized imitation. In several studies, it has been shown that reinforcement for some imitative behavior leads to a generalized set for imitative behaviors. A multiple-baseline design across behaviors might not be able to demonstrate that responses are not imitated until the contingency is applied to the specific imitative behavior. As soon as some imitative behavior is reinforced, other responses would change even though not reinforced (Baer, Peterson, & Sherman, 1967; Metz, 1965; Peterson & Whitehurst, 1971), unless they are topographically dissimilar responses (Garcia, Baer, & Firestone, 1971).

The problem of intercorrelations among responses has not been evident in the few multiple-baseline studies across behaviors (e.g., McAllister, Stachowiak, Baer, & Conderman, 1969; Wolf et al., 1968). However, it is a consideration an investigator should make when deciding on the type of design to best demonstrate the efficacy of experimental conditions (cf. Buell, Stoddard, Harris, & Baer, 1968; Pendergrass, 1972).

In the multiple-baseline design across individuals, baseline data are gathered for at least one behavior across several persons. After behavior stabilizes across subjects, the experimental condition is invoked for one subject while baseline conditions are continued for the other subject(s). Again, as the experimental condition is extended to include separate individuals, the response frequency changes. This demonstration shows that behavior of the subject does not change until he is included in the experimental condition.

As with the previous multiple-baseline design, one major aspect may make this design problematic. If it is possible that the alteration of the behavior of one subject will influence the behavior of other subjects, the design loses power. In this situation, implementation of the experimental condition for the first subject may dramatically alter the behavior of another subject for whom baseline conditions are continued. . . . Introducing contingencies for some individuals in a situation may be expected to alter the behaviors of other individuals under some circumstances, viz., when the behavior of one subject influences the behavior of an adjacent peer (Broden et al., 1970) or when social reinforcement provides a discriminative stimulus for probable reinforcement for an adjacent peer (Kazdin, 1973b) or when there is a limit to the amount of reinforcement available (Sechrest, 1963). In such situations, the use of a multiple-baseline design across individuals would not effectively demonstrate the specific effects of the experimental condition on the target behavior. The implementation of the contingency for the first subject might change the behavior of others, even though the baseline conditions were continued for the other subjects.

In the multiple-baseline design across situations, data are collected for a target behavior for one or more subjects across different circumstances or situations. For example, in altering the promptness of individuals in an elementary school situation, one might collect data (number of students late and number of minutes late) across several situations (arrival to class in the morning, after recess, after lunch, after assemblies). After collecting baseline data in all situations, the experimental contingency is instituted to control the behavior in one situation. Baseline data are continued for behavior in all other situations until each is consecutively included into the contingency. As with previous multiple-baseline designs, this design is more effective when there is little or no correlation of behavior across these situations. If behavior change in one situation is expected to alter behavior in another situation, this design is a less powerful demonstration of the effects of the contingencies. . . .

In the three basic types of multiple-baseline designs discussed, each has one potential weakness in powerfully demonstrating the effect of a particular experimental condition, viz., concomitant changes in the areas for which baseline data are collected. Whether this is the case in the particular instance the investigator decides to use a design must be determined primarily from experience. Concomitant changes that may occur as a result of implementing a contingency for one behavior (individual or situation) have to be determined empirically. In some instances, the investigator can rely on the well-documented experience of others. For example, if one were interested in evaluating classroom deportment in a multiple-baseline design across situations or time (such as morning and afternoon class periods), there already is consistent evidence showing that changes made in one of these time periods do not appreciably alter behavior in the other (Becker, Madsen, Arnold, & Thomas, 1967; Kuypers, Becker, & O'Leary, 1968; Meichenbaum, Bowers, & Ross, 1968; O'Leary et al., 1969).

The within-subject designs outlined above can be employed in most situations. In spite of the reasons outlined early in the paper as to the advantages of these designs, one must remain cognizant of the possible interaction obtained between the experimental manipulation and the design employed in determining behavior. There is evidence bearing on this from several quarters in the experimental literature. For example, in experiments varying conditioned stimulus intensity in eyelid conditioning and signal intensity in reaction-time experiments, the effects of variations of the stimuli depend upon whether they are evaluated within or between groups (Grice & Hunter, 1964). Similarly, the effects of different amounts of reinforcement in discrimination learning tasks differentially affect correct responses, again, depending on whether one group is exposed to different levels of reinforcement or separate groups are used (Lawson, 1957; Schrier, 1958). These experiments and others indicate that the effects obtained may be dependent upon the design of the experiment. There is a greater lesson to be learned from this than the simple recommendation that one should not become overly dependent on one design in examining the effects of a particular operation. Since the major interest in operant work is determining how environmental manipulations functionally control behavior, it is important to be more analytic about an experimental design that, in part, dictates the results. What about the design influences behavior, and how can these influences be brought under control, minimized, or altered? When an experimental design is examined in this light, it becomes another experimental operation that exerts some functional relation to behavior. When the design does determine the result in some way, it is important to determine how it accomplishes this and over what parametric levels of the experimental manipulation. Sidman (1960, pp. 334, 340) recommended comparing the effects of experimental manipulations when scheduled separately or as combined with other manipulations. This is similar to recommending a closer scrutiny of the effects of our designs.

## Evaluation of Results

Investigations of reinforcement programs in applied settings may introduce problems in evaluating the results. Initially, to discuss some of these problems, the distinction introduced by Campbell and Stanley (1963) on the validities of experimentation is useful. These authors refer to *internal validity* as the degree to which the results of an experiment are considered to be due to the experimental manipulation. *External validity* refers to the extent to which the findings obtained in a study may be extended or generalized to other groups and settings. Campbell and Stanley (1963) noted that the equivalent time-samples design (a version of the ABAB or reversal design) is quite strong with respect to the possible sources of threat to internal validity. In such designs, several rival hypotheses accounting for the results are ruled out. It is unlikely that events (outside of the experimental manipulation) that occur in time (history), growth or developmental processes within the subject (maturation), systematic shifts in performance over time resulting from the unreliability of measurement (e.g., regression and changes in the measurement device), selective loss of subjects (mortality), repeated assessment (testing), and other factors account for the results. As for external validity, however, they list some factors that may delimit the generalizability of the results. Both these types of validity will be discussed in light of research in reinforcement programs in applied settings.

Considering internal validity, investigators must be reasonably assured that there are no factors in the design that can account for the results other than the intended manipulated operation. This statement seems so basic that it might not warrant protracted discussion. However, in several studies it is evident that there are factors that covary with implementation of the experimental operation. In some instances, the operation of these extraneous factors plausibly are causative of the changes attributed to the experimental operation. If these extraneous factor(s) could not account for the change entirely, they can interact with the experimental operation as a codeterminant of the results. Examples of extraneous factors that covary with experimental conditions are evident in several studies. One obvious factor that covaries with conditions is instructions that convey to subjects how they are supposed to perform. For example, Ayllon and Azrin (1965) instructed subjects that they could continue to work even though they would receive token reinforcement for not working (i.e., a "vacation with pay," p. 366). The rapid changes noted in performance were attributed to the reinforcement contingencies. However, different instructions preceding each experimental phase appeared to contribute, in part, to the abrupt effect of contingent reinforcement. Previous work has shown that although instructions may not be sufficient to sustain performance relative to contingent operant consequences, they are effective in initiating behavior change (Ayllon & Azrin, 1964; Hopkins, 1968; Packard, 1970). Employing reinforcement contingencies alone results in behavior changes that are less dramatic than when accompanied by contingency instructions (Herman & Tramontana, 1971), although there are exceptions to this (Kazdin, 1973c). . . .

In considering external validity, several issues in reinforcement programs require mentioning. The question of the extent to which findings hold for other subjects and other settings than those that were included in an experiment are included in the issues discussed here.

First, there is a possibility of *multiple-treatment interference* (Campbell & Stanley, 1963), which may delimit generalization of the results. Whenever multiple phases are applied to a group, the conclusions derived from a later treatment may depend on previous phases because the effects of each are not erasable. For example, the effects of contingent reinforcement may be evaluated in a design in which it is preceded by noncontingent reinforcement, or punishment (e.g., verbal reprimand by teachers). The results can only be generalized to include other individuals exposed to a similar sequence of events. Also, the conclusions may be generalized only to conditions where the reinforcement condition is introduced repeatedly, interspersed with other conditions, and not to situations in which the reinforcement is continually present or introduced only once. For example, in two of their experiments, O'Leary and Becker

(O'Leary & Becker, 1967; O'Leary et al., 1969) implemented token reinforcement programs in classroom situations. In one study, instructions, praising appropriate and ignoring inappropriate behaviors along with token reinforcement, were introduced simultaneously; in the other study, these procedures were introduced sequentially in a cumulative fashion. In comparing these studies, it is evident that the simultaneous introduction of the conditions led to greater change than the sequential introduction of component parts. Thus, in generalizing the effects of token reinforcement procedures, one must be careful to specify the manner in which the component parts of the procedures (informative feedback, instructions, approval, ignoring) are introduced. The manner in which the program is introduced, as dictated by the experimental design, may have consequences as to the conclusions derived and their generalizability. . . .

## The Use of Control Groups

In discussions of work in the functional analysis of behavior in applied settings, the matter of control groups arises infrequently. There is great justification for ignoring the use of comparative groups in most instances. Treatises on experimental design (e.g., Underwood, 1957) usually recognize certain instances in which no control group is required to evaluate unambiguously the effect of the experimental manipulation. The design that fits this situation is an extended time-series design in which data are available for the subject(s) over a long period of time, or when data are available for a relatively short period, but behavior changes with the presentation and removal of the experimental variable (i.e., the ABAB design discussed earlier).

Other reasons have led investigators to eschew comparison groups stemming from philosophical or presuppositional considerations rather than simply convenience or design. The use of comparison groups usually implies a statistical evaluation of the data in terms of measures of central tendency and variability. Several assumptions are required for use of various statistical techniques, and risks attendant on their violation must be considered. Further, in the experimental analysis, the goal transcends obtaining mean differences between groups with exposure to an experimental operation and one that is not. Achieving functional control over behavior makes the investigator concerned with determining effective variables that will alter the individual's behavior. These variables necessarily entail within-subject manipulations. Also, examining group means does not really demonstrate that the experimenter achieved control over behavior in individual cases. There is the subject generality problem (Sidman, 1960) or representativeness of the findings. Comparisons of treated groups with untreated groups obscure a closer examination of the effect of treatment on those individuals in the experimental groups. Nevertheless, there are instances, particularly in recent years, that merit utilization of experimental groups in between- as well as within-subject comparisons. The salient instances will be presented.

Whereas the initial interest in operant work in applied settings was focused almost entirely upon examining effective experimental operations that functionally related to behavior, this interest has broadened (Staats, 1970). There is greater use of finding effective treatments that cannot easily be evaluated in single-subject or single-group designs. For example, Staats and his associates began work with reinforcement procedures on training reading skills by a careful scrutiny of the performance of individual subjects (e.g., Staats & Butterfield, 1965). This led to refinement and extensions of procedures which, though modified, were evaluated (statistically) as treatments and compared with a control group (e.g., Staats, Minke, & Butts, 1970). The extension of findings from an examination of single-group to between-group designs has been required in light of the greater aims of reinforcement procedures in applied settings. As a recent example of this, initial token reinforcement programs in psychiatric hospitals (e.g., Ayllon & Azrin, 1965) focused on evaluating the program on within-hospital behavior rather than global measures such as discharge and readmission rates (Ayllon & Azrin, 1968, p. 27). However, as the efficacy of the procedures evolved, it became important to determine how effective reinforcement procedures were relative to traditional techniques (Birky, Chambliss, & Wasden, 1971; Marks, Sanoda, & Schalock, 1968; Hartlage, 1970) and how well they fared when compared to untreated groups in terms of follow-up success (Stayer & Jones, 1969). Such comparisons, of course, imply the use of control groups. . . .

In advocating the use of control groups, it is important to recognize the limitations imposed by doing research in applied settings. Even if we might envision situations in which a comparison group would provide desirable information, there are usually restrictions as to the information it can provide. With relatively rare exceptions in the literature (e.g., Herman & Tramontana, 1971), subjects cannot be matched and assigned randomly to classes, hospital wards, institutional settings, or classrooms in which the procedures will be evaluated. In such instances it is desirable to select groups that will best control for the factors one is interested in controlling. For example, in a psychiatric setting, it is desirable to control for new staff, new ward facilities, and diagnostic group in evaluating the program. Some investigations in psychiatric settings have selected patients for the therapeutic program and placed them on a special ward (Heap, Boblitt, Moore, & Hord, 1970). This makes evaluation of any program ambiguous because the effect of ward change, in and of itself, may lead to behavior change (De Vries, 1968; Higgs, 1970). . . .

## Responses Assessed in Reinforcement Programs

The selection of responses to evaluate the efficacy of procedures is usually dictated by the purpose of the study and the goals of the treatment or training institution in which the program is conducted. The use of response frequency has been employed as the most useful measure of these responses, and its use has a number of features to recommend it (see Bijou et al., 1968, 1969; Ferster, 1953; Honig, 1966).

The focus on observable behaviors is perhaps one of the major advantages that accrue to behavior-modification procedures in general. This assessment procedure differs markedly from traditional approaches where inferential leaps may be made in diagnosing, treating, and assessing dynamics, dispositions, or traits (Mischel, 1968; Stuart, 1970).

In spite of the advantages of this assessment approach, the observations have been restricted to the single target behavior of initial focus. While changes in target behaviors are the *raison d'être* for undertaking treatment or training programs, concomitant changes may take place as well. If so, these should be assessed. It is one thing to assess and evaluate changes in a target behavior, but quite another to insist on excluding nontarget measures. It may be that investigators are short-changing themselves in evaluating the programs. Recently, other areas of behavior modification have attempted to assess behaviors that might change as a result of treatment but were not of direct therapeutic focus (e.g., Bandura, Blanchard, & Ritter, 1969; Kazdin, 1973a; Paul, 1967). To reiterate, the use of nontarget behavioral measures in reinforcement programs is to be encouraged. Yet, these measures are not to be made at the expense of the primary data on target performance.

There are several potential advantages in using measures of nontarget behaviors as well as the usual target response measures. One initial advantage is that such assessment would permit the possibility of determining response generalization. If certain response frequencies are increased or decreased, it would be expected that other related operants would be influenced. It would be a desirable addition to determine generalization of beneficial response changes by looking at behaviors related to the target response. In addition, changes in the frequency of responses might also correlate with topographical alterations. For example, a reduction of inappropriate responses may result in the concomitant reduction of the severity of the responses (Burchard & Tyler, 1965; Hawkins, Peterson, Schweid, & Bijou, 1966). . . .

## SUMMARY

In summing up, there are several advantages in using various within-subject designs. Generally, these designs are quite powerful in demonstrating the effect of a particular experimental operation. However, there are potential weaknesses of the designs currently employed. The choice of design may be influenced by the expectation or desirability of a reversal in behavior, if the experimental condition is withdrawn. In designs without a reversal of conditions (multiple-baseline designs), other problems may arise, such as interdependence of performance (across behaviors, individuals, or situations). Although these may prove to be infrequent in future research, their occurrence in a given instance may be fatal in evaluating the results.

In interpreting results of investigations in this area, it is important to be cognizant of potential influences that may covary with the presentations and withdrawal of experimental operations. Also, various elements of the experiment may delimit generalization of the results. Salient influences relevant to internal and external validity were discussed.

The use of control groups was advocated in examining certain effects of reinforcement programs. Although the functional analysis is the major aspect of the design, the proliferation of experiments in this area has led to questions that can, in many instances be adequately answered only by comparisons between or across groups. As a final point, the use of multiple-response measures was encouraged. Changes in target measures are the major point of undertaking reinforcement programs in applied settings. However, concomitant response changes may take place along with the target responses. If so, these should be documented.

## *REFERENCES*

Ayllon, T., & Azrin, N. H. Reinforcement and instructions with mental patients. *Journal of the Experimental Analysis of Behavior,* 1964, *7,* 327-331.

Ayllon, T., & Azrin, N. H. The measurement and reinforcement of behavior of psychotics. *Journal of the Experimental Analysis of Behavior,* 1965, *8,* 357-383.

Ayllon, T., & Azrin, N. H. *The token economy: a motivational system for therapy and rehabilitation.* New York: Appleton-Century-Crofts, 1968.

Baer, D. M., Peterson, R. F., & Sherman, J. The development of imitation by reinforcing behaviorial similarity to a model. *Journal of the Experimental Analysis of Behavior,* 1967, *10,* 405-416.

Baer, D. M., Wolf, M. M., & Risley, T. R. Some current dimensions of applied behavior analysis. *Journal of Applied Behavior Analysis*, 1968, *1*, 91-97.

Bandura, A. *Principles of behavior modification*. New York: Holt, Rinehart, & Winston, 1969.

Bandura, A., Blanchard, E. B., & Ritter, B. Relative efficacy of desensitization and modeling approaches for inducing behavioral, affective, and attitudinal changes. *Journal of Personality and Social Psychology*, 1969, *13*, 173-199.

Becker, W. C., Madsen, C. H., Arnold, C. R., & Thomas, D. R. The contingent use of teacher attention and praising in reducing classroom behavior problems. *Journal of Special Education*, 1967, *1*, 287-307.

Bijou, S. W., Peterson, R. F., & Ault, M. H. A method of integrating descriptive and experimental field studies at the level of data and empirical concepts. *Journal of Applied Behavior Analysis*, 1968, *1*, 175-191.

Bijou, S. W., Peterson, R. F., Harris, F. R., Allen, K. E., & Johnston, M. S. Methodology for experimental studies of young children in natural settings. *Psychological Record*, 1969, *19*, 177-210.

Birky, H. J., Chambliss, J. E., & Wasden, R. A comparison of residents discharged from a token economy and two traditional psychiatric programs. *Behavior Therapy*. 1971, *2*, 46-51.

Broden, M., Bruce, M., Mitchell, M., Carter, V., & Hall, R. V. Effects of teacher attention on attending behavior of two boys at adjacent desks. *Journal of Applied Behavior Analysis*, 1970, *3*, 199-203.

Buell, J., Stoddard, P., Harris, F., & Baer, D. M. Collateral social development accompanying reinforcement of outdoor play in a preschool child. *Journal of Applied Behavior Analysis*, 1968, *1*, 167-173.

Burchard, J. D. Systematic socialization: A programmed environment for the habilitation of antisocial retardates. *Psychological Record*, 1967, *17*, 461-476.

Burchard, J. D., & Tyler, V. O. The modification of delinquent behaviour through operant conditioning. *Behaviour Research and Therapy*, 1965, *2*, 245-250.

Campbell, D. T., & Stanley, J. C. Experimental and quasi-experimental designs for research and teaching. In N. L. Gage (Ed.), *Handbook of research on teaching*. Chicago: Rand McNally, 1963. Pp. 171-246.

DeVries, D. L. Effects of environmental change and of participation on the behavior of mental patients. *Journal of Consulting and Clinical Psychology*, 1968, *32*, 532-536.

Ferster, C. B. The use of the free operant in the analysis of behavior. *Psychological Bulletin*, 1953, *50*, 264-274.

Garcia, E., Baer, D. M., & Firestone, I. The development of generalized imitation within topographically determined boundaries. *Journal of Applied Behavior Analysis*, 1971, *4*, 101-112.

Grice, C. R., & Hunter, J. J. Stimulus intensity effects depend upon the type of experimental design. *Psychological Review*, 1964, *71*, 247-256.

Hartlage, L. C. Subprofessional therapists' use of reinforcement versus traditional psychotherapeutic techniques with schizophrenics. *Journal of Consulting and Clinical Psychology*, 1970, *34*, 181-183.

Hawkins, R. P., Peterson, R. F., Schweid, E., & Bijou, S. W. Behavior therapy in the home: Amelioration of problem parent-child relations with the parent in a therapeutic role. *Journal of Experimental Child Psychology,* 1966, *4,* 99-107.

Heap, R. F., Boblitt, W. E., Moore, C. H., & Hord, J. E. Behavior-milieu therapy with chronic neuropsychiatric patients. *Journal of Abnormal Psychology,* 1970, *76,* 349-354.

Herman, S., & Tramontana, J. Instructions and group *versus* individual reinforcement in modifying disruptive group behavior. *Journal of Applied Behavior Analysis,* 1971, *4,* 113-119.

Higgs, W. J. Effects of gross environmental change upon behavior of schizophrenics: A cautionary note. *Journal of Abnormal Psychology,* 1970, *76,* 421-422.

Honig, W. K. Introduction. *Operant behavior: areas of research and application.* New York: Appleton-Century-Crofts, 1966.

Hopkins, B. L. Effects of candy and social reinforcement schedule learning on the modification and maintenance of smiling. *Journal of Applied Behavior Analysis,* 1968, *1,* 121-128.

Kazdin, A. E. The effect of response cost and aversive stimulation in suppressing punished and nonpunished speech disfluencies. *Behavior Therapy,* 1973, *4,* 73-82. (a)

Kazdin, A. E. The effect of vicarious reinforcement on attentive behavior in the classroom. *Journal of Applied Behavior Analysis,* 1973, *6,* 71-78. (b)

Kazdin, A. E. The role of instructions and reinforcement in behavior changes in token reinforcement programs. *Journal of Educational Psychology,* 1973, *64,* 63-71. (c)

Kazdin, A. E., & Bootzin, R. R. The token economy: An evaluative review. *Journal of Applied Behavior Analysis,* 1972, *5,* 343-372.

Kuypers, D. S., Becker, W. C., & O'Leary, K. D. How to make a token system fail. *Exceptional Children,* 1968, *11,* 101-108.

Lawson, R. Brightness discrimination performance and secondary reward strength as a function of primary reward amount. *Journal of Comparative and Physiological Psychology,* 1957, *50,* 35-39.

McAllister, L. W., Stachowiak, J. G., Baer, D. M., & Conderman, L. The application of operant conditioning techniques in a secondary school classroom. *Journal of Applied Behavior Analysis,* 1969, *2,* 277-285.

Marks, J., Sonoda, B., & Schalock, R. Reinforcement *vs.* relationship therapy for schizophrenics. *Journal of Abnormal Psychology,* 1968, *73,* 397-402.

Meichenbaum, D. H., Bowers, K., & Ross, R. R. Modification of classroom behavior of institutionalized female adolescent offenders. *Behaviour Research and Therapy,* 1968, *6,* 343-353.

Metz, J. R. Conditioning generalized imitation in autistic children. *Journal of Experimental Child Psychology,* 1965, *2,* 389-399.

Mischel, W. *Personality and assessment.* New York: Wiley, 1968.

O'Leary, K. D., & Becker, W. C. Behavior modification of an adjustment class: A token reinforcement program. *Exceptional Children,* 1967, *9,* 637-642.

O'Leary, K. D., Becker, W. C., Evans, M. B., & Saudargas, R. A. A token reinforcement program in a public school: A replication and systematic analysis. *Journal of Applied Behavior Analysis,* 1969, *2,* 3-31.

O'Leary, K. D., & Drabman, R. Token reinforcement programs in the classroom: A review. *Psychological Bulletin,* 1971, *75,* 379-398.

Packard, R. G. The control of "classroom attention": A group contingency for complex behavior. *Journal of Applied Behavior Analysis*, 1970, *3*, 13-28.

Paul, G. L. Insight versus desensitization in psychotherapy two years after termination. *Journal of Consulting Psychology*, 1967, *31*, 333-348.

Pendergrass, V. E. Timeout from positive reinforcement following persistent, high-rate behavior in retardates. *Journal of Applied Behavior Analysis*, 1972, *5*, 85-91.

Peterson, R. F., & Whitehurst, G. J. A variable influencing the performance of generalized imitative behaviors. *Journal of Applied Behavior Analysis*, 1971, *4*, 1-9.

Phillips, E. L. Achievement Place: Token reinforcement procedures in a home-style rehabilitation setting for "predelinquent" boys. *Journal of Applied Behavior Analysis*, 1968, *1*, 213-223.

Schick, K. Operants. *Journal of the Experimental Analysis of Behavior*, 1971, *15*, 413-423.

Schrier, A. M. Comparison of two methods of investigating the effects of amount of reward on performance. *Journal of Comparative and Physiological Psychology*, 1958, *51*, 725-731.

Sechrest, L. Implicit reinforcement of responses. *Journal of Educational Psychology*, 1963, *54*, 197-201.

Sidman, M. *Tactics of scientific research*. New York: Basic Books, 1960.

Skinner, B. F. *Science and human behavior*. New York: Macmillan, 1953.

Staats, A. W. Reinforcer systems in the solution of human problems. In G. A. Fargo, C. Behrns, and P. Nolen (Eds.), *Behavior modification in the classroom*. Belmont, California: Wadsworth, 1970. Pp. 6-31.

Staats, A. W., & Butterfield, W. H. Treatment of nonreading in a culturally deprived juvenile delinquent: An application of learning principles. *Child Development*, 1965, *4*, 925-942.

Staats, A. W., Minke, K. A., & Butts, P. A token-reinforcement remedial reading program administered by black therapy technicians to problem black children. *Behavior Therapy*, 1970, *1*, 331-353.

Stayer, S. J., & Jones, F. Ward 108: *Behavior modification and the delinquent soldier*. Unpublished paper presented at Behavioral Engineering Conference, Walter Reed General Hospital, 1969.

Stuart, R. B. *Trick or treatment: how and when psychotherapy fails*. Champaign, Illinois: Research Press, 1970.

Surratt, P. R., Ulrich, R. E., & Hawkins, R. P. An elementary student as a behavioral engineer. *Journal of Applied Behavior Analysis*, 1969, *2*, 85-92.

Underwood, B. J. *Psychological research*. New York: Appleton-Century-Crofts, 1957.

Wahler, R. G. Setting generality: some specific and general effects of child behavior therapy. *Journal of Applied Behavior Analysis*, 1969, *2*, 239-246.

Wolf, M. M., Giles, D. K., & Hall, R. V. Experiments with token reinforcement in a remedial classroom. *Behaviour Research and Therapy*, 1968, *6*, 51-64.

Zimmerman, J., Struckey, T. E., Garlick, B. J., & Miller, M. Effects of token reinforcement on productivity in multiply handicapped clients in a sheltered workshop. *Rehabilitation Literature*, 1969, *30*, 34-41.

# Part II

---

# Behavioral Interviewing

Despite the increasing behavior therapy emphasis on assessment information obtained through direct observation of naturally occurring behavior, the interview is still the most frequently used assessment procedure. The changing emphasis on more direct samples of behavior has in some ways served to strengthen the role of interview information in assessment rather than to weaken it. This strengthening is the direct outcome of attempts to confirm and extend interview information through the use of independent data sources (Weller & Luchterhand, 1969) with a concomitant unwillingness to rely *solely* upon information obtained in the interview as a basis for assessment (Lytton, 1973).

The reliance upon interview information is especially predominant during the initial diagnosis phase of treatment. To the extent that assessment within a behavioral framework is an ongoing process that continues throughout the course of treatment, however, the interview is an integral assessment procedure throughout the successive phases of problem definition, treatment design, and program evaluation (Bean, 1970). The focus of this section, however, will be on the use of the interview primarily during the initial phase of problem diagnosis.

In general, the purposes of the initial interview are threefold:

1. To obtain a statement of the problem in the client's terms, along with an elaboration on the part of the client as to the degree to which the presenting problem is interfering with his current adjustment, and the amount of subjective distress he is currently experiencing.

2. To answer the question of eligibility for treatment. This will necessarily involve a judgment that attempts to relate the client's problems and resources for change to the therapist's specific skills and resources for bringing about change. Within a behavioral framework, it is assumed that the therapist's skills necessary for bringing about behavior change for particular types of problems are fairly well circumscribed, although by no means definitive. Consequently, the therapist is viewed not as an all-purpose clinician capable of taking on all comers, but rather as a specialist who is qualified to work with those types of problems for which he possesses the specific skills and sometimes the specific technology (e.g., aversive conditioning apparatus, bell and blanket, remote-controlled shocker). While it is possible that a behavior therapist

may possess a broad range of skills, it is also realistic to recognize that individuals who are highly skilled in contingency management may often be less skilled in using desensitization and other imagery procedures, and vice versa. In any event, the initial interview situation is frequently concerned with the question of eligibility conceptualized in this fashion.

3. To clarify the general goals and approach to be taken in therapy and to identify additional types of assessment information that are likely to be needed.

## SIMILARITIES WITH OTHER APPROACHES

Behavioral interviewing has many features in common with interview procedures used in other approaches, not the least of which is its inevitability of occurrence at some point in the assessment process. It is also the case that the interview situation is essential in establishing a working relationship with the client that may, at a very initial stage, determine the informativeness of later assessments and the eventual success of therapy (Lazarus, 1971).

Rimm and Masters (1974) point out that for any therapeutic process to succeed, a relationship characterized by interpersonal warmth between therapist and client is an essential, albeit not sufficient, condition. Although the nature of this relationship established during the initial interview is not characterized in terms of ''unconditional positive regard,'' the necessity of a warm relationship is supported by the following three points (Rimm & Masters, 1974): First, if the client likes the therapist, he is more likely to remain in treatment. Second, the client is placed in the situation of reporting highly charged and sometimes embarrassing information to the therapist; if the therapist is not receptive to the person, the likelihood that important information is divulged will be reduced. Finally, if the therapist establishes himself as a strong discriminative stimulus for responses that are ''pleasing'' to the client, his social reinforcement value is likely to be enhanced. As such, he is likely to be a stronger and more effective agent in attempting to maintain the client's behavior throughout the course of treatment.

## CHARACTERISTICS OF BEHAVIORAL INTERVIEWING

The behavior therapist is likely to convey to the client, at the outset, two major views. The first is that both the assessment and therapeutic processes represent a collaborative effort. Attempts to obtain assessment information will involve the client's active participation to the point that the client might be asked to monitor, record, and, at times, interpret his own behavior. Related to this is the second view conveyed to the client which stresses the need for specific and reliable information. The concerns and problems reported by the client will generally need to be followed up by assessment procedures that will permit a clear statement of the problem behaviors, antecedent stimuli, and consequent events. This assessment process may take some time, often more time than is expected by the client. For this reason, it is generally useful to clarify with the client, at an early stage, the importance of accurate assessment information.

While all interview situations are likely to involve some amount of interpretation, the type of interpretation within a behavioral interview is quite different from that involved in other interview approaches. The client's behavior and attitudes are assessed in relation to contemporaneous environmental events rather than in relation to some underlying personality structure. The therapist begins to formulate hypotheses in which the client's behavior is related to antecedent and consequent controlling events. In this regard, the behavior therapist will be less likely to focus on fantasy material and early experiences than will therapists with other orientations.

The initial interview is likely to be a somewhat stressful and anxiety-producing situation, regardless of the therapist's orientation or the particular interview format. However, the behavior therapist is likely to deal with initial anxiety differently from therapists of other persuasions. The stress is viewed as stemming from the problems that prompted the client to seek help, and from uncertainty on the part of the client or therapist in dealing with the interview situation. If a client initially demonstrates extreme anxiety, the therapist may employ relaxation procedures in an effort to assist the client in his efforts in initial problem presentation. This direct approach stands in contrast to other positions that view the field of interaction between the interviewee and interviewer as being marked by anxiety, which should be identified, explored, and interpreted with respect to its significance (Sullivan, 1954).

The behavioral interview places special demands upon the informant, particularly in terms of the type and form of verbal report information being requested. The behavior therapist is likely to use a language base consisting of objective descriptions of behavioral events in relation to specific situational determinants, in contrast to a language base involving subjective descriptions characterized by dispositional terminology and trait adjectives which is typically displayed by the client during initial contacts. This lack of congruence between the therapist's and client's language base may interfere with a behavioral formulation of the problem and require that the therapist use the interview session itself as a training situation for more objective reporting.

In this regard, it may be possible to develop preinterview training sessions that would lead to more objective reporting on the part of the client. For example, Truax, Wargo, Carkhuff, Kodman, and Noles (1966) reported using a ''vicarious therapy pretraining'' procedure, exposing groups of patients to taped excerpts of group therapy interactions in which patients were engaged in deep exploration of problems and feelings. As a function of this pretraining exposure, patients were reported to show greater intrapersonal exploration and positive changes on other self-report measures. While the content and goals of such pretraining for a behavioral interview would be quite different, it is possible that modeling exposure to a client reporting concerns in terms of objective behavioral descriptions related to specific situational occurrences later may facilitate such types of verbal report in the observer. In addition, response to such pretraining may provide an indirect estimate of the client's motivation for treatment, his susceptibility to the use of modeling procedures generally, and his general reactions to a behavioral formulation of problematic behavior.

A major strategy to reduce misunderstanding between therapist and client regarding information about behaviors obtained from verbal report involves a three-stage process:

1. Interviewing to assess problem areas, with a focus on specific behaviors, the settings in which they occur, and a description of how the behaviors are handled.

2. Setting up an occasion to observe and record the behaviors of the client. This may be done in the natural environment, such as home or school, or in a standardized clinic situation, through the use of direct observation and recording procedures (see Part V).

3. Arranging a follow-up interview after the observation to discuss with the client, i.e., the teacher, the parent, the spouse, the child (if appropriate), their impressions of what occurred in the session observed and recorded by the therapist.

The combined observations independently recorded by the therapist and the verbal reports obtained from the client not only serve to assist the therapist and client to communicate about their observations, but they also provide the therapist with additional information about what form of treatment may be most appropriate.

For example, if the therapist and client show high agreement between themselves regarding how they describe and interpret the client's behavior, then the therapist, in consultation with the client, can proceed to implement behavior-change techniques. In contrast, if there is wide discrepancy between the therapist and the client regarding how they describe and interpret the client's behavior, then the discrepancy should be attended to before more formal behavior change strategies are implemented. In parent-child behavior therapy, for example, it is not uncommon for a parent to demonstrate considerable difficulty in observing and describing what a child does. It seems apparent that an individual who has difficulty observing and describing behavior may also have substantial difficulty in knowing which behavior to attend to and when and how to consequate. It is for this reason that an interview procedure employed in conjunction with direct observation of a client's behavior can be a very useful assessment strategy.

The initial behavioral interview may also involve attempts to assess the motivation of the client for treatment. In most instances, the therapist is more likely to rely upon direct behavioral measures of motivation rather than indirect or subtle indicators. For example, it is not unusual for the behavior therapist to incorporate into the initial interview assessment a variety of conditions and pretreatment assignments which attempt to tap the client's motivation. These may include such things as requesting the client to deposit a sum of money to be returned upon completion of the various terms of the therapist-client contract, to gather observational data, or to read certain prescribed material. The fulfillment of such pretreatment assignments is viewed as a necessary condition for the development of a treatment program (Madsen & Madsen, 1974).

The behavioral interview tends to be less ritualistic with regard to being restricted to a particular time period or a particular place. The interview itself may take place in a variety of settings such as the home or classroom. In some instances, much interview information may be obtained over the telephone. In addition, the therapist may interview several individuals in order to obtain supplementary information regarding the environmental context for the client. He may frequently interview those individuals who serve as important reinforcement agents for the client. However, it should be noted that such reports may be subject to distortion (Bean, 1970). Since the behavior therapist often functions in a consulting role, there may be some reliance upon behavior analysts who serve an intermediary role between the supervising therapist and the client (Tharp & Wetzel, 1969).

## METHODOLOGICAL CONSIDERATIONS

In spite of its frequent use, the interview continues to present persistent methodological problems. One problem relates to the difficulty involved in studying interview behavior. Content analysis is especially difficult since the verbal material presented is typically idiosyncratic and variable from interview to interview. It is also extremely difficult to analyze nonverbal material. In this context, the research of Matarazzo and his colleagues (Matarazzo, Wiens, Matarazzo, & Saslow, 1968) highlight both the possibilities and complexities involved in studying noncontent material in interview research. Related to the fact that interview material is difficult to study is that records of what goes on in the interview itself are normally lost because there is typically not a permanent record obtained. These, and other issues have been carefully studied by Yarrow, Campbell, and Burton (1968). They conclude that reports made in the context of an interview about behavior and environmental events should not be taken as equivalent to information about the behavior itself.

There is also some question as to the reliability, over time, of interview information. The reliability question relates both to the behavior of the therapist and of the client. For example, Conger (1971) reports that the nature of the interview changes over the course of periods as short as thirty minutes. Moos and Clemes (1967) found that therapist behavior during the first half of an interview may be quite different from that during the second half. The fact that behavior is changing over time in the situation, and that the interview situation itself represents one of reciprocal influence, further contributes to difficulty of study.

Certain types of therapist bias may also confound the interview situation. For example, a behavior therapist oriented toward a "cognitive behavior modification" approach (Meichenbaum, 1974) may attempt to elicit different types of information than a therapist oriented toward a nonmediational operant conditioning approach. While such selective information gathering may be necessary for treatment, it is also possible that such therapist bias may serve to limit the types of information obtained and subsequently limit the potential usefulness of assessment information in designing the most efficient type of treatment program.

A more serious problem might occur if the therapist feels comfortable in dealing with certain categories of problems and creates a bias in which he responds selectively to problems presented by the client in this category and ignores or overlooks other concerns on the part of the client which may represent significant problems, but yet do not fall within the therapists's area of expertise. An example here might involve a therapist well trained in dealing with childhood problems, but less comfortable in dealing with marital conflict.

Another problem in the assessment interview is related to instances in which the therapist relies too heavily on well-established empirical relationships between presenting problems and treatment procedures early in assessment. For example, when a client reports the presence of a phobia, the therapist may immediately conclude that a desensitization procedure is warranted. A client reporting problems of bladder control may result in a quick decision to use a bell and blanket conditioning procedure. In many instances, this approach may be appropriate. However, it is possible that reliance on well-established procedures for certain classes of problems may tend to influence the therapist to omit or leave out a substantial amount of information that might assist him in formulating a treatment design based on assessment information rather than extra-assessment information.


## DESCRIPTION OF INTERVIEW MEASURES


The first paper in Part II provides an outline for behavioral diagnosis developed by Kanfer and Saslow (1965, 1969). The focus of this outline is similar to other behaviorally oriented interview guides that have been presented (Bersoff & Grieger, 1971; Peterson, 1968; Pomeranz & Goldfried, 1970; Storrow, 1967; Wahler & Cormier, 1970). The outline by Kanfer and Saslow provides a comprehensive statement of the types of information to be obtained in an interview situation which are necessary for a functional analysis involving descriptions of behavioral antecedents and consequences.

The outline itself covers several areas, including an initial analysis of the problem situation, further clarification, motivational analysis, developmental analysis, analysis of self-control, analysis of social relationships, and analysis of the social-cultural-physical environment. It should be noted that the framework presented is an exhaustive and comprehensive one, and it is not necessarily the case that all categories of information be obtained for all clients. In many instances, this may be neither feasible nor desirable. Rather, the outline serves as a general framework for the organization of interview questions and materials and highlights the types of interview information necessary for a functional analysis.

The generality of this outline is probably both a strength and a weakness. Its generality makes it appropriate for use across a wide range of problem areas, populations, and situations. At the same time, however, its scope sometimes makes it difficult to narrow in on areas of particular importance and to determine the specific way in which information will be obtained.

The paper by Holland represents an interview guide to be used in behavioral counseling with parents. Following through and elaborating on some of the major points made by Kanfer and Saslow, Holland describes a number of specific areas in which the interview should be focused to provide a functional analysis of child behavior. The interview guide goes beyond the phase of initial assessment in that a number of areas of questioning are related specifically to the management of behavior and the design of change programs.

The next paper, by Wolpe, provides an example of an initial interview with a depressed woman. Several important points are illustrated in this interview. An attempt is made on the part of the therapist to relate the reported symptomatology to specific situations and consequently to formulate a preliminary functional analysis. Also, the therapist attempts to examine the way in which the client perceives and interprets her own behavior. The interview ends with the therapist providing a behavioral interpretation of the interview information as well as some beginning statements concerning how the client may be helped.

In the last paper in Part II, Marlatt describes the development and use of the ''Drinking Profile,'' which is a questionnaire for the behavioral assessment of alcoholism. The procedure provides an extensive description of behavior and accompanying environmental conditions related to excessive drinking. While the profile may best be administered in the form of a structured interview, it would be possible for the informant to respond independently to a large number of the items presented. As such, this selection serves as a bridge between this section and the next on structured self-report measures. The Drinking Profile can be used to assess the long-term and naturalistic outcomes of programs for alcoholism, in contrast to other measures of drinking behavior, which have typically been analogous measures of short-term changes (Briddell & Nathan, 1975; Miller, 1973).

# 5

---

## An Outline for Behavioral Diagnosis

### Frederick H. Kanfer
### George Saslow

The analysis proposed here is not intended to lead to assignment of the patient to diagnostic categories. It should serve as a basis for making decisions about specific therapeutic interventions, regardless of the presenting problem. The compilation of data under as many of the headings as are relevant should yield a good basis for decisions about the areas in which intervention is needed, the particular targets of the intervention, the treatment methods to be used, and the series of goals at which treatment should aim.

### I. Initial Analysis of the Problem Situation

A preliminary formulation attempts to sort out the behaviors which are brought to the clinician's attention with regard to their eventual place in the treatment procedures. The patient's repertoire may be conspicuously different from what is required for adequate adjustment to his circumstances because of the unusual frequency with which various acts occur. Further, account is also taken of the extent of the behavioral repertoire which is nonproblematic and the presence of behaviors

This outline appeared previously in a paper in the *Archives of General Psychiatry,* 1965, *12,* 529-538, and in a chapter in C. M. Franks (Ed.) *Behavior-therapy: Appraisal and status.* New York: McGraw-Hill, 1969. Pp. 417-444. Reprinted by permission of McGraw-Hill Book Company.

This work was facilitated by Research Grant MH 6921-07 from the National Institutes of Mental Health, United States Public Health Service, to Frederick H. Kanfer.

representing special strengths, qualitatively or quantitatively, which would be available as resources in treatment. Although the classification of behaviors into excesses and deficits is conceptually useful, it is clear that in all but extreme cases humans have a rich and continually changing repertoire, and the interrelationships between the items in the repertoire cannot be ignored. The initial classification may not retain its appropriateness, once changes in the patient's life conditions and his overall activities begin to occur.

Since no objective frequency tables are available for reference, behavior items can be viewed either as excesses or as deficits, depending on the vantage point from which the imbalance is observed. For instance, excessive withdrawal and deficient social initiative, or excessive response to emotional stimulation and deficient self-controlling behavior, may be complementary. However, a decision about the starting point for treatment is necessary, committing the clinician to a set of priorities for treatment which can later be reviewed and changed.

Preference for viewing behavior as excessive or deficient is often determined by cultural valuation of the behavior, based on its consequences to other people. For example, in a child a physical blow in response to a critical remark can be regarded as excessive aggressive behavior, leading to the decision to reduce its occurrence by constraints or punishment. A clearly different consequence results from regarding the same behavior as a deficit in self-control, to be remedied by training the child to substitute acceptable alternative responses. Another choice resulting from the analysis may lie in a dual approach. The therapist may decide to train the child to discriminate among cues which indicate potential acceptance or rejection of the behavior by social members, e.g., the differential reinforcement potentials for physical blows in such sports as boxing, as contrasted to its consequences in conversation. Concurrently, major effort could be spent on remedying the relevant deficits in alternate social behaviors.

A. *Behavioral excess.*  A class of related behaviors occurs and is described as problematic by the patient or an informant because of excess in (1) frequency, (2) intensity, (3) duration, or (4) occurrence under conditions when its socially sanctioned frequency approaches zero. Compulsive hand-washing, combativeness, prolonged excitement, and sexual exhibitionism are examples of behavioral excesses along one or another of these four dimensions. Less obvious, because they often do not constitute the major presenting complaints and appear only in the course of the behavioral analysis, are examples of socially unacceptable solitary, affectionate, or other private behaviors. For instance, a housewife showing excessive solitary preoccupation can do so by excessive homemaking activities (1) several hours a day, (2) seven days weekly for most of the waking day, (3) to the extent that phone calls or doorbells are unanswered and family needs are unattended. From this example it is clear that both duration and intensity values of the behavior may jointly determine the characterization of the behavior as excessive.

B. *Behavioral deficit.* A class of responses is described as problematic by someone because it fails to occur (1) with sufficient frequency, (2) with adequate intensity, (3) in appropriate form, or (4) under socially expected conditions. Examples are: reduced social responsiveness (withdrawal), amnesias, fatigue syndromes, and restrictions in sexual or somatic function (e.g., impotence, writer's cramp). Other examples of behavioral deficits can be found in depressed patients who have no appropriate behavior in a new social environment, e.g., after changes from a rural to an urban area, from marital to single status, or from one socioeconomic level to another. "Inadequate" persons often are also found to have large gaps in their social or intellectual repertoires which prevent appropriate actions.

C. *Behavioral asset.* Behavioral assets are nonproblematic behaviors. What does the patient do well? What are his adequate social behaviors? What are his special talents or assets? The content of life experiences which can be used to execute a therapeutic program is unlimited. Any segment of the patient's activities can be used as an arena for building up new behaviors. In fact, his natural work and play activities provide a better starting point for behavior change than can ever be provided in a synthetic activity or relationship. For example, a person with musical talent, skill in a craft, physical skill, or social appeal can be helped to use his strengths as vehicles for changing behavior relationships and for acquiring new behaviors in areas in which some successful outcomes are highly probable. While a therapeutic goal may ultimately be the acquisition of specific social or self-evaluative behaviors, the learning can be programmed with many different tasks and in areas in which the patient has already acquired competence.

## II.    Clarification of Problem Situation

A.    Assign the classes of problematic responses to group $A$ or $B$ above, as study of the patient proceeds.

B.    Which persons or groups object to these behaviors? Which persons or groups support them? Who persuaded or coerced the patient to come to the clinician?

C.    What consequences does the problem have for the patient and for significant others? What consequences would removal of the problem have for the patient or others?

D. Under what conditions do the problematic behaviors occur (biological, symbolic, social, vocational, etc.)?

E. What satisfactions would continue for the patient if his problematic behaviors were sustained? What satisfactions would the patient gain if, as a result of psychiatric intervention, his problematic behavior were changed? What positive or aversive effects would occur for significant others if the patient's problematic behavior were changed? How would the patient continue to live if therapy were unsuccessful, that is, if nothing in his behavior changed?

F. What new problems in living would successful therapy pose for the patient?

G. To what extent is the patient as a sole informant capable of helping in development of a therapy program?

The questions raised here are derived from the assumption that maladjusted behavior requires continued support. It cannot be banished from the patient's life for all future circumstances. Change in it is related closely to the environment in which the person needs to live. Elimination of the problematic behavior is also impossible as long as powerful, and often undefined, reinforcing events operate. The answers to the above questions can help to bring about an early decision about the optimal goals within practical reach of the clinician and within the inevitably fixed boundaries of the patient's life pattern.

### III. Motivational Analysis[1]

A. How does the patient rank various incentives in their importance to him? Basing judgment on the patient's probable expenditure of time, energy, or physical discomfort, which of the following reinforcing events are relatively most effective in initiating or maintaining his behavior: achievement of recognition, sympathy, friendships, money, good health, sexual satisfaction, intellectual competence, social approval, work satisfaction, control over others, securing dependency, etc.?

[1] A Reinforcement Survey Schedule, recently prepared by J. R. Cautela and R. Kastenbaum (1967), provides a written instrument which may be of great value in obtaining specific information about some of the reinforcing stimuli elicited by items in this section.

B. How frequent and regular have been his successes with these reinforcers? What are his present expectations of success for each? Under what circumstances was reinforcement achieved for each of these incentives?

C. Under what specific conditions do each of these reinforcers arouse goal-directed behavior (biological, symbolic, social, vocational)?

D. Do his actions in relation to these goals correspond with his verbal statements? How does any definable discrepancy affect goals and procedures in therapy?

E. Which persons or groups have the most effective and widespread control over his current behavior?

F. Can the patient relate reinforcement contingencies to his own behavior, or does he assign reinforcement to random uncontrollable factors (''superstitious'' behavior, belief in luck, fate, miracles, etc.)?

G. What are the major aversive stimuli for this patient (1) in immediate day-to-day life, (2) in the future? Are there bodily sensations, conviction of illness, or fears of illness which serve as important aversive stimuli for change? What are his fears, the consequences which he avoids and dreads, the risks which he does not take?

H. Would a treatment program require that the patient give up current satisfactions associated with his problem, e.g., invalid status in the family or on the job; gratifications possibly due to unemployment; life restrictions and special privileges justified by his ''nervous'' status; illness as justification for failure to fulfill expectations of himself or others?

I. Which events of known reinforcing value can be utilized for learning new interpersonal skills or self-attitudes during treatment? In what areas and by what means can positive consequences be arranged to follow desired behaviors, replacing earlier aversive consequences?

## IV. Developmental Analysis

A. *Biological changes.*
   1. What are the limitations in the patient's biological equipment which may affect his current behavior (e.g., defective vision and hearing; residuals of illnesses, such as stroke, poliomyelitis, mononucleosis, glandular imbalances)? How do these limitations initiate or maintain

undesirable behaviors (e.g., behavioral constrictions due to fatigue, fear of overexertion, avoidance of social exposure of these deficits)? Can the patient's self-limiting expectations of the interfering consequences be changed?

2. When and how did biological deviations or limitations develop? What consequences did they have on his life-pattern and on his self-attitudes? What was done about them, by whom? Has he developed specific consistent response patterns toward some body structure or function?

3. How do these biological conditions limit response to treatment or resolution of his problems?

B. *Sociological changes.*

1. What are the most characteristic features of the patient's present sociocultural milieu (with regard to urban versus rural environment, religious affiliation, socioeconomic status, ethnic affiliation, educational-intellectual affiliation, etc.)? Are his attitudes congruent with this milieu? For instance, how is a college orientation of an adolescent accepted by his peer group in a poor neighborhood? How does the home and neighborhood environment respond to a patient's religious, social, and sexual activities and fantasies?

2. Have there been changes in this milieu which are pertinent to his current behavior? If so, how long ago, how permanently, and under what conditions did such changes occur? What immediate consequences did they have for the behavior of the patient? For example, what impact on a wife did a husband's rapid promotion have? Or a marriage into a different socioeconomic or religious group? Or a move from a rural southern community to an urban northern part of the United States?

3. Does the patient view these changes as brought about by himself, by significant persons, or by fortuitous circumstances? What attitudes does he have about these changes?

4. Are the patient's roles in various social settings congruent with one another? For example, is there role conflict between value systems of the patient's early and adult social environments? Are there behavioral deficits due to the changes (e.g., an inability to cope with new social demands, sexual standards, or affectional requirements, associated with rapid acquisition or loss of wealth, or geographic relocation)? If the roles are incongruent, is incongruence among these roles pertinent to his problem? Does the problematic behavior occur in all or only some of these different settings?

5. How can identified sociological factors in the problematic behavior be brought into relation with a treatment program?

C. *Behavioral changes.*

1. Prior to the time of referral did the patient's behavior show

deviations in behavioral patterns compared with developmental and social norms? If so, what was the nature of changes in social behaviors, in routine self-care behaviors, in verbal statements toward self and others? Under what conditions were these changes first noted?

2.   Do identified biological, social, or sociological events in the patient's life seem relevant to these behavior changes?

3.   Were these changes characterized by (a) emergence of new behaviors, (b) change in intensity or frequency of established behaviors, or (c) nonoccurence of previous behaviors?

4.   Under what conditions and in which social settings were these behavioral changes first noted? Have they extended to other social settings since the problematic behavior was first noted?

5.   Were the behavioral changes associated with the patient's exposure to significant individuals or groups from whom he learned new patterns of reinforcement and the behavior necessary to achieve them? Can the problematic behaviors be traced to a model in the patient's social environment from whom he has learned these responses?

## V.   Analysis of Self-Control

A.   In what situations can the patient control those behaviors which are problematic? How does he achieve such control, by manipulation of self or others?

B.   Have any of the problematic behaviors been followed by aversive consequences by others, e.g., social retribution, jail, ostracism, probation, etc.? Have these consequences reduced the frequency of the problematic behavior or only the conditions under which it occurs? Have these events modified the patient's self-controlling behavior?

C.   Has the patient acquired some measure of self-control in avoiding situations which are conducive to the execution of his problematic behavior? Does he do this by avoidance or by substitution of alternate instrumental behaviors leading to similar satisfactions?

D.   Is there correspondence between the patient's verbalized degree of self-control and observations by others? Can the patient match his behavior to his intentions?

E.   What conditions, persons, or reinforcers tend to change his self-controlling behavior (e.g., a child behaves acceptably at school but not at home, or vice versa)?

F.   To what extent can the patient's self-controlling behavior be used in a treatment program? Is constant supervision or drug administration necessary to supplement self-control?

## VI.   Analysis of Social Relationships

A.   Who are the most significant people in the patient's current environment? To which persons or groups is he most responsive? Who facilitates constructive behaviors? Who provokes antagonistic or problematic behaviors? Can these relationships be categorized according to dimensions which clarify the patient's behavioral patterns (e.g., does a patient respond in a submissive or hostile way to all older men)?

B.   In these relationships, by use of what reinforcers do the participants influence each other? For example, analysis may reveal a father who always bails out a delinquent son whose public punishment would be embarrassing to the father. Is the cessation of positive reinforcement or onset of punishment clearly signaled?

C.   What does the patient expect of these people in words and in action? On what does he base his verbal expectations?

D.   What do these people expect of the patient? Is there consistency between the patient's and others' expectations for him?

E.   How can the people who can influence the patient participate in treatment?

## VII.   Analysis of the Social-Cultural-Physical Environment

A.   What are the norms in the patient's social milieu for the behaviors about which there is a complaint?

B.   Are these norms similar in various environments in which the patient interacts, e.g., home and school, friends and parents, work and social milieu, etc.? If not, what are the major differences in behaviors supported in one but not in other environments?

C.   What are the limitations in the patient's environment which reduce his opportunities for continued reinforcement; are social, intellectual, sexual, vocational, economic, religious, moral, or physical restrictions imposed by his environment?

D. In which portion of the environment is the patient's problematic behavior most apparent, most troublesome, or most accepted? Can the congruence of several environments be increased or can the patient be helped by removal from dissonant environments? Does his milieu permit or discourage self-evaluation?

E. Does his milieu regard psychological procedures as appropriate for helping him solve his problems? Is there support in his milieu for the changes in attitudes and values which successful psychotherapy may require?

The preceding outline has as its purpose the definition of a patient's problem in a manner which suggests specific treatment operations and also suggests specific behaviors as targets for modification. It may also lead to the major conclusion that no such operations are possible. Therefore, the formulation is action oriented. It can be used as a guide for the initial collection of information, as a device for organizing available data, or as a design for treatment.

The formulation of a treatment plan follows from this type of analysis because knowledge of the reinforcing conditions suggests the motivational controls at the disposal of the clinician for the modification of the patient's behavior. The analysis of specific problem behaviors also provides a series of goals for psychotherapy or other treatment, and for the evaluation of treatment progress. Knowledge of the patient's biological, social, and cultural conditions should help to determine what resources can be used, and what limitations must be considered in a treatment plan.

The various categories attempt to call attention to important variables affecting the patient's current behavior. Therefore, they aim to elicit descriptions of low-level abstraction. Answers to these specific questions are best phrased by describing classes of events reported by the patient or observed by others, or from critical incidents described by an informant. The analysis does not exclude description of the patient's habitual verbal-symbolic behaviors. However, in using verbal behaviors as the basis for this analysis, one should be cautious not to ''explain'' verbal processes in terms of postulated internal mechanisms without adequate supportive evidence, nor should inference be made about non-observed processes or events without corroborative evidence. The analysis includes many items which are not known or not applicable for a given patient. Lack of information on some items does not necessarily indicate incompleteness of the analysis. These lacks must be noted nevertheless because they often contribute to the better understanding of what the patient needs to learn to become an autonomous person. Just as important is an inventory of his existing socially effective behavioral repertoire which can be put in the service of any treatment procedure.

This approach is not a substitute for assignment of the patient to traditional diagnostic categories. Such labeling may be desirable for statistical, administrative, or research purposes. But the current analysis is intended to replace other diagnostic formulations purporting to serve as a basis for making decisions about specific therapeutic interventions.

# 6

An Interview Guide for Behavioral
Counseling with Parents

*Cornelius J. Holland*

This paper outlines a procedure found helpful by the author as an interview guide when counseling parents for behavior problems of their children. A modified form of the present procedure based on "The Analysis of Human Operant Behavior" by Reese (1966) and *Child Development I* by Bijou and Baer (1961) was found to be readily understood by parents with secondary school educations who attended a clinical group led by the author to teach parents to apply behavioral principles, generally operant in nature, to a wide range of problems the parents were experiencing with their children.

The guide serves not only as a method for the interviewer to assemble the necessary data but simultaneously as a training aid for parents, especially when used in conjunction with such a book as *Living With Children* by Patterson and Gullion (1968). When the interview guide has been completed, most of the information necessary for behavioral analysis will have been gathered as well as a selection of the procedures required by the parents to bring about change.

The points for analysis should be carried out as exhaustively as possible before the actual reinforcement program is introduced by the parents. It is better to have too much information than too little, and only with patient and repeated observation of the behavior and the environmental conditions within which the behavior occurs will the necessary clarity of the determinants emerge. For example, behavior such as

Reprinted from *Behavior Therapy*, 1970, *1*, 70-79. Copyright © 1970 Academic Press, Inc. Reprinted by permission.

tantrums may be a function of either positive reinforcement or avoidance. Although the topography of the behavior is similar, it is important to locate and specify the major controlling stimuli, that is, whether they occur antecedent or consequent to the behavior in question, and whether they have positive reinforcing or aversive properties.

Not every point covered will be equally appropriate for every behavior problem. With some cases such as tantrums, simple extinction procedures may be sufficient; with others, such as attempting to shift behavior from competition to cooperation, extinction, punishment, and positive reinforcement may be indicated and subsequently used in the total program. Nevertheless, it is well to cover every point. Often a complete coverage introduces the possibility of using simultaneously two or three techniques for behavior modification and, as such, enhances the possibility of success.

Readers will recognize the outline to be focused on the single child. However, other children in the environment present no need for additional principles. If parents experience some difficulty in modifying a child's behavior because of the intrusions or interferences of a second child, they merely must see these intrusions as behaviors on the part of the second child and apply the same principles to them accordingly An example of this would occur when one sibling teases another and the teasing behavior is maintained by the reactions of the second child. In addition to reinforcing either positively or negatively nonteasing behavior of the first child, the parents may reinforce positively the second child whenever he does not react to the teasing in his usual manner, thus indirectly instituting an extinction procedure for the unwanted behavior.

A final point should be kept in mind. Although the author believes the outline follows the principles of reinforcement theory closely, the points covered are in a sequence which the author finds helpful to himself. Counselors who wish to use the outline may find other sequences more appropriate. It is also to be understood that the guide does not suggest the use of a mechanical gathering of information devoid of the rhythm and pace found in the counseling experience. The points covered in the guide are logical in nature and are not intended to place artifical constraints on the counselor or the parents. Neither are they intended as substitutes for the more traditional skills of a sensitive ear or a judicious tongue.

1. *Have the parents establish general goals and complaints.*   This step usually presents no problem for the parents or the psychologist since most of what the parents say concerning their child implicitly contains the present complaints (symptomatology) and goals (what the parents want the child to do or become). Usually much of this is revealed in the first interview. Subsequent interviews may serve to clarify, but it is the

author's experience that general complaints and goals are readily isolated even though not explicitly stated by the parents.

The above does not imply that the interviewer is merely a passive recipient of information. It is surprising how often parents voice complaints about their children without being able to state clearly what they want the child to do, even in the general way discussed here. It is the job of the interviewer to make this vagueness on the part of the parents known to them so that they may become more definite about it them-selves. Some problems with children probably find their inception just in this area, where demands are made by parents without any clear notion of what they want the child to do. Consider the frequent exhortation from parents for their child to be ''good'' without clarifying the terminal behavior which defines ''goodness'' for the parents. An interesting result of this clarification is that behavior often changes to some extent spontaneously in the desired direction before the parents put into operation any of the specific procedures for behavior change.

2. *Have the parents reduce the general goals and complaints to a list of discrete behaviors which require an increase or decrease in frequency.* A procedure commonly used and found by the author to be helpful is to have the parents make a list of five or ten behaviors they wish to increase and five or ten they wish to decrease, and then have the parents rank-order them in terms of severity or nuisance value. It has been the experience of the author that a generalized change in the child's behavior usually takes place after three or four behaviors have been systematically altered so that going through the entire list is unnecessary.

3. *Have the parents select from the ranked list a single problem behavior on which to concentrate their efforts.* The behavior that is selected is often the one causing the most difficulty or the one most dangerous to the child's welfare. This suggestion of focusing on a single problem while ignoring the others is one of the most important ways of bringing about some kind of manageable order into the entire attempt at behavior modification. Often parents who make contact with child guidance centers feel overwhelmed and confused by the difficulties their children are having or causing. By suggesting a focus on one problem behavior, the parents can be relieved of dealing with the many other problems for the present. Also by reducing the immediate requirements of the parents to more manageable proportions, it is more likely that any efforts at behavior change will meet with success. This in turn helps develop confidence in the methods used and, more importantly, gives the parents some sense of control over what they formerly considered an almost hopeless situation.

*4. Have the parents specify in behavioral terms the precise behavior that is presently occurring and which they desire to change.* This will require on the part of the parents a detailed observation of the behavior in concrete terms. By doing so the parents get closer to the actual behavior they want changed so that it becomes salient for them. Also, when they focus on the actual behavior, and not on inferences from the behavior, they are able to get a better idea of the frequency with which the behavior occurs. It is the change in frequency, consistent with operant psychology, which is the criterion of success or failure of the program.

*5. Have the parents specify in behavioral terms the precise behavior which they desire.* This rule is very similar to the requirements of Number 4, but here the parents must articulate in behavioral terms the terminal behavior, or goal, for any problem which they wish to modify. The task for the interviewer is to help make the goals as clear and precise as possible. Not only is this rule important in terms of measuring the success of the program, but it often reveals the first step toward the goal.

*6. Have the parents discuss how they may proceed to the terminal behavior in a step-by-step manner.* It is important for the parents to realize that it is often self-defeating to insist upon the terminal behavior immediately. For various reasons the child may not be capable of it either because the final behavior necessarily requires the foundation of prior learning, or the final behavior desired is of an aversive nature to the child.

Also important is the implication that in proceeding in such a step-by-step fashion the parents are required to make clear to themselves what is the first step toward the final goal. Often the first step or steps are already present in the child's repertoire but are ignored by the parents and thus remain at an operant level.

It is well, therefore, as an exercise for the parents to have them rehearse the steps required by the child in moving from his present behavior to the terminal behavior. By doing so, the parents are less likely to insist upon too much too soon and will also better appreciate approximations already being made by the child toward the terminal behavior.

*7. Have the parents list positive and negative reinforcers which they think will be effective in bringing about behavior changes.* Although the assumption being made throughout this interview guide is that behavior is maintained by environmental consequences of the behavior, it is not always easy for parents to isolate the reinforcers effective in controlling their children's behavior. Some of course are quite common, such as candy, but others and probably the more important ones are or may be quite specific to the child, such as being given the opportunity to make an independent choice. But it must be emphasized that discovering a reinforcer as being either positive or negative is an empirical matter for the most part which usually must be tested in a trial-and-error fashion. One complaint by parents heard by counselors in a guidance clinic is that what they consider rewarding for their children often has the opposite effect. An an extreme example, certain forms of praise or attention if applied following behavior may act as an aversive stimulus and thus be functionally punishing if the reinforcement history of the child were appropriate. More commonly, what are considered rewards by the parents are neutral for the children. There are, however, good guesses that can be made based on the fact that the child shares a common culture in which certain stimuli take on positive values for most of the children in it.

The task of the interviewer is to determine as completely as possible the total resources which are accessible to the parents or anyone else dispensing the reinforcers. It is helpful to explore systematically the social resources available to the parents, such as praise, attention, affection, or recognition; the physical resources available in the home such as radio, TV, games; and the activity resources available to the child, such as riding a bicycle or making a phone call. A list of these made by the parents is helpful in fitting the reinforcer to the desired behavior in as natural a manner as possible as well as helping the parents realize the many reinforcers available to them which may be made when any un-expected situation occurs which makes immediate reinforcement desirable.

8. *Have the parents discuss what deprivations are possible.*　The value of a reinforcer fluctuates with the child's being either deprived or satiated with it. Withholding toys, for example, will enhance the value of a toy when it is given following a behavior which is desired. If toys are given haphazardly, they should not be expected to be effective in behavioral control. The same can be said for affection or praise or any other stimulus serving as a reinforcer.

Many parents are reluctant to deprive their children of praise or affection for obvious reasons even though an indiscriminate use of these reinforcers may actually be doing harm to the child. It has been the experience of the author, however, that children whose behavior is being modified by these procedures do not suffer a loss of positive reinforcers in the long run; in fact, there is usually a gain when the problem behavior begins to diminish and the parents are more comfortable with the child. It has also been the experience of the author that deprivation of such activities as watching TV or using the phone are often the only deprivation necessary to bring about desired change. More importantly, the child is usually in some deprived state already. Some piece of sports equipment that the child greatly desired but cannot have at present is a deprived state for these purposes; also such things as a pet, a watch, a toy which the child values but does not have can be considered instances of deprived states. Therefore it is helpful to discuss with the parents the usually many things the child greatly desires but does not have, or is not obtaining as often as he desires.

9. *Have the parents clearly establish what they want to do, either to increase or decrease a behavior or to do both.* This information has already been determined from the ranked list of behaviors which the parents wish to change. It is introduced again because in many instances parents do not merely wish to decrease a behavior but also to increase an incompatible behavior. It is helpful if they have clear what is required for the total modification desired. Much of the success of this method depends on the readiness on the part of the parents to act immediately, either by reinforcing or withholding a reinforcer, and a clear notion of what they desire helps them to do so.

10. *Have the parents discuss the situation in which the desired behavior should occur.* The requirements for this step are to determine the discriminative stimuli for the desired behavior. If, for example, the parents desire to change their child's behavior from a withdrawn, isolated social style to one of more social participation with peers, the presence of the child's peers would be the discriminative stimuli at which time any increase in social participation would be reinforced. If the parents desire an increase in obedience on the part of their child, the situation or discriminative stimulus would be the verbal statement of the request or demand made by the parents. The behavior that is desired need not occur all the time but only under certain specifiable stimulus conditions, and isolating these stimulus conditions allows the parents to become aware of the precise circumstances in which reinforcement is to take place.

11. *Have the parents discuss the situation in which the undesired behavior should not occur.* The behavior that is unwanted and should be decreased occurs under specifiable stimulus conditions. These also have to be made known for they constitute discriminative conditions for some positive reinforcer which they must become aware of and withhold if possible. A not uncommon occurrence is found when children throw tantrums in stores but do not do so at home. The child has learned that tantrum behavior does not yield to positive reinforcers except under the discriminative conditions in which the mother will give in to the child in order to terminate the aversive tantrum which for the mother occasions social embarrassment.

12. *Have the parents determine a situation which increases the likelihood that some form or portion of the desired behavior occurs.* If, for example, the parents desire to increase their child's obedience, it is likely that sometimes the child is obedient. It is also likely that the obedience often goes unrewarded. It is precisely at these times that the program should focus its initial efforts, for strengthening the behavior under a structured situation will usually increase the likelihood of its occurrence under those conditions in which it is not now occurring.

Another example would be the attempt to increase cooperative behavior between sibs who show too much hostile competition. It is unlikely that competition occurs every time the children are together. Those times in which the children are together and are either cooperative or at least noncompetitive can be used by the parents as a situation in which they introduce some structure for the desired behavior. If the parents know, for example, that a certain toy or activity usually results in some cooperative behavior on the part of the sibs at least for a while, this could be used by the parents as the structured situation to begin the reinforcing of the desired behavior. If it were decided that the first step toward the final terminal behavior of prolonged cooperation was to have one minute of cooperative or noncompetitive play, the parents would reinforce after that period.

13. *Have the parents discuss how they may increase desired behavior by immediately giving a positive reinforcer following the behavior.* This of course is a basic principle of reinforcement theory. The crucial requirement is the immediate application of the reinforcer. The efficiency of this program depends on the availability to the parents of effective primary or secondary reinforcers which can be given immediately. Parents with whom the author has worked are usually quite able to develop star systems or other token economies, a certain number of which could be exchanged for backup reinforcers.

A most effective reinforcer of course is the verbal stimuli of the parents which constitutes praise or recognition. It has sometimes been found, however, that the parents' verbal behavior must first be paired with backup reinforcers for it to become effective as a viable acquired reinforcer in a program such as this.

It has also been found necessary at times to work out a system whereby any token reinforcer is at first able to translate almost immediately into a backup reinforcer which the child can enjoy. It is often too much to expect a child to accumulate 15 or 20 tokens in order to obtain a backup reinforcer when one of the problems the child is having is an intolerance for delay of gratification.

In any event, the parents should be instructed to give some form of praise whenever they give another reinforcer. Social reinforcers are ultimately more relevant because they are less arbitary and less artificial reinforcers in the child's broader social world.

14. *Have the parents discuss how they may increase desired behavior by immediately terminating a negative reinforcer following the behavior.* Both positive and negative reinforcement strengthen preceding behavior, and both can be employed effectively in the program, although usually the positive reinforcement method is the chief instrument for change. However, if parents insist on certain activities on the part of their children, such as doing the dishes, and the child finds this to be aversive, a relief from this chore can be an important source of negative reinforcement and could be effectively used.

15. *Have the parents discuss how they may decrease undesired behavior by withholding the reinforcers which follow it.* The requirements here on the part of the parents are to discover what stimuli are at present maintaining the undesired behavior, and to institute an extinction procedure. This often runs into several difficulties. The parents themselves may be providing the maintaining reinforcer. For example, a child of nine who was a chronic complainer apparently was being reinforced by his mother's concern and her getting upset. Since she had developed a habit of responding to him in this way, it was especially difficult to have her withhold this reinforcer. Again, children are often systematically taught by their parents that positive reinforcers will occur only under forms of tantrum behavior which are so shrill and upsetting to the parents that they cannot tolerate them for any length of time. It is important for the interviewer to show the parents that "giving in" after prolonged or especially shrill tantrums is a learning experience for the child leading to a prolonging or intensification of the undesired behavior.

   Another difficulty is that extinction procedures often increase the undesired behavior initially. In the example cited above with the nine-year-old boy, when the mother began to ignore him, his first reaction was to increase the complaining both in frequency and intensity.

   A third difficulty is that extinction is a vastly different procedure from intermittent reinforcement. Unless the parents are made to see the differential effects of each, withholding of the maintaining reinforcer may not be complete and may lead to a resistance to extinction. It is for the above reasons that the author has found extinction to be most effective when there exists the possibility of combining it with positive or negative reinforcement of incompatible behavior.

   The fourth difficulty, and perhaps the most serious, is the fact that often the parents do not have control over the maintaining reinforcer. Another way of saying that parents have lost control over their child's behavior is to say that the undesired behavior is being effectively controlled by other people, agencies, or circumstances. Although this situation introduces real difficulties, some of which may never be overcome, a solution can often be achieved by the reinforcement of incompatible behavior if the reinforcer used for the incompatible behavior is of greater value to the child than the reinforcer presently controlling the undesired behavior.

16. *Have the parents discuss how they may decrease undesired behavior by removing a positive reinforcer.* This is a punishment-by-loss technique which may prove effective in suppressing behavior long enough for the desired behavior to occur. Although many children who come to guidance clinics have been punished often enough already, the author believes such a procedure may at times be the only technique effective in suppressing a behavior whose necessity to change is obvious. Behaviors such as running out into the street between parked cars, fire setting, and physically abusive behavior toward another child readily come to mind as behaviors in which the parents cannot wait for the reinforcement of incompatible behavior to occur, or for extinction to take place.

The threat of punishment-by-loss can also be used, the threat being seen as a conditioned aversive stimulus. It must be discovered, however, whether or not threats from the parents have actually acquired aversive properties, as often threats have not been followed up by the parents in the past and are therefore looked on by the child not as a discriminative stimulus for punishment but as neutral stimuli.

17. *Have the parents discuss how they may decrease undesired behavior by time-out.* Time-out is any procedure in which the child is removed from the source of positive reinforcers. Putting the child in his room for a certain period of time or in the familiar corner is a common time-out procedure. It must be carried out in such a way, however, that the child does experience a loss of reinforcers; putting a child in his room where many of his toys are available to him could not be considered a time-out procedure.

Often when a child has been given a time-out period, at least if this has not been a common punishing procedure in the family, the child will react very strongly in a negative manner. It is well to establish at the beginning the time-out procedure as a punishment by making the relief from the room or corner contingent upon a set period of time in which none of the negative behavior has occurred. If it does occur, relief from the time-out period should be made contingent upon the absence, for a specified period of time, of the undesired negative behavior.

18. *Discuss with the parents how they may pattern the reinforcers they give to the child.* The parents should give reinforcers every time the

desired behavior occurs until it becomes strongly established, then they should give them randomly. This is the familiar shift from a continuous reinforcement schedule to a variable interval or variable ratio. There are no ready rules with which the author is familiar to move from a continuous to an intermittent schedule. It seems desirable, however, to tell the child that he shouldn't expect a reward every time the desired behavior occurs, even when the child is still being reinforced continuously. It also seems desirable to move from a continuous through a fixed schedule before establishing a random one.

19. *Have the parents discuss how they may vary the reinforcers they give to the child.* The parents will have available to them a list of reinforcers which they are reasonably sure are positive for the child. The parents have options of giving different amounts of the same reinforcers or different reinforcers. Varying the reinforcers enhances the probability that desired behavior, when it occurs, will be maintained for long periods of time.

20. *Have the parents discuss how they may apply two or more procedures simultaneously.* Success is enhanced by the parents having at their disposal as many procedures as can be applied to the behavior in question. The most obvious situation is an extinction procedure coupled with positive reinforcement of incompatible behavior, but other combinations are also possible and should be explored depending on the nature of the behavior the parents wish to change.

21. *Have the parents rehearse verbally the entire program.* This will require that they are able to specify clearly each step covered by the program. Such rehearsal enhances the success of the program by making salient to them such crucial issues as the terminal behavior stated in behavioral terms, any incipient behavior present, the initial steps toward the goal, the discriminative stimuli involved, and the reinforcers which must be withheld or supplied.

## REFERENCES

Bijou, S., & Baer, D. *Child development I: A systematic and empirical theory.* New York: Appleton-Century-Crofts, 1961.

Patterson, G. R., & Gullion, M. E. *Living with children: New methods for parents and teachers.* Champaign, Ill.: Research Press, 1968.

Reese, E. The analysis of human operant behavior. In J. Vernon (Ed.), *Introduction to psychology: A self-selection text.* Dubuque, Iowa: William C. Brown, 1966

# 7

## Transcript of Initial Interview
## in a Case of Depression

*Joseph Wolpe*

The interview recorded in the following transcript took place as a consultation-demonstration that was viewed on closed-circuit television by a group of psychiatric residents. In the one hour available, it was necessary both to reach an evaluation and make therapeutic recommendations. It was therefore not a typical first interview. Nevertheless, it followed the basic lines of behavioristic anamneses, being primarily directed at determining the stimulus conditions, external and internal, that elicit neurotic responses.

Several features of the behavior therapy approach will be apparent to the reader. He will see that, contrary to a fairly prevalent conception, the strategy does not consist of attacking target symptoms in isolation, and that all measures are planned within a broad conspectus of the patient's major functions and life situation. He will also note that pains are taken to ensure that the patient clearly understands the interrelations between stimulus conditions and responses, so that she can become an informed partner to the therapist in whatever therapeutic endeavors he may later undertake.

An important reason for selecting this case was the fact that its diagnosis was "depression." There are many who believe that such a diagnosis places behavior therapy out of its depth, for they suppose its applications to be confined to "simple" cases like phobias. What emerges here is that this woman's depression, like all other reactive depressions,

Reprinted from *Journal of Behavior Therapy and Experimental Psychiatry*, 1970, *1*, 71-78. Copyright © 1970 Pergamon Press Ltd. Reprinted by permission.

is clearly relatable to specific stimulus situations. Hers is one of the common class of depressions that are secondary to the evocation of anxiety or other emotional disturbance. In this case, the relevant anxiety was unadaptive—being evoked in the context of exposure to social groups or the context of sexual guilt. At other times the depression was related to a "normal" physiological response to sexual frustration.

Programs for procuring an adaptive modus vivendi for the patient were suggested for each of two alternative future life courses that she brought forward.

Dr:   How long have you been here Mrs. B?
Pt:   About 9 days.
Dr:   How old are you?
Pt:   41.
Dr:   Why are you here?
Pt:   I wasn't feeling too well, but I do feel much better now.
Dr:   Good. What was your complaint?
Pt:   Depression. I was very nauseous to my stomach, headaches, and my mouth was tightly closed. I cried constantly for about 10 days. I hadn't eaten for 4 days when I came in. But I do feel much better now.
Dr:   Good. How long were you feeling this way?
Pt:   It was sort of a downward thing, Doctor. I got the nausea about a month ago and it would keep getting worse. Well, about 6 weeks ago it started.
Dr:   What do you think started it?
Pt:   I am not sure. It could be one of several things. One thing that is bothering me, although I don't know if I am not making this one big thing and just looking at this. My husband and I have been separated for 2 years, and I have been dating a gentleman for 6 months. We have not had intercourse. I have had no affair with him. But one time (this is very hard for me to talk about) 6 or 7 weeks ago, I had my head on his lap one night and I don't know how it happened—his penis was out and I put my mouth down on it. I am shaken just talking about it.
Dr:   Now, what's wrong with that?[1]
Pt:   It is horrible.
Dr:   Why? I mean, was it unpleasant?
Pt:   Yes.

---

[1] During the next dozen interchanges (until "There is no union"), the therapist endeavors to reduce the patient's guilt about this sexual activity of hers—first, by putting its "wrongness" in question, and then by pinpointing the sources of her negative reaction. Eventually he is in a position to challenge the moral reasoning that is the wellspring of the guilt.

Dr: Let me get one thing straight. Was it physically unpleasant? Is that the point? Does it taste bad, for example?

Pt: Yes. It had like a urine taste to it.

Dr: Is that what upset you?

Pt: Yes. And we didn't do the act. I put my mouth down and drew it away. It was a split second like that, so that it was not oral.

Dr: It was just the taste? If it hadn't had any taste, would everything have been okay?

Pt: Well, it was sort of soft and mushy.

Dr: It was the physical unpleasantness of it? If it hadn't been physically unpleasant, you wouldn't have minded it?

Pt: Morally I would, because my conscience is just eating me away right now.

Dr. Your conscience? Will you explain that to me.

Pt: To me this is such a dirty thing.

Dr: What is?

Pt: I wouldn't have intercourse with this man, yet I went ahead and did this. If I had intercourse it would have been just as bad.

Dr: Why won't you have intercourse with this man? Do you like him?

Pt: Yes.

Dr: Would you like to have intercourse with him? If so, why won't you?

Pt: Because I am still a married woman, and I don't believe people should have intercourse unless they are married.

Dr: What do you mean by marriage? What is a marriage?

Pt: The union of two people.

Dr: Is there a union between you and your husband?[2] You are separated, there is no union. Tell me about that? Why are you separated?

Pt: I think—it was an accumulation of many things over the years. I had been ill for 5 years (off and on) with this depression—to one psychiatrist after another. I was in a hospital—I don't remember the name of the place. I think that he just got fed up with me being ill. I was a pest, a pain, a drag, I was always sick, and I think any man would have got fed up with it.

Dr: This is since 5 years ago when you were 36 years old?

Pt: Yes.

Dr: Can you say what made you depressed?

Pt: My husband owns a restaurant and he had an affair with one of the girls and wanted to marry her.[3] It ended up to be the biggest scandal. We live in a small town. The girl ended up in the hospital

[2] Her relationship with her husband is explored.

[3] This, of course, immediately makes it important to elucidate what the patient's husband found unsatisfactory about her.

with a nervous breakdown, and it was a year or so after. I just couldn't accept it.

Dr: Wait a minute. He had an affair, but before that you were quite happy and healthy.

Pt: I always kept myself so busy that I never realized the symptoms. I think I have always been depressed—all my life, but I got by. It wasn't that bad.

Dr: By depression,[4] what do you mean?

Pt: I never enjoy anything, Doctor. I can go out to a party and anticipate it and get all dressed, but the minute I get in there I want to go home.

Dr: Is there anything about parties that upsets you?

Pt: I don't only mean parties. It is just like when I went swimming with a group yesterday. I wanted to go, but as soon as I got there I wanted to go home.

Dr: Is there anything about groups that upsets you?

Pt: No. I just feel bored with it and I want to go home.

Dr: If there wasn't a group and there had been only one or two people, would the same thing have happened?

Pt: No.

Dr: Does this feeling have something to do with the number of people that you go to meet?

Pt: Yes. I guess so. If it is going to be a group. Now, today they told me there would be doctors in here with you and I was really frightened, but now that it is only you and I, that doesn't bother me.

Dr: So being watched by people bothers you?[5] And that has interfered with your enjoying group situations?

Pt: I don't know if it is that or if I am just bored. Just nothing interests me.

Dr: But if there are only one or two people, have you then been able to enjoy situations?

Pt: Yes, if I can converse with someone. What I want to tell you before I forget. This illness of mine is something I want. It is my security.

Dr: Is it?

Pt: Yes.

Dr: Did you come to that conclusion or did somebody tell you that?

---

[4] "Depression" is too easily taken for granted. It has different meanings for different people. Here, asking for its meaning leads to evidence of social anxiety which is then investigated.

[5] It is evident that she has a neurotic habit of responding with anxiety to being watched by several people. In such cases the anxiety is often found to increase as a function of the number of watchers.

Pt: No. I did.[6] It is my security, and when I am in the hospital I don't think I am sick or don't feel as though I am sick because I feel secure that I am here.

Dr: What do you mean when you say it is your security?

Pt: Like at home, it is something to hang on to. When I am sick I feel secure. It is a big point there. I know I want to be ill. Something inside of me wants to be ill. I am punishing myself, and the more angry I get at myself, I dislike myself intensely.

Dr: Wouldn't it be nice not to be ill?

Pt: That will never happen to me.

Dr: I wouldn't say that; but in some sense then it must be true that you prefer not to be ill?

Pt: Yes. There is a part of me that doesn't want to be ill. The confident side of me. When I have good days, I could lick the world. But when I have those down days I am ready to die.

Dr: Well, doesn't that mean you would really prefer to have good days all the time?

Pt: Yes.

Dr: And isn't that why you are here in the hospital, because you hope this may be brought about. Although I realize you are not very optimistic about this, this is why you are here. Let me see if we can piece this together clearly. You have always been aware that there are certain situations which you should have enjoyed but couldn't, and one of the things that got in the way was the presence of a number of people. (There may be other things too.) Are you saying that the fact that this happened may have been a kind of damper on your husband? It might have made him dissatified with you.[7] That might have been a reason for his having this affair.

Pt: That he was dissatisfied with me? Oh, yes. Our sexual life was very ·bad too.

Dr: Why, what was bad about it?

Pt: I never had a climax in 20 years. Never in my life have I had a climax.

Dr: Do you think you could have?

Pt: Yes.

Dr: What prevented you from doing so?

Pt: I don't think my husband knew enough.

Dr: Can you describe to me what used to happen?

Pt: Well, we would get in bed and he would kiss me and feel my

---

[6] Nevertheless, as she has previously had a considerable amount of psychoanalytically oriented psychotherapy, it is likely that the idea was originally planted by a therapist. The conversation that follows appears to uphold this inference.

[7] The reasons for her husband's dissatisfaction are brought out.

breasts and things like that, but it would last about 5 or 10 minutes and then he was ready to go and it was done. I think that maybe he was too small for me, because sometimes I could barely even feel it.

Dr:  And you would sort of be left high and dry?

Pt:  And then he is done and he turned over and went to sleep.

Dr:  Would you feel frustrated?

Pt:  Yes. For days.[8]

Dr:  Didn't he recognize that there was a problem. Did you tell him that this was not satisfactory to you?

Pt:  Yes, but I don't think he— —Since I have met this other man, from just the petting that we have done (I told you that we didn't have intercourse), I realize that my husband didn't know anything about making love. I don't know how I even got pregnant to tell you the truth. I mean other than the fact of the actual act, it could have been anybody getting me pregnant. I don't know why. I think that I didn't feel as a woman as I should because I never had a climax. I think that in doing what I did with this other man, I in a way wanted to prove that I was a woman, too.

Dr:  Well, why shouldn't you?[9]

Pt:  My conscience is just eating me alive.

Dr:  We will come back to that in a minute. Do you think (I am just asking you—I am not trying to suggest this to you), is it possible that because you found your sex life so unsatisfactory, you were not a very willing partner as far as your husband was concerned?

Pt:  Yes. That's true.

Dr:  So, we now have two reasons for him being dissatisfied with you, even though he himself was to blame for the one. You were a bit of a spoil-sport in company, and you weren't very willing in bed, so he may have become dissatisfied and that may have led to him going to another woman. Now, did he tell you this? Or did he, out of the blue, tell you, "I am tired of you and I want to marry this waitress"? Is that what happened or what?

Pt:  Yes, he did. I don't know how it came about. He said that he wanted to marry her. I took the car and I don't know where I drove that night. The next morning he changed his mind and asked for my forgiveness, and he went and told the girl that it was all over with. She ended up before the day was over in the hospital with a breakdown.

Dr:  You took him back?

---

[8] A major complaint against the husband is brought to light. Both parties thus have strong negative reactions in major recurrent situations. The elements are present for a vicious cycle of mutual repulsion that can generate growing negative emotions.

[9] Another attack is made on the "rationale" of her guilt from the therapist's authoritative pedestal.

Pt:  Yes, and a couple of months later I got pregnant and had my son. For a couple of years it was good after that.

Dr:  You really forgave him and you didn't think about it?[10]

Pt:  Oh no, I didn't forget it. I was (there is a word I could use for myself)—I let him live in hell because of it. I brought it up to him every time I could.

Dr:  From your point of view, in terms of the way you feel, you are not married to him any more. There is no relationship?

Pt:  But I never really let him go.

Dr:  That is just on paper. In fact, you have let him go. I mean, he is supporting you economically, but there is no relationship. There is no personal situation which you could call a marriage. It is just a piece of paper with money stuck on to it. Let me ask you this. Here is this other man; does he love you?[11]

Pt:  Yes.

Dr:  Is he in a position to marry you?

Pt:  Yes.

Dr:  Could he support you?

Pt:  Yes.

Dr:  Is there any good reason then why you shouldn't divorce your husband and marry him? Do you like him?

Pt:  Yes. I am very physically attracted to him, but he drinks —sometimes a little and sometimes a lot.

Dr:  If you were to marry him, would he give it up?

Pt:  I don't know. He has been a bachelor for 20 years.

Dr:  He wants to marry you?

Pt:  Yes.

Dr:  How old is he?

Pt:  He is 53, and I am 41.

Dr:  Well, that's not a bad difference.

Pt:  He doesn't look it. He looks very young and he is very vivacious. He is entirely different than I.

Dr:  Let me ask you this. Suppose he could put himself into a position where he could have treatment for his alcoholism? If you could have a reasonable assurance that he loved you enough to want to do something to give up the drinking and if this could be controlled, would you marry him?

Pt:  I don't know because I still love my husband.

Dr:  You still love your husband? But you also hate your husband?

Pt:  Do I? I don't know if I do.

Dr:  Well, the way you kept on attacking him until you separated.

---

[10] The therapist is not content with "it was good".

[11] In the following passages the potentialities of the other relationship are investigated.

Pt:  He left, but he would keep telling me to snap out of it and he was just disgusted.

Dr:  There is another possible solution to this problem. If you feel basically that you love your husband, and if it is conceivable that you could contemplate the fact that he had an affair without being distressed, then you could take him back.[12]

Pt:  I would take him back right now if he walked in.

Dr:  You would? And would you attack him every day?

Pt:  No.

Dr:  But would you feel okay about it?

Pt:  I think so. I can understand it better now.

Dr:  Even if you may be deceiving yourself in saying that you would comfortably take him back, it is possible for you to get treatment that would enable you to tolerate it and forgive it.[13] I believe that your husband had good reason to be dissatisfied with you. Now, it is very possible for him to be retrained sexually[14] so that you would not need to go on being frustrated. The question is: Is there any practical possibility of your making an approach to your husband to try to get things set right, or is he now tied up with somebody else?

Pt:  I don't know. He was. He was dating another waitress—he always has the waitresses. But I don't think so. We live in a small town and it took a lot of nerve for him to walk out and leave me, because there are people in town who still won't talk to him after 2½ years. It would take an awfully big man to come back and say—you know.

Dr:  Either he is mixed up with somebody else now or he is not. If he is not, then there is probably quite a good chance, but it depends on the way you approach it. I think you would need to make an approach and say that you now understand the situation and understand why he did what he did; that you can accept it; that you would like to come together with him and see whether a new future could be worked out between the two of you.[15] That accords with the way you feel, doesn't it?

Pt:  Yes. I would be very glad to do anything.

Dr:  Then, at the very least you should give yourself that chance. It may not work, he may refuse, but at least you should feel that you have done everything that is possible. Then, if he doesn't under

[12] In what follows the possibility of restitution of the marriage is explored.
[13] The rationality of what has happened would be driven home; and desensitization would subsequently be performed if nonrational emotional disturbance remained evocable by any aspects of these past developments.
[14] Means are proposed for overcoming the husband's impotence.
[15] It is generally a good rule to pursue objectives in the order of the patient's preferences.

any circumstance want to come back, you must cut your losses and resign yourself to not having him and see if you can find somebody else with whom you can make a life. Do you agree or not?

Pt: Yes. I am not getting anywhere, just standing still.

Dr: Well, that seems to be the logical sequence. You must make the approach to him, and tell him that you will accept it. The two of you should not only come together, but try to come together in such a way that, by getting psychiatric help,[16] you can remove the factors which led to the break-up of the marriage.

Pt: He doesn't believe in psychiatrists.

Dr: People often have good reason for this, because they have unsuccessful experiences; but I think what would happen here would be a constructive experience for both of you. It would really be quite different from the ordinary psychiatry that you have been thinking of.[17]

Pt: It is just that I have been to about 3 or 4 of them, and I just don't get over my problem. He has no faith in them, because they are not doing me any good. Yet, I realize that it could be that it is not the psychiatrist's fault, but it is just me. I just don't understand or I am not getting the point of what they are trying to tell me, or I just don't want to.

Dr: I don't think it is really that. It may have something to do with the approach of the psychiatrist. I am giving you a practical program.[18] Speak to your husband and say that you can accept what he did and that you want to do everything for yourself—to change yourself so that you can make the marriage work. Say that you have discovered that the two of you can get counsel to obtain the satisfactory sex life which you didn't have before. You would like to give it a go, that you feel much more mature, and so on. See what happens.

Pt: Well, I will do that. Right now he is very angry with me for coming to the hospital.

Dr: He is angry with you?

Pt: My whole family is angry. I have had hardly any visitors. They are all angry. I packed up and I left and came here myself and signed myself in.

Dr: You mean because it puts a blot on the family name?

Pt: Probably. I was in ——— Hospital, and I came out of there worse than I went in, and he just felt it wasn't going to do me any good

---

[16] The main targets, of course, are the patient's social anxieties and her husband's sexual inadequacy.

[17] This distinction often needs to be emphatically made and must sometimes be spelled out in detail.

[18] The targets of therapy are reiterated.

and that I should stay home and fight it. That is what he would tell me.

Dr:    At this stage, it may be a good idea for you to tell him that one of the results of your being in the hospital this time has been to reveal to you that you would like to give it another go with him and that there are ways to make it a success.

Pt:    But I feel dirty now.

Dr:    Look, in the same way that what he did with that waitress is understandable because of the unsatisfactory situation in which he found himself, what you have done is also understandable.[19] You would have been absolutely justified in having intercourse with this other man. There is no question about it. From the human point of view—you need companionship and love and so on, and if you are not getting it from your husband it is natural to do something else—the same way as when he wasn't getting affection from you, he got it from somebody else. From a rational point of view it is remarkable to me that you didn't have intercourse with this man. I think you should have.

Pt:    The problem is that I am really frustrated.

Dr:    Yes.

Pt:    It makes me nervous because we pet and then we stop. After all I am 41 years old, and it is not easy. You know, I have not had intercourse in 2½ years.

Dr:    Well that's ridiculous, and you should have, but now look—you have come to this point.[20] You have told me that you would rather have your husband. So you will try and get him to come back with you. You will try and overcome these things that have made you sort of a damping influence socially. This can be done very easily. This is a new kind of psychiatry which you can get right here. There may be other things I don't know about. We haven't been into them. These faults in you which have impaired the marriage can be overcome. Your husband's difficulty can be overcome. The other things which have interfered with marriage can be overcome. If he is prepared to go along with this, the marriage can be rebuilt. If he is not, then you have to cut your losses and get yourself another man. In any event, the fear that you have of being looked at needs to be overcome.

Pt:    Doctor, do you think it is fair for me to marry any man with this depression over me?

[19] The justifiability of her sexual behavior is reiterated.
[20] The sequential possibilities are brought together.

Dr: We know what the depression came from. At least we know some of the things that can cause it.[21] We haven't had much time together, so I haven't gone into many details. You have been depressed because you haven't enjoyed social situations due to tension in the presence of people; and that can be cured. If it is cured, that source of depression will be gone. You have also been depressed because you have been sexually frustrated. If the sexual situation can be remedied, that source of depression will be gone. If there are other things that I don't know about which can cause depression, they can be modified as well. The depression is not just a thing inside you which has got to be accepted. It is pretty clear that it comes from specified things that can be changed. Let me build a picture of a possible future. You have rejoined your husband. You no longer get disturbed by going into groups and crowds—you enjoy them. He has learned how to handle you sexually so that you have climaxes. Will there be any need for you to be depressed? But we have also noted another thing. You have a kind of anxiety at not having the approval of certain people.[22] Now this can be overcome, too, very simply.

Pt: Suppose things don't work out with my husband. What would happen if I really went through and did the whole sex thing with the other man? I don't know where I would go the next day.

Dr: Well, I don't think it is all that easy. You have an emotional attitude about it, and that would have to be overcome, so that you could accept sexual relations with this man without being disturbed. But now that you have told me that you want to go back to your husband, the immediate program is different. You may want to go ahead with this man later. Now you are going to make an approach to your husband. Therefore, why should we concern ourselves about this other thing now? I really don't want to pursue this any further. I wish you luck.

Pt: You have been very kind, doctor, Thank you.

---

[21] Knowing the sources of her depressions has the immediate effect of making individual attacks of depression easier for the patient to tolerate. The next stage in the therapist's strategy will be to decondition the unadaptive emotional habits that are the sources of depression. Systematic desensitization should be applied to the patient's interpersonal anxiety reactions. It would embrace her reactions to social disapproval, and her guilt in relation to having "transgressed" in various contexts of extramarital sex. A counter-conditioning schedule entailing the use of sexual responses will probably be needed to overcome her husband's sexual problem (Wolpe, 1969).

[22] This is a reference to her excessive concern about the opinions others have of her, which probably has a great deal to do with her sexual guilt reaction.

## REFERENCE

Wolpe, J. *The practice of behavior therapy.* Oxford: Pergamon Press. 1969.

# 8

## The Drinking Profile: A Questionnaire for the Behavioral Assessment of Alcoholism

*G. Alan Marlatt*

### Development of the Drinking Profile

The Drinking Profile was initially developed as a behaviorally oriented intake procedure for the assessment of alcoholism in hospitalized male alcoholics. The questionnaire was first used in a research study designed to evaluate the effectiveness of aversive conditioning treatment procedures with chronic alcoholics.[1] The present version of the Drinking Profile is an updated revision of this questionnaire and can be used with both male and female alcoholics or problem drinkers of any age. Although the form of the Profile is geared toward the hospitalized alcoholic, modifications can be made in those items that refer to current hospitalization (primarily in Section III-C) which would then make the questionnaire suitable for use with outpatients.

### Administration Procedures

The Drinking Profile is best administered in the form of a structured interview. A trained interviewer can help interpret items that the patient finds difficult to understand and can explore significant responses in more

The Drinking Profile may be used in its present form by researchers and treatment personnel without obtaining the permission of the author. References to the Drinking Profile should cite the present publication as the primary source.

[1] Marlatt, G. A. A comparison of aversive conditioning procedures in the treatment of alcoholism. Paper presented at the Western Psychological Association, Anaheim, California, May 1973. An expanded report of this research is currently under preparation for publication.

121

detail with the interviewee. In addition, several items require the administration of a "card sort" procedure, in which the patient is asked to sort and order alternative responses which are typed on 3×5 index cards (see Section II, items E-1 and E-2; and Section III, items A-1, B-8, and C-7). As a structured interview, the Profile takes between 45 and 60 minutes to administer with the average patient.

## Organization of the Drinking Profile

The Profile is divided into three main sections. Section I contains basic identification material, including such demographic information as age and residence, family status, employment status, and educational history. Considerable specification on residence is solicited in Part A, in order to facilitate post-treatment follow-up contact with the patient. Section II contains a variety of questions pertaining to drinking patterns and behavior, including the initial development of the drinking problem, typical drinking patterns (with separate items for steady drinkers and periodic or "binge" drinkers), symptoms and problems associated with drinking, periods of abstinence, and drinking settings. In section III, information is obtained concerning beverage preferences and drinking rates. Separate analyses of "favorite" and "most frequently consumed" alcoholic beverages are contained in Part A. Unless information concerning beverage switches as a function of treatment is required (as would be the case in aversion therapy), the section on "favorites" may be omitted to save time. Considerable detail is requested concerning drinking rates, so that the investigator can make some determination of pretreatment baseline estimates of drinking behavior. Part B of Section III contains items in which the patient is asked to specify his own reasons for drinking, in terms of both "internal" (intrapersonal feelings) and "external" (situational or environmental) factors. Finally, in Part C, questions relating to the patient's motivation for past and present treatment and expectations of treatment outcomes are presented.

## Scoring and Interpretation

Many of the items in the Profile are quantitatively specific and can easily be coded for purposes of computer analysis (see section on Drinking Profile Analysis). Quantification of drinking rates for fixed time periods (e.g., per day and per week) can be accomplished by transforming the raw data concerning consumption of various beverages into standard units (e.g., millilitres or grams of pure ethanol), based on the proof level of each beverage. Estimates of pretreatment consumption rates can then be compared with drinking rates during follow-up periods.

The open-ended questions can be assigned to coding categories based on content analysis procedures. In previous work, the author has established coding categories for each of these items. Independent raters were able to independently assign categories for these items with at least 80 percent agreement in each case. Copies of the coding categories, with scoring rules and examples, can be obtained upon request to the author.[2] Also available upon request are the following items: a shorter form of the Drinking Profile, a follow-up questionnaire designed to match items in the Profile which can be used to evaluate treatment outcome (both three-month and fifteen-month follow-up questionnaires are available), along with scoring rules and coding categories for the follow-up questionnaires.

[2] Address requests for these additional materials to the author, Department of Psychology, University of Washington, Seattle, Washington, 98195.

DRINKING PROFILE

Name of Patient:_____
                    (First)        (Initial)      (Last)
Interviewer:_____ Date:_____

Instructions to Patient

Your answers to the following questions are needed in order to
assist us in planning your treatment program.  Please try to
answer each question as accurately as possible.  If you have
trouble understanding any questions, feel free to ask for
further information.

I.  IDENTIFICATION MATERIAL

A.  Age and Residence

1.  Present Age:_____    Date of Birth: _____ _____ _____
                                        Day     Month    Year

2.  Local (present) Address:_____
    Local Telephone:_____

3.  Permanent Address (if different from No. 2 above):_____

    _____
    Permanent Telephone: _____ _____
                          Area    Number

4.  Name and address of a person through whom you can always be
    reached (should be different from No. 3 above):

    _____
    Telephone: _____ _____
                Area    Number

5.  Were you referred to this hospital by a doctor or other
    professional person?
    ___Yes  ___No (If yes, specify whom)_____
                                                 (Name)

    _____  _____
    (Title or Position)      (Building Title [clinic, depart-
                                             ment, etc.])

    _____
              (Street Address or Box No.)

    _____  _____  _____
    (City or Town)     (State)          (Zip Code)
    Telephone: _____ _____
                Area    Number

B.  Family Status

1.  Patient's Marital Status:  __Single  __Married  __Divorced
                               __Separated  __Widowed
    (If Married) Spouse's Name: _____  _____
                                    (First Name)      (Middle Name)
    Is your spouse currently living with you?  ___Yes  ___No
    Address (if different from patient's local address):
    _____
    Telephone:_____
    Do you have any children?  ___Yes  ___No
    (If yes, list name, sex, and ages of children):_____
    _____

2.  List other individuals living at the patient's current
    residence (use other side if necessary):
    Name:_____  _____  _____
              (Last)           (Initial)        (First)
    Age:_____  Sex:_____  Relationship:_____

C.  Employment and Income Information

1.  Major occupation or skill (whether or not presently
    employed):_____

2.  Title of present job (major job, if more than one):
    _____  ___unemployed  ___self-employed

3.  Name of employer or supervisor:_____  _____  _____
                                       (Last)  (Initial) (First)
    Name and address of firm or company (if applicable):
    _____
    Telephone:_____

4.  Average monthly income from this job:  $_____

5.  Length of time in present job:  _____  _____  _____
                                    (Years)  (Months)  (Weeks)

6.  Additional monthly income (list amounts and sources):
    _____  Total Monthly Income: $_____

7.  How many different jobs have you held in the past year?
    _____  In the last five years?_____

D.  Educational History

1.  Did you graduate from high school or equivalent?
    ___Yes  ___No
    If No, what was the highest grade attained in school?_____

2. Did you attend a college or university?  ___Yes  ___No
   If Yes, what was the highest year attained in college?
   _____ Major Subject:_____ Degree (if any):_____

3. List any further educational training (specify nature of
   training and degrees obtained):_____
   _____

## II. DRINKING PATTERNS

### A. Development of the Drinking Problem

1. Approximately how old were you when you first took one or
   more drinks? _____

2. Approximately how old were you when you first became
   intoxicated? _____
   Do you remember what you were drinking at that time?
   Beverage: _____

3. How would you describe the general drinking habits of each
   of your parents?
   The categories are: Non-drinker, occasional light social
   drinker, moderate to average social drinker, heavy and
   frequent social drinker, and alcoholism problem.  Which
   category best suits your Father (or guardian)?  Your
   Mother?  (Check categories below.)

   FATHER                              MOTHER

   ___Not applicable                   ___Not applicable
   ___Non-drinker (abstinent)          ___Non-drinker (abstinent)
   ___Occasional or light              ___Occasional or light
      social drinker                      social drinker
   ___Moderate or average              ___Moderate or average
      social drinker                      social drinker
   ___Frequent or heavy                ___Frequent or heavy
      social drinker                      social drinker
   ___Alcoholism problem               ___Alcoholism problem

4. Approximately how old were you when drinking first became
   a "real problem" for you; that is, when drinking began to
   have an effect on your life which you did not really approve
   of?  _____Age  ____Denies that it is a "real problem."
   At that particular time in your life, when drinking first
   became a real problem, were there any special circumstances
   or events which occurred which you feel were responsible
   for it becoming a problem?  (If Yes, summarize circumstances):_____
   _____

5. <u>Before</u> drinking became a real problem for you, how would you describe your drinking habits? (Attempt to fit the reply into one of the categories below):

___Cannot say
___Non-drinker or abstinent
___Occasional or light social drinker
___Moderate or average social drinker
___Frequent or heavy social drinker
___Other (Specify:_____)

B. <u>Usual Drinking Pattern</u>

1. What would you say best describes your overall drinking habits? Would you say that you were a <u>periodic, inter-mittent drinker</u> (one who drinks heavily on a binge or drinking bout every so often, with periods of little or no drinking between binges), or a <u>steady, regular drinker</u> (one who continuously drinks more or less the same amount on a day-to-day basis)?
   ___Periodic    ___Steady    ___Cannot say (or "both")

   a) <u>Section for Periodic Drinkers and Cannot Say Group</u>

      About how many drinking bouts have you had in the past six months? _____
      About how long does your average drinking bout usually last? _____Hours _____Days
      What is the longest bout you have ever had?
      _____Hours _____Days
      On the average, how much time goes by between drinking bouts? _____Days _____Weeks _____Months
      How would you describe the circumstances which mark the end of one of these drinking bouts? That is, what factors determine when you finally <u>stop</u> drinking?
      _____

   b) <u>Section for Steady Drinkers and Cannot Say Group</u>

      Are there any particular days of the week during which you drink more than on other days?
      ___Yes ___No (list days if Yes):_____

C. <u>Factors Associated with Drinking</u>

1. Do you sometimes take a drink in the morning, before breakfast? ___Yes ___No

2. Do you find that you are <u>unable</u> to stop drinking, once you have had one or two drinks on any occasion? ___Yes ___No

If Yes: Why do you think you are unable to stop after the first one or two drinks?_____

3.  After drinking for a period of time, have you ever had any of the following experiences? (Check for positive reply.)

   ___A hangover
   ___Nausea and/or vomiting
   ___An episode of the "shakes"
   ___A "blackout" (lapse of memory for events which occurred while drinking)
   ___Vague feelings of fear and anxiety
   ___A convulsion or seizure
   ___The "D.T.'s" (when you saw, felt, or heard things that were not really there)

   Is there anything else that happens to you after drinking? (If Yes, specify)_____

4.  Has drinking, in your opinion, been the cause of any of the following events in your life? (Check for positive reply.)

   ___Losing a job or jobs
   ___Getting arrested
   ___Becoming divorced or separated
   ___Losing a personal friend or friends
   ___Being broke or in financial debt
   ___Having a serious medical problem (Specify:_____)

D.  Periods of Abstinence

1.  Since drinking first became a real problem for you, what is the longest period of time during which you did not take a drink? _____Days _____Weeks _____Months _____Years
   _____Never abstinent
   When did this period end? _____Month _____Year

   a)  What would you say was the main reason or reasons for stopping drinking at that time?_____

   b)  What would you say was the main reason or reasons for starting to drink again after this period?_____
   _____

2.  Have you had a period of abstinence or nondrinking during the past six months? ___Yes ___No
   (Specify duration):_____

   a)  What would you say was the main reason for stopping drinking at that time?_____

b)  What would you say was the main reason for starting to
drink again after this period?_____

E.  Drinking Setting

1.  Card Sort Instructions: Drinking Locations

I am going to give you a set of cards, each of which has a
place or setting written on it where drinking might occur.
I want you to do two things with this set of cards.

First, I want you to sort the cards into two piles: place
those cards in one pile, here on the left, if they list
places where you have done at least some of your drinking
in the past six months or so; if they list places where you
have done no drinking in the past six months, then place
them in the other pile on the right.  Any questions?  All
right, begin sorting the cards.

(Wait until first sorting is complete)

Secondly, I want you to take the pile on your left, and
arrange the cards in order of where you have done most of
your drinking in the past six months.  Put the one card on
the top which lists the place where you do most of your
drinking and then sort the rest of the cards to represent
places where you do relatively less and less drinking.
The card on the bottom should list the place where you do
the least drinking of all.

(Indicate below, the ordering of the second card sort)

___Tavern or bar (if selected, ask which bar is the favor-
ite; location of bar; and name of bartender, if known):
Name of bar:_____
Location (city or town):_____
Name of bartender, if known:_____
___Restaurants (with meals)
___In your own home
___In other people's homes
___At work
___Private club or social fraternity
___Social events (such as weddings, parties, dances)
___While driving
___Out of doors
___List any additional places, if mentioned:_____

2.  Card Sort Instructions: Social Settings

Now I am going to ask you to do the same sort of thing with
another set of cards.  These cards have various persons
listed on them whom you may or may not drink with at
various times.

Again, I would first like you to sort the cards into two
piles: place those cards in a pile on the left, if they
list a person or persons with whom you have done at least
some of your drinking in the past six months or so; if they
list a person or persons with whom you have done no
drinking in the past six months, then place them in the
other pile on the right. Any questions? All right, begin
sorting the cards.

(Wait until first sorting is complete)

Secondly, I want you to take the pile on the left, and
arrange the cards in order of the people listed with whom
you have done most of your drinking in the past six months.
Put the one card on the top which lists the person or persons with whom you do most of your drinking; and then sort
the rest of the cards to represent people with whom you
do relatively less drinking. The card on the bottom should
list the person or persons with whom you do the least
drinking of all.

(Indicate below the ordering of the second card sort)

___I drink alone
___I drink with my wife (or husband)
___I drink with relatives other than my wife (or husband)
___I drink with a male friend or friends (no females
   present)
___I drink with a female friend or friends (no males
   present)
___I drink with friends of both sexes
___I drink with strangers, or people I meet after I have
   started drinking

F. Associate Behaviors

1. Do you smoke?  ___Yes  ___No (If Yes, how much do you smoke
   a day):
   ___Heavy (more than two packs)  ___Moderate (1-2 packs)
   ___Light (less than one pack)  ___Pipe or Cigars

2. Do you like to gamble?  ___Yes  ___No (If Yes, what type of
   gambling do you prefer?_____

3. Do you have any interests, hobbies, or other pasttime activities that take up some of your free time, and that are
   not connected with your drinking? (List):_____
   _____

III.  ATTITUDES AND PREFERENCES

A.  Preferences and Rates

1.  Card Sort Instructions: Beverage Preferences

Now I am going to give you another set of cards with
various kinds of alcoholic beverages printed on them.
Here we are interested in getting an idea of what your
favorite drinks would be, if you were in the mood for
drinking.

a)  First, I want you to look at the cards, to get an
    idea of the overall selection.  Then, I want you to
    sort the cards into two piles: place those cards in
    a pile on the left, if they list a beverage which you
    would like to drink, if you were in the mood to drink
    and were given a free choice of selection.  Pay no
    attention to the price or availability of each drink;
    We want your ideal preferences for drinks--as if you
    had a choice to select whatever you wanted from a
    liquor store, without worrying about money.

    Put the cards in a pile on the right if they list a
    beverage which you do not like to drink, when you are
    given a free choice of selection.  Any questions?
    All right, begin sorting the cards.

    (Wait until first sorting is complete)

    Now I want you to take the pile on the left, and
    arrange the cards in order of your favorite choices.
    Put the one card on the top which lists your most
    favorite beverage, if you had a free choice of what
    to drink.  Then sort the rest of the cards to repre-
    sent your second, third, and fourth choices, and so
    on through the pile.  The card on the bottom should
    list your least preferred choice.

    (Indicate on the main list, in the left column, the
    ordering of preferences.  Then take the first three
    preferred beverages, and obtain the favorite brand,
    if any; and the manner in which the subject prefers
    to drink each--i.e., with or without mixer, ice, etc.
    Specify brand names, if possible, for mixers.  List
    this information immediately below.)

    (i)  First Choice Beverage:_____
         Brand:_____ Preferred Manner of
         Drinking:_____

   (ii)  Second Choice:_____
        Brand:_____ Preferred Manner of
        Drinking:_____
  (iii)  Third Choice:_____
        Brand:_____ Preferred Manner of
        Drinking:_____

b) OK, now I want you to go through all the cards a second time. First, I want you to again sort the cards into two piles: place those cards in a pile on the left, if they list a beverage which you actually do drink from time to time. For many people the drink they would pick as their favorite beverage may not be the one they actually drink the most, due to reasons of cost and so forth. So, put those cards in the left pile which list beverages which you actually do drink in more or less amounts on different occasions. Put those cards in a pile on the right if they list a beverage which you never have drunk, as far as you can remember. Any questions? All right, begin sorting the cards.

(Wait until first sorting is complete)

Secondly, I want you to take the pile on the left, and arrange the cards in order of how frequently or how often you drink each beverage. Put the one card on the top which lists the beverage which you actually drink the most of all. Then sort the rest of the cards to represent which beverage you drink second most often, third most often, and so on, through the pile. The card on the bottom should list the beverage which you drink least frequently of all.

(Indicate on the main list, in the right column, the ordering of cards. Then take the first three most frequently consumed beverages and ascertain the brand most frequently consumed and the preferred manner of drinking, as before. List this information immediately below.)

   (i)  Most Frequently Consumed Drink:_____
        Brand:_____ Preferred Manner of
        Drinking:_____
   (ii)  Second Beverage:_____
        Brand:_____ Preferred Manner of
        Drinking:_____
  (iii)  Third Beverage:_____
        Brand:_____ Preferred Manner of
        Drinking:_____

BEVERAGE LIST

| Preference | Usage | |
|---|---|---|
| _____ | _____ | Blended Whiskey |
| _____ | _____ | Bourbon |
| _____ | _____ | Brandy |
| _____ | _____ | Gin |
| _____ | _____ | Rum |
| _____ | _____ | Scotch Whiskey |
| _____ | _____ | Tequila |
| _____ | _____ | Vodka |
| _____ | _____ | Liqueur |
| _____ | _____ | Beer and/or Ale |
| _____ | _____ | Malt Liquor |
| _____ | _____ | Red Dry Wine |
| _____ | _____ | Red Sweet Wine |
| _____ | _____ | White Dry Wine |
| _____ | _____ | White Sweet Wine |
| _____ | _____ | Sparkling Wine or Champagne |
| _____ | _____ | Special Fortified Wine (20% alcohol) |
| _____ | _____ | Nonbeverage Alcohol (e.g., shaving lotion) |
| _____ | _____ | Other (Specify):_____ |

2. What are your three favorite nonalcoholic beverages?
   (Specify brand, if possible.)
   First Choice:_____  Brand:_____
   Second Choice:_____  Brand:_____
   Third Choice:_____  Brand:_____

3. We are also interested in the <u>amount</u> of alcoholic beverages
   you consume on the average. For this reason, we would like
   you to estimate the average amount of alcohol you drank in
   a given time period.

   a) During an average <u>day</u> when you are drinking, how much do
      you drink? (Try to get specific units: number of bot-
      tles or cans of beer; pints or fifths of hard liquor,
      etc. Use other side, if necessary.)
      Beverage:_____  Amount:_____
      Comments:_____
      (and others)

   b) During an average <u>week</u> when you are drinking, how much
      do you drink?
      Beverage:_____  Amount:_____
      Comments:_____
      (and others)

   c) (For periodic drinkers only) About how long did your
      last drinking bout last?    ___Days    ___Hours

When did this bout start, approximately?
___Day ___Month ___Year
About how much alcohol did you drink at that time?
Beverage:_____ Amount:_____
Comments:_____
(and others)

4. Approximately how much do you spend on alcoholic beverages when you are drinking? Per day? $_____ Per week? $_____

B. Reasons for Drinking

1. In your own words, what is the main reason why you drink?

2. Are there any other reasons why you drink, which you consider important? If Yes, what are they?

3. Do you have inner thoughts or emotional feelings, or things within you as a person, which "trigger off" your need or desire to take a drink at a particular moment in time?

4. Are there any particular situations or set of events, things which happen to you in the outside world, which would be most likely to make you feel like having one or more drinks?

5. Can you describe a situation or set of events which would be least likely to make you feel like drinking? In other words, when do you least feel like drinking?

6. When you are actually drinking, what, for you, is the most positive or desirable effect of alcohol? In other words, what is the thing you like best about alcohol when you are drinking?

   Are there other positive or desirable effects which you get while you are actually drinking?

   In terms of your life as a whole, what do you see as the most positive effects or consequences of your drinking behavior?

7. When you are actually drinking, what, for you, is the most negative or undesirable effect of alcohol? In other words, what is the thing you like least about alcohol when you are drinking?

   Are there other negative or undesirable effects which you get while you are actually drinking?

In terms of your life as a whole, what do you see as the
most negative effects or consequences of your drinking
behavior?

8.  Card Sort Instructions:  Effects of Drinking

We are interested in knowing more about what kinds of
effects alcohol has on you when you are drinking.  I am
going to give you another set of cards with different
possible effects of drinking written on them.  I would like
you to sort these cards into two piles.  Place those cards
in a pile on the left, if they describe effects that alcohol has on you when you are actually drinking.  Put the
cards in a pile on the right which list effects which you
do not get from alcohol when you are drinking.  Any questions?  All right, begin sorting the cards.

| Positive Effects:<br>Tension Reduction | Negative Feelings:<br>Anger/Frustration | Negative Feelings:<br>Anxiety |
|---|---|---|
| ____Happy | ____Angry | ____Afraid |
| ____Relaxed | ____Sad | ____Nervous |
| ____Peaceful | ____Depressed | ____Tense |
| ____Calm | ____Lonely | ____Excited |
| ____Unafraid | ____Frustrated | ____Restless |

| Positive Feelings:<br>Socially Outgoing and<br>Positive Self-esteem | Negative Feelings:<br>Socially Withdrawn and<br>Negative Self-esteem |
|---|---|
| ____Secure | ____Insecure |
| ____Superior | ____Inferior |
| ____Outgoing | ____Withdrawn |
| ____Friendly | ____Unfriendly |
| ____Strong | ____Weak |

(Spread out chosen list of effects in front of subject)

Now, looking at these cards you have chosen, I want you to
pick out the five cards which represent the five most
accurate descriptions of effects which are true for you
when you are drinking.  (Wait until subject picks the five
cards.)  OK, now would you please arrange these five cards
in order from the most true effect for you to the least
true effect of the five cards.  Put the one card listing
the most true effect on the top, and the card with the
least true effect on the bottom, with the other three cards
arranged in the middle in terms of how accurately they
describe effects which you get from drinking?  Any questions?

(List the five cards in order of accuracy, below)
Comments, if any:

1._____     _____
2._____     _____
3._____     _____
4._____     _____
5._____     _____

C.  Motivational Aspects

1.  On your own and without any outside help, what steps, if
    any, have you taken in an attempt to stop drinking?

2.  Have you previously sought outside help, professional or
    otherwise, for your drinking problem?  ___Yes  ___No
    (If Yes, ask the subject to specify the nature of this
    help, as indicated below.)
    Date:_____ Nature of Contact:_____
    Results:_____
    (and others)

3.  Have you ever taken the drug Antabuse?  ___Yes  ___No
    (If Yes, specify dates): From_____ To_____
                             From_____ To_____

4.  Are you now a member of A.A. (Alcoholics Anonymous)?
    ___Yes  ___No
    If Yes, when did you first join?  Date:_____
    If No, have you ever been a member of A.A. in the past?
    ___Yes  ___No
    Specify dates, if Yes:  From_____ To_____

5.  What are the main reasons for seeking help for your drink-
    ing at this particular time?  In other words, what circum-
    stances led to your coming to this hospital at this time?

6.  a)  What do you see as the most ideal outcome of treatment
        here for you?  In other words, what would you consider
        to be the most desirable outcome of treatment in your
        case?

        In your honest and realistic opinion, what do you
        estimate your chances are from 1 to 10 of obtaining
        this outcome? _____

    b)  What is most likely to happen in your case, if this
        ideal outcome of treatment does not occur?

7.  Card Sort Instructions: Treatment Outcome

I am going to show you four cards, listing different possible outcomes of treatment for alcohol problems. I want you to arrange them in an order representing your preferences for what you would like as the eventual outcome of treatment at the top of the pile, and the least preferred outcome at the bottom.

(Number the order of preference below)

___I would like to stop drinking completely.
___I would like to become an occasional (light) social drinker.
___I would like to become a moderate (average) social drinker.
___I would like to become a heavy (frequent) social drinker.

8. In your own words, how would you define alcoholism?

9. Some people have said that alcoholism is a disease or sickness, while others have said that it is not a disease, but rather it is more like a bad habit a person has learned. Do you see it more as a disease or a bad habit?
   ___Disease    ___Bad Habit

10. Would you say that you are an alcoholic?   ___Yes   ___No
    Comments:

# Part III

---

# Self-Report Measures

Behavior-therapy assessments purport to rely less upon self-report measures of behavior than upon measures involving direct observation. In practice, however, it is evident that a great deal of assessment information is based upon information that is supplied directly by the client. A major concern in considering self-report data has been with respect to the degree to which such information is subjective and subject to distortion. For example, a recent statement by Katz and Woolley (1975) reflects the popularized view that client report data are, by definition, subjective in nature:

Subjective data refer to patient-rendered information, such as reports of mood, plans, concerns, and other statements that reflect on the patient's perception of the problem. This information is listed as subjective because it is obtained directly from the patient and in many cases, cannot be verified other than by what he says. (p. 121)

It should be recognized, however, that in terms of the above statement, all data are usually obtained directly from the patient, direct observational measures included, and therefore this characteristic is certainly not unique to patient self-report. A key issue, then, is whether information obtained through patient report is subject to independent verification. Clearly, there are many instances where such verification is possible; it would, therefore, be more descriptive of behavioral assessment to say that there is less of a tendency to rely upon self-report measures *in isolation,* than to say that behavioral assessment rejects self-report measures due to their subjectivity.

It is also evident that verbal report assessments, which frequently provide the only access route to the patient's perception of the problem, are likely to be viewed in an increasingly more important role concomitant with the increasing emphasis being placed upon cognitive mediational variables within a social-behavioral framework (Mahoney, 1974; Mischel, 1973).

The range of assessment procedures that may be characterized as self-report are numerous and diverse. They include interview measures, an individual's observation and coding or rating of his own behavior, and paper-and-pencil "tests." To a large extent, these different measures vary primarily in relation to the degree of response structuring provided for the informant, with interview measures typically being least structured and paper-and-pencil tests being most structured. All of these procedures can obtain some degree of objectivity to the extent that they can be independently verified, either through observation by an independent observer or through the use of a different measure of the same dimension. For example, McLean and Craig (1975) have demonstrated that some types of patient self-ratings are verifiable in that independent observers agree with the patient's own recording. Others have shown that self-report measures of child behavior may correlate highly with direct observational measures.

The self-report measures described in Part III are designed to obtain assessment information similar to that obtained in the interview, through the use of paper-and-pencil measures rather than through face-to-face therapist-client interaction. A major advantage of using paper-and-pencil measures is that they can be filled out by the client, thereby releasing therapist time for other activities. Basic information relating to problem areas can thus be obtained at a relatively low cost. In addition, paper-and-pencil measures represent a standardized technique for gathering information, which minimizes the possible influence of idiosyncratic response styles of the therapist. The standard format of these procedures, therefore, has the advantage of permitting cross-client comparisons. Although the behavioral approach, as described in this volume, is more concerned with individual assessment, there are instances in which comparisons across individuals may be useful, particularly in relation to the development of behavior-situation normative data (Mash, Hamerlynck, & Handy, 1976).

Structured self-report measures have been used across all stages of behavior-therapy assessment; however, the types of measures employed have varied as a function of assessment purposes. For example, paper-and-pencil measures used during the diagnosis phase of assessment have typically involved fairly global questionnaires designed to tap a large number of areas of functioning (e.g., life history questionnaires). The information from these types of self-reports are also used in designing treatment programs, often in conjunction with other more specific questionnaires (e.g., reinforcement surveys) and other assessment information (e.g., direct observation). Such global questionnaires are infrequently used in evaluative assessment because of their broad focus.

On the other hand, self-report measures have been used frequently in evaluative assessment. These measures, which relate to such variables as the client's moods, attitudes, and behavior, tend to have a much more restricted focus with respect to particular problem areas. Included here are such measures as anxiety questionnaires, fear survey schedules, and assertiveness questionnaires. Clearly, there is much overlap of assessment function for measures falling into the two broad categories described above; however, in general it can be said that global self-report question-naires have been used predominantly for diagnostic assessment, whereas more specific and restricted paper-and-pencil self-report measures have been used for evaluative assessment, frequently in conjunction with other behavioral measures.

The use of self-report measures during the initial stages of problem identification has much in common with the concept of the ''initial data base'' as it is employed within the context of the problem-oriented record (Grant & Maletzky, 1972), a procedure that has received widespread use in health-care programs, including behaviorally oriented psychiatric units (Grant, 1972; Katz & Woolley, 1975; McLean & Miles, 1974; Weed, 1968, 1969). The initial data base consists of preliminary information usually obtained from *all* clients, including historical information and information related to specific areas that are generally viewed as important across all cases in a particular setting. Aside from the fact that information involved in establishing an initial data base is considered relevant in all cases, such information must be clearly defined and obtainable with accuracy and clarity at minimal professional cost. As such, the initial data base is not overly elaborate but, rather, represents a starting point in a systematic effort to obtain functional clinical assessment information.

An example of a self-report assessment instrument that exemplifies the initial data base concept in behavioral assessment is the *Life History Questionnaire* (Lazarus, 1971; Wolpe & Lazarus, 1966). This questionnaire, which has been frequently used in a variety of clinical contexts, covers eight general areas, each dealing with a class of data considered essential as part of the assessment data obtained on every case. These areas include *general* background information such as marital status, living situation, and referral source; *clinical* information such as the client's statement of the problem, its severity and previous treatment for the difficulty; and *personal* data, including common problems in childhood and adolescence, history of hospitalization, a variety of symptoms including fears, and information about hobbies, interests, and use of free time. Also included are questions relating to *occupational data, sexual information, menstrual history, marital history,* and *family data.*

The concept of initial data base allows for variations in what constitutes an adequate data base to fit the needs and resources of various clinical settings and patient groupings. Consequently, the size of the initial pool of essential information may vary from a general description of a large number of areas, as in the ''Life History Questionnaire,'' or the initial data base may be more focused within a particular problem area. In this latter category are the marital precounseling inventories described by Stuart and Stuart in the first paper in Part III. These inventories, designed for the assessment of potential marital difficulty, involve an initial data base that includes aspects of current marital functioning, a focus on strengths and assets for change, and a delineation of precise therapeutic goals. The structure of these inventories is such that there are minimal demands on the therapist's time, maximal client involvement, and the provision of quantifiable data.

The reader will also note that the Drinking Profile, described previously in Part II (Marlatt), provides an initial data base for clients exhibiting problematic drinking behavior. In this context, it is important to note that the concept of initial data base as currently discussed does not necessarily specify how the information is to be obtained (i.e., via questionnaire, interview, observation, etc.). However, in terms of costs, a questionnaire—provided the information is accurate, clear, and quantifiable—probably represents the most efficient procedure for obtaining data of this sort.

Probably the major use of self-report paper-and-pencil measures in behavior-therapy research and application has been to assess situational factors or response characteristics associated with some of the more common presenting problems in clinical practice. In particular, the broad response classes of fear, anxiety, and assertiveness are extensively represented by the development of self-report inventories for their measurement. Such self-report inventories share with other behavioral assessment procedures the emphasis on identifying relationships between particular behaviors and environmental situations.

These self-report measures probably come closest to, and are often synonymous with, the types of "formal tests" frequently used in traditional assessment approaches. However, there are some consistent characteristics of self-report measures as they are used in a behavioral framework that set them apart from the traditional psychometric instruments.

The first is that the behavioral measures tend to have high content validity with respect to the behaviors of interest. For example, if the focus is on fears, the items included represent behavioral descriptions of a range of fearful behaviors and/or fear-producing situations, rather than a set of items that only indirectly attempt to predict the behaviors of interest.

Secondly, behaviorally oriented paper-and-pencil measures attempt to sample specific behaviors rather than general traits. Consequently, most of the measures are oriented toward obtaining information about specific problem areas rather than broad, trait descriptions of an individual's general level of functioning in relation to other persons.

Thirdly, paper-and-pencil measures employed within a behavioral framework examine responsiveness in relation to specific situations. For example, rather than providing a measure of general anxiety (e.g., *Taylor Manifest Anxiety Scale,* Taylor, 1953), behaviorally oriented measures such as the *S-R Inventory of Anxiousness* (Endler, Hunt, & Rosenstein, 1962) provide a format for the client to report on the anxiety he experiences in relation to specific situations.

A fourth characteristic of verbal report measures used by behavioral researchers and practitioners has been that they are usually used as part of a multiple assessment complex, rather than in isolation. That is, behavior therapists have been reluctant to rely solely upon such verbal self-report measures for formulating initial diagnosis or for evaluating treatment outcome. Although the measures are used, they are generally supplemented by more direct behavioral or physiological measures. For example, Hekmat (1972) employed a fear survey schedule and a semantic differential scale, along with a behavioral avoidance test, in an investigation of systematic desensitization. Similarly, Herman, Barlow, and Agras (1974) employed a number of dependent measures, including self-report, in a conditioning program for increasing heterosexual arousal in homosexuals. Liberman and Smith (1972) employed several measures in a case study of a patient exhibiting multiple phobias. Subjective fear was assessed using the target complaint scale (Battle, Imber, Hoehn-Saric, Stone, Nash, & Frank, 1966). In addition, behavioral observations of phobias were made during home visits, and additional data were obtained through interviews with neighbors of the patient.

An exhaustive description of the range of self-report/verbal report measures developed and used in conjunction with behavior-therapy programs of research and application would be a monumental task for a volume devoted exclusively to this topic and even more so in an introductory statement of the sort being presented in the present context. As is the case throughout this volume, no attempt will be made in Part III to be exhaustive. Rather, the measures presented here are intended to be representative of some of the more frequently used self-report assessments. In order to provide the reader with an overall context for considering these measures, a general overview of the diversity of applications of self-report measures in behavior-therapy assessment will be attempted.

The predominant position given to anxiety and fear-related phenomena in the work of Wolpe has resulted in the early development and extensive use of self-report measures of fear in behavior therapy research and application. A number of survey schedules have been developed and used for the assessment of fears both with adults (e.g., Geer, 1965; Lang & Lazovik, 1963; Wolpe & Lang, 1964) and with children (e.g., Scherer & Nakamura, 1968). The *Fear Survey Schedule III* (Wolpe & Lang, 1964) represents a pragmatic instrument derived from clinical practice, for clinical use. The 71 items of the schedule represent those that were most frequently reported in fifteen years of clinical practice. The schedule developed by Geer (1965), included here as paper 10, was constructed empirically from administration to a college student population. Both of these instruments represent global surveys that cover a wide range of feared objects and situations.

Fear survey schedules and self-ratings that focus on more specific content areas such as fear of snakes (e.g., Lutker, Tasto, & Jorgensen, 1972), spiders (e.g., Anthony & Duerfeldt, 1970), public speaking, acrophobia, agoraphobia, negative evaluation (e.g., Watson & Friend, 1969), etc. have also been employed. In addition, numerous studies have examined some of the psychometric properties of fear survey schedules (e.g., Farley & Mealiea, 1971; Klorman, Weerts, Hastings, Melamed, & Lang, 1974; Rubin, Lawlis, Tasto, & Namenek, 1969; Rubin, Katkin, Weiss, & Effran, 1968; Tasto & Hickson, 1970; Tasto, Hickson, & Rubin, 1971; Tasto & Suinn, 1972).

Other self-report measures have also been used in the assessment of fears, including semantic differentials (e.g., Bandura, Blanchard, & Ritter, 1969; Hekmat, 1972; Marks, 1965), rating scales, and fear thermometers designed to assess the client's momentary levels of fear in specific situations (e.g., Battle, Imber, Hoehn-Saric, Stone, Nash, & Frank, 1966; Kenny, Solyom, & Solyom, 1973; Lick & Bootzin, 1970; Walk, 1956). Fear-related self-report assessment used frequently with systematic desensitization procedures assesses the degree to which a client can visualize a fear-producing situation with emotion (Rimm & Masters, 1974). McCullough and Montgomery (1972) describe a procedure for assessing a client's proficiency in the use of imagery.

A number of self-report measures have also been developed for the assessment of assertiveness (e.g., Galassi, DeLo, Galassi, & Bastien, see paper 12; Lawrence, 1970; Lazarus, 1971; Hersen, Eisler, & Miller, 1973; Rathus, 1973; Wolpe & Lazarus, 1966, p. 41). In assessing assertiveness, McFall and Lillesand (1971) report the use of *The Conflict Resolution Inventory,* which consists of 35 items, each describing a situation where the person is requested to do something unreasonable, and an assessment is made of the person's ability to refuse.

Verbal report measures have also been frequently used in the assessment of anxiety (e.g., Cattell, 1957; Cattell & Rickels, 1965; Endler, Hunt, & Rosenstein, 1962; Kent, Wilson, & Nelson, 1972), test anxiety (e.g., Lomont & Sherman, 1971; Suinn, 1969a, 1969b; Suinn & Richardson, 1971), social anxiety (Borkovec, Stone, O'Brien, & Kaloupek, 1974; Glasgow & Arkowitz, 1975; Rehm & Marston, 1968; Watson & Friend, see paper 11), and more general mood states (e.g., Grim, 1971; Johnson & Spielberger, 1968; Zukerman & Lubin, 1965) including depressions (Beck, Weissman, Lester, & Trexler, 1974; Beck, Ward, Mendelsohn, Mock, & Erbaugh, 1961; Hamilton, 1960).

In addition to the use of structured self-report in the assessment of emotion and mood states as described above, these procedures have received extensive application in family and marital assessments. Stuart and Stuart (1975a) report the use of an inventory designed to obtain information in a premarital counseling situation. Self-report measures for assessment in marital counseling (Stuart & Stuart, 1972), family counseling (Stuart & Stuart, 1975b) and behavioral checklists (e.g., *Spouse Observation Checklist*, Wills, Weiss, & Patterson, 1974) for assessing marital satisfaction have also been developed. In addition, verbal report measures have been used to assess both sexual behavior and attitudes (Feldman & MacCulloch, 1971; Feldman, MacCulloch, Mallor, & Pinschoff, 1966; MacCulloch, Birtles, & Feldman, 1971; Stuart, Stuart, Maurice, & Szasz, 1975) in deviant and nondeviant populations.

Self-report measures that attempt to get at more specific areas of performance including social activity (Arkowitz, Lichtenstein, McGovern, & Heines, 1975; Glasgow & Arkowitz, 1975), academic performance (Goldfried & D'Zurilla, 1969), reactions to speech situations and speech deficits (e.g., Johnson, Darly, & Spriesterbach, 1963), and eating patterns (Wollersheim, 1970) have also been used, as well as measures that provide parental descriptions of child behavior (e.g., symptom checklists, Patterson, 1976).

In summary, it can be stated that behavioral researchers and practitioners have relied quite extensively on the use of structured self-report measures in the assessment process, despite the fact that they have frequently criticized the use of such information in terms of its subjectivity and unreliability. However, it would be accurate to say that the use of self-report measures by behavior therapists has more typically been in conjunction with direct corroborative measures (e.g., naturalistic observation) than has been the case for traditional assessment approaches. The fact that self-report measures can be shown to be objective through independent verification, are economical to use, are meaningful predictors of important behavior, and are frequently the only method of obtaining significant assessment information such as the client's perception of the problem, ensures that they will continue to receive continued use and further development as part of the behavior-therapy assessment process.

# 9

Prestructuring Behavior Therapy through
Precounseling Assessment

*Richard B. Stuart*
*Freida Stuart*

Clinical assessment can be considered to be a ''design for therapeutic action.'' It should begin with a question, the answer to which suggests an intervention program, otherwise it is a wasted experience in labeling for its own sake—of little benefit to the client and a tragic waste of clinical resources.

Action-oriented assessments have five features in common, whatever their theoretical orientation. First, they are phrased in terms oriented toward realistic, achievable goals. Second, they are sufficiently parsimonious so that they do not delay the initiation of service. Third, they are sufficiently broad in spectrum to include all of the clinically relevant dimensions of the client's behavior. Fourth, they are limited to valid and reliable data, with all inference being refutable in principle. And fifth, they conclude with a reversable hypothesis about the nature of the difficulty and what might be done to alleviate it.

Ignoring the first characteristic leads to a waste of clinical resources and to labeling without reason. Use of unnecessarily prolonged assessment procedures can only serve to delay the start of a service, sometimes irreparably. The treatment resulting from the assessment can be seriously weakened if it is based upon false (or unsubstantiated) data and if important information about the interactional context of behavior is not included in the assessment. And finally, because the only test of a clinical assessment is its use in the planning of service, it can best be evaluated in terms of the accuracy with which it predicts clinical change.

## Criteria for Effective Assessment

Clinicians vary greatly in their conception of the elements of an effective assessment protocol. The approach taken here focuses upon six primary criteria. A strong emphasis is placed upon an accurate description of current functioning. Historical data in this approach are held to a minimum for several reasons. The therapist is generally wholly dependent upon the client for these data and there is reason to believe that the past is always determined by its impact upon the future. That is, in the selective recall of past events, clients often deliberately or inadvertently relate those events that they believe will lead the therapist to share the image of themselves that they would like to communicate. Moreover, discussion of the past often discourages both client and therapist from the task at hand because it is often fraught with disappointments. Finally, the past is rarely relevant to the present because, as situations change, new behavioral capabilities are gained and others are lost. Therefore, reliance upon the past for information other than for the discovery of presently underutilized resources is often associated with greater problems than advantages.

In addition to its present focus, the present approach is also primarily concerned with strengths or with assets for change. Because our technology for behavioral suppression is limited in comparison with our ability to help clients to develop new behaviors, there is strong reason to concentrate both assessment and intervention efforts upon identifying positive targets for change, the attainment of which will place the client in receipt of a wider range of positive consequences.

The third criterion of assessment is its focus upon the delineation of precise goals for change. These goals lead to measureable changes in incremental steps so that a long period of time need not elapse before the assessment is repeated. Moreover, the goals must be agreeable to the therapist, to the client, and ideally to those with whom he shares his life space.

As a fourth criterion, the assessment protocol must make minimal demands upon the therapist's time. The reality is that the pressure of maintaining a human service program is great. If therapists allocate a large portion of their time to assessment, they will have proportionately less time to devote to behavior change efforts.

Related to the fourth criterion is a fifth: that the client should be maximally involved in the process of assessment. This reduces the likelihood of inaccurate judgement, provides the client with a reasonable opportunity to have the satisfaction of being heard, and increases the probability that the therapist and client will agree and be equally committed to treatment goals.

Finally, the outcome of the assessment process must be quantifiable. This permits efficient measurement of the attainment of therapeutic goals for each client. It also permits comparison of intervention efforts across clients and/or therapists at the same time that it permits normative comparisons so that each client's behavior can be viewed against the background of other clients from the same general group.

### The Research Press Pretreatment Questionnaires

Research Press has published four sets of pretreatment questionnaires adapted to each of four major interpersonal treatment goals: services for couples about to be married (Stuart & Stuart, 1975b), services to couples encountering marital discord (Stuart & Stuart, 1972), services to couples experiencing sexual problems (Stuart, Stuart, Maurice, & Szasz, 1975) and families seeking interaction change (Stuart & Stuart, 1975a). Each of these inventories is intended for completion by clients in advance of the first therapeutic session. Each person completes the forms and returns them independently of others in the family so that answers to the inventory questions cannot contribute in any way to added intrafamily conflict.

Because they are returned prior to the initial treatment session, each form equips therapists with core diagnostic information so that the process of behavioral change can begin immediately. In addition, each form offers the client an opportunity to learn something about the data base of the service that will be offered. That is, the kinds of questions asked alert the client to the salient dimensions of the treatment that is about to be offered. For example, Marital Precounseling Inventory asks clients to indicate what positive changes they would like to see in their spouses. But they are next asked how changes in their own behavior can make these changes more probable. In that way, the process of socializing them into their treatment roles is begun prior to their first therapeutic contact.

Each of these inventories is oriented toward a conception of the service to which it is adapted. For example, the marital treatment inventory starts with the assumptions that (1) all marital interactions are subject to open system influences; (2) reprogramming the social environment is the best means of modifying marital interaction; and (3) the environment can change through increasing the rate of positive behavioral exchanges, enhancing the process through which behaviorally relevant messages are sent and received, and through redefining the basic rules of the relationship. Accordingly, each section of the inventory is related to means of delineating positive behavior change goals, elucidating the present and ideal rules for interaction as viewed by both spouses. The inventory used for couples about to be married makes a similar set of assumptions in addition to focusing upon the need of couples to arrive at accurate expectations about each other's behavior at this critical time in their relationship. The family treatment inventory assumes that behavioral contracting and planned decision making are effective means of coping with family crises. And the Sexual Disfunction Inventory assumes that sexual interaction is an important form of communication, and it seeks to formulate goals for changing sexual experiences through techniques that are consistent with this assumption.

Because the inventories are often the client's first contact with the therapist, each of the inventories explains the nature of the information sought in each section and attempts to make the task informative for the client. For example, one series of questions on the family treatment inventory asks clients to communicate prestructured information as if they were applying for employment in their own family. In addition to creating interest, this concept also reinforces the reciprocal nature of interaction and the negotiation process through which it can be changed.

The inventories also devote a good deal of attention to an accounting of the client's resources for change. Each time that a target for change is solicited, respondents are asked to begin by indicating their present satisfactions in the area under discussion. For example, couples and families are asked to identify currently shared interests and to go further by suggesting personal interests that might be shared by others. In this way they can be helped to identify new areas of constructive stimulation that can be suffused into the exchanges between family members.

In addition, the inventories also permit a broad spectrum of assessment. In addition to including data pertaining to the expressed and implied contracts entered into by couples contemplating marriage, this inventory also assesses (1) the congruence of conceptions of interpersonal space on the assumption that couples about to be married would do well to conceive of their interpersonal worlds in terms which can be inter-translated; (2) relevant information about certain basic values; (3) data concerning family of orientation and any prior marriages; and (4) an examination of personal goals which marriage might facilitate or impede, among other things.

Further, each of the inventories also provides an opportunity to obtain the impressions of all the principals on certain issues. For example, the Sexual Counseling Inventory asks couples to rate their satisfaction with each of thirteen areas of communication about sex on a five-point Likert-type scale. Questions sample the extent to which each person believes that the other will agree with statements such as ''I find it easy to ask my partner to engage in sexual activity.'' Each spouse is then asked to indicate with a different symbol the way in which he or she believes that the other will answer the same question. That way it is possible to determine:

1. The husband's assessment of their communication about sex,
2. The wife's assessment of their communication about sex,
3. The husband's understanding of his wife's reactions in this area,
4. The wife's understanding of her husband's reactions in this area,
5. The areas in which they have relatively great agreement,
6. The areas in which they have relatively great disagreement,
7. Their general level of agreement as a couple,
8. Their general level of understanding as a couple.

Each of these quantitative indices can then be contrasted to yield pre- to post-treatment measures of change as well as providing an opportunity for comparison with associates of couples who do and/or do not encounter sexual problems.

But more than providing one means of evaluating the effectiveness of treatment, this kind of scaling also serves as a useful guide to the planning of intervention. Because this scale measures both agreement and understanding about major issues of interactional behavior it is possible to identify areas in which there is:

1. Both agreement and understanding,
2. Agreement but misunderstanding,
3. Disagreement and understanding,
4. Disagreement and misunderstanding.

When there is agreement and understanding, no clinical action is needed. When they agree but misunderstand one another, "pseudo-understanding" prevails and they have the potential of unexpected conflict. If they disagree and understand one another, there is a genuine conflict for which conflict management techniques are appropriate. And if they disagree and misunderstand each other there is a good chance that they have miscommunicated and are experiencing needless conflict. These imaginary conflicts can often be expeditiously resolved.

The therapeutic leads from this kind of analysis are somewhat indirect. They are far more direct, however, following from other questions on these inventories. For example, answers to the questions asking sexual partners whether they would like to "see their partner nude more often" or "touch partner's body except for genitals" as follows from the sexual inventory, yield precise and noninferential leads for the therapist.

While it would be desirable to have baseline data for these target behaviors, the fact is that clients are rather unlikely to supply this information in a reliable way. Therefore, the Research Press inventories all ask for general, retrospective information rather than specifically asking clients to keep precise behavioral records. These records can be kept when the therapist offers specified intruction and reinforcement for data collection, and records so kept are likely to be far more reliable than those collected prior to the onset of treatment.

## Conclusion

Assessment and treatment are closely interrelated processes. Treatment is offered in the process of elaborating an assessment as clients cannot help but be influenced by the kinds of questions asked and the content of their own answers. And the achievement of each new therapeutic goal requires continued assessment for the planning of the next. Therefore, it is naive to think of assessment as a temporarily isolated dimension of the process of treatment.

The approach to assessment contained in the Research Press inventories is "front-loaded" in the sense that its data are collected prior to the first contact. It blends idiographic and nomothetic data bases to the extent that individual assessments can be contrasted with those of comparable client and nonclient groups. It also permits the assessment of both behavioral and affective information so that the comprehensive effects of intervention can be studied.

For focal treatment problems additional data may be required, and, as a means of monitoring the impact of specific behavior change techniques, counts of these responses will be required in addition to inventory-produced data. Nevertheless, the inventories have proved useful in efforts to offer interpersonally oriented services, and they are to be found in an increasing number of service settings in North America.

## *REFERENCES*

Stuart, F. M., Stuart, R. B., Maurice, W. D., & Szasz, G., *Sexual adjustment inventory and guide.* Champaign, Ill.: Research Press, 1975.

Stuart, R. B., & Stuart, F. M. *Marriage pre-counseling inventory and guide.* Champaign, Ill.: Research Press, 1972.

Stuart, R. B., & Stuart, F. M. *Family counselling inventory and guide.* Champaign, Ill.: Research Press, 1975a.

Stuart, R. B., & Stuart, F. M. *Inventory and guide for couples planning to marry.* Champaign, Ill.: Research Press, 1975b.

# 10

---

## The Development of a Scale to Measure Fear

### James H. Geer

Most personality theories assign fear and anxiety central explanatory roles. This in part accounts for the recent proliferation of studies relating to anxiety (Houck, 1962). The focus of this paper is upon fear, and the paper describes the development of a scale to measure fear and presents several studies that have been employed in evaluating the scale.

Theories of personality differ in the way they describe fear and anxiety. Some theories use the concepts interchangeably, while others draw distinctions between the terms. For the purpose of this paper, fear is considered to be a negative emotional response evoked by a relatively specific stimulus. The difference between fear and anxiety is thus conceptualized as a difference in the specificity of the eliciting stimulus. Fear is a response to a specific stimulus and anxiety a response to a more general or pervasive stimulus. The validity of this distinction is not evaluated in this paper.

Akutagawa (1956) developed a Fear Survey that was constructed by selecting 50 items that he felt covered most commonly occurring fears. Lang and Lazovik (1963) used that scale in a study evaluating systematic desensitization therapy and reported that the scale indicated progress in therapy. They also reported that the scale correlated with standard

Reprinted from *Behaviour Research and Therapy*, 1965, 3, 45-53. Copyright© 1965 Pergamon Press Ltd. Reprinted by permission.

This research was supported in part by a grant from the United Health Foundation of Western New York and in part by a grant from the Graduate School, State University of New York at Buffalo.

Portions of this paper were read at the Midwestern Psychological Association Meeting, St. Louis, May, 1964.

anxiety scales. The scale presented in this paper is patterned after Akutagawa's scale and is called the Fear Survey Schedule-II (FSS-II).

In a recent paper, Wolpe and Lang (1964) presented a fear scale that was developed following the initial work on the FSS-II. Their scale, developed on the basis of clinical observation and theoretical conceptualizations, has been labelled the Fear Survey Schedule-III. Wolpe and Lang suggest that their scale be used as an adjunct to behavior therapy. The scale presented in this paper is designed primarily for use as a research tool.

## METHOD AND RESULTS

### Subjects

All 783 *S*s used in the studies reported in this paper were members of Introductory Psychology courses at The State University of New York at Buffalo.

### Item selection and analysis

Items for the FSS-II were selected on an empirical basis. Seventy-six male and 48 female *S*s were administered an open-ended questionnaire, identical to that used by Lang and Lazovik (1963) for subject selection, on which they were to list their fears. *S*s were instructed to rate the intensity of their fears on a three-point scale (Mild, Moderate, or Severe), and to include only fears that involved no actual danger or pain. Inspection of the questionnaires revealed that *S*s reported 111 different fears. Fifty-one of the fears occurred two or more times. These 51 fears were selected to make up the item pool for the development of the new scale. There were 18 fears in common between this pool and the original list compiled by Akutagawa, and there are approximately 20 fears in common between this pool and Wolpe and Lang's FSS-III.

Figure 1 presents a summary of the data relating to the frequency and intensity of fears as reported on the questionnaire. It appears that fears are quite common in the college undergraduate population. For example, 47 *S*s reported one or more fears as severe while less than 2 percent reported no fears at any intensity. Inspection of Figure 1 reveals a decreasing function between the number of fears at any given intensity and the number of *S*s reporting that intensity of fears.

The FSS-II, which consisted of the 51 fears that were found two or more times plus a rating scale for each fear, was administered to 161 male and 109 female *S*s. The rating scale for each item consisted of seven descriptions of different intensities of fear. *S*s were instructed to circle for each item the word that most nearly described the amount of fear they felt

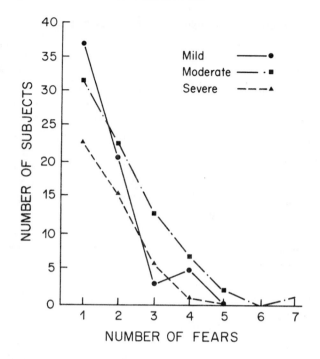

**FIGURE 1. Distribution of fears in a college population.**

toward the object or situation noted in the item. The descriptions of intensity were:

None  Very Little  A Little  Some  Much  Very Much  Terror

Table 1 contains a list of the items and several item statistics. In computing mean item scores, the score of 1 was assigned to the response "None" and the values 2 through 7 were consecutively assigned to the other descriptions. The item scores were correlated with the total score, and the results are listed in Table 1. With the single exception of Item 15, Roller Coasters, each item correlated significantly with ($p<0.01$) the total score for each sex. For women, item 15 correlated at a lower level of significance ($p<0.05$) with total score. It was decided, on the basis of the item analysis, to include all 51 items in the final form of the FSS-II.

The mean total score for men was 75.78 with a standard deviation of 33.84. The mean total score for women was 100.16 with a standard deviation of 36.11. A $t$ test was computed between those means and found to be significant ($t=5.22$ with 268 $df$, $p<0.001$), indicating that women report more intense fears than men. The individual items were therefore tested for a sex difference *beyond that expected on the basis of the sex difference* of the total scores. This was accomplished by

*TABLE 1.*   *Items and Item Statistics of the Fear Survey Schedule-II*

| | | Mean score | | Item-total score correlations | |
|---|---|---|---|---|---|
| | Item | Men | Women | Men | Women |
| 1. | Sharp objects | 1.60 | 1.87 | 0.477 | 0.434 |
| 2. | Being a passenger in a car | 0.60 | 0.93 | 0.411 | 0.527 |
| 3. | Dead bodies | 1.70 | 1.98 | 0.592 | 0.400 |
| 4. | Suffocating | 2.05 | 2.04 | 0.510 | 0.476 |
| 5. | Failing a test | 3.30 | 3.32 | 0.411 | 0.380 |
| 6. | Looking foolish | 2.79 | 2.94 | 0.467 | 0.575 |
| 7. | Being a passenger in an airplane | 1.26 | 1.79 | 0.513 | 0.448 |
| 8. | Worms | 0.27 | 1.32* | 0.355 | 0.402 |
| 9. | Arguing with parents | 1.27 | 1.37 | 0.493 | 0.287 |
| 10. | Rats and Mice | 1.03 | 2.33* | 0.568 | 0.316 |
| 11. | Life after death | 0.86 | 1.22 | 0.445 | 0.426 |
| 12. | Hypodermic needles | 1.50 | 1.89 | 0.607 | 0.312 |
| 13. | Being criticized | 1.98 | 2.30 | 0.612 | 0.573 |
| 14. | Meeting someone for the first time | 1.30 | 1.52 | 0.496 | 0.493 |
| 15. | Roller Coasters | 1.32 | 1.99 | 0.332 | 0.222 |
| 16. | Being alone | 0.70 | 1.23 | 0.548 | 0.489 |
| 17. | Making mistakes | 2.22 | 2.52 | 0.492 | 0.578 |
| 18. | Being misunderstood | 1.74 | 1.94 | 0.468 | 0.471 |
| 19. | Death | 1.96 | 2.39 | 0.538 | 0.659 |
| 20. | Being in a fight | 1.83* | 1.78 | 0.585 | 0.481 |
| 21. | Crowded places | 0.72* | 0.77 | 0.424 | 0.431 |
| 22. | Blood | 0.77* | 0.84 | 0.550 | 0.306 |
| 23. | Heights | 1.76 | 1.73 | 0.461 | 0.368 |
| 24. | Being a leader | 1.02 | 1.45 | 0.497 | 0.557 |
| 25. | Swimming alone | 0.96 | 1.43 | 0.474 | 0.395 |
| 26. | Illness | 1.25 | 1.86 | 0.568 | 0.426 |
| 27. | Being with drunks | 1.16 | 2.63* | 0.518 | 0.463 |
| 28. | Illness or injury to loved ones | 3.11 | 4.08* | 0.534 | 0.627 |
| 29. | Being self-conscious | 2.18 | 2.41 | 0.648 | 0.537 |
| 30. | Driving a car | 0.48 | 1.06 | 0.558 | 0.492 |
| 31. | Meeting authority | 1.27 | 1.66 | 0.546 | 0.514 |
| 32. | Mental illness | 1.29 | 1.97 | 0.516 | 0.519 |
| 33. | Closed places | 0.78 | 1.16 | 0.434 | 0.477 |
| 34. | Boating | 0.53 | 1.88 | 0.555 | 0.532 |
| 35. | Spiders | 1.20 | 2.19* | 0.466 | 0.472 |
| 36. | Thunderstorms | 0.45 | 1.03 | 0.482 | 0.428 |
| 37. | Not being a success | 2.79 | 2.28 | 0.442 | 0.597 |
| 38. | God | 1.35 | 1.50 | 0.382 | 0.313 |

| | | | | |
|---|---|---|---|---|
| 39. | Snakes | 1.97 | 3.05* | 0.482 | 0.482 |
| 40. | Cemeteries | 0.71 | 1.24 | 0.549 | 0.546 |
| 41. | Speaking before a group | 2.59 | 2.87 | 0.487 | 0.484 |
| 42. | Seeing a fight | 0.68 | 1.79* | 0.510 | 0.477 |
| 43. | Death of a loved one | 3.41 | 4.25 | 0.562 | 0.489 |
| 44. | Dark places | 0.95 | 1.67 | 0.576 | 0.481 |
| 45. | Strange dogs | 1.50 | 1.75 | 0.524 | 0.456 |
| 46. | Deep water | 1.22 | 2.02 | 0.515 | 0.607 |
| 47. | Being with a member of the opposite sex | 0.68* | 0.62 | 0.481 | 0.365 |
| 48. | Stinging insects | 1.80 | 2.38 | 0.565 | 0.495 |
| 49. | Untimely or early death | 1.89 | 2.66 | 0.555 | 0.654 |
| 50. | Losing a job | 1.95 | 2.02 | 0.475 | 0.566 |
| 51. | Auto accidents | 2.05 | 2.98 | 0.565 | 0.596 |

Note: All correlations are statistically significant at $p<0.01$ except number 15 for women which is significant $p<0.05$.
* Sex difference significantly larger than expected $p<0.01$.

computing the mean difference expected for the sexes, then subtracting that difference from the actual difference per item. The resultants were tested with $t$ tests and those items yielding a difference significant beyond the 0.01 level are designated as such in Table 1.

### Reliability

The internal consistency reliability of the FSS-II was estimated by applying the KR.20 formula. The overall $r$ was 0.939, the female $r$ was 0.928, and the male $r$ was 0.934. These data indicate that the FSS-II is a scale with high internal consistency reliability.

### Correlations with Other Personality Scales

The FSS-II was correlated with several personality inventories. Bendig's Pittsburgh Scales (1962) were given simultaneously with the first administration of the FSS-II. The correlations between the FSS-II and Bendig's scales were not computed separately for each sex, and the findings need to be replicated separately for each sex to extend and verify the results. The Emotionality scale of Bendig's inventory correlated significantly with the total score of the FSS-II ($r = 0.400$ with 267 $df$, $p<0.005$). The correlation between the FSS-II and the Social Extraversion-Introversion scale of Bendig's test was not significant ($r = 0.046$ with 267 $df$). This latter finding is in accord with Eysenck's (1961) expectations concerning extraversion and introversion. Eysenck suggests that extraversion-introversion is an independent personality dimension which is not related to neuroticism or scales of emotionality.

The FSS-II was correlated with the TMAS (Taylor, 1953). Ss employed in this evaluation were not the same Ss as used in the previous correlations. Correlations were computed separately for each sex. For males the correlation between the FSS-II and the TMAS was $r = 0.389$ with 150 $df$ ($p<0.005$); for females, the correlation was $r = 0.552$ with 55 $df$ ($p<0.005$). A test of the sex difference between the correlations was performed and found to be nonsignificant. Thus the FSS-II correlates significantly with the TMAS; however, there is no evidence that the size of the relationship between the FSS-II and the TMAS differs significantly with sex.

The FSS-II was also correlated with Welsh's A-Scale (Welsh, 1956). The Ss employed in the investigation of the correlation with the TMAS also were used in the examination of the correlation of the FSS-II with the A-Scale. The correlation for males between the FSS-II and the A-Scale was $r = 0.417$ with 150 $df$ ($p<0.005$); for females, the correlation was $r = 0.573$ with 55 $df$($p<0.005$). A test of the difference between these correlations was not significant, indicating again no evidence of a significant sex difference in the magnitude of the correlations.

The final set of correlations relates the FSS-II to social desirability. Ford (1964) has devised a forced-choice test of social desirability. This scale is similar to, and correlates highly with, the Marlowe-Crowne Social Desirability Scale (Crowne and Marlowe, 1960). The Ss employed in correlating the FSS-II and Ford's scale included some of those employed in computing the correlations between the FSS-II and the TMAS and A-Scale as well as some individuals who received only the FSS-II and Ford's scale. The correlation for males was $r = 0.231$ with 143 $df$ ($p<0.01$); for females the correlation was $r = 0.268$ with 60 $df$ ($p<0.05$), indicating that there is a low negative relationship between the FSS-II and social desirability.

## Validating Studies

Several items from the FSS-II were selected to be the basis of validating studies. The items were selected because they elicited a large number of fear responses and because they were amenable to laboratory study. Ss were selected on the basis of their response to specific items. In all studies "High Fear" Ss were those who responded to the selected item with the response of either "Much," "Very Much," or "Terror." In Study I, Ss were selected as being "Medium Fear" if their response to the appropriate item was either "A Little" or "Some." There were no medium fear Ss in Studies II and III. In all studies "Low

Fear'' *S*s were selected if their response to the appropriate item was ''None.''

The experimental procedures for the Studies were quite similar. The general paradigm was as follows. *S*s, naive as to the purpose of the investigation, were conducted to some known distance from a fear stimulus (a dog in Studies I and II and three rats in Study III). *S*s were then asked to approach the fear stimulus as close as they comfortably could. Two objective dependent variables were measured at that time. One, ''latency,'' was the time, in seconds, from the end of the instructions until *S* either touched the fear stimulus or was at his point of closest proximity to the fear stimulus. The second dependent variable taken during the ''Behavior Test'' was ''Distance.'' This measure was the distance, in inches, that *S* stopped from the fear stimulus.

Three other dependent variables were obtained following the behavior test. Each *S* rated, on a seven-point scale, the intensity of the tension or anxiety experienced when nearest to the fear stimulus. This dependent variable shall be called ''*S*'s rating.'' The intensity dimension used on that scale was identical to that used for the individual items of the FSS-II and was scored the same. A second measure was ''*E*'s rating'' and consisted of *E* rating *S*'s fear on a scale identical to that used for ''*S*'s rating.'' The last measure employed was Zuckerman's Affect Adjective Check List (AACL) (Zuckerman, 1960). *S* was instructed to complete the check list indicating the feelings that he experienced during the behavior test.

*TABLE 2.　Data Obtained from Approaching a Strange Dog*

| Fear level | Distance (in.) | Latency (sec.) | S's rating | E's rating | Adj. check list |
|---|---|---|---|---|---|
| *Combined sexes* | | | | | |
| High | 25 | 21.2 | 2.9 | 3.5 | 10.9 |
| Medium | 1 | 14.9 | 1.5 | 2.2 | 7.1 |
| Low | 0 | 11.2 | 0.5 | 0.9 | 4.6 |
| *Females only* | | | | | |
| High | 50 | 23.7 | 3.7 | 5.0 | 14.3 |
| Medium | 12 | 14.4 | 1.7 | 2.3 | 6.9 |
| Low | 0 | 10.1 | 0.0 | 0.6 | 3.7 |
| *Males only* | | | | | |
| High | 0 | 18.7 | 2.9 | 2.0 | 7.4 |
| Medium | 0 | 15.4 | 1.5 | 2.0 | 7.4 |
| Low | 0 | 12.3 | 0.5 | 1.1 | 5.6 |

Note: All data presented are means.

Study I used 21 male and 21 female *Ss* who were divided evenly into high, medium, and low fear groups. Their task was to approach a small female German Shepherd that was securely chained in one spot. *S*'s began their approach to the dog from a distance of 30 feet. Table 2 contains a summary of the results of Study I. A Kruskal-Wallace one-way analysis of variance by ranks for the data from combined sexes yielded significant *H*s in the expected direction for each dependent variable except distance. A sex difference was noted, and the data were analyzed separately for each sex. For women, each dependent variable yielded a significant *H* ($p<0.002$); while for men only *S*'s rating yielded a significant ($p<0.02$) *H*. Thus it would appear that the significant overall differences were primarily the result of the data for women. Correlations were computed between the five dependent variables for women and between latency, *S*'s rating, *E*'s rating, and AACL for men. Distance was excluded from the males correlations as all males touched the dog. All of the correlations were significant ($p<0.01$) revealing that all dependent variables were closely related. The actual correlations (Rhos) ranged from 0.52 to 0.92 with a median Rho of 0.75.

In Study II, 36 female *Ss* were employed. The independent variable was a time delay interposed between telling *S* of the nature of the study (approaching a dog) and the actual approach. Group I delayed 0 time, Group II 5 min, and Group III delayed 20 min. Equal numbers of high and low fear *Ss* made up each group. Table 3 contains the results of that study. With the exception of latency, significant differences in the expected directions were found between high and low fear *Ss* at each time-

TABLE 3.   Data from Approaching a Strange Dog after a Delay

| Fear level | Distance (in.) | Latency (sec.) | S's rating | E's rating | Adj. check list |
|---|---|---|---|---|---|
| No time delay | | | | | |
| High | 62.3 | 12.9 | 3.0 | 3.0 | 9.3 |
| Low | 0 | 9.8 | 0.5 | 0.5 | 3.6 |
| 5 min time delay | | | | | |
| High | 64.7 | 18.2 | 3.1 | 4.3 | 10.6 |
| Low | 0 | 18.8 | 0.8 | 2.3 | 5.3 |
| 20 min time delay | | | | | |
| High | 75.5 | 15.2 | 2.8 | 4.5 | 10.6 |
| Low | 6.3 | 20.6 | 1.1 | 2.1 | 5.6 |

Note: All data presented are means.

delay interval (Mann-Whitney $U$ test). The waiting period had no effect upon high fear $Ss$. Paradoxically, low fear $Ss$ rather than high fear $Ss$ displayed longer latencies ($p < 0.002$) after time delays. The fact that latency did not discriminate between high and low fear $Ss$ may have been a function of a change in instructions from Study I. In Study I, $Ss$ were given a second urging to approach the dog when they stopped. This was not done in Study II, and $E$ reported that determination of latency was made more difficult by this change.

Study III differed from Studies I and II in that three hooded rats from the Psychology Department's Animal Laboratory were used as fear stimuli. The animals were placed on a table three feet high. $Ss$ were told that the rats would not jump off the table. $S$'s starting point from the rats was one half of the distance employed in the dog studies. Forty female $Ss$ were used in this study; half were accompanied by a male $E$ and half were accompanied by a female $E$. The independent variable of sex of $E$ had no demonstrable effect; however, all five dependent variables, as tested by the Mann-Whitney $U$ test, significantly discriminated between high and low fear groups. Table 4 contains a summary of the results of Study III.

*TABLE 4.    Data from Approaching Rats with Different Sex Experimenters*

| Fear level | Distance (in.) | Latency (sec) | S's rating | E's rating | Adj. check list |
|---|---|---|---|---|---|
| | Male experimenter | | | | |
| High | 8.4 | 9.2 | 2.2 | 3.0 | 7.9 |
| Low | 0.0 | 5.5 | 0.2 | 0.5 | 4.2 |
| | Female experimenter | | | | |
| High | 16.8 | 10.2 | 1.9 | 3.5 | 9.3 |
| Low | 0.0 | 5.6 | 0.9 | 0.9 | 5.3 |

Note: All data presented are means.

## DISCUSSION

The statistics relating to the internal consistency of the FSS-II and the studies validating several of the individual items suggest that the FSS-II has good reliability and validity. The studies indicate that the FSS-II serves adequately to select individuals who differ on individual fears. As yet, the total score of the FSS-II has not been employed in a systematic manner; however, the correlations of the FSS-II with other personality scales indicate some of its potential usefulness.

It should be noted that fears, as measured by the FSS-II, are relatively stable phenomena. First, the manipulation of time delay and sex of $E$ had no observable effect upon high fear $Ss$. It may be that the variables selected were not relevant to fear. However, an equally tenable assumption is that fear is resistant to simple modification. Secondly, Studies II and III were conducted from 4 to 6 months following the administration of the FSS-II indicating that fears are stable over at least that period of time.

The correlations found among the various measures of fear indicate a relationship between traditional verbal measures of fear and observable behavioral measures of fear that is greater than might have been expected. The advantages of employing such measures as latency and distance are obvious and suggest that naturally occurring fears may provide a phenomenon that will be fruitful for further study.

One question that could be raised is that perhaps the reactions observed in the studies reported above are not specific to the item selected. If this were true the $S$ who rated ''Terror'' to any item would avoid other fear stimuli. An *ad hoc* evaluation of this suggestion was undertaken by examining the FSS-IIs of the low fear $Ss$. It was found that over 25 percent of low fear $Ss$ would have been classified a high fear $S$ to some item other than the critical item. These $Ss$ did not show more fear than other low fear $Ss$. A more systematic analysis of this question will be the object of subsequent research.

The correlation of the FSS-II with standard anxiety scales suggests that fears contribute substantially to general anxiety. This would be expected if fear and anxiety differ primarily in the dimension of specificity of eliciting stimulus. The more intense an individual lists his fears, the higher his score on tests of general anxiety.

The correlation of the FSS-II and a scale of social desirability indicates a low negative relationship. This would be expected since fears are generally not considered to be socially desirable. However, the size of the correlation indicates that most of the variance associated with the FSS-II is not accounted for by social desirability. The finding of no significant correlation between the FSS-II and extraversion-introversion conforms to Eysenck's theoretical position that suggests that the introversion-extraversion dimension is independent of neuroticism (anxiety).

A consistent finding is one of a sex difference in fear. The total score of the FSS-II differed for men and women, and individual items differed for men and women. On the behavioral tests of Study I women were more consistent in fearful behavior than men. The reasons for this discrepancy are not clear. Studies II and III controlled for the sex difference by using female $Ss$. Study III attempted to determine if the sex of the $E$ was a relevant factor in altering women's responses to a fear stimulus: the sex of $E$ yielded no significant differences. At this stage of investigation, it is not possible to explain the sex-linked differences. However, it appears likely that cultural differences account for the results. In our culture women are permitted to show fear while men are not.

The FSS-II is designed as a research tool. The total fear score may provide a useful personality variable for investigation and may prove useful in evaluating and extending theoretical conceptions concerning broad aspects of personality. In addition, the individual items provide a rough index of specific fears and may be used to select samples of college undergraduates for empirical investigations of fear. Research workers interested in behavior therapy as applied to fears or phobias may find the FSS-II of particular value.

*Acknowledgements*—The author wishes to acknowledge the assistance of the following individuals who acted as *E*s in the reported studies: Michael Singer, Patricia Ziel, and Phyllis Platt.

# REFERENCES

Akutagawa, D. A study in construct validity of the psychoanalytic concept of latent anxiety and test of a projection distance hypothesis. Unpublished doctoral dissertation, University of Pittsburgh, 1956.

Bendig, A. W. The Pittsburgh scales of social extraversion-introversion and emotionality. *Journal of Psychology*, 1962, *53*, 199-209.

Crowne, D. P., & Marlowe, D. A new scale of social desirability independent of psychopathology. *Journal of Consulting Psychology*, 1960, *24*, 349-354.

Eysenck, H. J. Classification and the problem of diagnosis. In H. J. Eysenck (Ed.), *Handbook of abnormal psychology*. New York: Basic Books, 1961.

Ford, L. H. A forced-choice, acquiescence-free, social desirability (defensiveness) scale. *Journal of Consulting Psychology*, 1964, *28*, 475.

Houck, L. D. *Biography on anxiety states*. Nutley, New Jersey: Roche Laboratories, Division of Hoffmann-La Roche Inc., 1962.

Lang, P. J., & Lazovik, A. D. The experimental desensitization of an animal phobia. *Journal of Abnormal and Social Psychology*, 1963, *66*, 519-525.

Taylor, J. A. A personality scale of manifest anxiety. *Journal of Abnormal and Social Psychology*, 1953, *48*, 285-290.

Welsh, G. S. Factor dimensions A and R. In G. S. Welsh and W. G. Dahlstrom (Eds.), *Basic readings on the MMPI in psychology and medicine*. Minneapolis: University Minnesota Press, 1956.

Wolpe, J. *Psychotherapy by reciprocal inhibition*. Stanford: Stanford University Press, 1958.

Wolpe, J., & Lang, P. J. A fear survey schedule for use in behavior therapy. *Behavior Research and Therapy*, 1964, *2*, 27-30.

Zuckerman, M. The development of an Affect Adjective Check List for the measurement of anxiety. *Journal of Consulting Psychology*, 1960, *24*, 457 462.

# 11

---

## Measurement of Social-Evaluative Anxiety

*David Watson*
*Ronald Friend*

Several lines of research and theory point to the potential heuristic value of the development of a scale or scales to measure anxiety experienced in social situations. Those studies on the effects of social censure on the performance of psychotics (Rodnick & Garmezy, 1957), on the effect of disturbed family and social relationships in psychopathology (Gerard & Siegel, 1950), and on the correlation between social incompetence and hospitalization (Zigler & Phillips, 1962) have all suggested that distressful social relationships may be one powerful determinant of psychopathology. A second line of research has followed the idea that some individuals are more anxious than others in social situations and might therefore be more persuasible (Sears, 1967), more concerned with others' evaluations of themselves (Diggory, 1966), or simply be upset at having to interact with other people (Byrne, McDonald, & Mikawa, 1963). A third line of evidence which points to the need for social anxiety scales is that which suggests that anxiety scales which confine their questions to specific situations or conditions (Endler & Hunt, 1966) have greater predictive validity for those specific situations than those scales which sparsely sample diverse situations. There do exist two sets of items which have been nominated as measuring social anxiety (Dixon, deMonchaux, & Sandler, 1957; Sears, 1967) but these items either are too few or have no underlying construct, nor have they been controlled

Reprinted from *Journal of Consulting and Clinical Psychology,* 1969, *33,* 448-457. Copyright © 1969 by the American Psychological Association. Reprinted by permission.
    This research was conducted while the first author was at the University of Toronto and was supported by Grant No. 67 from the Ontario Mental Health Foundation.

for response style problems such as acquiescence or social desirability, and they have never been validated.

Social-evaluative anxiety was initially defined as the experience of distress, discomfort, fear, anxiety, etc., in social situations; as the deliberate avoidance of social situations; and finally as a fear of receiving negative evaluations from others. The first two aspects were combined to compose a Social Avoidance and Distress (SAD) scale, and the last factor was employed to compose a Fear of Negative Evaluation (FNE) scale.

### Specification of the Constructs

The two scales were constructed at the same time. Three general goals were adopted: to suppress response style errors, to foster scale homogeneity, and to foster discriminant or convergent relationships with certain other scales. These goals can be approached by paying careful attention to the nature of the constructs from which the items follow.

Anxiety often is inferred from verbalized subjective distress, the execution of avoidance responses, impaired performance, or certain physiological signs. Almost all anxiety scales are a haphazard mixture of items asking $S$ to report on these four aspects of his behavior or experience. It was decided in the construction of the present scales to exclude items asking about physiological signs or impaired performance. This would make clear what behavior was used as a sign for membership in the class ''anxious''—subjective distress and avoidance—and what behavior was considered a correlate of class membership—impaired performance and physiological signs. The advantage of this specification is that one may later more easily distinguish between construct and predictive validity.

A second, rarely followed, requisite for careful delineation of a construct is the necessity for adequate definition of the range of the trait, particularly its opposite instance (Jackson, 1966a). To control for acquiescence response set in a true-false format, as was done here, one must have approximately half of the items worded so that answering ''false'' indicates presence of the trait, which requires an adequate definition of the opposite instance. For example, the opposite instance of social avoidance is not necessarily social approach, that is, affiliation, but simply a lack of avoidance. If the opposite instance of avoidance were allowed to be affiliation it would have obscured any possible discriminant relationship between the SAD scale and measures of affiliation. Particular attention was paid to wording items so that the opposite instance of a trait simply indicated absence of that trait, not the presence of some other trait.

Fear of negative evaluation was defined as apprehension about others' evaluations, distress over their negative evaluations, avoidance of evaluative situations, and the expectation that others would evaluate oneself negatively. The presence of high FNE does not necessarily imply that an individual evaluates himself negatively, or that he is concerned about revealing his inferiority (Dixon et al., 1957). Fear of loss of social approval would be identical to FNE, but the opposite instance of FNE is simply lack of anxiety about others' evaluations, not inevitably a desire for positive evaluation. High FNE differs from test anxiety in that it is not specific to testing conditions but may operate in any social, evaluative situation, such as being on a date, talking to one's superiors, or being interviewed for a job.

The SAD scale was divided into two subscales, social avoidance and social distress. The purpose was to create a general scale, so the respondent was not asked *why* he experienced distress or avoided social encounters. Social avoidance was defined as avoiding being with, talking to, or escaping from others for any reason. Both actual avoidance and the desire for avoidance were included. The opposite instance was simple lack of an avoidance motive, not desire to affiliate. Social distress was defined as the reported experience of a negative emotion, such as being upset, distressed, tense, or anxious, in social interactions, or the reported lack of negative emotion, such as being relaxed, calm, at ease, or comfortable. The opposite instance of distress was lack of unhappiness, not the presence of some positive emotion.

The item selection procedure was explicitly chosen to eliminate as much social desirability variance as possible, for questions about anxiety in social situations would tend to elicit great concern with issues of social desirability, and the additional variance would not have been helpful. In two other instances discriminant relationships were explicitly encouraged. Questions about *S*'s reaction to testing situations were excluded, as there are already several test-anxiety scales in existence, and because the social anxiety scales could be more explicitly oriented to social situations. Finally, the authors attempted to foster a discriminant relationship between the SAD and FNE scales themselves, in the hope that separating them would increase their heuristic value.

## CONSTRUCTION OF THE SCALES

Following the stringent criteria for evaluation of items suggested by Jackson (1966a), 145 items were selected by rational analysis from a much larger pool.[1] These were then subjected to an empirical test, and the

---

[1]The authors wish to thank Barney Gilmore, Stewart Page, and Sybil Paterson, who either contributed suggestions for items or aided in their evaluation.

final 58 items which survived as the two scales are presented in Tables 1 and 2. The scoring key is given after each item. The SAD scale is evenly divided between true and false items; the FNE scale has 17 true and 13 false items.

The 145 items initially selected were administered to 297 undergraduates at the University of Toronto. The Crowne-Marlowe (1964) Social Desirability scale and the first 10 items of Jackson's (1966b) Infrequency scale were also administered. The latter was used to control for pseudo-random responding, and *S*s who answered any of these items incorrectly were dropped from all analyses. Ninety-two *S*s were dropped for this reason or because they did not answer all items.

*TABLE 1.   Social Avoidance and Distress (SAD) Scale*

---

  1. I feel relaxed even in unfamiliar social situations.   (F)
  2. I try to avoid situations which force me to be very sociable.   (T)
  3. It is easy for me to relax when I am with strangers.   (F)
  4. I have no particular desire to avoid people.   (F)
  5. I often find social occasions upsetting.   (T)
  6. I usually feel calm and comfortable at social occasions.   (F)
  7. I am usually at ease when talking to someone of the opposite sex.   (F)
  8. I try to avoid talking to people unless I know them well.   (T)
  9. If the chance comes to meet new people, I often take it.   (F)
 10. I often feel nervous or tense in casual get-togethers in which both sexes are present.   (T)
 11. I am usually nervous with people unless I know them well.   (T)
 12. I usually feel relaxed when I am with a group of people.   (F)
 13. I often want to get away from people.   (T)
 14. I usually feel uncomfortable when I am in a group of people I don't know.   (T)
 15. I usually feel relaxed when I meet someone for the first time.   (F)
 16. Being introduced to people makes me tense and nervous.   (T)
 17. Even though a room is full of strangers, I may enter it anyway.   (F)
 18. I would avoid walking up and joining a large group of people.   (T)
 19. When my superiors want to talk with me, I talk willingly.   (T)
 20. I often feel on edge when I am with a group of people.   (T)
 21. I tend to withdraw from people.   (T)
 22. I don't mind talking to people at parties or social gatherings.   (F)
 23. I am seldom at ease in a large group of people.   (T)
 24. I often think up excuses in order to avoid social engagements.   (T)
 25. I sometimes take the responsibility for introducing people to each other.   (F)
 26. I try to avoid formal social occasions.   (T)
 27. I usually go to whatever social engagement I have.   (F)
 28. I find it easy to relax with other people.   (F)

---

### TABLE 2. Fear of Negative Evaluation (FNE)

1. I rarely worry about seeming foolish to others.   (F)
2. I worry about what people will think of me even when I know it doesn't make any difference.   (T)
3. I become tense and jittery if I know someone is sizing me up.   (T)
4. I am unconcerned even if I know people are forming an unfavorable impression of me.   (F)
5. I feel very upset when I commit some social error.   (T)
6. The opinions that important people have of me cause me little concern.   (F)
7. I am often afraid that I may look ridiculous or make a fool of myself.   (T)
8. I react very little when other people disapprove of me.   (F)
9. I am frequently afraid of other people noticing my shortcomings.   (T)
10. The disapproval of others would have little effect on me.   (F)
11. If someone is evaluating me I tend to expect the worst.   (T)
12. I rarely worry about what kind of impression I am making on someone.   (F)
13. I am afraid that others will not approve of me.   (T)
14. I am afraid that people will find fault with me.   (T)
15. Other people's opinions of me do not bother me.   (F)
16. I am not necessarily upset if I do not please someone.   (F)
17. When I am talking to someone, I worry about what they may be thinking about me.   (T)
18. I feel that you can't help making social errors sometimes, so why worry about it.   (F)
19. I am usually worried about what kind of impression I make.   (T)
20. I worry a lot about what my superiors think of me.   (T)
21. If I know someone is judging me, it has little effect on me.   (F)
22. I worry that others will think I am not worthwhile.   (T)
23. I worry very little about what others may think of me.   (F)
24. Sometimes I think I am too concerned with what other people think of me.   (T)
25. I often worry that I will say or do the wrong things.   (T)
26. I am often indifferent to the opinions others have of me.   (F)
27. I am usually confident that others will have a favorable impression of me.   (F)
28. I often worry that people who are important to me won't think very much of me.   (T)
29. I brood about the opinions my friends have about me.   (T)
30. I become tense and jittery if I know I am being judged by my superiors.   (T)

The Crowne-Marlowe scale provided an initial empirical criterion against which to evaluate the SAD and FNE items. Jackson's (1966a, 1967) item selection procedure was employed, to minimize covariation with social desirability as a response style. For every item for 205 *S*s a computer calculated the biserial correlation of the item with its own scale and the biserial correlation with all other scales in the samples. Items endorsed by less than 5% of the sample were dropped. Jackson's Differential Reliability Index (DRI) was calculated for each remaining item. In the first instance, the DRI was calculated for the item's own scale and the Crowne-Marlowe, giving an estimate of the amount of correlation between an item and its own scale with social desirability variance removed. The first criterion for selecting items was that this DRI be as high as possible and in all cases above .50. It would not have been possible to apply further criteria had not the original rational analysis provided a large number of items which passed this first hurdle.

The second criterion was that the probability of endorsement of each item must have been above 10% and as close to 50% as possible. Third, a discriminant relationship between the SAD and FNE was encouraged by using a DRI in which item-own scale correlation was estimated with variance attributable to the other scale removed, selecting those items with minimal common variance. Fourth, to control for acquiescence, items were selected by judging the adequacy of those representing the opposite instance of the trait. Finally, items were selected according to content dissimilarity and the representativeness of the situations about which the items inquired.

### Characteristics of the Scales

One of the major goals was to foster scale homogeneity. This can be expressed as the mean biserial correlation of each item with its own scale. The mean biserial correlation of the selected FNE items, corrected for presence of item in the total score, was .72; and of the selected SAD items, it was .77 ($N = 205$, $p < .01$). The product-moment correlation of the two subscales of the SAD, avoidance and distress, was .75. A second index of homogeneity is the $KR$-20 reliability statistic. The $KR$-20s of both the selected FNE and SAD items were .94. The $KR$-20 of the Crowne-Marlowe was .79. In a second sample of 154 $S$s the $KR$-20 of the FNE was .96 and that of the SAD was again .94. The two scales are very homogeneous.

A second goal was to minimize the relationship of the scales to social desirability. The product-moment correlations of both the FNE and SAD with the Crowne-Marlowe scale were $-.25$ ($N = 205$, $p < .01$). These correlations might have been less had the Crowne-Marlowe itself been more homogeneous. In any case, the relationship with social desirability has been minimized. Another goal had been to foster a discriminant relationship between FNE and SAD. In the first sample, the product-moment correlation between the two was .51 ($N = 205$, $p < .01$). A later sample of 42, with which a Spearman correlation was used, showed a correlation of .32 ($N = 42$, $p < .05$). The attempt to foster a discriminant relationship between SAD and FNE did not eliminate all the common variance, probably because some people score highly on SAD just because they are fearful in social-evaluative situations. However, the common variance has been minimized.

Neither of the scales was normally distributed. The distribution of the FNE was nearly rectangular. The mean was 15.47, the standard deviation was 8.62, and the median was 16. This rectangularity indicated that the entire range of the scale was well used. The distribution of the SAD was skewed. Although the modal score was zero, the mean was 9.11, the median was 7, and the standard deviation was 8.01. Separate analysis of the social avoidance and social distress subscales indicated that the distribution of social avoidance was most skewed. High levels of SAD were not as common as high levels of FNE. High levels of SAD may be more pathological. Variables determining extreme social withdrawal or distress, which might be termed schizoid, are probably not normally distributed within the general population, which would explain the skew in the SAD data. This lack of normality in the SAD may make easier the task of early identification of those who later show schizoid reactions.

There were differences between the sexes in scores on the two scales. The mean scores on the SAD were: males ($N = 60$), 11.20; females ($N = 145$), 8.24. This difference is significant ($t = 2.64, p < .01$). Males reported more social avoidance and distress than females. The mean scores on the FNE were: males, 13.97; females, 16.10. This difference approached significance ($N$ the same as before; $t = 1.76, p < .10$). In this case the direction was reversed, women reporting more fear of negative evaluation than men.

Data for test-retest reliability were gathered on a sample of 154 Ss in the summer school of the University of Toronto. The SAD and FNE scales were administered alone, during class time, and 1 month passed between administrations. The product-moment, test-retest correlation of the FNE was .78, and that of the SAD was .68. A second sample of 29 gave the figures .94 for FNE and .79 for SAD, but the larger size of the first sample makes it a better estimate. These figures indicated sufficient reliability.

## EXPERIMENTAL STUDIES[2]

The SAD and FNE scales were administered to 358 students in the summer school at the University of Toronto. From this pool Ss were drawn for three experiments, whose purpose was to validate the two scales.

[2]The authors wish to thank Betty Jean Findlay, Donna Hutchinson, and Mary Ann Linseman for serving as Es. The authors appreciated the useful advice of John Arrowood on the design of one of the studies.

## SAD and the Prospect of Working Alone or Together

Persons who are high on SAD would be expected to be uncomfortable in social situations, and to prefer to be alone. Even the prospect of having to be in a future social interaction might make those high on SAD anxious. In this study Ss were told that they would later be required to participate in a group discussion or write an essay alone, and the effect of this expectation on their performance, anxiety, and other attitudes was observed.

From the 82 Ss scoring zero or one on the SAD, 46 were randomly selected as the low anxious (LA) group; and from the 85 scoring 12 or above, 52 were selected as the high anxious (HA) group. Within these two groups Ss were randomly assigned either to an Essay or Group Discussion condition. The Ss participated in the study in heterogeneous groups varying in size from 6 to 15. All Ss had the same female E. The Ss were told that they would actually be in two experiments, one to occur immediately and the second afterward. In the Essay condition, Ss were informed that in the second experiment they would be placed alone in a cubicle where they would write an essay on an interesting, controversial topic. In the Group Discussion condition, Ss were told that they would be placed in a small group in which they would be expected to participate actively in a discussion of an interesting, controversial topic. Envelopes labeled ''Essay Writing'' or ''Group Discussion'' which ostensibly contained material for the later work were provided. The Ss then participated in what was for them the first of two experiments, in which they had administered to them the Digit Symbol subtest of the Wechsler Adult Intelligence Scale. If the Ss were very anxious, this would have been reflected in impaired performance on this test. The Ss then filled out a questionnaire. After this E said that the second experiment could not take place at that time, and elicited an indication of how interested Ss might be in returning for the second study. That concluded the experiment. All of the significant results came from the questionnaire, as the simple expectation of later social interaction apparently did not arouse the degree of anxiety necessary to interfere with performance at the Digit Symbol task.

The Ss indicated how interested they were in returning at a later date by checking a 5-point scale labeled ''Not at all'' at one end, and ''Very much'' at the other. Analysis of variance for unequal $N$ was performed on these and all other data. Table 3 presents the data. The difference between the HA and LA groups $(F = 9.49, df = 1/94, p < .01)$, indicated that as expected the HA Ss were less interested in returning. The overall difference between the Essay and Group Discussion conditions was also significant, but more interesting was the interaction

TABLE 3. *Questionnaire Data from Experiment I*

| Item | Condition | |
|---|---|---|
| | Essay | Group Discussion |
| Degree of interest in returning | | |
| HA | | |
| M | 2.67 | 2.39 |
| N | 24 | 28 |
| LA | | |
| M | 3.19 | 3.44 |
| N | 21 | 25 |
| Number of Ss choosing each condition | | |
| HA* | 27 | 24 |
| LA | 5 | 41 |
| Degree of concern | | |
| HA | 2.33 | 1.89 |
| LA | 1.28 | 1.16 |
| Degree of confidence | | |
| HA | 3.20 | 2.64 |
| LA | 3.28 | 3.68 |

*One S did not respond.

($F = 45.74$, $df = 1/94$, $p < .001$), which indicated that while HA Ss were more interested in returning if they were to be in the Essay condition, the LA Ss were more interested if they were to be in the Group Discussion. The Ss were also asked to indicate their choice of being in the Essay or Group Discussion conditions when they returned. The data, also in Table 3, were analyzed by chi-square ($x^2 = 19.11$, $df = 1$, $p < .001$). The LA Ss showed a much greater preference for the Group Discussion condition. These two analyses pointed up much greater interest in being sociable among LA Ss.

The Ss were asked how worried or concerned they were about the second experiment, and they responded on a 5-point scale as above. The HA Ss were more worried ($F = 26.38$, $df = 1/94$, $p < .001$). The Essay writing condition produced more concern than the Group Discussion condition ($F = 7.39$, $df = 1/94$, $p < .01$), perhaps because an essay is tangible and more easily evaluated while one's participation in a group discussion is not. If this is so, then it would explain the interaction effect

($F = 4.25$, $df = 1/94$, $p < .05$), in the direction opposite that expected, as the HA $S$s were most concerned in the Essay condition. The HA $S$s in that condition may have been worried about some possible later evaluation of their essay.

Another question asked $S$s to predict how uneasy or nervous they expected to feel in the second experiment, and they responded on a 5-point scale. There was a difference between the anxiety groups ($F = 26.77$, $df = 1/94$, $p < .001$), but no other effects. The means were: HA, 3.02 and LA, 1.80. In another question using a 5-point scale, LA $S$s reported that they expected to be calmer than HA $S$s did in the coming experiment ($F = 14.46$, $df = 1/94$, $p < .001$). The means were: HA, 2.98 and LA, 3.80. The HA $S$s expected to be more nervous, less calm, in the second experiment. A final question asked about the degree of apprehension felt about participating in the coming study. A 5-point scale was labelled ''apprehensive'' and ''confident'' at its extremes. The means are in Table 3. The LA $S$s reported more confidence ($F = 6.70$, $df = 1/94$, $p < .05$), and there was an interaction ($F = 4.92$, $df = 1/94$, $p < .05$) which showed the expected pattern: HA $S$s were more confident or less apprehensive if they were to be in the Essay condition, while LA $S$s were more confident if assigned to the Group Discussion.

To sum up, people who scored highly on the SAD scale were less likely to be interested in returning, and more likely to choose to be alone, both indexes of social avoidance. The HA $S$s were more worried and uneasy as well as less calm and confident—all indexes of distress—and these discomforts were magnified in the together condition. Two other studies provided modest additional validation for the two scales.

## SAD and Being Alone or Together

From the same distribution of SAD scores, 97 HA $S$s, with scores of 11 and above, and 58 LA $S$s, with scores below three, all of whom performed at the same tasks, were randomly assigned to work either alone, together in a cubicle with another person but without talking, or together and talking to the other person in the cubicle. The tasks were anagrams, risk-level, and the learning of paired-associative nonsense syllables. The experimental conditions produced results in the predicted directions, but were too weak to elicit enough anxiety to show significant effects on performance. In the Talking condition, the $S$s were encouraged to talk, but how much they actually talked was left up to them. When asked to indicate how much they had actually talked on a scale, labeled ''Briefly, occasionally, frequently, and almost all the time'' at its four points, HA $S$s reported significantly less talking ($t = 2.20$, $df = 42$, $p < .05$). The means were: HA, 2.7; LA, 3.3. Not talking to others is a kind of social avoidance, and the SAD scale is supported here in that it differentiates *S*s according to how much they report talking to others.

## FNE, Approval Seeking or Disapproval Avoiding

If fear of negative evaluation is an avoidance motive, then a person high in FNE might try to gain social approval simply as a way of avoiding disapproval. Individuals high on FNE might be expected to be most affected by the possibility of disapproval, while those low on FNE might be more affected by the possibility of gaining approval. This study attempted to manipulate these incentive conditions.

The *S*, seated alone in a cubicle, believed that the work he was doing was part of a group effort, and that his performance would be evaluated by an unseen, unknown group leader. From the top 25% of the same FNE distribution—scores above 18—and from the bottom 25%—scores less than 9—48 high FNE and 48 low FNE *S*s were randomly selected. Within each of these two groups *S*s were randomly assigned either to a condition in which they were told that their group leader might approve of their work, but would never disapprove of it (Approval), or to a condition in which the leader might disapprove, but would never approve (Disapproval). Actually there were no groups and *S*s never heard from their leader. The *S*s performed a letter-number substitution task for 4 minutes, the dependent variable being the number of items completed. Analysis of variance indicated that the only effect which approached significance was the interaction pattern ($F = 3.76$, $df = 1/92$, $p < .10$). The mean scores were: high FNE Approval, 148.2; high FNE Disapproval, 145.2; low FNE Approval, 132.9; low FNE Disapproval, 149.5. If this unexpected, borderline effect may be believed, it indicates that those high on FNE not only avoided disapproval but sought approval, while the low FNE *S*s were not approval seekers and were motivated to work hard on a relatively dull task only if disapproval were threatened.

On a questionnaire, *S*s were asked how nervous or uneasy they felt during the experiment, and they responded on a 5-point scale. As expected, those high on FNE reported more uneasiness ($F = 17.01$, $df = 1/92$, $p < .001$). The means were: high FNE, 2.5; low FNE, 1.6. The *S*s had also been asked how they evaluated their own performance and how they thought their group leader would evaluate their performance. Neither of these questions revealed differences between groups, but some *S*s—18 out of 96—reported that they expected the group leader to think less well of their work than they did. Of the 18, 10 were high FNE and 8 were low, which is a chance occurrence, but all 10 of the high FNE *S*s were in the Approval condition, while the low FNE *S*s were evenly divided between Approval and Disapproval. By Fisher's exact test this pattern is significantly different from chance ($p < .025$). If this post hoc analysis indicates a real difference, then it suggests a defensive sort of expecting the worst among some high FNE *S*s.

## CORRELATIONAL STUDIES

To check on certain discriminant or convergent relationships which had been specified, and to search for new relationships, the SAD and FNE scales were correlated with other measures. Table 4 presents the correlations of FNE and SAD with Taylor's (1953) Manifest Anxiety (*MA*) scale, Rotter's (1966) Locus of Control scale (LC), Alpert and Haber's (1960) Achievement Anxiety scale, divided into debilitating and facilitating anxiety subscales (AH− and AH+), the social and evaluative

*TABLE 4.  Correlation of FNE and SAD with Other Scales*

| Original sample* | | | | |
|---|---|---|---|---|
| | *MA* | LC | AH− | E-H** |
| FNE | .60 | .18 | .28 | .47 |
| *N* | 171 | 172 | 173 | 35 |
| SAD | .54 | *ns* | .18 | .45 |
| *N* | 171 | | 173 | 35 |

| Second sample** | | | | | | | |
|---|---|---|---|---|---|---|---|
| | ASI | Social Ap-proval | Affil-iation | Desir-ability | Auton-omy | Defend-ence | Achieve-ment |
| FNE | .39 | .77 | *ns* | −.58 | −.32 | .42 | *ns* |
| SAD | .76 | *ns* | −.76 | −.42 | *ns* | *ns* | −.33 |

| Third sample** | | | | | |
|---|---|---|---|---|---|
| | Aggres-sion | Domi-nance | Abase-ment | Exhibi-tionism | Impul-sivity |
| FNE | *ns* | −.50 | .29 | −.39 | *ns* |
| SAD | *ns* | *ns* | *ns* | *ns* | *ns* |

Note. — For the second sample, *N* = 42; for the third, *N* = 40.
[a] There were no significant correlations with AH+.
*if $r = .15, p < .05$; if $r = .19, p < .01$.
**if $r = .30, p < .05$; if $r = .39, p < .01$.

parts of the Endler-Hunt (1966) S-R Inventory of Anxiousness (E-H), Paivio's (1965) Audience Sensitivity Index (ASI), and 11 of the subscales of Jackson's (1966a, 1966b) Personality Research Form (Social Approval, Affiliation, Desirability, Autonomy, Defendence, Achievement, Aggression, Dominance, Abasement, Exhibitionism, and Impulsivity). The table presents only significant or borderline correlations.

There should be some common variance between a general and a more specific measure of anxiety. If the *MA* scale is a measure of general anxiety, then the FNE and SAD should have a moderate relationship to it, which was the case. An attempt was made to foster a discriminant relationship with test anxiety, and the low correlation of both the social anxiety scales with AH− indicates that this was accomplished. If the situation eliciting the state of anxiety is as important or even more important than the trait itself (Endler & Hunt, 1966), then fostering discriminant relationships between situationally specific scales is valuable. Indeed, Cherlin (1967) showed that, compared with other anxiety measures, only a measure of state anxiety in social situations correlated with behavior in those situations.

A scale measuring social avoidance would have to be negatively correlated with affiliation, and the SAD met this criterion. Whether lack of affiliation necessarily implies presence of social anxiety is a moot point. The problem is that a person low on both traits would answer the opposite-instance items of the two scales similarly, thus producing a spurious correlation, that is, a correlation between scales which did not imply a relationship between constructs. The present data indicate that it is impossible to be high on both traits which is as it should be, given the nature of the constructs, but whether it is possible to be low on both traits cannot definitely be answered by these data. This possible spurious correlation would be a general problem in specifying the relationship between scales which control for acquiescence by employing opposite instance items which inquire simply about the absence of the trait in question. Yet the paradox is that the best kind of item does just that to avoid confounding with another trait.

The Endler-Hunt items which were used here ask *S* to report how he would respond in social-evaluative situations such as going to meet a new date, going on an interview for a very important job, going into a psychological experiment, etc. The moderate correlation of the SAD and FNE scales with reported reactions in these situations supports the validity of the two scales.

Paivio's ASI scale inquires about both the reaction of *S* to audience situations and possible causes for that reaction. The evaluative nature of audience situations is indicated by the correlation of FNE and ASI. Note also the negative relationship of FNE and Exhibitionism. People who fear others' evaluations don't want to be the center of attention. The very high relationship between SAD and ASI delineates the experience of stage fright as intense discomfort and a desire to flee.

The high correlation of FNE and Social Approval was consistent with the tentative results of the third experiment, suggesting that people high in FNE are very concerned with gaining others' approval. It should be noted that one item is identical on the two scales, and that the wording of the opposite instance items again raises the possibility of a spuriously high correlation. High FNE may imply a desire for social approval, but it is not clear that the latter necessarily implies FNE, nor is it known if it is possible to be low on both traits. This correlation does not imply that FNE is heavily loaded with social desirability as a response set, which was minimized by the use of the Marlowe-Crowne scale in the item selection procedure. Rather, people who fear others' negative evaluations want their approval as a signal that the feared outcome has been avoided.

Jackson's Desirability scale, on its face, seems to measure the degree to which a person actually engages in socially undesirable behavior. Presumably both high levels of SAD and FNE are somewhat undesirable, hence the moderate relationship with Desirability. Note that this is not desirability as a response style, which was assessed by the Crowne-Marlowe scale. The remainder of the significant correlations gave validational support to the FNE and SAD scales in a fairly straightforward manner. People high on FNE tend to be defensive, not autonomous, not dominant, and perhaps self-effacing. Some of the Defendence items, in fact, inquire about defensiveness in evaluative situations. To be autonomous or dominant opens one to criticism which is exactly what the person high on FNE fears. The negative correlation of SAD and Achievement emphasizes the social nature of the competitive achievement motive.

One other validational study will be briefly reported. Summer school students at the University of Toronto were notorious for not keeping appointments to serve as $S$s in experiments. A test was made to see if this behavior was related to social anxiety. Fifty-two of the 81 high SAD $S$s, with scores above 10, versus 36 of 80 low SAD $S$s, scores below 3, appeared for an experimental appointment ($\chi^2 = 5.99$, $df = 1$, $p < .02$). There were no effects of FNE. Apparently these high SAD $S$s were sufficiently afraid of the $E$ or their professor (neither of whom had any power to enforce appearance for appointments) or the generalized other, to do what was asked of them. People high in SAD may be more ingratiating or conforming than others.

## DISCUSSION

As expected, people high on SAD did avoid social situations, and were anxious in social interactions. Individuals high on FNE became nervous in evaluative conditions, and seemed to seek social approval. Both scales showed correlations with other relevant measures. The results lend validity to the two scales.

It is worth mentioning constructs which might have been embodied in the two scales but were not: fear of revealing one's inferiority, concern about the appearance of one's body, fear of lack of control of bodily processes, fear of one's unmanageable motives, inadequate expectations concerning what others will do; not knowing how to behave in social situations. These and other notions may express some of the origins of social anxiety. They were not included in the present construct to avoid begging the question of origins, but now that relatively unambiguous measures of the trait have been developed it will be possible to explore the relationships between variables. For example, one may ask how fear of others' evaluations is related to self-evaluation.

Social anxiety is a variable which may act as a moderator in a number of social situations. For example, the threat of negative evaluation might increase the chances of eliciting compliant behavior *if* the individual is in a state of anxiety and appraises that he can reduce anxiety through compliance. Thus FNE or SAD might act as moderator variables in studies on ingratiation, conformity, persuasibility, the demand characteristics of experiments, social approval seeking, social comparison processes, etc. Studies of the social processes within groups, such as the study of communication, might use the SAD as a moderator variable. In general, the FNE might be relevant in any potential evaluative situation, and the SAD could be useful in studies of social interaction.

The situation eliciting social anxiety is important, and one would expect to find that different situations have differential effects on individuals. The potential item universe from which items were selected for the FNE and SAD was intended to be all social situations, though only a few situations were unsystematically sampled by the items actually chosen. The sex of the person with whom $S$ is interacting, his status relative to $S$, whether he is a friend or stranger, in public or private conditions, under evaluative or nonevaluative circumstances, with covert or overt evaluation—all of these varied conditions will differentially affect people high or low in social anxiety. In an evaluative situation, how do the characteristics of the evaluator affect a person's anxiety level, and how does the behavior of the anxious person affect the judgment of the evaluator? Social avoidance and distress, measured by the SAD, may be a general reaction for some people, while for others it may be specific to certain conditions, such as dealing with authorities or members of the opposite sex.

Very little is known about the development of high levels of social anxiety, or about what effect they have on individuals. The amount of FNE may be a simple function of the amount of prior disapproval received, or a more complicated function combining prior disapproval with desire for approval. It seems best to conceive it as acquired on the basis of some sort of frustration or punishment. The relationship between approval seeking and disapproval avoiding is unclear. Individuals with high levels of FNE may seek nonevaluative social situations. They may fear not only obvious evaluative conditions, but also expect and fear evaluation where none is intended. The amount of SAD may also be a function of prior frustration or punishment in social interaction. The motives or frustrations underlying the acquisition of high SAD are unclear. A person with high SAD is clearly isolated and often fearful. The relationship of social anxiety to psychopathology is hinted here: the SAD scale may make it possible to study not simply the schizoid versus the normal, but intermediate types as well. Hopefully the development of the FNE and SAD scales will make it possible to study several of the interactions of personality and social variables discussed here.

## REFERENCES

Alpert, R., & Haber, R. N. Anxiety in academic achievement situations. *Journal of Abnormal and Social Psychology*, 1960, *61*, 207-215.

Byrne, D., McDonald, R., & Mikawa, J. Approach and avoidance affiliation motives. *Journal of Personality*, 1963, *31*, 21-37.

Cherlin, D. L. Anxiety and consultant differences in self-study groups. Unpublished doctoral dissertation, Yale University, 1967.

Crowne, D. P., & Marlowe, D. *The approval motive: Studies in evaluative dependence.* New York: Wiley, 1964.

Diggory, J. C. *Self-evaluation, concepts and studies.* New York: Wiley, 1966.

Dixon, J. J., deMonchaux, C., & Sandler, J. Patterns of anxiety: An analysis of social anxieties. *British Journal of Medical Psychology*, 1957, *30*, 107-112.

Endler, N. S., & Hunt, J. McV. Sources of behavioral variances as measured by the S-R Inventory of Anxiousness. *Psychological Bulletin*, 1966, *65*, 336-346.

Gerard, D. L., & Siegel, J. The family background of schizophrenia. *Psychiatric Quarterly*, 1950, *24*, 47-73.

Jackson, D. N. A modern strategy for personality assessment: The Personality Research Form. Research Bulletin No. 30, 1966, Psychology Department, University of Western Ontario. (a)

Jackson, D. N. *Personality research form.* Goshen, N. Y.: Research Psychologists Press, 1966. (b)

Jackson, D. N. Acquiescence response styles: Problems of identification and control. In I. A. Berg (Ed.), *Response set in personality assessment.* Chicago: Aldine, 1967.

Paivio, A. Personality and audience influence. In B. Maher (Ed.), *Progress in experimental personality research.* Vol. 2. New York: Academic Press, 1965.

Rodnick, E., & Garmezy, N. An experimental approach to the study of motivation in schizophrenia. *Nebraska Symposium on Motivation,* 1957, *5,* 109-184.

Rotter, J. B. Generalized expectancies for internal versus external control of reinforcement. *Psychological Monographs,* 1966, *80* (1, Whole No. 609).

Sears, D. O. Social anxiety, opinion structure and opinion change. *Journal of Personality and Social Psychology,* 1967, *7,* 142-151.

Taylor, J. A personality scale of manifest anxiety. *Journal of Abnormal and Social Psychology,* 1953, *48,* 285-290.

Zigler, E., & Phillips, L. Social competence and the process-reactive distinction in psychopathology. *Journal of Abnormal and Social Psychology,* 1962, *65,* 215-222.

# 12

## The College Self-Expression Scale:
## A Measure of Assertiveness

*John P. Galassi*
*James S. DeLo*
*Merna D. Galassi*
*Sheila Bastien*

Assertive training is one of the earliest of the therapeutic procedures developed by behavior therapists (Salter, 1949). Assertiveness has been defined by Alberti and Emmons (1970) as "... behavior which enables a person to act in his own best interests, or stand up for himself without undue anxiety, to express his rights without denying the rights of others." Wolpe (1969) states that appropriate assertiveness denotes "... the outward expression of practically all feelings other than anxiety. ... It may express friendly, affectionate, and other nonanxious feelings."

In spite of both its early development and the fact that assertive training appears to be one of the most promising contributions by behavior therapy to date (Bandura, 1969; Mischel, 1968; Ullmann & Krasner, 1965), research on assertiveness has been slow to emerge. Perhaps one of the factors that has retarded its investigation is the absence of a standardized instrument which is designed to serve diagnostic purposes and to measure change. Previous research has relied upon instruments which were unstandardized (e.g., Lazarus, 1966), which were not designed specifically to measure the construct (e.g., Hedquist & Weinhold, 1970), or which tapped only limited aspects of assertiveness (e.g., McFall & Lillesand, 1971).

Reprinted from *Behavior Therapy*, 1974, 5, 165-171. Copyright © 1974 by Academic Press, Inc. Reproduced by permission.

The authors are indebted to Martha DeLo for her contribution to the study.

TABLE 1.   The College Self-Expression Scale

---

The following inventory is designed to provide information about the way in which you express yourself. Please answer the questions by checking the appropriate box from 0-4 (Almost Always or Always, 0; Usually, 1; Sometimes, 2; Seldom, 3; Never or Rarely, 4) on the computer answer sheet. Your answer should reflect how you generally express yourself in the situation.

---

1. Do you ignore it when someone pushes in front of you in line?
2. When you decide that you no longer wish to date someone, do you have marked difficulty telling the person of your decision?
3. Would you exchange a purchase you discover to be faulty?   (R)
4. If you decided to change your major to a field which your parents will not approve, would you have difficulty telling them?
5. Are you inclined to be over-apologetic?
6. If you were studying and if your roommate were making too much noise, would you ask him to stop?   (R)
7. Is it difficult for you to compliment and praise others?
8. If you are angry at your parents, can you tell them?   (R)
9. Do you insist that your roommate does his fair share of the cleaning?   (R)
10. If you find yourself becoming fond of someone you are dating, would you have difficulty expressing these feelings to that person?
11. If a friend who has borrowed $5.00 from you seems to have forgotten about it, would you remind this person?   (R)
12. Are you overly careful to avoid hurting other people's feelings?
13. If you have a close friend whom your parents dislike and constantly criticize, would you inform your parents that you disagree with them and tell them of your friend's assets?   (R)
14. Do you find it difficult to ask a friend to do a favor for you?
15. If food which is not to your satisfaction is served in a restaurant, would you complain about it to the waiter?   (R)
16. If your roommate without your permission eats food that he knows you have been saving, can you express your displeasure to him?   (R)
17. If a salesman has gone to considerable trouble to show you some merchandise which is not quite suitable, do you have difficulty in saying no?
18. Do you keep your opinions to yourself?
19. If friends visit when you want to study, do you ask them to return at a more convenient time?   (R)
20. Are you able to express love and affection to people for whom you care?   (R)
21. If you were in a small seminar and the professor made a statement that you considered untrue, would you question it?   (R)
22. If a person of the opposite sex whom you have been wanting to meet smiles or directs attention to you at a party, would you take the initiative in beginning a conversation?   (R)

23. If someone you respect expresses opinions with which you strongly disagree, would you venture to state your own point of view? (R)
24. Do you go out of your way to avoid trouble with other people?
25. If a friend is wearing a new outfit which you like, do you tell that person so? (R)
26. If after leaving a store you realize that you have been "short-changed," do you go back and request the correct amount? (R)
27. If a friend makes what you consider to be an unreasonable request, are you able to refuse? (R)
28. If a close and respected relative were annoying you, would you hide your feelings rather than express your annoyance?
29. If your parents want you to come home for a weekend but you have made important plans, would you tell them of your preference? (R)
30. Do you express anger or annoyance toward the opposite sex when it is justified? (R)
31. If a friend does an errand for you, do you tell that person how much you appreciate it? (R)
32. When a person is blatantly unfair, do you fail to say something about it to him?
33. Do you avoid social contacts for fear of doing or saying the wrong thing?
34. If a friend betrays your confidence, would you hesitate to express annoyance to that person?
35. When a clerk in a store waits on someone who has come in after you, do you call his attention to the matter? (R)
36. If you are particularly happy about someone's good fortune, can you express this to that person? (R)
37. Would you be hesitant about asking a good friend to lend you a few dollars?
38. If a person teases you to the point that it is no longer fun, do you have difficulty expressing your displeasure?
39. If you arrive late for a meeting, would you rather stand than go to a front seat which could only be secured with a fair degree of conspicuousness?
40. If your date calls on Saturday night 15 minutes before you are supposed to meet and says that she (he) has to study for an important exam and cannot make it, would you express your annoyance? (R)
41. If someone keeps kicking the back of your chair in a movie, would you ask him to stop? (R)
42. If someone interrupts you in the middle of an important conversation, do you request that the person wait until you have finished? (R)
43. Do you freely volunteer information or opinions in class discussions? (R)
44. Are you reluctant to speak to an attractive acquaintance of the opposite sex?
45. If you lived in an apartment and the landlord failed to make certain necessary repairs after promising to do so, would you insist on it? (R)
46. If your parents want you home by a certain time which you feel is much too early and unreasonable, do you attempt to discuss or negotiate this with them? (R)

TABLE 1. (Cont.)

47. Do you find it difficult to stand up for your rights? (R)
48. If a friend unjustifiably criticizes you, do you express your resentment there and then? (R)
49. Do you express your feelings to others? (R)
50. Do you avoid asking questions in class for fear of feeling self-conscious?

(R) = Reverse scored.

The present study reports on an instrument which was designed specifically to measure assertiveness, as it is broadly defined above, in college students. The successful expression of personal feelings, values, and attitudes constitutes a particularly important developmental task (Coons, 1970) for this population.

## METHOD

### The Scale

The College Self-Expression Scale (CSES) is a 50-item, self-report measure (see Table 1). It utilizes a five-point Likert format (0-4) with 21 positively worded items and 29 negatively worded items. The scale attempts to measure three aspects of assertiveness: positive, negative, and self-denial. Positive assertiveness consists of expressing feelings of love, affection, admiration, approval, and agreement. Negative assertions include expressions of justified feelings of anger, disagreement, dissatisfaction, and annoyance; whereas, self-denial includes overapologizing, excessive interpersonal anxiety, and exaggerated concern for the feelings of others. The scale also indicates a subject's level of assertiveness vis-à-vis a variety of role occupants: strangers, authority figures, business relations, family and relatives, like and opposite sex peers. Items for the scale, in part, were derived or modified from work by Lazarus (1971), Wolpe (1969), and Wolpe and Lazarus (1966). A total score for the scale is obtained by summing all positively worded items and reverse scoring and summing all negatively worded items. Low scores are indicative of a generalized nonassertive response pattern.

### Procedure

Normative data were collected on four separate samples: 91 students enrolled in an introductory psychology course at West Virginia University, 47 upper division and beginning graduate students enrolled in a personality theory course and an introductory testing course at West Virginia University, and 41 elementary and 82 secondary school student teachers at Fairmont State College.

Test-retest reliability data were collected for the first two samples of students over a 2-week period. Pearson product-moment correlation coefficients were computed for each group on total scores for the two occasions. Two types of validity data, construct and concurrent, were obtained for the scale.

Construct validity was established by correlating the CSES with the 24 scales of the Adjective Check List (Gough and Heilbrun, 1965). The Adjective Check List (ACL) consists of 300 common adjectives which compose 24 personality scales, 15 of which operationalize constructs of Murray's need-press system. The ACL was administered to 72 of the 91 Psychology I students.

Concurrent validity was obtained by correlating the CSES scores of the combined sample of 121 student teachers with ratings of their assertiveness made by immediate supervisors. Each student was rated on a five-point CSES Behavioral Rating Form for Observers.[1]

TABLE 2.   *Means and Standard Deviations on the College Self-Expression Scale*

| Sample | Sex | N | Mean | SD |
|---|---|---|---|---|
| W.V.U. Psych. I | Male | 58 | 121.97 | 14.12 |
| Pretest | Female | 33 | 117.91 | 16.01 |
| | | 91 | 120.31 | 18.05 |
| W.V.U. Psych. I | Male | 58 | 124.16 | 19.58 |
| Posttest | Female | 33 | 120.82 | 20.11 |
| | | 91 | 121.95 | 19.73 |
| W.V.U. Upper division and | Male | 19 | 133.00 | 11.96 |
| graduate students | Female | 28 | 124.75 | 17.55 |
| Pretest | | 47 | 128.09 | 15.46 |
| W.V.U. Upper division and | Male | 19 | 132.74 | 14.11 |
| graduate students | Female | 28 | 123.39 | 20.62 |
| Posttest | | 47 | 127.17 | 18.68 |
| Fairmont State Elementary | Male | 7 | 123.14 | 27.73 |
| Student teachers | Female | 34 | 122.44 | 17.17 |
| | | 41 | 122.56 | 18.94 |
| Fairmont State Secondary | Male | 36 | 128.75 | 18.27 |
| Student teachers | Female | 46 | 118.46 | 17.77 |
| | | 82 | 122.98 | 18.61 |

## RESULTS AND DISCUSSION

### Normative Data and Reliability

In all of the samples, males achieved slightly higher scores than females (Table 2). The test-retest reliability coefficients for samples one and two were 0.89 and 0.90, respectively.

[1] Available from the authors upon request.

## Construct Validity

As expected, the College Self-Expression Scale correlates positively and significantly with the following Adjective Check List Scales: Number checked, Defensiveness, Favorable, Self-Confidence, Achievement, Dominance, Intraception, Heterosexuality, Exhibition, Autonomy, and Change (Table 3). Gough and Heilbrun's (1965) definitions of these scales suggest characteristics which typify assertiveness. The assertive individual is expressive, spontaneous, well defended, confident, and able to influence and lead others.

Significant negative correlations were obtained with the Unfavorable, Succorance, Abasement, Deference, and Counseling Readiness Scales. These results are consistent with nonassertiveness and indicate an inadequate and negative self-evaluation, feelings of inferiority, a tendency to be over-solicitous of emotional support from others, and excessive interpersonal anxiety (Counseling Readiness).

Descriptions of the Self-Control, Lability, Endurance, Order, Nurturance, Affiliation, and Aggression scales by Gough and Heilbrun (1965) suggested that these variables would not be significantly related to

TABLE 3.   *Intercorrelations between the College Self-Expression Scale and the Adjective Check List Scales*

| | Number checked | Defensiveness | Favorable |
|---|---|---|---|
| CSES | 0.33 | 0.35 | 0.30 |
| | Unfavorable | Self-confidence | Self-control |
| CSES | − 0.25 | 0.46 | − 0.11 |
| | Lability | Personal adjustment | Achievement |
| CSES | 0.21 | 0.22 | 0.34 |
| | Dominance | Endurance | Order |
| CSES | 0.46 | 0.16 | 0.10 |
| | Intraception | Nurturance | Affiliation |
| CSES | 0.22 | 0.15 | 0.22 |
| | Heterosexuality | Exhibition | Autonomy |
| CSES | 0.46 | 0.48 | 0.24 |
| | Aggression | Change | Succorance |
| CSES | 0.17 | 0.43 | − 0.31 |
| | Abasement | Deference | Counseling readiness |
| CSES | − 0.35 | − 0.29 | − 0.43 |

$r \leq 0.23$  $p < .05$             $r \leq 0.33$  $p < .005$

$r \leq 0.29$  $p < .01$             $r \leq 0.39$  $p < .001$

responses on the CSES. This, in fact, was the case. The confirmation of a nonsignificant correlation between Aggression and the CSES is of especial importance since aggressiveness is often mistaken for assertiveness.

The correlation between Personal Adjustment and assertiveness, although positive, did not achieve significance. However, the correlation of the CSES with other scales, notably the Counseling Readiness and Unfavorable Scales, suggests poorer adjustment on the part of low scorers of the CSES.

### Concurrent Validity

The correlation between supervisor and self-ratings on assertiveness was 0.19, $p < .04$. Although this correlation is significant, it is low. However, the nature of the interaction between supervisor and supervisee may have vitiated this correlation. This interaction was for the most part limited to the subject's performance as a classroom teacher. The supervisor had limited information in regard to the subject's ability to function with peers, family, etc., which the CSES also taps. In light of the high construct validity with the Adjective Check List, it would be expected that the use of raters, who are trained in observation and evaluation of the construct of assertiveness and who are acquainted with the subject's behavior in a variety of situations, would undoubtedly raise the concurrent validity correlation coefficient.

### CONCLUSION

The College Self-Expression Scale provides a useful measure of assertiveness for clinician and researcher alike. The scale can be utilized by therapists to determine quickly the type of assertive responses which a client fails to emit, as well as the interpersonal situations in which appropriate assertiveness is not forthcoming. For those who wish to do research on assertive training, the CSES is a valuable instrument for initial subject selection and for the measurement of change.

## REFERENCES

Alberti, R. E., & Emmons, M. L. *Your perfect right: A guide to assertive behavior.* San Luis Obispo, California: Impact, 1970.

Bandura, A. *Principles of behavior modification.* New York: Holt, Rinehart, and Winston, 1969.

Coons, F. W. The resolution of adolescence in college. *Personnel and Guidance Journal,* 1970, *48,* 533-541.

Gough, H. G., & Heilbrun, A. B., Jr. *The adjective check list manual.* Palo Alto, California: Consulting Psychologists Press, 1965.

Hedquist, F. J., & Weinhold, B. K. Behavioral counseling with socially anxious and unassertive college students. *Journal of Counseling Psychology,* 1970, *17,* 237-242.

Lazarus, A. A. Behavioral rehearsal vs. non-directive therapy vs. advice in effecting behavior change. *Behaviour Research and Therapy,* 1966, *4,* 209-212.

Lazarus, A. A. *Behavior therapy and beyond.* New York: McGraw-Hill Book Company, 1971.

McFall, R. M., & Lillesand, D. B. Behavior rehearsal with modeling and coaching in assertion training. *Journal of Abnormal Psychology,* 1971, *77,* 313-323.

Mischel, W. *Personality and assessment.* New York: Wiley, 1968.

Salter, A. *Conditioned reflex therapy.* New York: Capricorn Books, 1949.

Ullmann, L. P., & Krasner, L. *Case studies in behavior modification.* New York: Holt, Rinehart, and Winston, 1965.

Wolpe, J. *The practice of behavior therapy.* New York: Pergamon Press, Inc., 1969.

Wolpe, J., & Lazarus, A. A. *Behavior therapy techniques: A guide to the treatment of neuroses.* New York: Pergamon Press, 1966.

# Part IV

---

# Assessment for Potential Reinforcers

Notions of reinforcement and the application of the reinforcement principle have occupied a central position in the theoretical, experimental, and practical developments surrounding behavior therapy. Naturally occurring as well as arbitrarily arranged consequent stimulus events have been observed both to increase and to decrease the probability with which behavior occurs (Glaser, 1971). The manner in which consequences are provided, that is, scheduling and timing, will influence specific behavioral properties such as rate and resistance to extinction. Glaser (1971) defines a reinforcer as ''an event, stimulus, or state of affairs that changes subsequent behavior when it temporally follows an instance of that behavior'' (p. 1). He also notes that, throughout the various theoretical interpretations of reinforcement mechanisms, this description of reinforcing situations has remained relatively consistent. It is this operational definition that we will use in discussing the assessment of potential reinforcers, since it is most relevant for treatment.

In an applied context, the uses and misuses of reinforcement terminology have served as a basis for probably unjust criticisms of behavior therapy. More importantly for present purposes, misunderstandings and inappropriate conceptualizations of reinforcement have probably impeded the development of adequate devices for the assessment of potentially reinforcing consequences. Therefore, before discussing some of the specific assessment devices that have developed, an attempt to clarify some of these misunderstandings is necessary.

In spite of the fact that reinforcing events have consistently been defined in terms of their functional relationship to behavior, there has been a persistent tendency to equate reinforcers with stimuli that look, sound, taste, feel, or smell either good or bad. For example, Madsen and Madsen (1974) present an extensive listing of ''approval'' and ''disapproval'' responses that are further elaborated in terms of words spoken, written symbols, nonverbal expressions, physical contact, activities, and things. To the extent that events having such absolute properties may be correlated with consistent response strengthening or weakening properties when presented contingently following behavior, this focus may yield useful assessment information. However, such a focus has also had at least two negative effects. First, it has probably served to limit the assessment of a wide range of events whose absolute stimulus properties do not fit the stereotype of "reinforcers" yet might be functionally effective in bringing about behavior change. Secondly, it has, to some extent, limited the development of assessment devices designed to establish the functional effectiveness of a variety of consequences *prior* to intervention. The first effect has probably been reduced somewhat by attempts to incorporate the "Premack principle" into behavior programs. The second effect has particular importance from the standpoint of program efficiency.

In most situations, reinforcer assessments attempt to define events that *if* presented contingently following a response, will alter it in some way. For this reason, we speak of assessing for *potential* reinforcers. This means that almost any event may serve this function. Therefore, not only is the assessment of events with perceived positive or negative properties limiting, but it is also limiting to assess *only* consequent events. There are numerous antecedent events with discriminative stimulus ($S^D$) properties which, if presented following a behavior, could influence responding.

Another important factor in assessing potential reinforcers relates to whether the assessment deals with events that are currently present in the person's life situation or events that, while not currently present, if available, could serve as potential reinforcers in a therapeutic program. To the extent that behavior-change programs have emphasized the utilization of naturally occurring events in the alteration of behavior, assessing events in the current situation is extremely important, especially from the standpoint of treatment generalization. However, it is necessary to consider that there are events that *could be* extremely potent reinforcers if they were made available. Therefore, not only is an examination of responsiveness to current stimulus events important but, also, assessment should involve an estimate of responses to a variety of events that might not be immediately accessible to the individual.

A major problem involved in attempting to assess for potential reinforcers is the high likelihood that the reinforcing properties of a given stimulus are dependent upon additional stimuli that may be available in the situation. The reinforcement value of any stimulus is likely related to and dependent upon other events in the situation. In contrast to laboratory investigations, in which a single event is presented contingently upon a response, a naturalistic situation provides a host of available alternative situations and responses. This type of complexity creates a situation in which it is difficult to assess the reinforcing properties of any stimulus in an isolated fashion. The major problem from an assessment standpoint, however, is to determine what clusters of stimuli are functionally related. This point has been made by Costello (1972), who considers depression as an instance involving not so much the loss of available reinforcers, but rather a loss in reinforcer effectiveness. Essentially, the notion here is that, if the critical event for some parts of the situation is no longer present, other parts may lose their reinforcer effectiveness. This point is extremely important in relation to the assessment of reinforcers and points to the importance of assessing events in the context of other circumstances that usually surround them.

Another general point to consider in assessing reinforcing events is the high degree of variability that characterizes the description of social events. It is fairly easy to describe and quantify static events such as tangible or food reinforcers that might be used in laboratory situations or in simple reward programs with children. However, when one is considering the assessment of more subtle types of social reinforcers, it is likely that the stimulus event will not appear in an identical form on successive occasions. Rather, it is more likely that the class of stimuli ''social praise'' may serve to reinforce an individual's behavior; however, the specific event occurring within this class may vary significantly from occasion to occasion. The assessment problem here is related to the identification of classes of events that are functionally related in terms of similar reward properties.

Most of the work that has been done in attempting to identify reinforcers has tended to have as its focus the assessment of positive events. For example, the reinforcement survey schedules included in Part IV (see Clement & Richard and Cautela & Kastenbaum) are primarily concerned with the individual's preferences for a variety of ''positive'' stimuli. This focus has likely been supported by the persistent emphasis that has been placed upon the use of positive reinforcement programs for behavior change in contrast to programs based upon aversive control. This emphasis may have limited the development of assessment instruments that attempt to identify negative controlling variables in the person's life situation. With a few minor exceptions—for example, the use of certain types of aversive control for self-destructive behavior and a number of aversive conditioning programs with specific disorders (e.g., alcoholism, sexual deviation)—the emphasis more than likely involves introduction of positive controls. However, in many situations the therapeutic program is designed in such a way as to utilize intrinsic or naturally occurring events as the primary vehicle for change. That is, an attempt is made to alter the current events surrounding the individual's inappropriate behavior. In this regard, much has been written (Skinner, 1953, 1972) about the prevalent use of aversive control in many human situations. To the extent that aversive control is part of the complex of variables maintaining a behavior, efforts to develop measures for assessing the degree of aversive control are critical if there is to be change. Some work has focused on this type of question, including that of Patterson (1971, 1973) who has, through observational measures, identified a variety of behaviors that have both response suppressing and facilitating properties and also would likely be classified as aversive stimuli. Other investigators (McLean, 1975) have presented data to support the frequent reliance on aversive controls in marital interaction. In summary, the high prevalence of aversive control in naturalistic situations is somewhat at odds with the relative lack of sophistication in the assessment of aversive controlling events. Clearly this is one area in which additional work is needed. For the most part, any attempt to assess the empirical reinforcing properties of the stimulus requires that the stimulus event be presented following a behavior. While this approach is not problematic within a laboratory framework, it can be problematic in clinical situations. Especially where there is possible danger to the individual or where there is an urgency or need for an efficient change program, the assessment of a reinforcer through direct application may not always be possible. What would seem to be needed is a way to make some probability statement about the likelihood that an event will serve as a reinforcer prior to actual contingent application of that event.

Such a probability statement made on an a priori basis is possible through the application of some of the notions presented by Premack (1959, 1965, 1971). These would seem to be particularly applicable to human situations in that they emphasize the relative properties of any reinforcing stimulus. The reinforcement properties of a stimulus are related to the availability of other stimuli in the situation. The same event may serve either as a reinforcer or a punisher, depending upon its probability relationship to the response that is being consequated. The Premack notion, frequently summarized under the heading of ''The Premack Principle,'' states that for any set of responses the most probable response in a free-choice situation will serve to reinforce less probable behaviors when presented at a subsequent time in a contingency relationship. Premack has also extended this notion (Premack, 1971) to state that less probable responses, if presented contingently, will serve to punish more probable responses. It is important to note that these reinforcement relationships are assumed to hold regardless of the manner in which any of the reponses were originally acquired. This notion is referred to as the ''Indifference Principle.'' From an assessment standpoint, a Premackian analysis would essentially involve observing the organism behaving in a free-choice situation and noting the duration of time that is spent in a variety of behaviors or activities. Presumably the behaviors that occurred with the greatest duration are the behaviors that would serve to reinforce less probable responses.

In spite of its seeming applicability to human clinical situations, the number of direct applications of the Premack principle as an assessment or treatment procedure has been quite limited. Several studies (Homme, 1965, 1970; Johansson, Lewinsohn, & Flippo, 1969) have used the Premack principle with both children and adults (for a review, see Danaher, 1974). It should be noted, however, that in most of these studies the initial duration assessment of behavior has been done in a way that does not conform to some of the specific assessment requirements outlined by Premack. Danaher (1974) discusses some of these points in detail. Frequently, people have employed verbal reports or preference measures of behavior and have attempted to employ them within a Premackian framework. For example, the article by Daley included in Part IV attempts to use a Premackian analysis for visual symbolic stimuli. However, there is little empirical support for the assumption that a highly preferred activity assessed through symbolic-verbal report measures is equivalent in its empirical properties to a highly preferred activity assessed using a duration measure.

The assessment procedures in Part IV serve as a bridge between the previous sections dealing with interview/self-report assessments and the following section, Part V, dealing with observational measures, since attempts at assessing potential reinforcers have involved the use of both. It is also useful to make the distinction between assessing for potential reinforcers with child populations versus adult populations since (1) the types of procedures that have been used with children have been different from those used with adults and (2) at a conceptual and methodological level there are reasons for using different procedures with children than with adults. These conceptual points will be elaborated in discussing the procedures in this section.

## ASSESSING POTENTIAL REINFORCERS FOR CHILDREN

A number of different reinforcer assessment approaches have been used with children. These include the interview, survey schedules and questionnaires involving verbal report from other individuals, verbal report measures in which the child is asked to respond directly, direct observations of child behavior, and, finally, direct exposure to reinforcing events. Each of these topics will be treated separately below.

1. *Interviews.* As is the case for general assessment, the interview is the most frequently used procedure for obtaining initial information regarding the range of potential events which may be reinforcing to a child. In most instances, interview information, especially for younger children, is likely to be obtained from a second party informant, usually

the child's parents or teacher (Holland, 1970). While interviews with children are frequently used with children of an older age, the apparent unreliability of verbal report measures with young children has resulted in an infrequent use of this type of procedure for this age group. The information relating to reinforcing events obtained in the interview is similar to that outlined in Part III by Kanfer and Saslow. Essentially, the parent is asked to report on the range of objects, people, places, activities, etc., that the child frequently engages in, or that the child prefers or enjoys. In many instances, the verbal report measure will be later substantiated by direct behavior sampling across a variety of situations.

One of the possible difficulties relating to the use of parental or teacher verbal report is the likelihood that they will tend to think more in terms of absolute reinforcement properties than of functional reinforcement properties. Consequently, these types of reports are more likely to divulge events that have positive features but may not necessarily be exercising positive (response strengthening) control over the child's behavior. One of the problems associated with using second-party report may be that the informants have had limited opportunity to observe the child in many situations that may be quite important for the identification of reinforcing events. This would be especially the case where powerful peer reinforcers are present. Clearly, peer interaction—playground interaction and so forth—may not be available for observation by second-party informants.

2. *Second-Party Verbal Report Measures.* Survey schedules have been developed (see Clement & Richard, paper 13) for obtaining information from parents and from teachers regarding the child's likes and dislikes. As was the case for interviews, such likes and dislikes may be expressed as objects, events, activities, places, people, etc. Again, it is often assumed that preferred events will serve to strengthen responses that they follow, whereas nonpreferred events will have a weakening effect. Given the problems associated with the reliability and validity of verbal report data, as presented in the previous section, this assumption is suspect. In addition, there is little direct information showing a relationship between stated preferences for an event as reported by a second party and the event's response-strengthening properties. The verbal report measure of potential reinforcers is clearly not a behavioral measure in the sense of designating functionally effective reinforcers. However, such verbal report measures can be extremely useful in identifying possible areas that may be followed up. In addition, the verbal report measures given by second-party informants may be extremely useful in helping to identify the perceptions of the informant of the kind of things he thinks the child will find reinforcing. It is of clinical importance, therefore, to identify whether or not there is a consistency or discrepancy between the parents'

view and the teacher's view of events that are reinforcing for a child, and whether or not these events are actually reinforcing or whether the perceptions of a teacher or parent are substantially different from the perceptions and behavior of the child. In this regard, second-party verbal report measures may also be extremely useful in the planning of treatment programs (Ellett & Bersoff, 1973).

3. *Verbal Report Measures with the Child as Respondent.* For the reasons mentioned above, these types of measures have not been frequently used. However, there have been a few attempts to obtain direct verbal report measures from the child. Notable here is the "Mediator-Reinforcer Incomplete Blank" (MRB) described by Tharp and Wetzel (1969) and also some of the applications of the Children's Reinforcement Survey Schedule described by Clement and Richard (see paper 13). As described by Tharp and Wetzel (1969):

The MRB is a 34-item incomplete-sentence blank. Items were devised to give pertinent information on reinforcers and mediators. A few examples: (a) "Two things I like to do best are_____"; (b) "I will do almost anything to get_____"; (c) "The only person I will take advice from is_____"; (d) "The thing I like to do best with my father is_____". (p. 75)

A point to be made in relation to both these measures is that there is very little reliability or validity information associated with their use. So, while their clinical applicability seems promising in terms of their extensive application, the usefulness of these procedures awaits a more direct empirical test.

One possible positive outcome associated with getting such children's responses directly may be that it makes the child a more willing participant in relation to a forthcoming treatment program. For example, actively including the child in decisions relating to possible events that he finds rewarding may serve as a cue for additional later payoffs. This may make the child more receptive to later programs for behavior change. Other nonspecific factors associated with the use of such direct types of verbal report measures may be ways of getting indirect information regarding the child's motivation for change, as well as how he responds to a structured task situation. Component responses involved in having a child complete such a survey schedule would, in some ways, simulate certain kinds of classroom tasks in which the child is asked to work on an assignment. As such, some other indirect, yet important, behaviors that are over and above the information that would be obtained about reinforcing events may also be assessed through the use of the survey.

Other assessment procedures that involve a child's response, but to pictorial rather than verbal symbolic stimuli, have also been developed.

For example, in the "Reinforcer Event Menu" procedure (Homme, 1970) presented by Daley in Part IV, the child is shown a number of pictures of children engaged in different activities and is asked to pick out the ones that are most preferred. The problems here again relate to the reliability and validity of preference measures of behavior as a measure of reinforcer effectiveness.

Other assessment procedures in this category have attempted to expose the child directly to the actual stimulus event, without necessarily providing him with the opportunity to engage in the activity. An example of this may be a case in which the child is presented with two toys and is asked to indicate which of the two he prefers. Problems with this type of assessment are similar to those with other types of preference measures and again relate to reliability and validity considerations.

4. *Direct Observation of Child Behavior.* Consistent with a Premack approach are attempts to identify potential reinforcers by directly observing the child behaving in a number of situations. These situations may represent naturalistic circumstances, for example, the home or classroom, or they may also represent structured situations designed to get at information about the reinforcing properties of more discrete stimulus events. In the latter category, certain events are introduced into the situation, are freely available, and an attempt is made to observe the degree to which the child engages in those activities.

First, in relation to observation of the child in interaction situations, the focus is on the identification of naturally occurring reinforcing events in the situation. An attempt is made to identify both social and nonsocial consequences for behavior that are perhaps serving as maintaining stimuli for the child's responses. In addition to this, direct estimates of the child's own responses are made in order to determine the kinds of activities that the child prefers. The direct observation measures discussed in Part V are clearly valuable instruments for identifying possible reinforcers, although they may not specifically be designated as such. Direct observational procedures with children provide an initial basis for identifying aversive consequences for the child and also enhance the possibilities for identifying a variety of contextual stimuli that may serve to heighten or diminish the effectiveness of potentially reinforcing events.

Some of the disadvantages of using direct observation procedures as a way of assessing reinforcers are: (1) it is still necessary to demonstrate that the events do in fact show functional control over the behavior; (2) there are problems to be discussed, relating to the reactivity of observation instruments as well as their reliability and validity; and (3) observational procedures may be inefficient. This is especially so under naturalistic conditions where the behaviors of interest and consequences of interest may not occur at an extremely high rate. For this reason, it is possible to set up structured situations that increase the probability that the child will be able to sample certain types of consequences and have the opportunity to engage in certain types of behavior. For example, if we were interested in examinining the degree to which the child engages in play activity as a preferred event, then by providing a direct situation, either in the home or in a structured clinical setting where a number of attractive toys are freely available, as well as additional alternatives, we could obtain free-choice measures.

5. *Exposure to Reinforcing Stimuli.* An extension of the semi-structured observation procedure described above involves the attempt to assess reinforcer effectiveness in relation to behavior influence by presenting a particular stimulus event contingent upon the occurrence of a response on the part of the child in a given situation (Ferster & DeMyer, 1962; Kubany & Sloggett, 1973). This procedure is clearly closest to a laboratory analogue or laboratory definition of reinforcement and also to the definition of reinforcement that is likely to be most relevant from the standpoint of treatment. These types of assessment represent a miniature treatment situation in which there is a direct attempt to alter an ongoing response. The difference here, however, is that the responses that have been used tend to be analogue responses; that is, they may not be the responses of interest for the treatment program. Furthermore, in most instances, investigators have looked at the short-term effects of the stimulus events rather than at long-term changes.

An example of this type of assessment procedure, in which a simple marble-dropping task was used, is reported by Patterson and Fagot (1967). The child was initially observed during a baseline period in which he dropped marbles into two holes in a box. Following this baseline period, the parent, who was in the situation with the child, was told to use social reinforcement, that is, praise contingent upon a marble-dropping response in what was the nonpreferred hole during the baseline. Such a procedure gives a direct (but admittedly short-term) estimate of the social reinforcement properties of the parent. Presumably, if the number of marbles dropped into the nonpreferred hole increases with contingent parental approval and decreases subsequently when parental approval is withdrawn, a direct test of reinforcer effectiveness for this variable is obtained. In spite of the fact that such simple operant, as well as more complex analogue, assessments with children would be a potentially rich source for obtaining information about potential reinforcers in other situations, this type of procedure has not been frequently reported. This suggests that many behavioral practitioners in applied situations may shortcut their assessment of potential reinforcers by relying too heavily on interview-verbal report information, which is much more easily obtained, but may not be as strong a predictor of eventual behavioral change as more direct tests.

The ''Positive Reinforcement Observation Schedule (PROS)''

described by Bersoff and Moyer in Part IV represents an attempt to assess reinforcing events using a number of different methods and also to obtain reliability and validity information. The categories of positively reinforcing behaviors described are rated as such by teachers, are reliably observable, and have response-strengthening properties when presented contingently following behavior. This approach of multiple evaluation of the instrument offers a promising direction for future developments.

## ASSESSMENT OF REINFORCING EVENTS FOR ADULTS

The types of assessment used with adults have been similar to those reported above for children, with a lesser emphasis on second-party informants and direct observational measures (where the reactivity of observation is likely to be greater), and a greater emphasis on the use of self-observation procedures. Each of the types of procedures that have been used with adults is discussed separately below.

1. *Interviews.* The interview procedure is a frequently used assessment device for assessing potentially reinforcing events as they relate to the problematic behaviors of adults. The format in which an interview procedure may be used for motivational analyses has been given in the previous section and follows the outline presented by Kanfer and Saslow (see Part II). This model structures the information obtained by the interviewer along the lines of determining the pattern of consequences that typically follow the behaviors that represent the complaints or concerns reported by the client. The use of the interview provides sufficient flexibility so that the interviewer may be able to get some idea about the possible maintaining events for the problematic behaviors in question. Typically, the interviewer also attempts to obtain information from the client regarding his likes and dislikes. This provides the interviewer with preliminary information about possible events that may be included in the design of a treatment program.

2. *Reinforcement Survey Schedules.* A number of schedules have been described in which a range of activities is presented and the individual is asked to indicate his degree of enjoyment for each. Probably the two most frequently used schedules of this sort are the ''Reinforcement Survey Schedule'' (Cautela, 1972; Cautela & Kastenbaum, see paper 14) and the ''Pleasant Events Schedule'' (MacPhillamy & Lewinsohn, 1973). Both of these measures describe the individual's preferences for certain types of events, while not necessarily determining the actual frequency with

which the behavior occurs. So, for example, it might be reported that the individual enjoys sexual behavior very much, but the actual frequency of the behavior is not established. Some attempts have been made to modify the survey schedules to include frequency measures (McLean, 1970).

The Reinforcement Survey Schedule (RSS) was constructed through the selection of items on an a priori basis, and in this regard it is non-empirical. The construction of the Pleasant Events Schedule is more empirical in that university students were asked to generate events, experiences, and activities that they found to be pleasant, rewarding, or fun. In either case, however, the items reflect verbal preferences rather than a demonstration of functional effectiveness.

In spite of the fact that these verbal report measures would seem to have enormous clinical utility, there is relatively little reliability or validity information associated with their use. An exception to this is a number of studies (Kleinknecht, McCormick, & Thorndike, 1973; Thorndike & Kleinknecht, 1974) that have been done with Cautela and Kastenbaum's schedule. Kleinknecht, et al. (1973) demonstrated that stated preferences of college students on the RSS were fairly stable over a five-week period, and Thorndike and Kleinknecht (1974) have explored the use of cluster analysis of the RSS as a possible way of forming homogeneous reinforcer groupings that might be useful in the development of treatment programs.

The utility of the RSS has been supported in a number of studies. For example, Cautela (1970) reports the use of the schedule as an assessment device in a number of programs involving both covert (Cautela, Steffen, & Wish, 1970) and overt techniques. Cautela and Wisocki (1971) also report the use of the schedule in programs involving token economies (Herr, 1969), alcoholism (Keehn, Bloomfield, & Hug, 1970), and imaginal procedures with children (Krop, Calhoon, & Verrier, 1971).

In addition to the usefulness of reinforcement surveys for the identification of motivational variables in change programs, such schedules can also be used with both adults and children to identify possible areas for behavior change. For example, with some individuals (e.g., depressives) the absence of a variety of reinforcing activities may be part of their behavioral difficulties. Consequently, these measures may be useful in the identification and designation of treatment goals.

A factor to consider in the use of reinforcement survey schedules is that the items on the schedule may not indicate the actual maintaining events for the problematic behaviors. This does not play down the importance of such scales in assessment, but it does point up the need for the behavior therapist to recognize that the potentially reinforcing events as indicated by the person's response to the scales may or may not relate to the pattern of reinforcing events in the natural environment that serve to control and maintain problematic behavior.

3. *Direct Observation.* Direct observation for the assessment of potential reinforcers has been used less frequently for adults than for children. Presumably, adults are better able to report on events that affect them and are also more likely to show reactive effects to the presence of an observer. Some investigators (McLean, 1975; Wills, Weiss, & Patterson, 1974) have developed analogues for obtaining direct measures of marriage partners dealing with conflict and/or problem-solving situations. Such measures may provide information regarding the pattern of aversive consequences and potential positive reinforcers that might be related to the problematic dyadic relationship.

4. *Self-Observation and Daily Records.* Self-observation procedures have been used fairly extensively, both as a change procedure and for monitoring change (Thoresen & Mahoney, 1974; Mahoney & Thoresen, 1974). Such self-observation approaches have been used less frequently for identifying reinforcers, although they could be used for this purpose. Especially when self-monitoring involves daily activity schedules, there are possibilities for identifying reinforcers based upon those things that the client spends most of his time doing.

5. *Exposure to Reinforcing Stimuli.* Exposure to reinforcing stimuli has taken two forms. Under one condition, the individual is exposed to a stimulus, and a direct measure of his reaction is taken. Studies that expose individuals to sexually arousing stimuli, to fearful stimuli (Lang & Lazovik, 1963; Miller & Nawas, 1970) as in the case of behavioral avoidance tests, or to other preferred stimuli, such as alcohol, with concomitant measure of drinking behavior being taken (Briddell & Nathan, 1975), would fall into this category. The second set of procedures has involved direct exposure to selected events administered contingently on selected client behavior (Robinson & Lewinsohn, 1973; Zifferblatt, 1972). This procedure is closest to the laboratory definition of reinforcement and has been applied with alcoholics. Weiss (1969) discusses the use of such operant measures in the assessment of potential reinforcers. It is possible that such measures may be useful in predicting treatment success; however, their use has been quite limited.

# 13

## Identifying Reinforcers for Children: A Children's Reinforcement Survey

*Paul W. Clement*
*Robert C. Richard*

The Children's Reinforcement Survey is presented as one tool of many to be used in performing a functional analysis of a child's behavior. This chapter covers technical considerations regarding the Survey, its weaknesses and its strengths, and information apart from reinforcers which may be of interest to the clinician.

Many kinds of information are needed in a comprehensive behavioral analysis, and Kanfer and Saslow (1965, 1969) provided an extensive list of the types of data which should be gathered. A major component in their outline is a "motivational analysis," and the key element in the motivational analysis is "incentives" (that is, potential reinforcers). In 1967 Cautela and Kastenbaum (1967) published their Reinforcement Survey Schedule for identifying incentives. Since their Survey focused on reinforcers primarily for adults, there was need to develop a similar tool for children.

Preliminary work on developing such a device began at the Child Development Center in late 1968. Refinement and field testing took place throughout 1969 and the first half of 1970. During this period of development two behavioral publications appeared which also dealt with identifying reinforcers for children.

Preparation of the Children's Reinforcement Survey was supported in part by grant MH 14395-03 from the National Institute of Mental Health, United States Public Health Service. The junior author is now affiliated with RAFA Counseling Associates, 3490 Buskirk Avenue, Pleasant Hill, California.

In their book, *Behavior Modification in the Natural Environment,* Tharp and Wetzel (1969, pp. 225-226) presented a Mediator-Reinforcer Incomplete Blank. Their Blank used an incomplete sentences format which appears most appropriate for school-age children who can write. An interviewer, however, can record a child's oral responses to the sentence stems. There are 34 basic stems on the Blank, and at the very end there is space for the child to rank his/her reinforcers by preference.

A short time later Holland (1970) published An Interview Guide for Behavioral Counseling with Parents. His section on "positive and negative reinforcers" provided general guidelines for data gathering, rather than a fixed format.

In October 1970 the Children's Reinforcement Survey was printed by Clement and Richard. Their Survey was designed for use by an informant, such as a parent, or by the target child. The Children's Reinforcement Survey was designed as one of several tools that may be used to perform a functional analysis of a child's behavior. The other tools[1] that are routinely used at Fuller's Child Development Center are (1) a Face Sheet which provides identifying data on the child and his/her family; (2) Release of Information forms; (3) two copies of the Devereux Child Behavior Rating Scale (Spivack & Spotts, 1966), one copy for each parent to fill out independently; (4) a Devereux Elementary School Behavior Rating Scale (Spivack & Swift, 1967), for the child's teacher; (5) a Parents' Evaluation of Child's Behavior form for identifying the child's specific behavioral excesses, deficits, and assets; and (6) a Medical Evaluation Form to be completed by the pediatrician.

These preceding tools are normally completed before the initial interview takes place with the parents. Interviews are used to elicit additional data for treatment planning and evaluation. In addition to an extensive use of interviews, direct observations of the child's behavior in the natural environment are basic sources of data for virtually all cases. These observations are normally used within the context of an experimental analysis of the child's behavior using an ABAB or multiple-baseline design (see Leitenberg, 1973, for examples).

The Children's Reinforcement Survey is of primary help in identifying potentially reinforcing events that may be explored within an experimental analysis of the child's behavior. A sample Survey[2] appears in Figure 1.

---

[1] Samples of items (1), (2),(5), and (6) may be obtained from the senior author.

[2] Figure 1 may be reproduced *as is* without obtaining prior approval of the authors.

# CHILDREN'S REINFORCEMENT SURVEY

Paul W. Clement and Robert C. Richard
Child Development Center
Graduate School of Psychology
Fuller Theological Seminary
Pasadena, California

Child's name _____   Date of rating _____

Birthdate _____   Grade _____

Name of person filling out this survey

What is your relationship to the child (i. e., mother, father, teacher,

etc.)?_____

### INTRODUCTION

Many psychologists believe that one of the best ways to understand the personality of a child is to identify the people, places, things, and activities to which he is attracted. Such people, places, things, and activities are called reinforcers. Behavior that is followed by a reinforcer will occur more frequently in the future. If we want to teach a child new behaviors or if we want to strengthen old behaviors, we should follow these behaviors with a reinforcer. This survey has been designed to help parents, teachers, and child workers to identify the more effective reinforcers for their children.

First Printing - October, 1970

*FIGURE 1.    Sample of the Children's Reinforcement Survey.*

A.  PEOPLE

List below the 10 people with whom your child spends the most time each week. Put the person with whom he spends the most time after "1". Put the person with whom he spends the second most time after "2", and so on. In making the list, consider brothers, sisters, parents, relatives, playmates, etc.

1. _____     6. _____

2. _____     7. _____

3. _____     8. _____

4. _____     9. _____

5. _____    10. _____


There may be other people (children or adults) with whom you think he would like to spend more time each week, but doesn't get to. List below any such persons with whom you feel your child would like to spend more time than he presently gets to.

1. _____     4. _____

2. _____     5. _____

3. _____     6. _____


B.  PLACES

List below the 10 places where your child spends the most time each week. Put the place he spends the most time after "1", second most time after "2", etc. In making the list consider such places as bedroom, family room, kitchen, back yard, playground, classroom, baseball field, etc.

1. _____     6. _____

2. _____     7. _____

3. _____     8. _____

4. _____     9. _____

5. _____    10. _____

There may be other places where he would like to spend more time, but doesn't get to. List such places below.

1. _____  4. _____

2. _____  5. _____

3. _____  6. _____

C.  THINGS

List below the 10 things with which your child spends the most time each week. Put them in order beginning with the thing with which he spends the most time. In making the list consider such things as specific toys (identify each kind), pets, books, puzzles, mechanical objects, musical instruments, bicycle, etc.

1. _____  6. _____

2. _____  7. _____

3. _____  8. _____

4. _____  9. _____

5. _____  10. _____

List below the things your child does not own or to which he does not have ready access which he would most like to have.

1. _____  4. _____

2. _____  5. _____

3. _____  6. _____

List below your child's 10 best-liked foods and drinks. Include candy, desserts, and other treats in the list. Record the items according to preference beginning with the most preferred first. Include items which you may not allow your child to have very often, but which fall high on his list of preferences.

1. _____   6. _____

2. _____   7. _____

3. _____   8. _____

4. _____   9. _____

5. _____   10. _____

D. ACTIVITIES

List below the 10 activities on which your child spends the most time. Put them in order according to their frequency. By activities, we mean such things as doing homework, working puzzles, going to movies, reading, watching sports, playing sports, watching TV, singing, dancing, playing a musical instrument, hiking or walking, fishing, swimming, camping, riding a bike, sleeping, taking a bath, talking to other people, going to church, going shopping, being alone by himself, etc.

1. _____   6. _____

2. _____   7. _____

3. _____   8. _____

4. _____   9. _____

5. _____   10. _____

List below any activities in which you think he would like to engage more frequently than he presently does.

1. _____   4. _____

2. _____   5. _____

3. _____   6. _____

## Technical Considerations

No manual has been written to accompany the Children's Reinforcement Survey, but it has been used for a few thousand cases by dozens of clinicians in many agencies across the United States during the past few years. Data on the ways different clinicians and researchers have used the survey have not been reported. There are no standardized procedures for administering and scoring it; no one has attempted to establish norms for the reinforcers that get listed.

The Survey is worded so that it is appropriate for children of any age, provided that an informed adult is available to fill in the blanks. Most children are able to fill in the Survey on their own by the age of nine or ten; however, the authors have tended to ask the parents to complete the survey for children through age eleven or twelve.

*Validity.* No formal validity studies (in the usual psychometric sense) have been done on the Children's Reinforcement Survey. However, since it is usually used within the context of an experimental analysis of behavior, every case in which the Survey has been used has provided a partial validity study on some of the data produced in the Survey. These data which come out of the Survey and out of the applied behavioral analyses speak to all three of the more common forms of validity: (1) content validity, (2) criterion-related validity, and (3) construct validity.

*Reliability.* As with validity, no formal reliability studies on the Children's Reinforcement Survey have been reported. Since there is a single form of the Survey and because of its contents, internal consistency is not a very relevant concept concerning the reliability of the Survey. Comparisons of parents' or children's responses over time would be the more appropriate way to measure the reliability of the Survey, but such a study is yet to be done. Inter-rater reliability would also be easy to determine by having mothers and fathers independently fill out the survey and then calculating their level of agreement.

## Discussion

*Weaknesses.* The Children's Reinforcement Survey only provides a list of potential positive reinforcers: it does not identify negative reinforcers. This particular deficiency in the Survey occurs, however, by design. One of the assumptions underlying the Survey is that most contingency management programs for children will be based upon positive reinforcement and/or punishment Type II (e.g., time out or response cost) rather than on negative reinforcement and/or punishment Type I.

Other shortcomings include the following: (1) There is no manual accompanying the Survey; therefore, the user receives minimal guidance in how to administer the Survey and no direction in how to interpret the data obtained. (2) As previously indicated, no formal reliability or validity data have been published on this tool. (3) There is only one form of the Survey. (4) No normative data are available on responses to the items in the survey; however, it was designed for gathering idiographic rather than nomothetic information. (5) When the parents, rather than the target child, fill out the Survey, the psychological consultant may miss items that the child wants but has not made public. Obviously an interview with the child would increase the chances of obtaining such data.

Although the Children's Reinforcement Survey may identify a child's major reinforcers, it does not provide information on how the child perceives the relationship between his own actions and the production of positive reinforcers. A large literature has accumulated on perceived "locus of control" of reinforcement, with Rotter's work (Rotter, 1966) being the most important. Knowing where a child falls on the internal-external (I-E) dimension of perceived locus of control of reinforcement may make a difference in how he responds to a particular reinforcer and treatment program.

*Strengths.* In addition to having a number of deficiencies, the Survey has several strong points: (1) It is a flexible tool which can be used by a wide range of informants (e.g., target child, parents, teacher, psychiatric technician, child peers, etc.) and in a wide range of settings (e.g., home, school, residential treatment setting, etc.). (2) It is fast, requiring only 10-15 minutes to complete. (3) It is inexpensive. (4) No technical sophistication is needed to fill in the Survey. (5) Use of the survey saves consulting time, thereby reducing the cost of professional services to the child's family. (6) The Survey is empirically oriented and helps focus all concerned parties on observable events. (7) Closely related to the preceding point is the fact that the Survey's data are usually directly related to overt behaviors. Use of the Survey encourages an experimental analysis of these relationships.

*Miscellaneous points.* Not only is the Survey useful in identifying reinforcers, but it may also provide additional kinds of information. For example, not all parents fill in all of the blanks in the Survey; therefore, the extent to which parents complete the items may be used as a predictor of later parental cooperation in carrying out the treatment program. Also what the parent doesn't say may carry significance, such as when the parent lists no playmates under "People" but the clinician knows from other sources that the target child spends a few hours each day with selected friends. Such a discrepancy in data may indicate that the parent is minimally involved with and informed about his/her own child. One method for identifying such discrepancies is to have the parents and the target child fill out separate Surveys.

Just as with the parents, the child's ability to fill in the Survey may provide an index to his/her ability to participate in planning his/her own treatment.

Since behavioral treatment programs with children are usually (or at least partially) conducted in the natural environment, the ''People'' section of the Survey is useful for identifying potential therapeutic agents. The assumption is that, other things being equal, the more available person is a better potential therapeutic agent than the less available person.

The prospective user of the Children's Reinforcement Survey should keep in mind that it may identify reinforcers but it does not identify *reinforcement contingencies* in the child's natural environment. The determination of such contingencies usually necessitates an experimental analysis of the child's behavior.

In addition to, and sometimes as part of, such an experimental analysis, several data-gathering procedures are used at the Child Development Center in addition to those already mentioned: (1) behavioral rehearsal and role playing, (2) observations of contrived social situations using family members and/or child peers, (3) video recording, (4) audio recordings, (5) monitoring of autonomic and related functions, (6) self-observation, and (7) testing with standardized psychometric tools.

In using any of these approaches we admonish ourselves to be as simple-minded as possible, creative, sensitive to the special circumstances facing the child and his/her family, and focused on what can be determined empirically. As with any tool, however, the Children's Reinforcement Survey is only as good as the person using it. Although the ability to describe behaviors in simple terms is a prerequisite for being an effective behavior modifier, being stupid is not. The Survey is intended for use by professionals who have solid grasp of the experimental analysis of behavior.

## REFERENCES

Cautela, J. R., & Kastenbaum, R. A Reinforcement Survey Schedule for use in therapy, training, and research. *Psychological Reports,* 1967, *20,* 1115-1130.

Holland, C. J. An interview guide for behavioral counseling with parents. *Behavior Therapy,* 1970, *1,* 70-79

Kanfer, F. H., & Saslow, G. Behavioral analysis: An alternative to diagnostic classification. *Archives of General Psychiatry,* 1965, *12,* 529-538.

Kanfer, F. H., & Saslow, G. Behavioral diagnosis. In C. M. Franks (Ed.), *Behavior therapy: Appraisal and status.* New York: McGraw-Hill, 1969.

Leitenberg, H. The use of single-case methodology in psychotherapy research. *Journal of Abnormal Psychology,* 1973, *82,* 87-101.

Rotter, J. B. Generalized expectancies for internal versus external control of reinforcement. *Psychological Monographs,* 1966, *80* (1, Whole No. 609).

Spivack, G., & Spotts, J. *Devereux Child Behavior Rating Scale manual.* Devon, Pa.: Devereux Foundation, 1966.

Spivack, G., & Swift, M. *Devereux Elementary School Behavior Rating Scale manual.* Devon, Pa.: Devereux Foundation, 1967.

Tharp, R. G., & Wetzel, R. J. *Behavior modification in the natural environment.* New York: Academic Press, 1969.

# 14

## A Reinforcement Survey Schedule for Use in Therapy, Training, and Research

*Joseph R. Cautela*
*Robert Kastenbaum*

The assumptions and procedures of behavior therapy differ in many crucial aspects from traditional approaches (Eysenck, 1960; Wolpe, 1958). However, in one aspect, psychotherapy based on reciprocal inhibition agrees with a number of therapeutic models. Both the more conventional models and the reciprocal inhibition approach place great emphasis on the concept of anxiety as an explanatory construct. Wolpe (1958, p. 33) defines neurosis as "... any persistent habit of unadaptive behavior acquired by learning in a physiologically normal organism. Anxiety is usually the central constituent of this behavior, being invariably present in the causal situations." Anxiety is reduced by the application of the reciprocal inhibition procedures. These procedures are based upon the assumption that, "if a response antagonistic to anxiety can be made to occur in the presence of anxiety-provoking stimuli so that it is accompanied by a complete or partial suppression of the anxiety responses, then the bond between these stimuli and the anxiety responses will be weakened" (Wolpe, 1958, p. 71).

As can be seen from the above description of neurotic behavior it is important for the therapist employing reciprocal inhibition procedures to identify the stimuli that precede anxiety responses. What is needed is a full picture of the stimulus antecedents of the neurotic reactions. This

Reprinted with permission of author and publishers: Cautela, J. R., & Kastenbaum, R. A Reinforcement Survey Schedule for use in therapy, training, and research. *Psychological Reports*, 1967, *20*, 1115-1130.

The work reported here was supported in part by USPHS Grant MHO-1520, Cushing Hospital, Framingham, Massachusetts.

picture should not only include the identification of the stimuli but also the extent of the anxiety reaction. Many times it is arduous and time-consuming to obtain a total view of the anxiety components by use of interview procedures. Consequently fear survey schedules (Geer, 1965; Wolpe & Lang, 1964) have been developed for use by reciprocal inhibition therapists.

In practice, one often finds that it is also necessary to develop *new* behavior (approach responses) as well as to eliminate unadaptive fear responses. This leads to the necessity for using both reciprocal inhibition and operant conditioning techniques in dealing with many individual cases. As indicated above, reciprocal inhibition procedures require the identification of stimuli which precede anxiety responses. In the employment of operant conditioning techniques it is also important to identify possible reinforcing stimuli. Unless reinforcing stimuli are identified, it is exceedingly difficult to shape new responses. This is equally true concerning the treatment of neurotics in a private clinical setting and the rehabilitation of institutionalized patients.

In operant therapy the crucial procedure is the manipulation of reinforcing stimuli to extinguish unadaptive behavior or shape new responses. Often one finds there are classes of stimuli which seem reinforcing to many individuals, such as smiling and paying attention. There are also idiosyncratic reinforcers, i.e., stimuli that are especially reinforcing to one particular individual. For one person, jazz music may have some reinforcing value; for another person classical music may be reinforcing and jazz music aversive. It would be quite helpful for use in combined reciprocal inhibition and operant conditioning therapeutic approaches to employ a Reinforcement Survey Schedule to identify possible reinforcing stimuli together with their relative reinforcing values. Most of the behavior therapy done with psychotics has employed operant procedures (Ayllon & Michael, 1959) with some success. Operant procedures should also be promising for use with other institutionalized groups such as geriatric patients and juvenile offenders. At present the authors are exploring the use of behavior therapy with geriatric patients and one of the authors (Cautela) is using behavior therapy techniques with delinquents in both group and individual settings.

While the Reinforcement Survey Schedule (RSS) offered here was developed primarily within a behavior therapy model, one need not exclude other theoretical frameworks and empirical applications. It is often assumed, for example, that behavior therapy and developmental theory make a number of mutually incompatible assumptions and have very little subject matter in common. But the RSS can be employed to advantage in either conceptual framework. The RSS is also intended to be useful to investigators who favor an eclectic viewpoint. Although terminology may differ from theory to theory, most psychologists recognize the importance of identifying those stimuli which are associated with the probability of response occurrence. In this paper we are chiefly concerned with those stimuli which can be used to evoke adaptive responses in contrast to stimuli which tend to evoke maladaptive responses (anxiety stimuli).

## Description of the Reinforcement Survey Schedule

The RSS is divided into four major sections (see Table 1). In the first three sections the respondent is asked to rate items on a five-point scale representing the degree to which the stimuli give joy or other pleasurable feelings. The extreme points of the scale are "not at all" and "very much."

Section I consists of items that actually can be presented to an *S* or client in many conventional settings. Thus, for example, item one, "Eating," includes six specific kinds of food which a therapist might present to his client in the course of a session. There are 10 items in Section I, some of which are further subdivided. The total number of rating decisions in Section I is 33. An attempt has been made to provide a comprehensive sampling of areas of possible pleasure within the scope of a relatively few items. The items in Section I can be presented in three ways: (1) actually presenting the objects themselves; (2) presenting a facsimile of the object, for example, a picture of a beautiful woman or handsome man; (3) presenting the objects in imagination.

Section II consists of items which, for most practical purposes, can be presented only through facsimile or imagination. Usually these items will be presented in imagination. There are 44 items in Section II, eight of which have subcategories. The total number of rating decisions is 106. It is obvious that the range of possible stimuli is greatly increased when we include imagination as a means of manipulating stimuli. It is important to note that both reciprocal inhibition procedures and new operant approaches employ the manipulation of covert stimuli (Homme, 1965) as a useful way to influence behavior; also, developmental-field theory gives particular emphasis to the structure of inner experience as a way of evaluating the level and style of functioning (Kastenbaum, 1965, 1966a).

Although it would be possible to develop a scale with fewer sub-items, it was considered useful to provide information that is reasonably specific so there will be less of a gap between RSS rating and its clinical implementation. For example, it may be only moderately helpful to know a person enjoys reading very much, but quite helpful to know the particular kind of reading that is especially enjoyable, e.g. *True Confessions* or science fiction. Section II items include both active and spectator pursuits, solitary and interpersonal activities. These items en-

## TABLE 1.   Reinforcement Survey Schedule

The items in this questionnaire refer to things and experiences that may give joy or other pleasurable feelings. Check each item in the column that describes how much pleasure it gives you nowadays.

|  | Not at all | A little | A fair amount | Much | Very much |
|---|---|---|---|---|---|
| **SECTION I** | | | | | |
| 1. *Eating* | | | | | |
| a. Ice cream | ___ | ___ | ___ | ___ | ___ |
| b. Candy | ___ | ___ | ___ | ___ | ___ |
| c. Fruit | ___ | ___ | ___ | ___ | ___ |
| d. Pastry | ___ | ___ | ___ | ___ | ___ |
| e. Nuts | ___ | ___ | ___ | ___ | ___ |
| f. Cookies | ___ | ___ | ___ | ___ | ___ |
| 2. *Beverages* | | | | | |
| a. Water | ___ | ___ | ___ | ___ | ___ |
| b. Milk | ___ | ___ | ___ | ___ | ___ |
| c. Soft drink | ___ | ___ | ___ | ___ | ___ |
| d. Tea | ___ | ___ | ___ | ___ | ___ |
| e. Coffee | ___ | ___ | ___ | ___ | ___ |
| 3. *Alcoholic beverages* | | | | | |
| a. Beer | ___ | ___ | ___ | ___ | ___ |
| b. Wine | ___ | ___ | ___ | ___ | ___ |
| c. Hard liquor | ___ | ___ | ___ | ___ | ___ |
| 4. *Beautiful women* | ___ | ___ | ___ | ___ | ___ |
| 5. *Handsome men* | ___ | ___ | ___ | ___ | ___ |
| 6. *Solving problems* | | | | | |
| a. Crossword puzzles | ___ | ___ | ___ | ___ | ___ |
| b. Mathematical problems | ___ | ___ | ___ | ___ | ___ |
| c. Figuring out how something works | ___ | ___ | ___ | ___ | ___ |
| 7. *Listening to music* | | | | | |
| a. Classical | ___ | ___ | ___ | ___ | ___ |
| b. Western country | ___ | ___ | ___ | ___ | ___ |
| c. Jazz | ___ | ___ | ___ | ___ | ___ |
| d. Show tunes | ___ | ___ | ___ | ___ | ___ |
| e. Rhythm & blues | ___ | ___ | ___ | ___ | ___ |
| f. Rock & roll | ___ | ___ | ___ | ___ | ___ |
| g. Folk | ___ | ___ | ___ | ___ | ___ |
| h. Popular | ___ | ___ | ___ | ___ | ___ |
| 8. *Nude men* | ___ | ___ | ___ | ___ | ___ |

TABLE 1.  *(Contd.)*

|  | Not at all | A little | A fair amount | Much | Very much |
|---|---|---|---|---|---|
| 9. *Nude women* | —— | —— | —— | —— | —— |
| 10. *Animals* | | | | | |
| a. Dogs | —— | —— | —— | —— | —— |
| b. Cats | —— | —— | —— | —— | —— |
| c. Horses | —— | —— | —— | —— | —— |
| d. Birds | —— | —— | —— | —— | —— |

SECTION II

| | Not at all | A little | A fair amount | Much | Very much |
|---|---|---|---|---|---|
| 11. *Watching sports* | | | | | |
| a. Football | —— | —— | —— | —— | —— |
| b. Baseball | —— | —— | —— | —— | —— |
| c. Basketball | —— | —— | —— | —— | —— |
| d. Track | —— | —— | —— | —— | —— |
| e. Golf | —— | —— | —— | —— | —— |
| f. Swimming | —— | —— | —— | —— | —— |
| g. Running | —— | —— | —— | —— | —— |
| h. Tennis | —— | —— | —— | —— | —— |
| i. Pool | —— | —— | —— | —— | —— |
| j. Other | —— | —— | —— | —— | —— |
| 12. *Reading* | | | | | |
| a. Adventure | —— | —— | —— | —— | —— |
| b. Mystery | —— | —— | —— | —— | —— |
| c. Famous people | —— | —— | —— | —— | —— |
| d. Poetry | —— | —— | —— | —— | —— |
| e. Travel | —— | —— | —— | —— | —— |
| f. True confessions | —— | —— | —— | —— | —— |
| g. Politics & history | —— | —— | —— | —— | —— |
| h. How to-do-it | —— | —— | —— | —— | —— |
| i. Humor | —— | —— | —— | —— | —— |
| j. Comic books | —— | —— | —— | —— | —— |
| k. Love Stories | —— | —— | —— | —— | —— |
| l. Spiritual | —— | —— | —— | —— | —— |
| m. Sexy | —— | —— | —— | —— | —— |
| n. Sports | —— | —— | —— | —— | —— |
| o. Medicine | —— | —— | —— | —— | —— |
| p. Science | —— | —— | —— | —— | —— |
| q. Newspapers | —— | —— | —— | —— | —— |
| 13. *Looking at interesting buildings* | —— | —— | —— | —— | —— |

*TABLE 1.  (Contd.)*

|  | Not at all | A little | A fair amount | Much | Very much |
|---|---|---|---|---|---|
| 14. *Looking at beautiful scenery* | —— | —— | —— | —— | —— |
| 15. *T.V., movies, or radio* | —— | —— | —— | —— | —— |
| 16. *Like to sing* | —— | —— | —— | —— | —— |
| a. Alone | —— | —— | —— | —— | |
| b. With Others | —— | —— | —— | —— | |
| 17. *Like to dance* | | | | | |
| a. Ballroom | —— | —— | —— | —— | —— |
| b. Discotheque | —— | —— | —— | —— | —— |
| c. Ballet or interpretive | —— | —— | —— | —— | —— |
| d. Square dancing | —— | —— | —— | —— | —— |
| e. Folk dancing | —— | —— | —— | —— | —— |
| 18. *Performing on a musical instrument* | —— | —— | —— | —— | —— |
| 19. *Playing sports* | | | | | |
| a. Football | —— | —— | —— | —— | —— |
| b. Baseball | —— | —— | —— | —— | —— |
| c. Basketball | —— | —— | —— | —— | —— |
| d. Track & field | —— | —— | —— | —— | —— |
| e. Golf | —— | —— | —— | —— | —— |
| f. Swimming | —— | —— | —— | —— | —— |
| g. Running | —— | —— | —— | —— | —— |
| h. Tennis | —— | —— | —— | —— | —— |
| i. Pool | —— | —— | —— | —— | —— |
| j. Boxing | —— | —— | —— | —— | —— |
| k. Judo or karate | —— | —— | —— | —— | —— |
| l. Fishing | —— | —— | —— | —— | —— |
| m. Skin diving | —— | —— | —— | —— | —— |
| n. Auto or cycle racing | —— | —— | —— | —— | —— |
| o. Hunting | —— | —— | —— | —— | —— |
| p. Skiing | —— | —— | —— | —— | —— |
| 20. *Shopping* | | | | | |
| a. Clothes | —— | —— | —— | —— | —— |
| b. Furniture | —— | —— | —— | —— | —— |
| c. Auto parts & supply | —— | —— | —— | —— | —— |
| d. Appliances | —— | —— | —— | —— | —— |
| e. Food | —— | —— | —— | —— | —— |
| f. New car | —— | —— | —— | —— | —— |
| g. New place to live | —— | —— | —— | —— | —— |
| h. Sports equipment | —— | —— | —— | —— | —— |

*TABLE 1.  (Contd.)*

|  | Not at all | A little | A fair amount | Much | Very much |
|---|---|---|---|---|---|
| 21. Gardening | —— | —— | —— | —— | —— |
| 22. Playing cards | —— | —— | —— | —— | —— |
| 23. Hiking or walking | —— | —— | —— | —— | —— |
| 24. Completing a difficult job | —— | —— | —— | —— | —— |
| 25. Camping | —— | —— | —— | —— | —— |
| 26. Sleeping | —— | —— | —— | —— | —— |
| 27. Taking a bath | —— | —— | —— | —— | —— |
| 28. Taking a shower | —— | —— | —— | —— | —— |
| 29. Being right | | | | | |
|    a. Guessing what somebody is going to do | —— | —— | —— | —— | —— |
|    b. In an argument | —— | —— | —— | —— | —— |
|    c. About your work | —— | —— | —— | —— | —— |
|    d. On a bet | —— | —— | —— | —— | —— |
| 30. Being praised | | | | | |
|    a. About your appearance | —— | —— | —— | —— | —— |
|    b. About your work | —— | —— | —— | —— | —— |
|    c. About your hobbies | —— | —— | —— | —— | —— |
|    d. About your physical strength | —— | —— | —— | —— | —— |
|    e. About your athletic ability | —— | —— | —— | —— | —— |
|    f. About your mind | —— | —— | —— | —— | —— |
|    g. About your personality | —— | —— | —— | —— | —— |
|    h. About your moral strength | —— | —— | —— | —— | —— |
|    i. About your understanding of others | —— | —— | —— | —— | —— |
| 31. Having people seek you out for company | —— | —— | —— | —— | —— |
| 32. Flirting | —— | —— | —— | —— | —— |
| 33. Having somebody flirt with you | —— | —— | —— | —— | —— |
| 34. Talking with people who like you | —— | —— | —— | —— | —— |
| 35. Making somebody happy | —— | —— | —— | —— | —— |
| 36. Babies | —— | —— | —— | —— | —— |
| 37. Children | —— | —— | —— | —— | —— |
| 38. Old men | —— | —— | —— | —— | —— |
| 39. Old women | —— | —— | —— | —— | —— |

## TABLE 1.    (Contd.)

|                                        | Not at all | A little | A fair amount | Much | Very much |
|----------------------------------------|:----------:|:--------:|:-------------:|:----:|:---------:|
| 40. Having people ask your advice      | ___ | ___ | ___ | ___ | ___ |
| 41. Watching other people              | ___ | ___ | ___ | ___ | ___ |
| 42. Somebody smiling at you            | ___ | ___ | ___ | ___ | ___ |
| 43. Making love                        | ___ | ___ | ___ | ___ | ___ |
| 44. Happy people                       | ___ | ___ | ___ | ___ | ___ |
| 45. Being close to an attractive man   | ___ | ___ | ___ | ___ | ___ |
| 46. Being close to an attractive woman | ___ | ___ | ___ | ___ | ___ |
| 47. Talking about the opposite sex     | ___ | ___ | ___ | ___ | ___ |
| 48. Talking to friends                 | ___ | ___ | ___ | ___ | ___ |
| 49. Being perfect                      | ___ | ___ | ___ | ___ | ___ |
| 50. Winning a bet                      | ___ | ___ | ___ | ___ | ___ |
| 51. Being in church or temple          | ___ | ___ | ___ | ___ | ___ |
| 52. Saying prayers                     | ___ | ___ | ___ | ___ | ___ |
| 53. Having somebody pray for you       | ___ | ___ | ___ | ___ | ___ |
| 54. Peace and quiet                    | ___ | ___ | ___ | ___ | ___ |

### SECTION III— Situations I Would Like To Be In

How much would you enjoy being in each of the following situations?

1. You have just completed a difficult job. Your superior comes by and praises you highly for "a job well done." He also makes it clear that such good work is going to be rewarded very soon.

not at all (  )     a little (  )     a fair amount (  )     much (  )     very much (  )

2. You are at a lively party. Somebody walks across the room to you, smiles in a friendly way, and says, "I'm glad to meet you. I've heard so many good things about you. Do you have a moment to talk?"

not at all (  )     a little (  )     a fair amount (  )     much (  )     very much (  )

3. You have just led your team to victory. An old friend comes over and says, "You played a terrific game. Let me treat you to dinner and drinks."

not at all (  )     a little (  )     a fair amount (  )     much (  )     very much (  )

4. You are walking along a mountain pathway with your dog by your side. You notice attractive lakes, streams, flowers, and trees. You think to yourself, "It's great to be alive on a day like this, and to have the opportunity to wander alone out in the countryside."

not at all (  )     a little (  )     a fair amount (  )     much (  )     very much (  )

5. You are sitting by the fireplace with your loved one. Music is playing softly on

the phonograph. Your loved one gives you a tender glance and you respond with a kiss. You think to yourself how wonderful it is to care for someone and have somebody care for you.'

not at all ( )  a little ( )  a fair amount ( )  much ( )  very much ( )

6. As you are leaving your place of worship, a woman turns to you and says, "I want you to know how much we appreciate all that you did for us in our time of trouble and misery. Everything is wonderful now. I'll always remember you in my prayers."

not at all ( )  a little ( )  a fair amount ( )  much ( )  very much ( )

A. Now place a check next to the number of the situation that appeals to you most.

## SECTION IV

List things you do or think about more than:

| 5 | 10 | 15 | 20 times a day? |
|---|----|----|----------------|
| _____ | _____ | _____ | _____ |
| _____ | _____ | _____ | _____ |
| _____ | _____ | _____ | _____ |
| _____ | _____ | _____ | _____ |
| _____ | _____ | _____ | _____ |
| _____ | _____ | _____ | _____ |
| _____ | _____ | _____ | _____ |
| _____ | _____ | _____ | _____ |

compass objects, people and psychological states (such as "being perfect"). Some items portray the respondent in an initiating role with respect to other people, while other items portray the person in a recipient role.

Section III differs from the preceding section in that it presents *situations* rather than discrete objects and activities. While experimental procedures often focus upon a single reinforcing stimulus, it is often the case in an individual's daily life that he is confronted with a combination of stimuli and responses from a variety of sources. Most behavior in daily life occurs in "situations." It is, therefore, considered useful to sample a variety of situations of psychosocial fields for their possible reinforcing value, as will be seen below. The analysis of response contingency in relationship to field situations is a particularly important meeting place for behavior theory and developmental-field theory. Section III presents six brief "Situations I would like to be in." Each situation is constructed from at least three specific reinforcing stimuli. For example, Item 1 combines the satisfaction of having completed a difficult job, praise and appreciation from a superior, and a promise of future reward. Table 2 details the particular reinforcing stimuli for each situation in Section III. As will be seen in Table 2, each situation was constructed to convey a distinct theme.

*TABLE 2.   Percentage of Extreme Responses for Situational Themes and Respective Components for Section III.*

| Situation no. | Theme | M of specific reinforcers | | Specific reinforcers | |
|---|---|---|---|---|---|
| 1. | Occupational Success 80.6 | 74.6 | (24)* (30/b) | Completion of difficult job Praise: About your work | 69.1 80.0 |
| 2. | Favorable Social Attention 70.3 | 65.1 | (42) (31) (30) | Somebody smiling at you Somebody seeking you out for company Heard so many good things about you | 80.6 56.4 58.4 |
| 3. | Successful Competitive Performance 64.8 | 44.4 | (19) (30/e) (31) (3) | Playing a sport Praise: About your athletic ability Sought out for company Promise of food (1) and drink | 30.2 43.6 86.6 35.8 |
| 4. | Pleasure from Nature 69.1 | 56.1 | (23) (14) (10a) (54) | Hiking or walking Looking at beautiful scenery Accompanied by your dog Peace and quiet | 38.2 70.3 54.5 61.2 |
| 5. | Loving Intimacy 91.5 | 66.5 | (46) (7) (43) | Close to your loved one Listening to music Making love | 74.5 40.7 84.2 |
| 6. | Faith and Good Works 51.5 | 51.3 | (51) (35) (53) | Coming from place of worship Making somebody happy, and helping them Having somebody pray for you | 23.6 92.1 38.2 |

*Numbers in parentheses refer to specific reinforcers that are also presented as separate items in Sections I or II of the RSS.

After responding to each situation separately, $S$ is asked to indicate which situation appeals to him the most. From the nature of the items in Section III, it appears obvious that these items will usually be presented in imagination.

In Section IV, $S$ is asked to list the things he does or thinks about more than certain designated frequencies from 5 to 20. In practice, we have found that this section may require some elaboration with particular populations. For example, with a number of juvenile offenders the authors found it necessary to give illustrations and examples. This section was included so that Premack's *Differential Probability Hypothesis* (1959) may be used to manipulate behavior. The *Premack Differential Probability Hypothesis* states that if two responses occur with different probabilities, the response with the highest probability can be used to reinforce the response with the lower probability. For example, if someone smokes 40 cigarettes a day, ''high probability,'' smoking may be made contingent upon reading a page in a book, ''low probability.'' These responses may include thoughts, activities such as walking, aggressive behavior, or derogatory remarks made to oneself. If these responses are available to the therapist or researcher they can be used to increase the probability of behavior that has a low frequency. In the geriatric population, putting one's feet on the floor can be a low probability response which has to occur before the person takes a drink of water. This section can be particularly valuable in teaching the patient self-control responses and also in establishing therapeutic activity which can occur in the absence of the researcher or therapist.

## Administration of Scale

The RSS is given either individually or in group settings. When $Ss$ present problems in comprehension or communication, it is suggested that the size of the group be reduced. The authors' experiences suggest that administration time for college students is approximately 20 minutes and for juvenile offenders approximately 30 minutes. The extra time needed for juvenile offenders is for definition of items. This is especially true with youthful offenders from 12 to 17 of average intelligence. For certain populations who are illiterate or unable to read the questionnaire for one reason or another, the test has to be administered orally. In our experience a minimum of seventh grade education is needed to have a fairly good comprehension of the questionnaire. It is recommended that the scale (RSS) be administered to children of high school age or younger only with the knowledge and consent of parents or guardians.

## Uses of the RSS

The RSS can be used in three general areas: private practice, institutional practice, and research.

*Private practice.* The RSS can be helpful in establishing rapport during the first few interviews by referring to some of the objects and activities which the client has rated as liked "very much." This use of the RSS to establish rapport is especially relevant in dealing with delinquent, highly anxious, or geriatric patients. With the delinquent and the highly anxious person, one of the frequent problems is in establishing a warm, trusting relationship. With the geriatric patient there is frequently such a low baseline of social interaction that the client must be coaxed back to an attitude of relating to others. It is easy enough during the interview to allude to some of the items because of the scale's broad coverage of possible reinforcing objects or activities.

Lazarus and Abramowitz (1962) have developed a method to countercondition anxiety by use of emotive imagery. The client is asked to approach in imagination a fearful stimulus while in the presence of a stimulus that he regards as highly desirable. For instance, if a boy has a fear of dogs and he has a great admiration for sports cars, then he can be asked to imagine that he is driving a sports car past a dog. The pleasure desired from driving the sports car counter-conditions the fear aroused by perceiving the dog. Gradually the proximity of this boy to the dog is increased until he is able to picture the dog sitting next to him in the car without experiencing anxiety. Other reinforcing stimuli can also be included to accompany this fear-arousing situation.

Many times when dealing with anxious individuals, the anxiety is so great that it hinders the interview procedure. One of the authors has used the emotive imagery technique to reduce anxiety to such an extent that the interview could be continued in a fruitful manner. A knowledge of the possible reinforcing stimuli can also be quite helpful in shaping behavior during an interview. Whenever the patient exhibits bodily or verbal behavior considered desirable by the therapist, the latter then mentions one of the objects that is liked very much by the client. This can be done in a smooth manner if the therapist is quite familiar with the client's RSS responses. For example, when a young patient makes self-enhancing responses such as "I think I'm getting more confident," the therapist may respond, "That's great! When you get so that you can walk out in the open, I'll buy you an ice cream."

Another way to initiate new behavior, other than reinforcement strategies, is through use of behavior rehearsals. For example, a client may be fearful in social situations such as a cocktail party because he is afraid of being ridiculed. The therapist might structure a behavior rehearsal in such a manner that it includes a number of highly reinforcing stimuli, e.g., those described in Situation 2, Section III of the RSS. The client's reaction to his own judgment on the RSS may also prove useful in a therapeutic situation. For example, either spontaneously or with the therapist's assistance he may become aware of how much he depends' upon a very limited class of reinforcers. This realization may induce him to consider the possibility of expanding his sphere of pleasurable activities.

*Institutional practice.* The RSS can be employed in institutional settings much in the same manner as in individual therapy. The RSS might also be a useful addition to training programs and demonstration projects which have the intention of helping the caretaking personnel to realize how important a part they play in shaping the behavior of the patient. Just at that point in the training program when the personnel are beginning to see themselves in a more socially active role, frequently there is a lack of specific information as to how one might proceed. The RSS can provide a set of concrete suggestions for working with individual patients, thus closing the gap between a project's stimulating effects and the actual implementation of its objectives. Additionally, the use of the RSS in institutions will force the staff and ward personnel to come to an agreement as to what is and is not desirable behavior.

One might consider the possibility of administering the RSS to personnel as well as patients to determine the areas of agreement and conflict. Thus for example, it might turn out that for a given population of institutionalized people those objects and activities which are most reinforcing for the residents may be least reinforcing for the staff, or vice versa. When one has the choice of assigning particular staff members to a patient, there is a possibility of matching therapist and patient on the basis of the RSS profile. However, we do not mean to imply there will be a perfect and positive relationship between a person favoring certain reinforcers for himself and his approving these reinforcers for someone else, particularly when there is a staff attitude which regards the patients or inmates as representing a population vastly different from themselves. The staff will sometimes insist upon the withholding of certain reinforcers that are felt to be "too good" for the inmates. The optimal relationship between the RSS score of the therapist and the RSS score of the patient in terms of the therapeutic outcome will have to be determined by appropriate research.

*Research.* The RSS has research potential in a number of ways. It offers the possibility of comparing different populations with respect to the (1) *number* of reinforcers they favor; (2) *specific content* of reinforcers; (3) the tendency toward extreme as compared with graduated or differentiated preference; and (4) their relative amenability to each of the specific therapeutic approaches. Thus for example, juvenile offenders may in general prove to be rather easily accessible when using reinforcers which can be presented palpably (Section I) but may be almost impervious at the beginning to reinforcers which require satisfaction from stimulations presented in imagination (Section II or III). Furthermore, the progress of an individual through his therapeutic experiences might be traced through the increase in number and quality of reinforcers which now matter to him. It is apparent that such developmental concepts as differentiation and versatility of functioning could be related to operational specifications in the RSS.

It might prove important to determine the personal and social correlates of different RSS profiles. One person may select relatively few reinforcers but emphasize these with extreme ratings, while another person selects a broader range but with less extreme preferences. These simple ratings might therefore provide data to life style. The RSS scores will have special value for studying the life style of the aged since there is little information available on this topic at the present time. Specific questions would include whether or not a person with few but intense sources of satisfaction will cope with problems associated with the aging process more adequately than a person with more numerous but less intense sources of satisfaction. We might expect these two kinds of people to cope quite differently with the progressive reduction of sources of satisfaction.

It would be of great interest to compare RSS scores with a number of other relevant variables.

1. *Treatment outcome:* Ss can be given the RSS pre- and post-treatment.

2. *Fear survey schedule:* One would expect an inverse relationship between scores of the RSS and the fear survey schedule. But it is not at all unlikely that some individuals will have both high and low responses on both scores.

3. *S's baseline of activity:* A measure of this activity has been developed by Kastenbaum, et al. This measure has been designated the VIRO Scale. The measure of the client's vigor, intactness, relationship, and orientation during the interview situation itself are provided by this procedure.

4. *Different diagnostic categories:* It would be interesting to compare individuals designated as psychopaths with Ss diagnosed as having anxieties and neurosis. Eysenck (1960) has noted significant differences in conditionability scores between psychopaths and highly anxious individuals. It might be important to learn whether or not apparent differences in conditionability are associated with differences in the range, level, and intensity of reinforcers available to them. Individuals who have suffered cerebral vascular accidents and other impairments affecting their

nervous system may either attempt to maintain their previous level and style of functioning or may share either temporary or permanent manifestations of regression. The RSS might offer a way of determining whether or not a person has now centered his sources of gratification around relatively simpler and more childlike reinforcers or whether he is still attempting to maintain his adult self-demands despite impairment.

5. *Social research:* On a broader level, we might wish to trace the temporal pattern of social integration for immigrants or minority group members. For example, Negroes living in a ghetto-like situation might select reinforcers that are not typical for middle-class society in general. The same Negroes or their children may shift their reinforcers as they become more integrated into the larger society.

Some observers have gone so far as to describe the aged as a minority group (Kogan & Shelton, 1962). We might be able to trace the aged person's perception of his changing status in terms of what he still hopes to get out of life. Is there a certain age level at which the person relinquishes the idea of having a new car, engaging in loving intimacy, etc.? Or does he perhaps maintain the full range of previous reinforcers in his outlook? This might be a greater source of conflict for the aged individual who maintains most of his full range of reinforcers, yet, in practice, is cut off from these reinforcers by those who have a negative stereotype of the aged. We have here the possibility of investigating the discrepancy between the individual's own view of what he expects to get from life and the way he is perceived by others, as well as the consequences of an aging person's holding a congruent or discongruent view from society.

6. *Brain pathology:* It could be hypothesized, based upon research such as Goldstein's (1944), that brain-damaged individuals would prefer palpable items more than non-brain-damaged people. One might, also, expect the degree of brain damage to be related to the ratio of scores between Section I and Section II.

7. *Developmental variables:* The RSS also can be used to test critical questions in male-female development. We can learn, with some precision, at what point in their childhood the boy and girl begin to develop along different pathways, especially in relation to changes in content and intensity with which the reinforcers are favored. Perhaps a separate RSS will be needed to assess this range and quality of reinforcers for children.

When the RSS is used with adolescents or elderly people, a variation might be considered. After completing the RSS to represent his present orientation, the adolescent can be asked to project ahead as to what he thinks he would like when he grows up, while the aged person can be asked to tell which of these reinforcers were important to him when he was younger. This allows us to manipulate the future in helping the child and manipulate the past in helping the aged person, including the possibility of bringing to the child some foretaste of the adult pleasures that he is seeking and returning to the older person some vibrant memories of bygone days.

## Illustrative Data

The RSS was administered to 111 male undergraduates and 54 female undergraduates. A chi-square analysis for the frequency of choice for each response category showed no significant difference ($p > .05$, $N = 165$), that is, there was no tendency to pick any one category, such as "a fair amount," over any other category.

Comparisons of Sections I, II, and III of the RSS reveal some interesting data with respect to percentage of choice for each response category.

Section I, which consists of palpable or concrete items, has a lesser percentage of "very much" responses as compared with Section II, which contains mostly items that would involve symbolic manipulation. Preliminary data from a population of juvenile offenders indicate a greater percentage of "very much" choices for Section I over Section II. It appears from these data that Section I-type items are more effective reinforcers for delinquents than are Section II-type items. Just the reverse seems to be the case for college undergraduates. These results are consistent with investigations that report primary reinforcers to be more effective for delinquent as compared with nondelinquent populations (Johns & Quay, 1962; Bandura, 1961). Time perspective research also has revealed a similar tendency for delinquent youths to be relatively less oriented toward goals and gratifications in the future and relatively more oriented toward immediate gratifications and tension release (Barndt & Johnson, 1955). One might expect that preference for Section I over Section II items would be characteristic of culturally deprived and less mature individuals as might be predicted from data on time perspectives (LeShan, 1952; Kastenbaum, 1966b).

It can also be seen from Table 3 that the percentage of choice for the "very much" items for Section III is greater than Sections I and II combined. This finding is probably associated with three factors: (1) In each of the Section III situations there are a number of possible reinforcing items. It appears that the items in these situations have a cumulative effect, although perhaps not simply additive. (2) The situations require more imaginative manipulation than do the items in either Section I or Section II. (3) Presentation of a number of discrete reinforcing items in the form of a unified story may constitute a "reinforcing field." This "reinforcing field" might be regarded as somewhat analogous to a Gestalt grouping. The reinforcing value of each item is determined by its position within a

TABLE 3.   Percent of Choice for Each Response Category for Males and Females

| Section N | No response | Not at all | Little | Fair amount | Much | Very much | Much and very much 2 |
|---|---|---|---|---|---|---|---|
| I   N = 165 | 1.4 | 16.4 | 22.7 | 26.2 | 19.7 | 13.6 | 16.6 |
| M = 111 | 1.1 | 15.1 | 23.3 | 28.1 | 20.3 | 12.1 | 16.2 |
| F = 54 | 2.0 | 19.7 | 21.0 | 23.0 | 17.6 | 16.7 | 17.1 |
| II   N = 165 | 1.5 | 17.6 | 17.4 | 23.2 | 20.0 | 20.2 | 20.1 |
| M = 111 | 1.1 | 16.0 | 18.6 | 24.2 | 22.1 | 18.1 | 20.1 |
| F = 54 | 2.0 | 22.3 | 15.0 | 20.7 | 15.8 | 24.2 | 20.0 |
| III   N = 165 | 0.0 | 2.3 | 11.0 | 15.4 | 26.7 | 44.6 | 35.7 |
| M = 111 | 0.0 | 2.9 | 11.3 | 17.4 | 28.0 | 40.4 | 34.2 |
| F = 54 | 0.0 | 11.2 | 10.2 | 11.1 | 24.1 | 53.4 | 38.8 |
| $M_m$ | .73 | 11.33 | 17.73 | 23.23 | 23.47 | 23.50 | 23.49 |
| $M_f$ | 1.33 | 17.73 | 15.40 | 18.27 | 19.17 | 31.43 | 25.30 |
| $M_{tot.}$ | 1.03 | 14.53 | 16.21 | 20.75 | 21.32 | 27.47 | 24.39 |

(symbolic) configuration as well as its reinforcing value as established without consideration of context. From a developmental standpoint, one would expect relatively mature individuals to respond to a larger variety of reinforcing fields than would relatively immature individuals. The implication of the relatively greater choice of the ''very much'' response category for Section III is that a reinforcing field probably would be more effective in shaping behavior than discrete presentations of reinforcing stimuli. The present findings tend to support the value of emotive imagery in counterconditioning. As previously noted, the use of emotive imagery involves the presentation of reinforcing stimuli symbolically within a vignette.

A comparison of male and female responses for each category, as presented in Table 3, indicates that the females tend to choose a greater precentage of ''very much'' responses for each of the three sections. The greatest difference occurs for Section III. Although there is no obvious explanation for the differences in male and female responses on the ''very much'' category, some speculation can be offered in this regard. Perhaps there is no ''real'' difference in choice, but the females might be less inhibited in expressing extreme response choices, in keeping with more liberal cultural sanctions for expressing affect by women than by men. Perhaps, however, the sex differences in response are related to a relatively greater dependency on vicarious satisfaction through wishing and fantasy behavior on the part of women who, in Western culture, have not been allowed as many sources of satisfaction as the male.

Clues to the differential reinforcing value of different kinds of people may also be found in RSS data. The present findings, for example, suggest that Old Men (Sec. II, Item 38) and Old Women (Sec. II, Item 39) have rather little value as positive reinforcers for the behavior of young adults. "A little" and "a fair amount" were the most frequently cited response categories for both of these items. By contrast, "very much" and "much" were the two most popular responses for Items 36 and 37: Babies and Children. Furthermore, Old Men and Old Women were less preferred than Dogs (Sec. I, Item 10-A), although slightly more than Birds (10-D) and Cats (10-C).

These findings tend to support a recent study which found that the "psychological distance" between the efforts one would make to save a young man and an old man was significantly greater than the distance between an old man and a pet dog or cat (Kastenbaum, 1964). The situation that is suggested by these illustrative data requires more extended discussion than what can be offered here. It might simply be noted that the RSS could serve as a measure of attitude change toward the aged before and after particular individuals are exposed to desensitization concerning the aged. Additionally, the young adults who presently find old men and old women to be without much reinforcement value will one day themselves fall into these categories—a circumstance that holds rich theoretical and empirical possibilities.

# REFERENCES

Ayllon, T., & Michael, J. The psychiatric nurse as a behavioral engineer. *Journal of the Experimental Analysis of Behavior,* 1959, *2,* 323-334.
Bandura, A. Psychotherapy as a learning process. *Psychological Bulletin,* 1961, *58,* 143-159.
Barndt, R. J., & Johnson, D. M. Time orientation in delinquents. *Journal of Abnormal and Social Psychology,* 1955, *51,* 589-592.
Eysenck, H. J. *Behavior therapy and the neuroses.* Oxford: Pergamon, 1960.
Geer, J. H. The development of a scale to measure fear. *Behavior Research and Therapy,* 1965, *3,* 45-54.
Goldstein, K. The mental changes due to frontal lobe damage. *Journal of Psychology,* 1944, 187-208.
Homme, L. E. Perspectives in psychology: XXIV. Control of coverants, the operants of the mind. *Psychological Records,* 1965, *15,* 501-511.
Johns, P., & Quay, R. The effect of social reward on verbal conditioning in psychopathic and neurotic military offenders. *Journal of Consulting Psychology,* 1962, *26,* 217-220.

Kastenbaum, R. The interpersonal context of death in a geriatric hospital. Paper read at the 17th Annual Meeting, Gerontological Society, 1964, New York.

Kastenbaum, R. Engrossment and perspective in later life: a developmental-field approach. In R. Kastenbaum (Ed.), *Contributions to the psychobiology of aging.* New York: Springer, 1965. Pp 3-18.

Kastenbaum, R. Developmental-field theory and the aged person's inner experience. *Gerontologist,* 1966, 6, 10-13. (a)

Kastenbaum, R. The meaning of time in later life. *Journal of Genetic Psychology,* 1966, *109,* 9-25. (b)

Kogan, N., & Shelton, F. C. Beliefs about "old people": a comparative study of older and younger samples. *Journal of Genetic Psychology,* 1962, *100,* 93-111.

Lazarus, A., & Abramowitz, A. The use of "emotive imagery" in the treatment of children's phobias. *Journal of Mental Science,* 1962, *108,* 191-195.

LeShan, L. L. Time orientation and social class. *Journal of Abnormal and Social Psychology,* 1952, 47, 589-592.

Premack, D. Toward empirical behavior laws: I. Positive reinforcement. *Psychological Review,* 1959, 66, 219-233.

Wolpe, J. *Psychotherapy by reciprocal inhibition.* Stanford: Stanford University Press, 1958.

Wolpe, J., & Lang, P. A fear survey schedule for use in behavior therapy. *Behavior Research and Therapy,* 1964, 2, 27-30.

# 15

## The "Reinforcement Menu": Finding Effective Reinforcers

### Marvin F. Daley

A concept of reinforcement has been developed by Premack which states that "for any pair of responses, the more probable one will reinforce the less probable one (Premack, 1965)." Taking Premack literally, *any* behavior can be used as a reinforcer of *any* other lower probability behavior at the instant that the behavior is a higher probability one. It is not necessary when attempting to modify behavior to depend wholly on candy or trinkets as reinforcers, as did early investigators. It is necessary only that the contingency manager be able to identify what students *are doing* most frequently in a given environment.

Homme (1963) observed children in a preschool nursery. The children would run around the room, scream, push a chair across the floor, and play games. All these behaviors were occurring most of the time. As one would expect, the instruction, "come and sit down," would go unnoticed. Applying the Premack principle, the contingency manager allowed the children to engage in their usual behaviors contingent or dependent upon the subjects doing a very small amount of what the experimenters instructed them to do. A typical early con-

From "The 'Reinforcement Menu': Finding effective reinforcers" by Marvin F. Daley, in *Behavioral counseling: Cases and techniques,* edited by John D. Krumboltz and Carl E. Thoreson. Copyright © by Holt, Rinehart and Winston, Inc. Reprinted by permission of Holt, Rinehart and Winston, Inc.

Mrs. Cheryl Vajanasoontorn played a major role in conducting a part of the research on which the report is based.

Editors' Note: "Contingency manager" as used here stresses the importance of controlling the consequences of certain behaviors, that is, seeing to it that certain things happen when behavior occurs.

tingency required the children briefly to sit quietly in chairs and look at the blackboard. The behavior was followed quickly by the command, "Everybody run and scream now." Immediate control over the situation was obtained. The time spent sitting in chairs was progressively increased, and training in school skills was begun. The experimenters reported that they were able to teach the entire first grade repertoire to these students in about one month of training.

In another experiment, Homme (1965) was able to demonstrate that preschool Indian children could make substantial improvements in learning English when taught by a contingency management system.

Still another twist for gaining better control over the contingency management has been to develop a kind of "menu" of activities that represent high probability response (Addison & Homme, 1966). The menu has been put in a book form with systematic line drawings or stick figure sketches of the activities. The subject is presented with the menu before executing the task to be learned and is allowed to select from it an event which for him at that moment is a high probability event. Upon completion of the task, he is allowed to go to the reinforcement area, and his selection is immediately made available. Homme has suggested that certain reinforcing events could be "daily specials" to be made available on a restricted basis. With contingency management and the Premack principles, the teacher is in a position to deliberately, systematically, and efficiently modify behavior.

One of our first experiments was designed to parallel the regular classroom situation. Five 8- to 11-year-old mentally retarded children from the Cache Valley Day Care and Training Center served as subjects. They were very difficult to motivate and often displayed nonacceptable behavior in the school atmosphere.

Extensive observations were carried out producing 22 items which, because of their high frequency of occurrence, were considered to be high probability behaviors:

| | | |
|---|---|---|
| a. Talking | i. Dancing | q. Using colored pencils |
| b. Writing | j. Walking | r. Singing |
| c. Coloring | k. Drawing on board | s. Swinging on door |
| d. Drawing | l. Telephoning | t. Moving chair |
| e. Reading | m. Puzzle | u. Erasing blackboard |
| f. Swinging feet | n. Blocks | v. Looking out window |
| g. Record | o. Jumping | w. RE book |
| h. Hugging | p. Drinking | |

A menu depicting these activities in color was prepared by an artist and enclosed in a single book with one activity per page. The book indicating the reinforcing events is called an RE menu for short (see accompanying illustration).

# REINFORCEMENT MENU

The RE menu was introduced to the class by encouraging them to name the activity involved while the RE menu was held before them and the pages turned. The children were then told, "You are going to be able to have time to do whatever you want to do that is in this book. Every time you finish your work, you will get to look at our book and pick what you want to do for four minutes. I will tell you when your time is over to do what you want to do."

The lesson activity was presented, and upon completion of the exercise the children were told, "Here is the book. Now you can pick what *you* want to do for four minutes. . ." The children were shown the RE materials and were given the next exercise. From here on the children took turns being first to use the menu upon completion of the task.

Lessons were taken directly from the Peabody language development kit (Dunn & Smith, 1965). The stated purpose of the kit is: (1) "to stimulate the over-all oral language facility of the disadvantaged and retarded," (2) "to develop their verbal intelligence through training," and (3) "to enhance their school progress." Each lesson contained an average of three exercises, for example, following directions, identification, classification. In one case, a card is held up and the instruction given to the group to "pick out food eaten for breakfast," "pick out food eaten for snacks." Experimental sessions were 60 minutes long and comparable to a regular class period.

Initially RE activity was made available after every five minutes of work. By the eleventh hour each task was 30 minutes long. The experimenter-instructor was able to gradually shape larger and larger amounts of work to be accomplished before making available the RE menu. Attention span and work output had been increased greatly. After 15 sessions, the children were re-evaluated by means of the Utah verbal language development scale. The range of improvement was 20 years 0 months to 2 years 6 months.

## REFERENCES

Addison, R. M., & Homme, L. E. The reinforcing event (RE) menu. *National Society for Programmed Instruction Journal*, 1966, *5*, 8-9.

Dunn, L., & Smith, J. *Peabody language development kit manual for level #1.* Minneapolis: American Guidance Service, 1965.

Homme, L., DeBaca, P., Devine, J., Steinhorst, R., & Rickert, E. Use of the Premack principle in controlling the behavior of nursery school children. *Journal of Experimental Analysis of Behavior*, 1963, *6*, 544.

Homme, L. E. *System for teaching English literacy to preschool Indian children.* Westinghouse Reasearch Laboratories Contract 14-20-065001506. Bureau of Indian Affairs, Final Report, October 11, 1965, 1-15.

Premack, D. Reinforcement theory. In David Levine (Ed.), *Nebraska symposium on motivation.* Lincoln, Nebraska: University Press, 1965. Pp. 123-188.

# 16

---

## Positive Reinforcement Observation Schedule (Pros): Development and Use

*Donald N. Bersoff*
*Dale Moyer*

This article describes an attempt to develop, validate, and establish the reliability of an instrument that can be used as a mediator reinforcement preference scale and as an observation schedule to obtain frequency and rate of positive reinforcement (PR) emission in a variety of settings. Many useful observation schedules are available, but they either fail to include nonverbal reinforcement (e.g., Amidon & Flanders, 1967; Brophy & Good, 1969) or are not inclusive enough to guide observations of all possible types of reinforcement emission (e.g., O'Leary & Becker, 1967). The PROS attempts to correct both these deficiencies.

The scale consists of ten categories of positively reinforcing behaviors that may be emitted by mediators (i.e., classroom teachers, psychologists during individual testing, behavior modifiers). These behaviors appear to possess reinforcing qualities that are both powerful and durable. However, the authors make no assumption of the trans-situational nature or generalized effectiveness of these categories. An assumption of the PROS is that reinforcement is relational rather than an absolute property of any activity. The PROS merely represents diverse consequating events, all of which may potentially serve a reinforcing function in a given situation. The 10 PR categories, their symbols, and definitions are found in Table 1.

This is an expanded version of a paper presented at the annual meeting of the American Psychological Association, Montreal, August 1973 under the title, Positive Reinforcement Observation Schedule (PROS): Development and applications to educational settings.

TABLE 1.   *Positive Reinforcement Observation Schedule (PROS):*
*Definitions and Symbols*

### Positive Categories

*CRD Administration of Concrete Rewards (Direct):*   Giving of direct concrete rewards such as candy, money, or free time. This category also consists of those instances when the teacher/tester gives concrete but symbolic rewards (such as giving flashcards to a child contingent upon correct answer to that card) which have no backup or other value.

*CRT Administration of Concrete Rewards (Token):*   Giving of symbolic rewards which will be redeemed for direct concrete rewards at some future time. Common examples are poker chips, tallies, colored sticks, stars, stickers, etc.

*AAB Affirmation of Appropriate Behavior:*   Verbal contact indicating approval, commendation to a child that his responses are correct or acceptable, or that his behavior is appropriate. Verbal affirmation may either be loud or soft, and consists of such examples as "That's good," "Fine," "You're studying well." (Adapted from Brophy & Good, 1969; O'Leary & Becker, 1967.)

*RP Rapport-Praise:*   Evaluative reactions which go beyond the teacher/tester's level of simple affirmation or positive feedback by verbally complimenting the child. RP communicates a positive evaluation or a warm personal reaction to the child and not merely an impersonal communication. Teacher/tester responses are considered RP if the verbal content (Yes, Umhumm, Fine, Good) or nonverbal content (headnod) is accompanied by nonverbal communication of warmth, joy, or excitement. (Adapted from Brophy & Good, 1969.)

*FA+ Positive Facial Attention:*   Looking at a child when teacher/tester is smiling or attending to what the child is doing or what the child is saying. Teacher/tester might nod head, wink, or give other indication of approval while smiling. Concerted looking or attending to a child also belongs in this category but a five-second interval must elapse between one attend episode and another for this category to be scored again. (Adapted from O'Leary & Becker, 1967.)

*PC+ Positive Physical Contact:*   Actual physical contact such as patting, embracing, holding arm, taking hand, etc. as a sign of approval. (Adapted from O'Leary & Becker, 1967.)

*AF Accepts Feelings:*   Teacher/tester accepts and clarifies the feeling tone of the child in a nonthreatening manner. Feelings or student emotions may be positive or negative. Predicting or recalling feelings is included. The teacher/tester accepts feelings when he says he understands how the child feels, that he has a right to these feelings, and that he will not punish the child for his feelings. (Adapted from Amidon & Flanders, 1967.)

*AI Accepts Ideas:*   Clarifying, building, or developing ideas suggested by the child. Teacher/tester may paraphrase the student's statement, restate the idea more simply, or summarize what the student has said. The key teacher/tester behaviors are clarifying and developing ideas. Simple restatement without building such as when teacher/tester verbalizes student answer during recording on chalkboard or test booklet is not scored. (Adapted from Amidon & Flanders, 1967.)

*AM Adjuvant Mastery:*   Urging, prompting, fostering, promoting confidence and success, providing encouragement for response production. When the child refuses to answer, the teacher/tester may suggest guessing, give encouragement ("You just got the last one"), or systematically employ a graded series of suggestions.

*AE Aiding by Example:*   Demonstration of appropriate behavior by teacher/tester when the child is either nonresponsive or incorrect in exhibiting expected response.

### Neutral Categories

*AQ Asks Questions:* Asking questions by teacher/tester following student behavior concerning that behavior. In this category neither positive nor negative evaluation of the child is present in the question.

*NVR Non-Germane Verbal Response:* A response by teacher/tester which is neither criticism nor affirmation of behavior initiated by the child.

### Negative Categories

*A- Admonishment:* Verbal response by a teacher/tester indicating to a child that his responses are incorrect, unacceptable, or inappropriate, such as "No," "You're being bad," "That's wrong."

*FA- Negative Facial Attention:* Nonverbal response by teacher/tester indicating to child that his responses are incorrect, unacceptable, or inappropriate, such as frowning, grimacing, shaking head, pointing finger.

## VALIDITY AND RELIABILITY OF THE PROS
## AS A REINFORCEMENT PREFERENCE SCHEDULE

In order to validate the scale, that is, to establish outside verification that others, in addition to the authors, considered these categories as reinforcers, two categories which were assumed to be ''neutral'' and two categories which were assumed to be ''negative'' (punishing stimuli) were added to the scale. The total of 14 categories were constructed in a paired comparisons format (see Edwards, 1957) with each category being compared to each other for a total of 91 pairs [N(N − 1)]. The scale was administered to a wide variety of *S*s (n = 147) and scale weights and rankings derived for each category. The test of validity assumed that if the ten original categories were accepted by others to be positive reinforcers, they would be ranked 1-10, the neutral stimuli would be ranked 11 and 12, and the two negative stimuli would be ranked 13 and 14. The two neutral and two negative categories with their symbols and definitions are also found in Table 1.

Of course, in the directions preceding the scale there was no indication that some of the categories were considered positive, neutral, or negative. The order of presentation of the definitions for all 14 categories, as well as the order of pairing, was determined by random selection. The directions read, in part:

Defined below are 14 categories that may possibly be subsumed under the rubric of positive reinforcement as administered by a teacher or psychologist (tester). The aim of this scale is to determine which of these categories you consider to be the most potent positive reinforcers with *children.*

In filling out the scale use the following definition of positive reinforcement:

TABLE 2.   Ranks and Scale Weights
for All 14 PROS Categories

| Category | Rank | Scale Weight[1] |
|---|---|---|
| Rapport-Praise   (RP) | 1 | 75.8 |
| Affirmation of Appropriate Behavior   (AAB) | 2 | 71.6 |
| Accepts Ideas   (AI) | 3 | 66.9 |
| Accepts Feelings   (AF) | 4 | 65.3 |
| Positive Facial Attention   (FA+) | 5 | 59.5 |
| Concrete Reinforcement Direct   (CRD) | 6 | 57.5 |
| Aiding by Example   (AE) | 7 | 55.3 |
| Adjuvant Mastery   (AM) | 8 | 54.5 |
| Positive Physical Contact   (PC) | 9 | 52.0 |
| Concrete Reinforcement Token   (CRT) | 10 | 49.5 |
| Asks Questions   (AQ) | 11 | 43.7 |
| Non-Germane Verbal Response   (NVR) | 12 | 22.0 |
| Negative Facial Attention   (FA−) | 13 | 15.1 |
| Admonishment   (A−) | 14 | 11.4 |

[1] Theoretical range is 0 to 100 with a mean of 50.

*Behavior by teacher/tester following student response for the purpose of strengthening or accelerating appropriate behavior* (italics in the original).[1]

Following a technique devised by Dunn-Rankin (1965), scale weights and rankings were determined for all 14 categories. The results are presented in Table 2.

Inspection of Table 2 indicates reasonable support for the scale's validity. All 10 of the presumptive PR categories were judged by the *S*s to be potentially reinforcing. While it would have been ''purer'' if CRT had been weighed a little higher and AQ weighted somewhat lower to make it more ''neutral,'' the two neutral categories did end up 11th and 12th and the two negative categories were ranked 13th and 14th. Additionally, it will be noted that all 10 PR categories achieved scale weights at or above the mean (theoretical mean = 50) although by chance it would be expected that only seven of the categories would be above the mean.

Substantiating the need for scaling in addition to ranking is the fact that the 10 PR categories were neither all considered equally potent as

[1] Complete directions and a copy of the original scale in paired comparisons format may be obtained by writing the senior author, Department of Educational Psychology, College of Education, Athens, Georgia 30601.

reinforcers nor distributed along equal intervals. Differences between PR categories ranged from 0.8 (AE and AM) to 5.8 (FA+ and AF).

It can be expected that specific scale weights and rankings of the PR categories will change with repeated validation studies. The precise weightings and rankings are dependent on both the nature of the judging *Ss* (that is, teachers, psychologists) and the target group about whom these judges are making reinforcement preferences (that is, elementary vs. high-school children). The measure of the scale's validity lies in the proposition that under any validation procedure similar in intent to the original, PR categories presently ranked 1-10 will again be ranked 1-10, although possibly in different order. The same would be true for the neutral and negative categories. A recently completed study (Byalick & Bersoff, in press), in part a replication of the validation procedure described here, supports the proposition. In that study, using 60 teachers as the validation group, the 10 putative PR categories were again ranked 1-10, followed by the neutral and negative categories.

Having established some consensual validation that the 10 categories were perceived by others to be PRs, the next task was to obtain some measure of reliability in terms of stability of reinforcement choice. Possibly, the paired comparisons scales were filled out capriciously and the initial choices selected unthinkingly, perversely, or at random. To establish an indication of the stability of preference, a subsample of 38 *Ss*, taken from the original validation sample, was administered the PROS and readministered it 15 days later. The *Ss*, graduate students in a child development class, were given no indication that their original performances would be checked.

Two procedures were chosen to establish reliability. In the first method, the percent of agreement among the pairs from first to second administration was calculated for each *S*. In the second method, the rank order correlation coefficient ($r'$) between first and second administration was calculated for each *S*. Table 3 presents the reliability data and summarizes the results using these techniques.

The percent of disagreement is largely a function, upon inspection, of closeness of scale weights. That is, those pairs in which choices were made between stimuli close in scale weights were more often reversed on second administration than those pairs in which the stimuli had highly disparate scale weights. For example, the pair in which reversals were most often made (17 reversals in 38) was the item in which the two stimuli compared were AE and AM, ranked 7 and 8 and yielding scale weights of 55.3 and 54.5, respectively. On the other hand, absolutely no reversals were made for the item in which AAB and A-, ranked 2 and 14 with respective scale weights of 71.6 and 15.1, were compared. Secondly, reliability may be somewhat underestimated by the fact that some learning about reinforcement could have taken place during the

TABLE 3.   Reliability Measures (Stability of Preferences) for PROS Scale; 15-Day Test-Retest

| Ss (N = 38) | Pairs Agree | Pairs Disagree | Percent Agree | |
|---|---|---|---|---|
| 1 | 73 | 18 | 80.2 | .790 |
| 2 | 73 | 18 | 80.2 | .851 |
| 3 | 87 | 4 | 95.6 | .969 |
| 4 | 74 | 17 | 81.3 | .890 |
| 5 | 75 | 16 | 82.4 | .908 |
| 6 | 80 | 11 | 87.7 | .890 |
| 7 | 76 | 15 | 83.5 | .836 |
| 8 | 70 | 21 | 76.9 | .813 |
| 9 | 77 | 14 | 84.6 | .954 |
| 10 | 81 | 10 | 89.0 | .973 |
| 11 | 65 | 26 | 71.4 | .715 |
| 12 | 65 | 26 | 71.4 | .870 |
| 13 | 71 | 20 | 78.0 | .717 |
| 14 | 82 | 9 | 90.1 | .902 |
| 15 | 77 | 14 | 84.6 | .927 |
| 16 | 78 | 13 | 85.7 | .851 |
| 17 | 74 | 17 | 81.3 | .758 |
| 18 | 86 | 5 | 94.5 | .963 |
| 19 | 63 | 28 | 69.2 | .852 |
| 20 | 69 | 22 | 75.8 | .605 |
| 21 | 78 | 13 | 85.7 | .907 |
| 22 | 75 | 16 | 82.4 | .812 |
| 23 | 67 | 24 | 73.6 | .842 |
| 24 | 69 | 22 | 75.8 | .764 |
| 25 | 82 | 9 | 90.1 | .885 |
| 26 | 83 | 8 | 91.2 | .943 |
| 27 | 69 | 22 | 75.8 | .753 |
| 28 | 73 | 18 | 80.2 | .758 |
| 29 | 65 | 26 | 71.4 | .710 |
| 30 | 79 | 12 | 86.8 | .925 |
| 31 | 63 | 28 | 69.2 | .808 |
| 32 | 80 | 11 | 87.9 | .927 |
| 33 | 84 | 7 | 92.3 | .964 |
| 34 | 75 | 16 | 82.4 | .861 |
| 35 | 74 | 17 | 81.3 | .850 |
| 36 | 80 | 11 | 87.8 | .956 |
| 37 | 73 | 18 | 80.2 | .726 |
| 38 | 82 | 9 | 90.1 | .996 |
| Range | | | 69.2−95.6 | .605−.996 |
| $\overline{X}$ | | | 82.33 | .882 |
| Mdn | | | 82.4 | .857 |

two-week interval between retesting. The class used as *S*s met every day during a summer session, so it is quite possible for there to have been effects on retesting due to increased knowledge of learning theory and behavior modification. Notwithstanding these explanations, the PROS as a reinforcement preference scale appears to have reasonable reliability as well as validity.

## OBSERVABILITY OF PROS EVENTS

While the test-retest reliability of the PROS in its form as a preference schedule has been reasonably established, the question still remains if those behaviors designated as PRs can be observed and reliably recorded. Classroom settings were used to demonstrate that PROS events could be reliably observed. Three different data collection programs with a variety of observers[2] provided the evidence.

### Study 1

An observer ($O_1$) experienced in the use of the PROS as an observation instrument trained a second observer ($O_2$). After practice through trial runs and discussion in which recording differences were clarified, the two *O*s made observations of the frequency of the PROS events emitted by teachers in five regular elementary classrooms (grades 1-4, 6). The average number of students per classroom was 22. The observers waited 15 minutes after entering the classrooms before recording and then tallied PR emission for 30 continuous minutes. Approximately 40 PR per classroom were recorded. The five data collection periods occurred during a 25-day period. The correlation for each observation session between $O_1$ and $O_2$, as well as the average correlation for all five observations, are reported in Table 4.

### Study 2

A procedure similar to Study 1 was used in a more extensive test. Observer $O_1$ now trained a third observer ($O_3$) who in turn trained observers 4-7. Reliability checks were obtained between $O_1$ and $O_3$ on one occasion and between $O_3$ and $O_{4-7}$ on at least three occasions. PR

[2]Grateful appreciation is expressed to the following observers: Robert Byalick, Malinda Hennen, Gail Mayshark, Vicki NeSmith, Mildred Neville, Jean Rasheed, Maggie Weshner.

emission by teachers in third- and fourth-grade classrooms was used as the data in this study. Each classroom averaged 28 students. Os waited 10 minutes before recording and then tallied continuously for 14 minutes. The average number of PR per classroom was 15. The correlations obtained are found in Table 4.

## Study 3

Studies 1 and 2 demonstrated that two trained Os can record almost equal frequencies across 10 PR categories in periods ranging from 14 to 30 minutes. In addition, since high reliability coefficients were obtained among seven different Os, there is evidence that the PROS is neither a difficult instrument to teach nor to learn.

Study 3 was initiated to discover if Os could not only record equal frequencies over time but also if they could observe and record the same PR behaviors sequentially, a more rigorous test of the observability of PROS events. A time-sampling format for the PROS categories was devised (similar to that used to obtain reliability of observations by O'Leary, Becker, and their co-workers, e.g., O'Leary & Becker, 1967; O'Leary, Becker, Evans, & Saudergas, 1969). In Study 3 the measure of reliability was percent agreement between two Os. An agreement was scored if both Os recorded the same teacher PR behavior(s) within the same 20-second observation interval. A disagreement was scored if one O recorded different PR behavior(s) within the same interval. Percent agreement was calculated by dividing the total number of intervals into the number of intervals in which agreement occurred. Observations were made continuously during 20-second intervals for 14 minutes on eight separate occasions using $O_{3-7}$. The raw data were the same as in Study 2. Precise percents are reported in Table 4, but all Os obtained agreements far exceeding the 80% usually accepted as reliable (O'Leary & Becker, 1967). Percent of agreement was also calculated for each PROS category; in none of the 10 categories was agreement below 80%.

## REINFORCING FUNCTIONS OF PROS EVENTS

The PROS has been characterized as consisting of 10 categories of behaviors that may potentially serve a reinforcing function in a given situation, and it has been shown that a large number of judges substantiate the authors' judgment that those behaviors are identifiable as positive reinforcers. Yet to be demonstrated is that these behaviors can actually serve a reinforcing function; that is, that their use by a behavior

TABLE 4. *Reliability of the PROS when used as an Observation Scale*

| Recording Session | Observers | | | | | | | | | | | |
|---|---|---|---|---|---|---|---|---|---|---|---|---|
| | $O_1 \times O_2$ | | $O_1 \times O_3$ | | $O_3 \times O_4$ | | $O_3 \times O_5$ | | $O_3 \times O_6$ | | $O_3 \times O_7$ | |
| | r | % Agree | r | % Agree | r | % Agree | r | % Agree | r | % Agree | r | % Agree |
| 1 | .97 | — | .89 | — | .95 | — | .62 | — | .99 | 97 | .91 | — |
| 2 | .88 | — | — | — | .75 | 94 | .98 | 96 | .98 | 88 | .87 | 97 |
| 3 | .99 | — | — | — | .96 | 97 | .98 | 95 | — | — | .64 | 96 |
| 4 | .95 | — | — | — | .94 | — | .97 | — | .88 | — | .99 | — |
| 5 | .94 | — | — | — | — | — | — | — | — | — | — | — |
| Average r[1] | .96 | — | .89 | — | .92 | — | .95 | — | .97 | — | .92 | — |

[1]Calculated using Fisher's transformation.

249

mediator can accelerate some predesigned desired behavior. While each of the categories have been demonstrated by other researchers (Amidon & Flanders, 1967; Bandura & Walters, 1963; O'Leary, Becker, Evans, & Saudergas, 1969; O'Leary & Drabman, 1971) to have reinforcing functions, a more specific proof was felt to be necessary. Other researchers may have demonstrated the reinforcing power of categories similar to the PROS but may have defined them differently or had different purposes in mind when applying them to a classroom situation. Thus, a small experiment was initiated to empirically demonstrate the reinforcing functions of the behaviors defined in the PROS.

Academic functioning, specifically arithmetic achievement, was chosen as the behavior to be accelerated. Baseline data were obtained on two measures:

1. Rate of PR emission (as defined by the PROS) by a teacher in a third grade classroom.
2. Rate correct of arithmetic problems (a mixture of the four fundamental arithmetic processes) attempted by students (N = 26) in the same classroom.

Two PR emission rates and three measures of arithmetic performance were obtained under baseline conditions. The intent of the experiment was to demonstrate that increased PR emission by the teacher during arithmetic instructional periods would increase arithmetic achievement, tested immediately after instruction, by the students.

During the baseline period the teacher was not aware that her reinforcement emission rate was being observed nor did she have any knowledge of the PROS. She was, however, a volunteer in a behavior-modification project.

After obtaining the baseline measures, a conference was held with the teacher and the three consultants involved in the behavior-modification project.[3] The categories included in the PROS were explained to her, examples given of specific behaviors described by these categories, and feedback was communicated concerning her rate of reinforcement emission during baseline. Two major factors were particularly noted. One was that the teacher was using very few of the PROS events and that only one-fourth of the children were receiving PR. A videotape training session was held in which the teacher was instructed to use all of the PROS categories and to attempt to reinforce each child in the classroom at least once during a 30-minute period. Inspection of the tape indicated that she successfully accomplished both these objectives.

Concurrently during this teacher training period, the children were

[3] The help of School District 5, Anderson, S. C., and particularly Joyce Johnson, teacher, Mary Beth Rigsby, and Beatrice Thompson, Pupil Personnel Specialists, is deeply acknowledged.

taught to record the results of their arithmetic tests on a simple graph using a rate/minute measure. As each child would finish the tests in his own time, rate correct rather than simple frequencies were deemed the most appropriate measure.

After training was complete the experimental phase began. The rate of teacher PR emission was recorded on three separate occasions during an arithmetic instructional period. At least one consultant was present in the classroom three times a week during the experimental phase, and thus the teacher was unaware of when, or if, her PR emission was being recorded. At the same time, nine arithmetic tests were administered over a 10-week interval and the rate correct was determined for each. It should be noted that the arithmetic tests were taken mainly from the students' workbooks and that they became progressively more difficult.

The results of the experiment indicate that manipulation of PR emission by the teacher significantly increased arithmetic achievement of her students. The rate of teacher PR emission during the experimental phase quadrupled when compared to baseline conditions. During the baseline phase her rate of PR emission as measured by the PROS was .70 (or 7 PRs every 10 minutes), emitting 32 PROS events in a total of 46 minutes over two recording sessions. During the experimental phase her rate was 2.81, or 216 PROS events in 77 minutes over three recording sessions. Moreover, the teacher used more of the PROS categories and was successful in spreading the effect of her PR emission. No child was neglected during the experimental phase, whereas almost three-quarters of the class received no PR behavior from the teacher during baseline.

At the same time that the teacher quadrupled her rate of PR emission, the students increased their rate correct on arithmetic tests from a mean of 1.20 (SD = .57) during baseline to 2.03 (SD = 1.31) during the experimental phase. A $t$-test comparing these means yielded a $t$ of 7.36, a result with very high statistical significance. An initial hypothesis could attribute part of the increase to the novelty of graphing one's own test results, a kind of Hawthorne effect. However, the students did less well on the first two tests than on any of the others. The rate correct for arithmetic achievement during baseline and experimental conditions are presented in Table 5.

While statistically significant results were obtained, it must be pointed out that a rate increase that was not quite doubled from baseline to experimental conditions is, on the surface, not all that remarkable. However, the results become somewhat more academically significant when it is remembered that the students were working and being tested on progressively harder material. Over the 10-week experimental phase the students moved from simple addition to division and multiplication. Still, this demonstration of the reinforcing functions of PROS events is not definitive, and further experiments in which the PROS categories are

TABLE 5   Arithmetic Achievement Test Rate Correct
During Baseline and Experimental Conditions

| Condition | | $\overline{X}$ Rate Correct[1] |
|---|---|---|
| Baseline Test | 1 | 1.18 |
| | 2 | 1.65 |
| | 3 | .77 |
| Baseline Mean = 1.21, SD = .57 | | |
| Expmental Test | 1 | 1.21 |
| | 2 | 1.31 |
| | 3 | 2.68 |
| | 4 | 1.40 |
| | 5 | 3.09 |
| | 6 | 2.33 |
| | 7 | 2.59 |
| | 8 | 1.63 |
| | 9 | 1.83 |
| Expmental Mean = 2.03, SD = 1.31 | | |

[1] Because of absences N varies from 20 to 27.

more systematically manipulated are needed. Yet, by objective data (and the teacher's subjective report of greater overall effectiveness in her teaching and positive feeling about managing the class), there is support for the genuineness of the reinforcing functions of those mediator behaviors described by the PROS.

## POSSIBLE USES OF THE PROS

In its paired comparisons format, the PROS may be used as an attitude scale to assess the reinforcement preferences of those who will effect the behavior of others. It can be used more directly as an observation schedule. Possible applications in both of these formats follow.

*As a Preference Scale.*   A recently completed investigation by the senior author being prepared for publication uses the PROS as an attitude scale to measure disparity of reinforcement preferences between behavioral consultants and mediators (consultees). The nature, direction, and implications of these disparities will be detailed in the article but the findings lead to the strong recommendation that reinforcement preferences of the mediator be assessed before an intervention approach is recommended, so that the consultants do not suggest reinforcers that are devalued by the consultee with a resultant refusal or resistance to participate in the modification procedure.

Another use is in the assessment of attitude change before, throughout, and after training in behavioral approaches. Such an application is currently being used in a graduate course in behavioral management. It can be applied as easily in the in-service training of teachers and paraprofessionals. In this regard it may also be used as a diagnostic device. If, through use of the PROS, mediators are found to be resistant to the emission of CRD and CRT, and the trainer assumes that token systems are indeed valuable in classroom management, more time could be spent in explaining the rationale and demonstrating the efficacy of such an approach.

Alternately, the PROS may be used, not as a mediator-preference schedule, but as a target (child) preference schedule. Tharp and Wetzel (1969) indicate that in using a behavior-modification approach, the target's hierarchy of valued reinforcements must be delineated. They suggest the use of a structured interview session. The PROS may prove to be a more economical vehicle for this purpose. However, the definitions for each PR category would have to be retranslated commensurably with the reading ability of the target,[4] or presented in miniature situation form.

*As an Observation Schedule.* The PROS, most potentially valuable applications lie in its use as a method to guide observations in training and research and as a clinical tool in assessing teacher- and/or parent-child interaction. As a training device, let us assume one is interested in increasing the rate of PR emission in teachers to accelerate student behavior. Using an observation sheet as suggested in Figure 1, the frequency and rate/minute of each category of PR can be tallied at various stages of training. This direct and continuous measurement of behavior (cf., Bersoff & Ericson, 1972) provides immediate information as to trainee performance and the potential for on-the-spot teaching of target behavior in the trainee through telecoaching.

Similarly, the PROS may be used to assess parent-child interaction. Either in the natural setting of the home, in a carefully constructed miniature situation, or in a more open-ended clinical interview, the PROS can provide clues as to parental consequation of both appropriate and

[4]Such a rewording has been done for adolescent delinquents by Moyer. This scale can be obtained by writing the junior author, 676 Harley Drive, Columbus, Ohio 43221.

## TESTING OBSERVATION

Date_____ Observer_____ Tester_____ Child_____

| Category | | Freq | Rate |
|---|---|---|---|
| RP | | | |
| AAB | | | |
| AI | | | |
| AF | | | |
| FA+ | | | |
| CRD | | | |
| AE | | | |
| AM | | | |
| PC+ | | | |
| CRT | | | |
| | Total | | |

Time Go:_____

Time Stop:_____

Total Time:_____

*FIGURE 1.    Sample observation sheet for obtaining PR rate and frequency during testing situation.*

inappropriate behavior. For example if a child is emitting some form of aggressive behavior (pushing, shoving, striking) toward siblings, the PROS could be used to determine the particular categories and rates of PR being administered by environmental mediators (parents and siblings) which may be accelerating the maladaptive behavior at the expense of the desired or more ''appropriate'' behavior.

In general, the PROS can be used to examine the effects of predesignated categories and rates of PR contingent upon the child's behavior which sustains, perpetuates, or accelerates that behavior. In addition, it can be used to specify which PRs are most effective in consequating different behaviors within the same child, on the premise that there are intra-target differences in potentially potent reinforcers dependent on the particular behavior to be consequated.

The PROS is also currently being used in training graduate students in school psychology who have little background in education. As a systematic observation device it has directed attention to the nature of teacher-child interaction as evidenced by kind and rate of reinforcement delivery by teachers. These students have noted some interesting and apparently consistent behavior in teachers. For example, when they do reinforce, teachers do so individually, engaging in very little group reinforcement, raising questions concerning the economical use and delivery of PR with consequent implications for the training of student teachers. It has also been noted that teachers rely mainly on what could be called the ''distant reinforcers'' such as FA+ and AAB and very rarely use the more ''proximity reinforcers'' such as PC+, CRT, or CRD.

The PROS has been used to substantiate the hypothesis that it is invalid to extrapolate about a child's academic functioning in the classroom from his performance on individual intelligence tests (Bersoff, 1971) in part because the rate of PR emission in the testing situation far exceeds that found in the classroom. Rigsby (1972) found that testers emit significantly more PRs than teachers toward the same child in the same time span during similar academic activities, with the rate being 20 to 30 times higher in some cases.

Another recently completed study with the PROS involved an investigation of the congruence between teacher preference and actual teacher behavior (Byalick & Bersoff, in press). The design was enhanced by including a biracial sample of teachers and pupils to determine the nature of reinforcement delivery between teachers and students of different races. The junior author is exploring the nature of reinforcement preferences among different kinds of delinquents and the disparity between delinquent reinforcement preferences and actual PR delivery by mediators of delinquents' behavior.

Potential research possibilities using the PROS include objective substantiation of the self-fulfilling prophecy and teacher expectation effect in psychologist and teacher as observed through intra-tester and intra-teacher differences among children (that is, verbal vs. relatively nonverbal children; retarded vs. normal children; white vs. minority group children). Certainly, of immediate interest would be some cross-validation studies of the PROS by other, possibly more dispassionate, researchers than the present authors. The latter would appreciate any such results to include with their own ongoing cross-validations.

## CONCLUSION

The PROS appears useful in measuring both attitudes (preferences) and actual behavior with regard to PR. The PR categories represent potentially reinforcing events that form a natural part of spontaneous interpersonal relationships. As such, the PROS can be used in both natural settings such as the classroom and home, as well as in other situations where parent- and/or teacher-child interactions can be observed. As a direct monitor and feedback device of PR emission, it is useful in assessment, training, and remediation.

## *REFERENCES*

Amidon, E. J., & Flanders, N. A. *The role of the teacher in the classroom.* Minneapolis: Association for Productive Teaching, 1967.

Bandura, A., & Walters, R. H. *Social learning and personality development.* New York: Holt, Rinehart and Winston, 1963.

Bersoff, D. N. "Current functioning" myth: An overlooked fallacy in psychological assessment. *Journal of Consulting and Clinical Psychology,* 1971, *37,* 391-393.

Bersoff, D. N., & Ericson, C. R. A precise and valid measure of behavior and behavior change in the classroom. *Journal of School Psychology,* 1972, *10,* 161-163.

Brophy, J. E., & Good, T. L. Teacher-child dyadic interaction: A manual for coding classroom behavior. Report Series No. 27, December 1969, University of Texas, Research and Development Center for Teacher Education.

Byalick, R., & Bersoff, D. N. Reinforcement practices of black and white teachers in integrated classrooms. *Journal of Educational Psychology,* in press.

Dunn-Rankin, P. "The true probability distribution of the range of rank totals and its applications to psychological scaling." Unpublished doctoral dissertation, Florida State University, 1965.

Edwards, A. L. *Techniques of attitude scale construction.* New York: Appleton-Century-Crofts, 1957.

O'Leary, K. D., & Becker, W. C. Behavior modification of an adjustment class: A token reinforcement program. *Exceptional Children,* 1967, *33,* 737-742.

O'Leary, K. D., Becker, W. C., Evans, M. B., & Saudergas, R. A. A token reinforcement program in a public school: A replication and systematic analysis. *Journal of Applied Behavior Analysis,* 1969, *2,* 3-14.

O'Leary, K. D., & Drabman, R. Token reinforcement programs in the classroom: A review. *Psychological Bulletin,* 1971, *6,* 379-398.

Rigsby, M. B. "Positive reinforcement emission in two different academic evaluation settings." Unpublished masters thesis, Clemson University, 1972.

Tharp, R. G., & Wetzel, R. J. *Behavior modification in the natural environment.* New York: Academic Press, 1969

# Part V

---

## Observational Assessment

Examples: "You did that stupidly." "You're playing like a monkey."
"You did a crummy job." "I don't like what you're doing." "I hate
when you do that." "You did that wrong."

DV. Dependency. This category is coded whenever a child verbally
insists upon or urges a task that he/she is capable of doing himself or
redoes situations or behavior. A DV category covers two criteria.

Probably the major contrast between assessment procedures used in the context of behavior therapy and procedures employed in other forms of treatment has been an extensive reliance upon direct observational measures for the description of behavior and situations. The use of direct observational procedures is certainly not new, having been extensively used for some time in the fields of child development (Arrington, 1932; Jersild & Meigs, 1939) and ethology. What is relatively new is the use of direct observational measures in conjunction with clinical assessment and treatment.

Weick (1968) has defined an observational method partly in terms of the process of recording behaviors and settings that are consistent with empirical aims. Wiggins (1973) notes that observational methods are important in almost every area of psychology and emphasizes the consideration of methods that are consistent with the empirical aim of personality assessment, "the prediction of socially relevant criterion measures" (p. 277). In the current discussion we have defined the empirical aims of behavior-therapy assessment as involving diagnosis, design, and evaluation, and it is in this context that a variety of observational methods shall be considered.

A number of authors have provided extensive definitions and discussions of direct observational methods (Heyns & Lippitt, 1954; Hutt & Hutt, 1970; Jones, Reid, & Patterson, 1974; Weick, 1968; Wiggins, 1973; Wright, 1960). While there are minor variations in definition among authors, in the present context a direct observational procedure is defined as a method for obtaining samples of behaviors and settings determined to be clinically important (in relation to diagnosis, design, and evaluation), in a naturalistic situation or in an analogue situation that is structured in such a way as to provoke information about behaviors and settings comparable to what would have been obtained "in situ." Direct observational methods involve the recording of behavior at the time it occurs, not retrospectively, the use of trained and impartial observers following clearly specified rules and procedures for recording, and behavioral descriptions that require a minimal degree of inference (Jones,

Reid, & Patterson, 1974, p. 4). In addition, the observations to be recorded may be both of verbal (Lewinsohn, see paper 21; Rubin & Stolz, 1974) and/or of nonverbal (Dooley, 1975; Eisler, Hersen, & Agras, 1973) behavior.

A major focus in the use of direct observational methods is the effort to obtain information that enables the therapist to make statements about the behavior of an individual in the situation in which the behavior occurs (Mischel, 1973). Consequently, there has been an emphasis on data collection in the natural environment (Tharp & Wetzel, 1969). It is presumed that such naturalistic measures will necessarily involve fewer inferences than would information obtained in the clinic or laboratory setting. Furthermore, to the extent that there are idiosyncratic variables in the natural environment that may contribute to the maintenance of maladaptive behavior, direct observation would seem to provide a more direct measure than information obtained through the use of standardized tests involving normative comparisons.

The uses of direct observational measures in behavioral assessment are as follows:

1. To assist the behavior therapist in identifying relevant target behaviors for treatment.

2. To identify possible events in the natural environment that may serve as maintaining stimuli for these behaviors.

3. To identify additional antecedent and consequent stimulus events that might be used to bring about behavior change.

4. To provide a basis for evaluating therapeutic outcome by obtaining a base rate of the behavior prior to, during, and following the implementation of a behavior-change program.

5. To obtain information through one measure, which may then be compared with other independently obtained measures in order to examine the convergent validity of the diagnosis or the outcome of treatment.

6. To obtain over the course of treatment ongoing information that can be used to provide feedback to both the therapist and client regarding progress.

7. To utilize the above information to make changes in the treatment program where expected goals are not met.

It should be noted that while the use of direct observation methods in behavioral assessment represents a contrast with more traditional approaches, such procedures also share much in common with most other assessment devices. Like other forms of assessment including intelligence testing and personality assessment using both projective and nonprojective tests, the use of direct observational procedures requires sophistication both in terms of the procedure itself and in the training necessary for using the procedure. Such procedures are not exempt from the basic psychometric questions of reliability, validity, objectivity, sampling, and, to some degree, normative information. One of the criticisms levied against traditional psychometrics has been the considerable time and manpower costs involved in their development, use, and interpretation. It should be noted that direct observational measures, rather than being a more economical source of information, may be as expensive, or more expensive, when used appropriately. It is not uncommon that investigators attempting to use observational measures have given up and turned to simpler questionnaire measures because of some of the practical and methodological difficulties encountered (e.g., Boren & Jagodzinski, 1973).

A wide range of observational procedures has been developed for obtaining information to be used in the ways indicated above. For the most part, these procedures may be categorized both in terms of their structural properties and with respect to the range of behavioral and situational content that is included in the code system. It should be noted that decisions relating to the structural format of the procedure are probably more straightforward than decisions relating to content. Very often structural decisions tend to be a function of available resources, whereas content decisions are a matter of individual interpretation. Typically, content decisions are made in an arbitrary manner based upon face validity, in spite of the fact that empirical selection based upon the predictive value of various categories would make for a much stronger assessment procedure.

Questions relating to structural properties of coding systems refer to such variables as the number of behavior and/or situation categories to be included in the code system, the manner in which the relationship between behavior and situation is structured (continuous-sequential versus discrete recordings), the complexity of the behaviors coded, and the temporal demands that are imposed on the system and subsequently placed on the observer.

The basic types of behavior-recording procedures are continuous recording (ongoing narrative), direct measurement of permanent products, event recording, duration recording, interval recording, time sampling, and mixed systems that combine two or more of the former procedures. Alevizos and Berck (1974) and Cooper (1974) have provided descriptions for each of these procedures as well as systematic guidelines for their selection and use. The description by Alevizos and Berck (1974) is presented in Table 1, and their flow chart depicting a number of decision-making points that permit the selection of an appropriate recording technique is presented in Figure 1.

*TABLE 1. Behavior Recording Techniques*

| Method and Definition | Purpose | Application |
|---|---|---|
| **CONTINUOUS RECORDING [Running Narrative]**<br><br>The observer writes a narrative describing in sequence all behaviors observed. These observations can be organized into a 3-column chart ["ABC" chart] consisting of the events occurring prior to the behavior [Antecedents], the subject's responses [Behaviors] following these antecedents, and the events that follow the behavior [Consequences]. | 1. Allows further specification of conditions in which the behavior occurs, including cues, verbal prompts, and the possible reinforcers that maintain behavior<br><br>2. Provides general information necessary for choosing an efficient recording method [e.g., is frequency, duration, or intensity the critical variable?] | 1. Prior to assessment and modification, when unfamiliar with the subject<br><br>2. When the behaviors need to be more precisely defined [e.g., when two observers cannot agree on what is an instance of the behavior] |
| **DIRECT MEASUREMENT OF PERMANENT BEHAVIORAL PRODUCT**<br><br>A simple observation of a "physical" product of the behavior [e.g., the weight of an obese person, the test scores of an underachieving student, or the number of tokens spent]; usually measured at the end of a predetermined time period | 1. When available, it can provide a very direct measure of an effect of the behavior<br><br>2. Provides a means of measuring behavior which tends not to influence its occurrence or rate<br><br>3. Provides a standard of comparison or rough validity check on other measures | 1. When other methods may interfere with the behavior under observation<br><br>2. When too difficult or too time-consuming to observe behavior directly<br><br>3. Since the product is quantifiable, use with another method whenever possible |

## EVENT RECORDING

The observer simply counts each occurrence of the behavior during a predefined time period, often extended over a whole day if the behavior is of low frequency

Gives an accurate record of frequency within a designated time period, thus estimating the rate at which the behavior occurs

1. When behavior is of moderate to low frequency, and occurrences are similar in length

2. Can be used by a trained observer to record more than one behavior or more than one subject when the behavior is very easy to observe [e.g., one can record different subjects engaging in the same simple behavior (such as patients entering the nurses' station), or one can record more than one simple behavior for a single subject (such as a child crying or calling out in class)]

## DURATION RECORDING

The observer measures the total length of time that the behavior occurs during a predefined observation period

1. Provides a record of how long the behavior occurs within a given time period

2. Can provide a more accurate measure, especially when frequency alone is unrepresentative [see 4th application in adjacent box]

1. Only when behavior has an easily determined beginning and end

2. Ordinarily used with one subject

3. For behaviors with variable durations [e.g., a behavioral deficit of low frequency (poor eye contact)]

4. For a behavioral excess of long duration and moderate to low frequency [e.g., when a child is out of his seat for long periods at a time]

265

| Method and Definition | Purpose | Application |
|---|---|---|
| **INTERVAL RECORDING**<br><br>The observer divides the observation period [e.g., ½ hour] into a number of equal time intervals, usually ranging from 5 seconds to 1 or 2 minutes. He then notes whether or not the defined behavior(s) occurs in each interval. Interval length should be such that a behavior typically occurs only once in each interval | Gives a rough estimate of the frequency of the responses and the latency between responses | 1. By establishing a code for the behaviors, multiple behaviors may be recorded for multiple subjects [e.g., observe 1-5 behaviors for a different subject for each interval. Repeat process after each subject is observed]<br>2. When event and duration recording do not work<br>3. For behaviors with highly variable frequencies<br>4. Behavior need not have easily determined beginning and end |
| **TIME SAMPLING**<br><br>Brief observations are made at specified times throughout the subjects' active daily hours. These times can be evenly spaced or randomly selected | 1 Very brief, providing staff with additional time for other duties or other observations<br>2. Provides a schedule for use of other recording methods [e.g., counting the frequency of prompted verbalizations at randomly sampled times throughout the day] | 1. For multiple subjects and/or multiple behaviors<br>2. When behaviors have moderate to high frequency<br>3. When behavior can be prompted by staff [e.g., delusional speech of patient when questioned] |

Reprinted, by permission, from Alevizos, P.N., and Berck, P. L. An instructional aid for staff training in behavioral assessment. Unpublished manuscript, Camarillo Neuropsychiatric Institute Research Program, 1974. Described in a Communication, Journal of Applied Behavior Analysis. 1975, 7, 472 & 660.

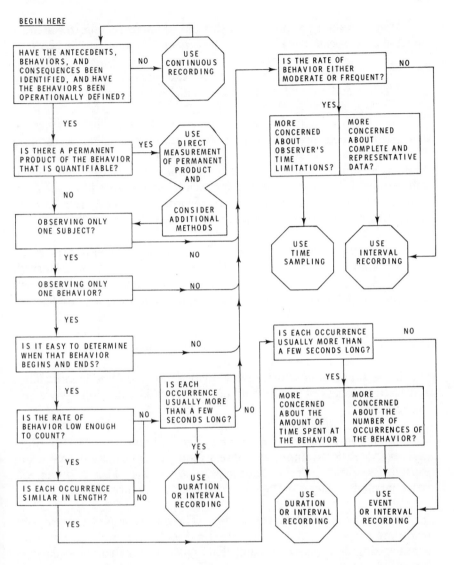

*Fig. 1.   A flow chart providing a simplified method of selecting an appropriate recording technique. Beginning with the box in the upper left-hand corner, the observer answers each successive question until reaching the appropriate recording method.*

*Reprinted, by permission, from Alevizos, P.N., and Berck, P. L. An instructional aid for staff training in behavioral assessment. Unpublished manuscript, Camarillo Neuropsychiatric Institute Research Program, 1974. Described in a Communication, Journal of Applied Behavior Analysis. 1975, 7, 472 & 660.*

While it is not the purpose of this introductory section to elaborate on all of these specific techniques, a few general comments are in order.

The type of recording system selected for use depends upon a number of broad factors and their interaction. These include:

1. *The stage of the assessment process.* In the early stages of assessment when problem definition is the major goal, a running narrative probably provides the most information about behavior and its context. It is likely that a good deal of this initial observation information will be discarded as unnecessary for treatment design and/or program evaluation; however, such continuous recording provides a rich base for generating assessment and treatment hypotheses.

2. *Characteristics of the behaviors being observed.* Such factors as the rate at which behavior occurs, the number of behaviors being observed, the complexity of the behavior, and other qualitative characteristics will determine which type of recording technique will be most applicable.

3. *Characteristics of the situation in which observation is to occur.* The degree to which an observer is intrusive in a situation (i.e., home versus classroom), the number of individuals being observed, the degree to which the situation is structured or unstructured, and the identifiability and distinctiveness of situational cues will also designate one procedure over another.

4. *Characteristics of the observer.* The amount of observer time available, both for training and observation, the information processing capabilities of the observer, and the prior experience of the observer will be a contributing factor in the selection of one procedure over another.

5. *Resources for data summarization.* The more complex the behavior recording procedure, the greater the time and manpower resources for summarizing and analyzing data. This could mean that some delay is introduced between assessment and treatment when recording procedures are complex.

The factors designated above should serve to make the point that there is never an ''ideal'' coding system for a given situation. Within limits, the system that is ''optimal'' for a given situation reflects not only the information yield of the recording procedure, but also a number of pragmatic considerations related to the therapist's or investigator's time and resources. Such considerations are as important a part of the assessment enterprise as considerations relating to reliability and validity.

Voluminous amounts of reliable data that cannot be summarized may be as useless as unreliable data.

## METHODOLOGICAL CONSIDERATIONS IN THE USE OF DIRECT OBSERVATION

The emphasis on observational procedures in behavior-therapy assessment has led to an increasing concern for methodological problems associated with their use (Johnson & Bolstad, 1973; Jones, 1973; Jones, Reid, & Patterson, 1974; Lipinski & Nelson, 1974; Lytton, 1971; Mash, 1976; O'Leary & Kent, 1973; Patterson & Harris, 1968). These problems include factors influencing observer accuracy, difficulty of choosing an appropriate interobserver reliability measure, observer bias, reactive effects of being observed, and demand characteristics of the observation situation. Extensive treatment of these issues is provided in the articles mentioned above. While it is not the purpose of this introduction to provide an exhaustive treatment of methodological difficulties inherent in the use of observational procedures, a summary of some of the major points should alert the reader to specific and recurrent problems.

The primary methodological requirement for any observational procedure is reflected in the simple requirement of observer accuracy. Observer accuracy usually reflects the extent to which an observer agrees with another observer (interobserver agreement), with a criterion coding protocol (criterion-observer agreement), or with himself on successive scorings of the same stimulus materials (intraobserver agreement). The most frequently used measure is that of interobserver agreement.

At the simplest level one might assume that observer accuracy is a direct function of the amount of training received by an observer. The greater the amount of training, the more accurate the observer. However, a number of studies have demonstrated that observer accuracy is a function of the complex interaction between coding procedure characteristics, observer characteristics, and conditions of observation (Mash & McElwee, 1974). Before commenting further on some of these factors, it should be pointed out that even if observer accuracy were simply a function of practice (amount of training), there is very little systematic data relating training conditions to the later performance of observers. In fact, with a few exceptions (Budd, Rogers, & Schilmoeller, 1972), detailed descriptions of observer training procedures have been relatively sparse. Studies that have attempted to relate training conditions to later performance have tended to show that different conditions may result in observers who may code the same information differently (Mash & Makohoniuk, 1975; Mash & McElwee, 1974; Wildman & Erickson, 1975). Such variables as the nature of behavior observed during training and whether the observer is trained by others or self-trained have been implicated. In any event, it would appear that more systematic attention needs to be given to some of the problems involved in training observers.

Another methodological consideration relates to the choice of an appropriate interobserver reliability measure. Repp, Dietz, Boles, Dietz, and Repp (1973) have shown that different ways of calculating interobserver agreement may lead to different outcomes. In general, the observer accuracy measure selected will vary, depending upon the nature of the recordings and the way in which the data will be used. For extensive treatments of this issue the reader is referred to Hartmann (1974), Johnson and Bolstad (1973), and Long (1962).

There is also an increasingly large number of studies that have shown that an observer accuracy measure may be a "fickle figure" (Kent, O'Leary, & Kanowitz, 1974; O'Leary & Kent, 1973; Reid, 1970; Reid & DeMaster, 1972; Romanczyk, Kent, Diament, & O'Leary, 1973; Taplin & Reid, 1973; Wildman, Erickson, & Kent, 1975). The general conclusions to be drawn from these studies are that accuracy measures obtained under conditions where the observer is aware that his performance is being monitored may be much higher than under conditions where the observer believes that his performance is not being monitored. This latter condition is the more frequent one, in that often observers are trained to perform at a criterion level and then left on their own for much of the data-collection process. The findings from these studies suggest that reliability assessment itself may be a reactive process and that it may be necessary to monitor the observer's performance continually, or at least to employ periodic spot-check procedures.

Other studies (Kass & O'Leary, 1970; Mash & Makohoniuk, 1975; Skindrud, 1972, 1973) have shown that observers may show biases in the way in which they record information. For example, Kent, O'Leary, Diament, & Dietz (1974) have reported data indicating that observers may show certain expectation biases related to beliefs about the outcome of treatment. In addition, the "observer drift" phenomenon in which two observers continue to agree with one another but move away from the scoring criterion originally designated has also been identified as a methodological problem (Johnson & Bolstad, 1973).

The methodological difficulty associated with observation procedures which has probably received the most discussion, if not the most research has been the observer's influence on the observation situation. This reactivity question is frequently encountered both in terms of clients who question whether an outside observer will see them as they "really are," and with respect to more basic questions relating to the validity and generalizability of information obtained by observation.

One of the troublesome features related to the question of observer effect is that the empirical studies are few in number and typically have had mixed results. In part, this is related to the fact that the design for answering the question of observer effect requires that a measure of performance be taken in the absence of an observer. This means that individuals in the situation are to be unaware that they are being observed, which creates a host of ethical concerns. Because of this problem a number of investigators have attempted to vary the *level* of intrusiveness of the observation condition in a way that the observee is unsure of the particular times at which observation is taking place. These applications have involved the use of wireless transmitters (Johnson, Christensen, & Bellamy, 1975) or recorders that come on at periodic intervals that are unknown to people in the setting (Bernal, Gibson, Williams, & Pesses, 1971). Other investigators have attempted to get at this question by having a person in the setting record behavior without others being aware (Patterson & Harris, 1968). Still others have attempted to use stability in the data collected (sometimes following a period of instability) as an indicator that habituation is occurring. All of these approaches have their limitations, but still provide useful information in an otherwise difficult area.

Findings concerning the nature of an observer's effect on performance have been equivocal. A number of studies (Bernal, Gibson, Williams, & Pesses, 1971; Hagen, Craighead, & Paul, 1975; Moos, 1968; Purcell & Brady, 1966; Soskin & John, 1963) have found minimal effects. Other studies have shown reactivity to an observer's presence (Bechtel, 1967; Cox, 1968; Dubanoski & Parton, 1971; Martin, Gelfand, & Hartmann, 1971; Mash & Hedley, 1975; Mercatoris & Craighead, 1974; Patterson & Harris, 1968; Roberts & Renzaglia, 1965; White, 1973). In general, the conclusion to be drawn from the existing literature is that the presence or absence of observer effect, its magnitude, directionality, and persistence appear to be a function of the complex interaction between observer, performer, and situation characteristics. In those instances where observational assessment is to be used, an attempt to assess the effect of the observer in relation to variables under each of these broad headings should be attempted.

Other methodological problems that have been considered include the observee's tendency to "fake" behavior in a way consistent with certain ends, for example, acceptance into treatment (Johnson & Lobitz, 1972), the need to find ways of dealing with baseline instability (Jones, 1972) and with low-rate behaviors (Royer, Flynn, & Osadca, 1971), and data differences occurring from differences in observational and computational procedures (Gaines, 1973; Hawn, Brown, & LeBlanc,

1973; Martin & Gonzalez, 1975; Thomson, Holmberg, & Baer, 1973; Wodarski, Feldman, & Pedi, 1974). In sum, the information presented in this section should alert the user of observational procedures to a number of methodological issues inherent in their use, many of which are unresolved.


## GENERAL CONSIDERATIONS


*Who observes?* Most frequently, observational data are obtained by an "outside" observer who is trained in the use of a particular procedure. However, there are numerous reports that have attempted to use individuals in the situation as data collection agents, usually by having them employ a fairly simple code system. The most common applications of this sort have involved parents or teachers recording the behavior of children and individuals recording their own behavior (self-monitoring). These applications have tended to have somewhat different goals.

Having parents record the behavior of their child (e.g., Eyberg & Johnson, 1974; Mash, Handy, & Hamerlynck, 1976; Patterson, 1974; Peine, 1972) has been used for multiple purposes. These include providing information for diagnosis and design questions, assessing the parents' motivation to participate, monitoring the progress of treatment, teaching parents more effective "tracking" skills, providing feedback and reinforcement to the parent for positive changes that may occur, and providing an independent data source for comparison with observational measures obtained through other procedures, in order to establish the convergent validity of measures of treatment effectiveness (Eyberg & Johnson, 1974; Johnson & Christensen, 1974; Patterson, 1974). Similar purposes may be ascribed to teacher recording of student behavior, with perhaps a greater emphasis being placed upon the use of such measures for evaluating the outcome of specific programs (Kubany & Sloggett, 1973). Apart from the methodological questions associated with using individuals in the situation as data collection agents, an overriding concern has been the time-consuming nature of such observations. Typically, much reinforcement must be given in order to maintain these recording behaviors. Frequent contact either in person or via the telephone is often needed.

Probably the most frequently employed observational procedure for adult populations has been some form of self-monitoring in which the individual is asked to observe and record his own behavior. The use of self-monitoring has likely increased, concomitant with the increasing emphasis on cognitive processes and self-control in behavior change programs (Mahoney, 1974; Mahoney & Thoresen, 1974; Thoresen &

Mahoney, 1974; Watson & Tharp, 1972). In addition, a number of technical aids have been developed to assist in self-recording (e.g., Lindsley, 1968). Self-monitoring has been used both for behavioral assessment, particularly in relation to outcome evaluation, and as a behavior-change procedure (Kazdin, 1974). There have been numerous applications of self-monitoring procedures across a wide range of problems and situations. While it is not possible to review all of these studies in this introduction, the reader is directed to the texts cited above for excellent and extensive reviews and discussions of the topic. It should be pointed out that self-monitoring procedures present a set of somewhat unique methodological problems related to the reliability of data obtained in this manner and the reactivity of the procedure. A number of studies have attempted to examine these questions (Gottman & McFall, 1972; Johnson & White, 1971; Lipinski & Nelson, 1974; Nelson, Lipinski, & Black, 1975; Nelson & McReynolds, 1971; Romanczyk, 1974; Simkins, 1971a, 1971b).

*Where to observe?* The behavioral emphasis on the contemporaneous antecedent and consequent stimulus events designates the natural environment (home, school, work, etc.) as the most appropriate arena for observational assessment. However, despite the potentially rich data yield, observation in the natural environment is not an easy matter. Apart from the reactivity problems that more than likely make most naturalistic assessment pseudo-naturalistic (Lytton, 1971), a major concern is with the efficiency of the sampling procedure. That is, it may be necessary to observe for inordinately long periods of time before the behaviors or situations of interest are likely to occur. This is especially the case when one is interested in low-rate behaviors and is exemplified by observations of family interaction in which a relatively small proportion of observed behavior is of interest and a good deal of the observation time is characterized by nonresponding.

Attempts to deal with this problem have involved the development of analogue observation situations designed to provoke the behaviors of interest, usually by providing cues that are associated with the occurrence of particular responses (Martin, Johnson, Johansson, & Wahl, 1976). In observing children, frequently in interaction with their parents, a number of studies (e.g., Eyberg & Johnson, 1974; Johnson & Brown, 1969; Wahler, Winkel, Peterson, & Morrison, 1965) have discussed the use of "standard situations" designed to simulate frequently occurring life situations. These situations have involved such things as having a parent involved in free play with the child, command-compliance situations in which the parent is instructed to have the child follow a series of simple requests, and presentation of taped excerpts or vignettes (both audio and video-taped) of child behavior to which the parent is asked to provide a typical response. Such analogous assessments represent a more economical assessment procedure than naturalistic observation, but they are useful only to the extent that behavior in response to such "contrived" circumstances correlates with naturally occurring behavior. There is little systematic information relating to this question. However, what data does exist suggests that the correlation may be slight (Martin, et al., 1976), even though some studies (e.g., Martin, Dysart, & Gonzalez, 1975; Rapoport & Benoit, 1975) have found some correspondence between clinic-analogue measures and home observations. The lack of a clearly demonstrated relationship between analogue and "real life" measures probably reflects more the methodological inadequacies and sparcity of studies than conclusive findings, and because of the efficiency of these procedures this would seem to be an area worthy of further exploration.

The use of analogue situations in assessing adult behavior has been extensive; however, the direct use of these situations for systematic behavior observation has been less frequent. Often, the analogue situations used were concerned with some research hypothesis rather than with clinical assessment per se. Many studies have reported the use or behavioral avoidance tests as an analogue assessment for fears (e.g., Bernstein & Nietzel, 1974; Borkovec, Stone, O'Brien, & Kaloupek, 1974). Others studies have relied upon the use of analogues in assessing interpersonal competence (e.g., Goldfried & D'Zurilla, 1969; McFall & Marston, 1970; McFall & Lillesand, 1971), marital conflicts (Olson & Ryder, 1970), drinking behavior (Briddell & Nathan, 1975), stuttering (Daly & Frick, 1970), response to social reinforcement (Weiss, 1969), response to interpersonal situations (Hersen, Eisler, & Miller, 1973), responsiveness to sexual stimuli, and fears (Rutner & Pear, 1972). Other studies have attempted to simulate family interactions through the use of role-playing procedures. In addition, almost any therapy interaction involving the use of behavior rehearsal or role playing constitutes a potential analogue assessment procedure. As was the case for analogues involving child behavior, the major question is concerned with the generalizability of such assessment information for predicting behavior in naturalistic circumstances.

*Behavioral norms.* One of the persistent questions for observational assessment has been determining the significance of obtained levels of responding with respect to what constitutes a "typical" or "average" response level for a given population or situation. Given the highly idiosyncratic and individualistic approach to assessment taken by behavioral practitioners, there is some question as to whether normative information of this sort is necessary or useful. For example, of what functional value is it for a particular four-year-old child who is exhibiting ten hitting responses a minute, to know that most four-year-olds show a hitting rate of one response every sixty minutes? To a large extent the answer to this type of question relates to the way in which this information is used. If it is used directly as an indicant of what an individual client should be doing, then clearly this is a misuse, in that what the individual should be doing is a function of the complex interaction between individual and both micro- and macro-social criteria.

On the other hand, such normative information might be useful in providing broad guidelines for the terminal level of behavior change when considered in conjunction with other social criteria. A number of studies have provided norms for observational data taken across situations (Bernal, Delfini, North, & Kreutzer, 1976; Johnson, Bolstad, & Lobitz, 1976; Pelc, 1973) and populations (Delfini, Bernal, & Rosen, 1976; Sallows, 1973; Terdal, Jackson, & Garner, 1976). The usefulness of such normative information in the assessment process is yet to be demonstrated.

*Technical aids.* Observational assessments are often dependent upon technical aids for the coding and storage of behavioral data. Apart from the use of audio and video recording devices that serve to preserve the behavior but not transform it, a variety of counters and timers have been developed for observational use. A number of such technical aids, including wrist counters, digital counters, tally boards, and timers for recording behavior in the classroom, are described by Cooper (1974). Further devices of this sort are presented in a number of technical notes reported in the *Journal of Applied Behavioral Analysis* (1968-1976).

## OBSERVATIONAL ASSESSMENT: PROCEDURES

Observational procedures have been developed for coding behavior across a variety of populations and settings. For the most part, observational procedures have been used predominantly with children. A major reason for this has probably been the concern for reactivity of observational measures, and the assumption is frequently made that children will be less influenced than adults by the presence of an observer. While there are virtually no direct data to support this notion, there are a number of studies, as previously reported, that have shown children to be influenced by the presence of an observer. Consequently, the question of whether observational measures have greater application with children is an open one.

The simplest types of observational codes have typically involved taking rate measures on a few behaviors within the context of a single-subject research study. In this regard the range of code procedures is as diverse as the range of single-subject applications (see *Journal of Applied Behavior Analysis* for representative types of studies) that have been carried out. Beyond the use of observational measures in this fashion, a large number of more complex code systems have been developed. These code systems have typically involved the inclusion of multiple situational and behavioral codes. Such procedures have been developed for observation of family interaction (e.g., Bernal & North, 1972; Bernal, Kreutzer, North, & Pelc, 1973; Lavigueur, Peterson, Sheese, & Peterson, 1973; Lewinsohn & Shaffer, 1971; Mash, Terdal, & Anderson, 1973; Mash & McElwee, paper 20; Patterson, Ray, Shaw, & Cobb, 1969), in the classroom (e.g., Barocas & Weiss, 1974; Becker, Madsen, Arnold, & Thomas, 1967; Bernal & North, 1972; Cobb, 1970; Cobb & Hops, 1971; Cobb & Ray, 1970; Cotler, Applegate, King, & Kristal, 1972; Ferber, Keeley, & Shemberg, 1974; Gagne, 1973; Goodwin & Coate, 1971; Kuypers, Becker, & O'Leary, 1968; McNamara, 1971; O'Leary & Becker, 1967), for ward activities (Cataldo & Risley, 1974), for token programs (Henderson & Scoles, 1970; O'Leary, Becker, Evans, & Saudargas, 1969; Tanner, Parrino, & Daniels, 1975), of marital interaction (Carter & Thomas, 1973; Hops, Wills, Patterson, & Weiss, 1971), in occupational therapy workshops (Katz, Johnson, & Gelfand, 1972), staff-resident interaction in a detention center (Gambrill, 1975), and with autistic children (Boer, 1968; Lovaas, Koegal, Simmons, & Long, 1973). This listing, which is by no means exhaustive, serves to give some representation of the types of observational code systems employed for behavior-therapy assessment.

The observational systems presented in this section were selected to provide a sampling of procedures that vary along a number of dimensions. The first relates to the complexity of the system. Observational procedures include those based upon simple event recording to approaches involving the classification of multiple behaviors for groups of individuals (see Mash & McElwee, paper 20). Another dimension is that of situational diversity. Procedures represented include measures for recording behavior in the home (Mash & McElwee) and classroom (see papers 17, 18). The methods presented have also been used across a range of populations (e.g., child, adult, family, etc.).

The article by Ray (see paper 17) describes a direct observational procedure for use in the classroom (Cobb & Ray, 1970) which possesses several unique features. The procedures make it possible for an observer to code the behavior of groups of individuals by sequentially observing different individuals. The code system also looks at antecedent consequent responses to behavior as well as the agent (teacher or peer) who is interacting with the child. The procedure provides for the delineation of broader situational contexts within the classroom, reflecting the degree of structure and make-up of different activities. Behavioral information about *all* children in the classroom helps to place the behavior of any one child in the context of a specific reference norm. However, the use of the recording procedure is time-consuming, and requires a trained observer. It would not, for example, be possible for a teacher to record behavior with this procedure while she was conducting a class.

The coding procedure described by Kubany and Sloggett (see paper 18) is specifically designed to be used by the teacher. It makes minimal demands on teacher time, making it possible for her to continue her regular teaching duties while periodically making an entry for a given child. Entries are made in conjunction with a timer that provides explicit cues for sampling, and the amount of sampling necessary would depend upon the amount of time the student is in the class. The procedure minimizes the amount of professional observer time needed and centers the data collection procedures around the teacher as primary agent in the classroom.

The response-class matrix presented by Mash, Terdal, and Anderson (see paper 19) is a procedure designed to record parent-child interaction. The use of the matrix permits an examination of behavior along with antecedent and consequent responses. While developed specifically for use with parent-child interaction, the structural aspects of the procedure would be applicable for other populations, if appropriate content changes were made. The procedure is less complex than others that have been developed for recording interaction, and as such it can be used following a minimal period of training.

The family interaction code by Mash and McElwee (see paper 20) is an extension and adaptation of the manual for coding family interaction developed by Patterson, Ray, Shaw, and Cobb (1969). The procedure is a fairly complex code involving 42 behavioral categories. Records are obtained for sequential events, which permits an examination of behavior in relation to antecedent and consequent. The code also provides an additional procedure for obtaining ongoing information about location and activities to provide further contextual information. The usefulness of this type of sequential coding procedure has been documented in a large number of studies reported by Gerald R. Patterson and his associates (e.g., Patterson, 1974, 1976).

The procedure requires highly trained coders who require continual practice in recording. For this reason, the code system in its totality is probably more suitable as a research tool than as a clinical assessment procedure. However, the carefully defined and conceptualized system of behavioral categories could serve as a pool from which to draw specific codes for the development of simpler code systems.

The coding procedure developed by Lewinsohn (see paper 21) was designed for the observation of interpersonal behavior involving verbal exchanges. This system has been used primarily with populations of depressed individuals (Libet & Lewinsohn, 1973) and looks at both the verbal content emitted by an individual and reactions of others to this behavior. In a broad sense, behaviors are coded in terms of positive and negative reactions; however there are categories involving further differentiation within categories. The system also requires a good deal of observer training.

A system for recording individual behavioral data in a token program is reported by Milby, Willcutt, Hawk, MacDonald, and Whitfield (see paper 22). This code system is designed in such a way that it can be used to monitor treatment as well as facilitate the operation of a token system through the clear identification of behaviors and reinforcers and the use of the actual tokens as the record-keeping system.

# 17 (Part 1)

## Naturalistic Assessment in Educational Settings: The Classroom Behavior Observation Code

*Roberta Shockley Ray*

The educational setting has become a major focus of behavioral intervention programs and social learning research. The emphasis on assessment of behavior in situ which characterizes both behavioral intervention and research has encouraged the rapid development of procedures for collection of observational data in the school setting. Teachers wearing event counters strapped on their wrists, students plotting behavioral records on graph paper, and observers carrying interval timers and coding forms are becoming increasingly familiar figures in the classroom.

Numerous systems for collection of observational data in the classroom have been developed over the last ten years. Emphases on the single subject design and on specificity of target responses have resulted in proliferation of *specific* behavior codes, such as the tantrum coding system developed by Brawley and his colleagues (Brawley, Harris, Allen, Fleming, & Petersen, 1969) and the system for observation of isolate behaviors used by Allen, Hart, Buell, Harris, and Wolf (1964).

To a somewhat lesser extent, investigators have designed *general* response codes applicable to a wide range of classroom situations and behaviors. Two such broad-based systems have been described by Bijou, Peterson, Harris, Allen, and Johnson (1969) and by Becker and his colleagues (Becker, Madsen, Arnold, & Thomas, 1967). The observation code that is the focus of this description is a further example of a general response code that was designed for the evaluation of behavioral intervention and for the study of socialization processes.

## Development of the Classroom Behavior
## Observation Code

This code is one of a series of observational assessment systems developed to describe the behavior of "conduct-disordered" boys and their peers and teachers in the classroom. It is a modification and extension of an earlier classroom observation system developed by Ray, Shaw, and Patterson (1968). The most recent code in this series, a further modification of the Cobb and Ray coding system, is currently being used in the assessment of activity level and attending behavior in hyperactive boys (Ray, Kantosky, Clement, & Morse, 1975).

The Classroom Behavior Observation Code is a broad band-width instrument designed to meet multiple clinical and research data needs. It was our objective to develop an observational assessment procedure that would provide data for:

1. Behavioral analyses specifying setting determinants of behavior, deficient and excessive responses in contrast to a "normal" peer group, and social consequences maintaining behavior patterns.
2. Evaluation of behavioral intervention programs with aggressive, hyperactive boys (e.g., Patterson, Cobb, & Ray, 1972).
3. Studies of the relationship of observed behaviors to academic performance (e.g., Cobb, 1972).
4. Studies of the effects of changes in classroom structure and teaching strategies on observed behavior (e.g., Ray, Shaw, & Cobb, 1970).

The coding system may be characterized as a *time-sampling procedure* in which a *nonparticipant observer,* utilizing a *paper-and-pencil format,* codes *classroom structure and activity, subjects' and peers' behaviors, and responses to those behaviors* from the *teacher and other students.*

*Time sampling procedure.* The coding manual suggests a time interval of six seconds for coding each behavior-response unit. During each interval only one subject or peer behavior and the associated student and teacher responses to that behavior are to be coded. Although the time-sampling procedure could be altered to fit the requirements of other coding situations, the six-second interval appears to be sufficiently long to allow for complete coding of a behavior-response unit. The interval is also sufficiently short to make it unlikely that two observers will code different behavior-response units in the same time interval.

*Nonparticipant observer.* In contrast to the classroom observation procedure suggested by Kubany and Sloggett (1973), this coding system requires a trained observer who does not interact with the subjects of the data collection. Although the use of a nonparticipant observer may be an unnecessary luxury in some simple behavior-modification programs, this procedure permits the collection of extensive data necessary for the evaluation of complex intervention programs, the analysis of classroom interaction, or answering research questions. The required observer-training is fairly brief and may be completed as successfully by volunteer classroom aides or student tutors as by ''professional'' observers.

*Paper-and-pencil format.* The coding system is most frequently used in the format shown in the manual. The only additional requirement is the provision of a time signal, commonly an auditory signal supplied via earphone from an interval timer or a cassette recorder playing a prerecorded tape with time-interval signal tones. Alterations to the format are easily made to accommodate encoding by a variety of electro-mechanical recording devices.

*Classroom structure and activity.* Behavior analysts, teachers, *and* children frequently comment on the importance of situational determinants of behavior. Using this observation system, the first task of the observer is to code the classroom situation as structured or unstructured and the student activity as individual or group. At each activity transition, the observer again codes setting determinants. Coding for situational determinants could be elaborated to include any stimulus conditions hypothesized to be relevant to the behavioral output of the code: for example, language, arts, and math instruction might be coded as setting variables on the assumption that they may be powerful differential determinants of achievement behaviors in girls and in boys.

*Subjects and peers.* The code was originally designed to describe the behavior of the target child (subject or *S* on the coding sheet) and a composite peer (*P*), an average of all same-sex peers in the classroom. The purposes of this comparison were to study the behavioral effects of a ''deviant child'' label and to provide normative data on the level of ''appropriate'' and ''inappropriate'' behaviors in the classroom. It should be clear, however, that the use of the coding procedure does not predetermine the selection of students to be observed. The system user might elect to observe only one subject, one subject and one peer, or to compare high and low achievers; appropriate selection of subjects should be determined by the research or clinical questions to be answered.

*Behaviors and responses.* During each interval one subject behavior and any clear response to that behavior are coded. Nineteen behaviors and responses are defined in the coding manual. Users who consider additions, subtractions, or combinations of codes should be aware of the hierarchical arrangement of behavior codes and the ipsative quality of the system. Given these considerations, altering the number or order of behaviors will alter the probability of observing other behaviors. This alteration has implications for the calculation of reliability and stability data as well as for the comparison of findings across studies employing a different number of codes. These limitations should be considered prior to any alteration of the categories defined in the manual.

*Teacher and other students.* Responses that appear to be immediate consequences of recorded subject behaviors are coded as teacher or peer behaviors. This recording of responses may provide the information necessary to understand the conditions maintaining a pattern of behavior or to design a consequence-alteration treatment program. Teachers have found an analysis of the immediate consequences they supply for appropriate and inappropriate behaviors helpful in the design of a behavioral self-change program.

## Observer Training

Over the course of several studies of classroom interaction and outcome of behavioral intervention programs, a large number of observers have been trained in the use of the Classroom Behavior Observation Code. School counselors, volunteer classroom aides, "professional" observers associated with research or intervention projects, and high school students working as tutors in elementary classrooms have participated in a four-stage program including:

1. Coding manual training.
2. Videotape training.
3. Classroom training.
4. Accuracy retraining.

During the first stage of training, observers study the coding manual, learning definitions of behavior categories and becoming familiar with the coding form used in data collection. Also at this stage, practice in coding from a written classroom "scenario," such as that included as an example of behavior coding in the manual, clarifies distinctions among the various behavior categories and provides the observer with an opportunity to learn the process of scanning the coding form to locate the correct time intervals and behavior symbols.

In the second stage, training progresses to the observation of videotaped and precoded classroom interactions. Videotapes may present either "'actual'' classroom behaviors or a simulated classroom setting in which behavior scripts are acted out. Simulation tapes present some advantages for training in that scripts may be written to ensure inclusion of examples of all behavior categories and subject-teacher-peer interactions at a predetermined base rate and level of complexity. Although observer training may be accomplished solely in situ or by "live" role-playing, the use of videotapes provides the opportunity to "stop action" for discussion of coding disagreements, ensures the exact repetition of behavioral sequences which may be judged critical in clarifying a distinction between behaviors, and allows the option to precode tapes for observer accuracy checks. Videotape training also facilitates the simultaneous training of larger groups of observers than could be trained in a classroom setting.

Observers-in-training are sent into the classroom with experienced observers during the third stage of the training program. Practice sessions are short and interspersed with feedback sessions with the experienced observer. It may be advantageous to order the classroom settings to be observed in terms of the probable complexity of the behaviors to be coded. For example, training observations might begin with coding one subject only during periods of structured individual and group activities, followed by unstructured individual and group activities, and finally, by including interval-to-interval alternation between subject and peers.

A total of six to ten hours of training (manual, videotape, and in situ) has been sufficient for observers to achieve approximately an 85% level of inter-observer agreement.

The fourth stage of observer training continues throughout the data-collection process. Periodic retraining is essential to maintaining observer accuracy (agreement with predetermined criterion coding of behavior sequences). Research in observer agreement and accuracy indicates that pairs of observers may maintain a high level of intra-pair agreement and concurrently become less accurate in terms of agreement with criterion protocols (Reid & DeMaster, 1972). This research on observer drift underlines the necessity for continuing training on criterion-coded videotapes or classroom scripts in addition to frequent field studies of inter-observer agreement.

## INTER-OBSERVER AGREEMENT AND STABILITY

Extensive data on inter-observer agreement and the stability of behavior codes are presented in several research reports (Cobb, 1972; Patterson, Cobb, & Ray, 1972).

Inter-observer agreement is computed by assigning agreement or nonagreement status to each scored interval. Inter-observer agreement is expressed as a percentage where

$$\text{Observer agreement} = \frac{\text{Agreement intervals}}{\text{Agreement} + \text{nonagreement intervals}} \times 100$$

This method of computing observer reliability yielded mean agreement across behavior categories of 88% (Cobb, 1971) and 84.5% (Patterson, Ray, & Cobb, 1972). Agreement figures for individual codes have been found to range from 75% to 100% (Cobb, 1972).

The stability of behavior codes has been the subject of one study of the observation system (Cobb, 1972). One-hundred-and-twenty fourth graders were observed over a period of ten days for an average of 14 minutes of data collection on each child. Comparing behavior category rates for alternate days, Cobb found a median correlation of .56. The magnitude of individual category stability coefficients was significantly related to the base-rate occurrence of the behavior (r = .64, p < .05). These results indicate that a longer period of observation will be required to establish stability in low-rate behaviors. Intervention studies would commonly include longer periods of observation than those in the Cobb study.

For use in intervention studies, the Classroom Behavior Observation Code produces a large number of scored intervals within the span of a typical baseline period in the classroom. A baseline observation on one target child for 20 minutes per day over a five-day week yields 600 coded behaviors and up to 600 responses each from the peer group and the teacher.

Code users should conduct their own studies of inter-observer agreement, observer accuracy, and stability of behaviors in addition to becoming familiar with currently available data.

The following section presents the manual for the Classroom Behavior Observation Code. The manual includes a description of the coding procedure and format, definitions of behavior categories, and a classroom "scenario," precoded on a sample coding form.

You are invited to try it in your own classroom data-collection program. Perhaps you will find you agree with Yogi Berra, who is reputed to have said, "You can see a lot by observing."

# REFERENCES

Allen, K. E., Hart, B. M., Buell, J. S., Harris, F. R., & Wolf, M. M. Effects of social reinforcement on isolate behavior of a nursery school child. *Child Development,* 1964, *35,* 511-518.

Becker, W. C., Madsen, C. H., Jr., Arnold, C. R., & Thomas, D. R. The contingent use of teacher attention and praise in reducing classroom behavior problems. *Journal of Special Education,* 1967, *1,* 287-307.

Bijou, S. W., Peterson, R. F., Harris, F. R., Allen, K. E., & Johnson, M. S. Methodology for experimental studies of young children in natural settings. *Psychological Record,* 1969, *19,* 177-210.

Brawley, E. R., Harris, F. R., Allen, K. E., Fleming, R. s., & Peterson, R. F. Behavior modification of an autistic child. *Behavioral Science,* 1969, *14* (2), 87-98.

Cobb, J. A. The relationship of discrete classroom behaviors to fourth-grade academic achievement. *Journal of Educational Psychology,* 1972, *63,* 74-80.

Kubany, E. S., & Sloggett, B. B. Coding procedure for teachers. *Journal of Applied Behavior Analysis,* 1973, *6,* 339-344.

Patterson, G. R., Cobb, J. A., & Ray, R. S. Direct intervention in the Classroom: A set of procedures for the aggressive child. In F. W. Clark, D. R. Evans, & L. A. Hamerlynck (Eds.), *Implementing behavioral programs for schools and clinics.* Champaign, Ill.: Research Press, 1972.

Ray, R. S., Kantosky, M. A., Xlement, R. L., & Morse, E. "Classroom observations of activity level and attending behavior." Unpublished coding manual, University of Wisconsin, Madison, 1975.

Ray, R. S., Shaw, D. A., & Cobb, J. A. The Work Box: An innovation in teaching attentional behavior. *The School Counselor,* 1970, *18,* 15-35.

Ray, R. S., Shaw, D. A., & Patterson, G. R. "Observation in the school: Description of a coding form." Unpublished coding manual, Oregon Research Institute, Eugene, 1968.

Reid, J. B., & DeMaster, B. The efficacy of the spot-check procedure in maintaining the reliability of data collected by observers in quasi-natural settings: Two pilot studies. *Oregon Research Institute Research Bulletin,* 1972, *12,* No. 8.

# 17 (Part 2)

## The Classroom Behavior
## Observation Code

*Joseph A. Cobb*

*Roberta S. Ray*

This manual is a guide to be used in connection with the observation of classroom behaviors. The code has been developed to provide a precise record of behavioral rates in the classroom. Many behaviors have been defined previously by Ray, Shaw, and Patterson (1968).

### PROCEDURE

The observer will look at the subject and each same-sex peer in alternating six-second intervals, i.e., subject, peer; subject, peer; subject, peer; etc. The observer will code the appropriate behavior by placing a circle around the category on the coding sheet. If there is a response to the behavior by another person which can be discerned by the subject, the response is to be coded. A vertical line ( | ) is to be placed through the

This code is adapted from a system which appeared in J. A. Cobb & R. S. Ray. Manual for coding discrete behaviors in the school setting. In F. W. Clark, D. R. Evans, & L. A. Hamerlynck (Eds.), *Implementing behavioral programs for schools and clinics.* Champaign, Ill.: Research Press, 1972. Pp. 187-194. Copyright © 1972 Research Press Company. Reprinted by permission.

Inquiries concerning this code system should be directed to Dr. Roberta S. Ray, Department of Psychology, University of Wisconsin, 1202 West Johnson Street, Madison, Wisconsin, 53706.

symbol of the response on the coding sheet if the response is by the teacher; if the response is by a peer, a horizontal line (−) is used.

A signalling device (clipboard with built-in interval timer and earphone jack) is provided to produce an auditory signal every six seconds so the observer will know when to code a child's behavior. An efficient procedure for coding is to observe the child for a few seconds after the auditory signal occurs and check to see if there is a response from the environment; then code the behavior observed as well as the response; if there is no immediate response, but a response occurs before the end of the six-second interval, code that response, wait for the next auditory signal, and repeat the procedure for the next person. Once all same-sex peers have been coded in the classroom, the observer will begin coding in the same order of peers on the same coding sheet as in the original sequence. Sometimes the original order will be difficult to maintain due to movement in the classroom; in these cases the observer should attempt to sample all peers, regardless of order, before returning to coding the same peer twice. If a peer leaves the room or is unobservable for other reasons, do not leave the space blank, just continue and code the next peer.

## CODING CATEGORIES

Space is provided on the sheet for the academic activity, the structure provided by the teacher, and the type of work (group, individual, and transitional) that was occurring at the time of coding. The observer is to fill in the academic activity, e.g., reading, arithmetic, social studies, etc., the type of structure, and the type of work. When changes occur in the latter two areas while the sheet is being coded, a symbol is to be placed at the beginning of the subject or peer line in which the change occurred. The symbol should be the first letter of the five categories used to characterize the situation. For instance, if the teacher is lecturing to the class and then begins to have them work on individual work assignments at a point where only part of the class has been coded, an ''I'' is placed in front of the child's number at which point group work changed to individual work.

The definitions for the five categories are as follows:

*Structured.* The teacher has provided clear guidelines for the children to follow in carrying out tasks.

*Unstructured.* The guidelines for the child's behavior are vague or unclear to the observer, i.e., the students may determine what they want to do in terms of academic activity and/or nonintellectual behaviors.

*Group.* The class is involved as one unit in academic activity, e.g., teacher lecturing, student reciting while entire class listens. Also,

"Group" is to be coded when there are small groups in the class, as often occurs in reading.

*Individual.* The majority of the students are doing work by themselves at desks, e.g., social study projects are being done by each student. "Individual" can be checked even though the student asks for and receives help from other peers and/or teachers.

*Transitional.* This category should be checked when the class is between activities, e.g., waiting for recess, lining up for lunch, class returning from recess, teacher has indicated reading period is finished but has provided no directions for the next activity. As soon as teacher provides directions for the next activity, the "Transitional" category is to be omitted and either the "Group" or the "Individual" category checked.

It is essential that only one behavior be coded for each subject. Although there will be instances in which more than one behavior code is applicable, the observer should code only one. To facilitate a consistent choice of categories among observers, the codes are ordered in the manual as well as on the code sheets in an hierarchical fashion for appropriate and inappropriate behaviors. The observer is to move from left to right until the first applicable code category is reached; that category is to be marked and no other.

The same procedure is to be followed for coding a peer and/or teacher response. The rule to keep uppermost in mind regarding the choice of response is that the response is *specifically* directed at the subject. For example, if the student is attending to his work and a peer drops a book with a loud noise, the student's behavior is coded but not the peer's behavior as the behavior was not directed at the subject; however, if the peer dropped the book on the student's desk, then that response would be coded.

In the following list the code definitions are applicable to both behavior of the subject and to responses from teachers and peers unless noted otherwise:

*AP Approval.* Used whenever a person gives a clear gestural, verbal, or physical approval to another individual. "Approval" is more than attention, in that it must include some clear indication of positive interest or involvement. Examples of "approval" are smiles, head nods, hugs, pats on the back, and phrases such as "That's a good boy," "Thank you," "That's right," and "That's a good job."

*CO Complies.* This category can be checked each time the person does what another person has requested, e.g., the teacher asks class to take out notebooks and pupil does; she asks for paper to be turned in and pupil obeys; pupil asks for pencil and teacher or peer gives him one; teacher tells class to be quiet and pupil is quiet.

*TT+ Appropriate talking with teacher.* This category can be checked when the pupil talks with the teacher, whether in private as in independent work situations or answers questions in other situations. If the teacher is *interacting* with the child when the child is talking appropriately, the *response* is coded TT+. The reason for coding the subject's behavior and the response in the same category is the difficulty of differentiating other responses in quick verbal interchanges; of course, if other responses are appropriate, e.g., AP, DI, or AT, and can be clearly differentiated, they preclude coding the response as TT+.

*IP+ Appropriate interaction with peer.* Coded when the pupil is interacting with peer and is not violating classroom rules. Interaction includes verbal and nonverbal communication, e.g., talking, handing materials, working on project with peer. The response for the peer is IP+ if the peer is *interacting* with the subject. The main element to remember in applying this code is that *an interaction is occurring* or one of the persons is attempting to interact. If two students are working on a social studies project, the code is IP+; if they are talking to each other or organizing a notebook *together,* the code is IP+; but if the subject is simply writing a report and the peer is writing, then the appropriate code is AT.

*VO Volunteers.* Coded when student indicates that he wants to make an academic contribution, e.g., teacher asks a question and he raises his hand.

*IT Initiation to or by teacher.* Pupil or teacher initiates or attempts to initiate interaction with each other, but not in conjunction with volunteering. Pupil may go to teacher's desk during independent study or raise his hand and seek assistance in solving an arithmetic problem; as a response, teacher may initiate interaction with pupil. This behavior is not inappropriate unless specified as such by the teacher. Frequency count of this behavior may be helpful in analysis of "dependency."

*AT Attending.* This category is used whenever a person indicates by his behavior that he is doing what is appropriate in a school situation, e.g., he is looking at the teacher when she is presenting material to the class; he is looking at visual aids as the teacher tells about them; he has his eyes focused on his book as he does the reading assignment; he writes answers to arithmetic problems; the teacher or peer looks at the child reciting. "Attending" is to be coded as a *response* when there is an indication that the subject is aware that a teacher or peer is attending to him; thus, when a child is working and the teacher looks at him, the child must make some recognition of the attending on the teacher's part, e.g., he looks at the teacher.

*PN  Physical negative.*   Use of this category is restricted to times when a person attacks or attempts to attack another person with the possibility of inflicting pain. Examples include slapping, spanking, kicking, biting, throwing objects at someone, etc.

*DS  Destructiveness.*   Use of this category is applicable when a person destroys or attempts to destroy some object, e.g., breaking a pencil in half, tearing a page from a book, carving name on desk, etc. This category is not to be used when the person is writing an answer or working out a problem on a desk with a pen or pencil.

*DI  Disapproval.*   Use this category whenever the person gives verbal or gestural disapproval of another person's behavior or characteristics. Shaking the head or finger are examples of gestural disapproval. "I do not like that tone of voice," "You didn't pass in your homework on time," "Your work is sloppy," "I don't like you" are examples of "disapproval." In verbal statements it is essential that the content of the statement explicitly states disapproval of the subject's behaviors or attributes, e.g., appearance, attitudes, academic skills, etc.

*NY  Noisy.*   This category is to be used when the person talks loudly, yells, bangs book, scrapes chairs, or makes any sounds that are likely to be actually or potentially disruptive to others.

*NC  Noncompliance.*   To be coded whenever the person does not do what is requested. This includes teacher giving instructions to entire class and the subject does not comply.

*PL  Play.*   Coded whenever person is playing alone or with another person and the classroom rules do not allow playing, e.g., playing tic-tac-toe in class, throwing a ball in classroom, etc. When coding P.E. or recess activities, approved play is to be coded as AT; nonapproved play is to be coded as PL.

*TT— Inappropriate talk with teacher.*   Used whenever content of conversation is negative toward teacher by pupil or when classroom rules do not allow interaction with teacher. Examples are, "I'm tired of this lesson," "I won't go to the principal's office," etc. This category should not be used if DI is appropriate.

*IP- Inappropriate interaction with peer.*   Coded whenever peer or pupil interacts with or attempts to interact with each other, and classroom rules are being violated. Examples include behaviors and/or responses such as touching a peer to get his attention, calling peer by name, talking to peer, looking at peer *when the student should be working.*

*IL Inappropriate locale.* This category is not to be used if rules allow for pupils to leave seats without permission and what the pupil is doing is not an infraction of other rules, e.g., a pupil goes to sharpen pencil would not be classified IL unless he stopped and looked at neighbors on the way or unless this activity takes permission from teacher, etc.

*SS Self-stimulation.* A narrow class of events in which the person attempts to stimulate himself repetitively in such ways as swinging his feet, rubbing his nose, ears, forehead, tapping his fingers, scratching, rubbing a pencil eraser back and forth across the desk, to such an extent that attention to other activities is precluded.

*LO Look around.* Coded when person is looking around the room, looking out the window, or staring into space when an academic activity is occurring.

*NA Not attending.* This category is to be used when person is not attending to work in individual work situations or not attending to discussion when teacher is presenting material. This category is applicable to those situations in which the subject is working on the wrong assignment. Care should be taken in using this category. Be sure that *no other category* is appropriate before checking it.

## PRACTICE SCRIPT

The following is a description of a hypothetical situation in a school setting. The coding of each sequence is on an accompanying coding sheet (see Fig. 1).

The observer has entered the classroom and will be coding the first sheet of the observation. The teacher is presenting a lesson in arithmetic to the whole class.

The subject is looking out the window and the teacher says, "Jimmy, don't you ever pay attention to what's going on?" (Interval 1).

The first male peer is looking at the teacher. (2)

The subject looks at the teacher. (3)

The second male peer is scratching and looking at his arm. (4)

The subject talks to a peer while the teacher is still presenting the lesson. The peer talks with the subject. (5)

The third male peer answers a question from the teacher. The teacher smiles and says, "Fine." Some of the children look at the interaction between the peer and the teacher. (6)

The subject pushes a book off his desk onto the floor. Several peers giggle. The teacher says, "That's enough of that, Jimmy." (7)

The fourth male peer is rolling a ball down the aisle to his buddy. The buddy rolls the ball back. (8)

The subject raises his hand in response to a question asked of the class by the teacher. (9)

The fifth male peer picks up a piece of paper at the teacher's request. The teacher says, "Thank you." (10)

The subject rummages through his desk while the teacher is presenting the lesson. (11)

The sixth male peer is walking around the room. Several of his classmates look at him. (12)

The subject looks at the teacher. (13)

The seventh male peer hits the child next to him. The child hits him back. (14)

The subject raises his hand as the teacher is talking. She does not look at him. (15)

The eighth male peer looks at the teacher. (16)

The subject still has his hand raised. The teacher asks him what he wants. (17)

The first male peer looks at the teacher. (18)

Subject stomps his foot on the floor. Several peers look at him. (19)

With the teacher's permission, the second male peer explains the lesson to a neighbor, who responds with questions. (20)

Subject stares at the child sitting next to him. The child does not respond. (21)

The third male peer talks to the teacher about the lesson. She answers. (22)

Subject talks to child sitting next to him. The child responds. Teacher says, "Stop that talking." (23)

The fourth male peer looks around the room. (24)

The subject is reading a comic book. (25)

The teacher has told the fifth male peer to sit up straight in his chair. He still slouches in chair. (26)

The subject is still reading a comic book. The teacher takes the book away from him. (27)

The sixth male peer says to the teacher, "That's a nice dress you're wearing." The teacher looks at the child and smiles. (28)

The subject yells, "I want to go to recess!" The teacher says, "Speak in a lower tone of voice, Jimmy." (29)

The seventh male peer rubs a pencil eraser back and forth on the desk. (30)

The subject looks at the clock while the teacher is giving the lesson. (31)

The eighth male peer looks at the teacher. (32)

Subject passes a note to peer. Peer accepts note. (33)

The first male peer tears a page out of his book. (34)

The subject sits quietly in chair, looking at teacher. (35)

OBSERVER _J. Doe_ SHEET NO. _1_ SUBJECT _Jimmy_

DATE _3/15/75_ ACADEMIC ACTIVITY _arithmetic_

Structured _✓_ Unstructured_____ Group _✓_ Individual_____ Transitional_____

| Student | | Interval | | Student |
|---|---|---|---|---|
| S | AP CO TT+ IP+ VO AT PN DS D(I) | 1 | NY NC PL TT- IP- IL SS (LO) NA IT | S |
| P | AP CO TT+ IP+ VO (AT) PN DS DI | 2 | NY NC PL TT- IP- IL SS LO NA IT | P |
| S | AP CO TT+ IP+ VO (AT) PN DS DI | 3 | NY NC PL TT- IP- IL SS LO NA IT | S |
| P | AP CO TT+ IP+ VO AT PN DS DI | 4 | NY NC PL TT- IP- IL (SS) LO NA IT | P |
| S | AP CO TT+ IP+ VO AT PN DS DI | 5 | NY NC PL TT-(IP-) IL SS LO NA IT | S |
| P | A(P) CO (TT+) IP+ VO -AT- PN DS DI | 6 | NY NC PL TT- IP- IL SS LO NA IT | P |
| S | AP CO TT+ IP+ VO AT PN (DS) D(I) | 7 | -NY- NC PL TT- IP- IL SS LO NA IT | S |
| P | AP CO TT+ IP+ VO AT PN DS DI | 8 | NY NC(PL) TT- IP- IL SS LO NA IT | P |
| S | AP CO TT+ IP+ (VO) AT PN DS DI | 9 | NY NC PL TT- IP- IL SS LO NA IT | S |
| P | A(P) (CO) TT+ IP+ VO AT PN DS DI | 10 | NY NC PL TT- IP- IL SS LO NA IT | P |
| S | AP CO TT+ IP+ VO AT PN DS DI | 11 | NY NC PL TT- IP- IL SS LO(NA) IT | S |
| P | AP CO TT+ IP+ VO -AT- PN DS DI | 12 | NY NC PL TT- IP-(IL) SS LO NA IT | P |
| S | AP CO TT+ IP+ VO (AT) PN DS DI | 13 | NY NC PL TT- IP- IL SS LO NA IT | S |
| P | AP CO TT+ IP+ VO AT (PN) DS DI | 14 | NY NC PL TT- IP- IL SS LO NA IT | P |
| S | AP CO TT+ IP+ VO AT PN DS DI | 15 | NY NC PL TT- IP- IL SS LO NA (IT) | S |
| P | AP CO TT+ IP+ VO (AT) PN DS DI | 16 | NY NC PL TT- IP- IL SS LO NA IT | P |
| S | AP CO TT+ IP+ VO AT PN DS DI | 17 | NY NC PL TT- IP- IL SS LO NA (IT) | S |
| P | AP CO TT+ IP+ VO (AT) PN DS DI | 18 | NY NC PL TT- IP- IL SS LO NA IT | P |
| S | 'AP CO TT+ IP+ VO -AT- PN DS DI | 19 | (NY) NC PL TT- IP- IL SS LO NA IT | S |
| P | AP CO TT+(IP+) VO AT PN DS DI | 20 | NY NC PL TT- IP- IL SS LO NA IT | P |
| S | AP CO TT+ IP+ VO AT PN DS DI | 21 | NY NC PL TT-(IP-) IL SS LO NA IT | S |
| P | AP CO (TT+) IP+ VO AT PN DS DI | 22 | NY NC PL TT- IP- IL SS LO NA IT | P |
| S | AP CO TT+ IP+ VO AT PN DS D(I) | 23 | NY NC PL TT-(IP-) IL SS LO NA IT | S |
| P | AP CO TT+ IP+ VO AT PN DS DI | 24 | NY NC PL TT- IP- IL SS(LO) NA IT | P |
| S | AP CO TT+ IP+ VO AT PN DS DI | 25 | NY NC PL TT- IP- IL SS LO (NA) IT | S |
| P | AP CO TT+ IP+ VO AT PN DS DI | 26 | NY(NC) PL TT- IP- IL SS LO (NA) IT | P |
| S | AP CO TT+ IP+ VO AT PN DS D(I) | 27 | NY NC PL TT- IP- IL SS LO (NA) IT | S |
| P | (AP) CO TT+ IP+ VO AT PN DS DI | 28 | NY NC PL TT- IP- IL SS LO NA IT | P |
| S | AP CO TT+ IP+ VO AT PN DS D(I) | 29 | (NY) NC PL TT- IP- IL SS LO. NA IT | S |
| P | AP CO TT+ IP+ VO AT PN DS DI | 30 | NY NC PL TT- IP- IL(SS) LO NA IT | P |
| S | AP CO TT+ IP+ VO AT PN DS DI | 31 | NY NC PL TT- IP- IL SS(LO) NA IT | S |
| P | AP CO TT+ IP+ VO (AT) PN DS DI | 32 | NY NC PL TT- IP- IL SS LO NA IT | P |
| S | AP CO TT+ IP+ VO AT PN DS DI | 33 | NY NC PL TT-(IP-) IL SS LO NA IT | S |
| P | AP CO TT+ IP+ VO AT PN (DS) DI | 34 | NY NC PL TT- IP- IL SS LO NA IT | P |
| S | AP CO TT+ IP+ VO (AT) PN DS DI | 35 | NY NC PL TT- IP- IL SS LO NA IT | S |

*FIGURE 1.* Coding sheet.

# 18

## Coding Procedure for Teachers

*Edward S. Kubany*
*Barbara B. Sloggett*

On-going observation and objective evaluation have been hallmarks of behavior modification research and application. However, in most classroom experiments dealing with frequently occurring deviant behavior, the record keeper has been an outside observer, typically a psychologist or research assistant (Kubany, Weiss, & Sloggett, 1971; Wasik, Senn, Welch, & Cooper, 1969). Such extravagant and often inconvenient use of outside personnel is certainly justifiable for research purposes but is probably uneconomical for widely accepted practical application.

In most cases, the teacher has not been solicited as an observer on the assumption that she has too much else to do; she cannot conduct her class efficiently and record behavior reliably at the same time. When teachers have been recruited for observing purposes they have usually been asked to obtain only a simple frequency count of a target behavior, and the reliability of these observations is often in doubt. Even wrist counters are easily forgotten under the pressures of teaching, and observational reports from teachers are often vague. ("I think he had two

Reprinted from *Journal of Applied Behavior Analysis,* 1973, 6, 339-344. Copyright © 1973 by the Society for the Experimental Analysis of Behavior, Inc. Reprinted by permission.

This study was partially supported by the Social Welfare Development and Research Center, University of Hawaii.

The authors wish gratefully to acknowledge the assistance of Mrs. Annette Murayama and the editorial advice of Ronald Gallimore.

or three tantrums last week.'') When the referrals have concerned questions such as what percent of the time a student spends on-task or disrupting the class, outside observers have been employed almost exclusively.

The present report describes an easily learned observing and recording procedure that can be utilized by the regular classroom teacher without requiring her to deviate more than momentarily from regular classroom routine. The procedure can yield an objective statement as to approximately how much time a given student spends doing his work, wasting time, and bothering others.

### The Code Sheet and Timer

The code sheet shown in Figure 1 was designed to accommodate different kinds of classroom situations. Depending upon which one of the three coding columns is utilized, the teacher observes and records a student's behavior on either a 4-, 8-, or 16-minute variable interval schedule. If the teacher has the problem student for only one class period

Date_____
Student_____
Teacher_____
Starting Time_____
Activity_____

| COMMENTS | FOUR | EIGHT | SIXTEEN |
|---|---|---|---|
| | 2 | 12 | 12 |
| | 5 | 2 | 8 |
| | 7 | 10 | 28 |
| | 1 | 4 | 2 |
| | 3 | 6 | 24 |
| | 6 | 14 | 6 |
| | 4 | 8 | 24 |
| | 6 | 2 | 6 |
| | 4 | 10 | 30 |
| | 1 | 14 | 12 |
| | 2 | 8 | 16 |
| | 5 | 10 | 4 |
| | 3 | 6 | 8 |
| | 7 | 4 | 30 |
| | 2 | 12 | 28 |
| | 1 | 4 | 6 |
| | 7 | 12 | 24 |
| | 3 | 14 | 16 |
| | 4 | 2 | 12 |
| | 5 | 6 | 2 |

FIGURE 1.    Teacher's observation code sheet. Four-, 8-, and 16-minute variable interval schedules.

daily, it would be advisable to use the 4-minute recording schedule. On the other hand, if the teacher has the student in her class all day long, she might choose to use the 8- or 16-minute schedule. The numbers beside each space on the code sheet designate the number of minutes for which a kitchen timer is to be set. One of the three time schedules should be selected, and then only that column should be utilized. At the beginning of the class period, the time should be set for a time interval that corresponds to one of the numbers in the selected column. When the timer ''goes off,'' it should be reset without delay at the next number (immediately below) in the same column.

The timer should be placed in such a position that the clock face is not visible to the class. With the clock face out of sight and the intervals variable, the student has no way of telling when the timer will ''go off.''

## Observing and Recording

When the timer bell rings, the teacher glances at the student and identifies what he is doing *at that instant.* Is he: (1) ''On-task'' (A) —that is, doing what the teacher wants him to do; (2) ''Passive'' (P)—not doing what he should be doing, but not disrupting others; or is he (3) ''Disruptive'' (D)—e.g., out of seat, talking without permission, or making other noise. The teacher enters the appropriate code symbol—either ''A,'' ''P,'' or ''D'' in the space next to the number representing the timer interval just passed. The timer should then be reset without delay.

To minimize the time spent recording, it is recommended that the teacher carry a pencil and a clipboard with the code sheet attached. To minimize any inconvenience, the teacher might allow a conscientious student to set and reset the timer. It would sit on his desk, and he also would have a code sheet so that he would know how to schedule the appropriate time intervals.

## Initial Instructions to Class

''May I have your attention please? Every once in a while this timer will ring. Do not pay any attention to it. I am doing this to keep track of certain things I want to do. Simply disregard the bell and continue with your work.'' After the first several times the timer rings, certain class members may attend to the bell and even make comments about it. The teacher should ignore all references to the timer. In a short period of time, the class should adapt to the bell, and it will not disrupt the students when they are working.

## Interpretation and Validity of the Recording

For any given day, and for longer periods of time, it is possible to calculate the approximate percentage of time that the student spends "on-task," "passive," and "disruptive." Simply divide the total number of spaces marked "A," "P," or "D," by the total number of observations. For example, if seven out of 10 observations are coded as "on-task," the student may be estimated to have been on-task approximately 70% of the time.

Although the teacher will record relatively few observations at infrequent intervals, there is evidence that the percentages yielded are likely to reflect the total population of behaviors occurring during the entire period. In a classroom study by Kubany et al. (1971), observations were made and recorded over a 50-day period. During the daily 20-minute observation sessions, an outside observer would glance at the first-grade subject every 15 seconds, classify his behavior at that moment, and then record on the code sheet. During the 20-minute session the boy's behavior was observed and coded 80 times, and the daily percent of "disruptive" behavior was estimated and plotted graphically. Using the variable-interval 4-minute (VI 4-min) schedule on the teacher's observation code sheet, a sampling of these daily recordings was used for

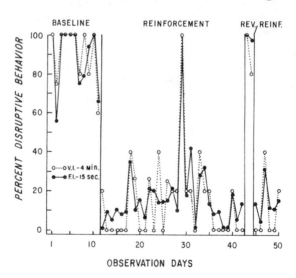

FIGURE 2.    *Graphic comparison of results obtained under two different observational schedules. Daily percentages of observations per 20-minute session during which student's behavior was coded as disruptive, obtained with FI 15-sec and VI 4-min observational schedules.*

recalculating the daily percentages of "disruptive" behavior. For example, the percentage of "disruptive" behavior for day one of baseline was computed on the basis of observations recorded only at the 2-, 7-, 14-, 15-, and 18-minute junctures (five times during 20 minutes). Figure 2 shows graphically how the percentages compare under the two different recording schedules. One can see that making only four or five observations per 20-minute session yielded a record remarkably similar to the one in which 80 observations were recorded.[1] These comparisons are summarized in Table 1. During baseline the average percent of "disruptive" behavior was calculated as 88% based on the fixed-interval 15-second (FI 15-sec) schedule. Based on the VI 4-minute schedule, the percentage was 90—only two percentage points difference. During the first intervention period, the percentages were 17 and 19, under the FI and VI schedules respectively. A similar correspondence of results was obtained during the reversal and second reinforcement periods.

Under certain circumstances, the teacher's code may yield even more representative information than that garnered from an outside ob-

TABLE 1. A Comparison of Results Obtained Using Two Different Observation Schedules

|  | Daily mean percent of observations coded as disruptive | |
|---|---|---|
|  | 4-min Variable-Interval schedule (four or five observations per 20-min session) | 15-sec Fixed-Interval schedule (80 observations per 20-min session) |
| Baseline (11 days) | 88 | 90 |
| Reinforcement (31 days) | 17 | 15 |
| Reversal (two days) | 99 | 95 |
| Reinforcement (six days) | 13 | 16 |

[1]One implication of this finding is that many researchers may have spent more time observing than was necessary in order to make reliable inferences about the frequency of occurrence of certain behaviors. Elementary probability theory tells us that even with relatively few randomly selected observations, there is good reason to expect that the observed relative frequency will be quite close to the true state of affairs (Hays, 1963).

server who spends 20 or 30 minutes in the classroom daily. Intervention programs frequently run all day, and there certainly is no basis for assuming that the 20- or 30-minute observation period is a random sample of the total population of behaviors of concern. On the other hand, the teacher is in a position to collect data all day on a systematic interval basis that can be representative of the entire population of relevant behaviors. And different patterns of behavior at different times of the day might provide insights about reinforcing stimuli or sources that maintain inappropriate behavior.

Finally, when the teacher is the observer, neither the teacher nor the students have to adapt to visitors in the classroom, and there need be no concern about possible experimental effects due to the presence of an outside observer (Surratt, Ulrich, & Hawkins, 1969).

## Alternate Procedures

When a misbehavior of interest occurs only sporadically (e.g., swearing, fighting, occasional outbursts, or tantrums), it might be preferable to record simply whether or not the behavior of interest occurs or does not occur during an entire interval period (that is, from one bell ring to the next). Say, for example, that the problem behavior is "Swearing," and the first timer setting is 10 minutes. If swearing occurs at any time during this 10-minute interval, the teacher immediately records the symbol "Y" (Yes) in the recording space for that interval. It is no longer necessary to record any further swearing behavior for that 10-minute interval. The Symbol "Y" simply means that at least one swearing behavior occurred during the entire time interval. If no swearing behavior had occurred during the entire interval, the teacher should record the symbol "No" (No) when the timer bell rings.

It would also be possible to use both of the two general coding procedures simultaneously. For example, the teacher would record "on-task" behavior when the bell sounds—at the end of an interval—and record "fighting" behavior if and when it occurred during that interval.

## Recording as the Basis for Reinforcement

Once a baseline of target behavior has been obtained, the teacher may utilize the observing procedure as an explicit basis for dispensing reinforcement for appropriate behavior. For example, if the target student is behaving appropriately when the bell rings, he might earn a point, which could be "backed-up" by or redeemed for an infinite variety of privileges or tangible reinforcers. The reinforcers might be dispensed in the classroom, or a note indicating the daily number of points earned might be sent home for redemption there. The teacher would then have additional motivation to continue recording, because setting the timer is an integral part of remediation. As long as the teacher goes along with the intervention procedures, she would at the same time be collecting evaluation data.

Timers set on variable-interval schedules have been used successfully in numerous studies as the basis for dispensing token reinforcement (Broden, Hall, Dunlap, & Clark, 1970; Schmidt & Ulrich, 1969; Wolf, Giles, & Hall, 1968; Wolf, Hanley, King, Lackowicz, & Giles, 1970; Wolf & Risley, 1967). In none of these studies, however, was the bell ring related to the evaluation/recording procedures. In each case, an outside observer coded the target behaviors.

### Illustrative Example

During the last month of the school year, a seventh-grade social studies teacher was experiencing difficulty with a particular student "who never does her work" (Sloggett and Kubany, 1970). The teacher's coding procedure was described to the teacher and on the first day of observation, an outside observer (a new-teacher supervisor) established interrater reliability with the teacher. Utilizing the VI 4-min schedule, the teacher and the teacher trainer agreed on eight of nine observations (89%) during the 50-minute class period. Figure 3 shows that during a six-day baseline, the remiss student was "on-task" when the timer sounded 53% of the time. During the remainder of the observations, the coded behaviors were relatively equally distributed as "out of seat," "passive," and "disruptive." As an intervention procedure, it was decided to award the entire

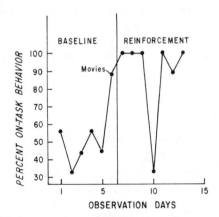

FIGURE 3.    Daily percentage of observations that student's behavior was coded as on-task. Her behavior was coded eight or nine times per 50-minute class period on a VI 4-min schedule.

class 1 minute of free time for card playing at the end of the class period each time the referred girl was "on-task" when the timer sounded. Figure 3 shows that during the intervention period, on-task behavior increased to an estimated 89%. It might be added that the teacher reported that, for her, recording the data and resetting the timer were not inconvenient and did not require her to deviate from her regular routine. She also reported that after the first few bell rings, the class paid no attention to the ringing bell.

## DISCUSSION

One of the distinctive features of this coding procedure is that it relieves the teacher of the responsibility of keeping track of when to record. The timer bell provides an explicit discriminative stimulus for observing/recording behavior.

Of course, it should be stressed that development of this procedure was motivated primarily to minimize the amount of professional time necessary to implement behavioral intervention programs in the classroom and still maintain a rigorous means for monitoring and evaluation.

## REFERENCES

Broden, M., Hall, R. V., Dunlap, A., & Clark, R. Effects of teacher attention and a token reinforcement system in a junior high school special education class. *Exceptional Children,* 1970, *36,* 341-349.

Hays, W. L. *Statistics for psychologists.* New York: Holt, Rinehart and Winston, 1963.

Kubany, E. S., Bloch, L. E., & Sloggett, B. B. The good behavior clock: A reinforcement/timeout procedure for reducing disruptive classroom behavior. *Journal of Behavior Therapy and Experimental Psychiatry,* 1971, *2,* 173-179.

Schmidt, G. W., & Ulrich, R. E. Effects of group contingent events upon classroom noise. *Journal of Applied Behavior Analysis,* 1969, *2,* 171-179.

Sloggett, B. B., & Kubany, E. S. *Training the school counselor as a behavioral consultant: A participative-modeling approach.* Unpublished paper presented at Hawaii Psychological Association, Honolulu, May, 1970.

Wasik, B. H., Senn, K., Welch, R. H., & Cooper, B. R. Behavior modification with culturally deprived school children: two case studies. *Journal of Applied Behavior Analysis,* 1969, *2,* 181-194.

Wolf, M., Giles, D., & Hall, R. V. Experiments with token reinforcement in a remedial classroom. *Behavior Research and Therapy,* 1968, *6,* 51-64.
Wolf, M., Hanley, E., King, L., Lackowicz, J., & Giles, D. The timer-game: A variable interval contingency for the management of out-of-seat behavior. *Exceptional Children,* 1970, *36,* 113-117.
Wolf, M., & Risley, T. *Analysis and modification of deviant child behavior.* Unpublished paper presented at American Psychological Association, Washington, D.C., 1967.

# 19

The Response-Class Matrix:
A Procedure for Recording Parent-Child
Interactions

*Eric J. Mash, Leif Terdal and
Kathryn Anderson*

Observational procedures, for use with behavioral treatment approaches, have ranged from single-behavior/single-person recordings to multiple-behavior/multiple-person recordings. The simpler schemes, while easier to apply methodologically (i.e., obtaining observer agreement, time for observer training, etc.), are restricted in terms of their informational output. They do not provide systematic information about the antecedents or consequents for a given behavior and thus limit the user in formulating a functional analysis. The more complex schemes, while providing an enormous amount of information about behavior and its social context, are extremely difficult to implement from a methodological standpoint and require a sophisticated data storage and report system before the obtained information can be interpreted. The present report describes a procedure for monitoring dyadic interactions which provides immediate information about behavior and its context, and yet from a methodological standpoint can be easily implemented in a wide range of situations.

Reprinted from the *Journal of Consulting and Clinical Psychology,* 1973, *40,* 163-164. Copyright © 1973 by the American Psychological Association. Reprinted by permission.

This work was carried out at the Multi-disciplinary Clinic of the University of Oregon Medical School, Crippled Children's Division and was supported by Health Services and Mental Health Administration, Maternal and Child Health Services Project #920.

| Child's antecedent | MOTHER'S CONSEQUENT | | | | | | |
|---|---|---|---|---|---|---|---|
| | Command | Command question | Question | Praise | Negative | Inter-action | No response |
| Compliance | | | | | | | |
| Play | | | | | | | |
| Competing | | | | | | | |
| Negative | | | | | | | |
| Interaction | | | | | | | |
| No response | | | | | | | |

*FIGURE 1.    Response-class matrix.*

The general form of the recording procedure uses two matrices—one in which the behaviors of a member of the dyad are designated as antecedents and the behaviors of the other member are designated as consequents, and the other in which the antecedent-consequent relationship is reversed. Two recorders, using a time sampling procedure, each make a single mark in one of the matrix cells every 10 seconds, recording only the first scorable behavior unit to occur during that interval. The two matrices taken together provide a three-term contingency record (Holland & Skinner, 1961) in that it is possible to look at the events that precede a behavior, the behavior, and the events that follow.

Figure 1 shows a matrix of one form of the recording procedure which has been used extensively in observing mother-child interactions. Six child behaviors are given in the row margins, and seven parent behaviors are given in the column headings. For the companion matrix (not shown), the row and column headings would be reversed. Using these 6 × 7 and 7 × 6 matrices, the interobserver agreement measures[1] for the individual behavior categories have ranged from 78% to 96% following 4 to 6 hours of training.

Using this method one can look at the patterns of social interaction

[1]Observer agreement was calculated as the number of agreements/sum agreements and disagreements.

between members of a dyad and obtain some estimate of both antecedent and consequent stimulus control. Such information can be used in the planning of treatment and evaluation of outcome, both in research and applied programs.

## REFERENCE

Holland, J. G., & Skinner, B. F. *The analysis of behavior.* New York: McGraw-Hill, 1961.

# 20

## Manual for Coding Interactions

*Eric J. Mash*
*John D. McElwee*

The behavior-coding system described in this manual is designed to provide a sequential description of social interaction in a variety of settings. The behavior codes represent a number of behavioral events that often occur during social interaction between and among family members, and also in the school setting between teachers and students or between peer group members. Two main considerations have determined the present status of the coding system: the behavioral categories should be applicable across a variety of settings without much alteration; the behavior categories should require very little inference on the part of the observer (that is, the behavior should be observable).

The manual is divided into five main parts: Part I includes definitions, rules, and specific procedures for the coding of social interactions; Part II includes definitions, rules, and specific procedures for situational coding; Part III includes definitions, rules, and specific procedures for proximity recording; Part IV includes rules and the specific procedures that are adopted for an observation session; Part V includes the definitions for each behavioral category, situation, and location.

This manual is a revised form of the Manual for Coding Family Interaction, Sixth Revision, by G.R. Patterson, Roberta Ray, D. Shaw, and J. Cobb, and developed at the Oregon Research Institute, Eugene, Oregon. We would like to extend our appreciation to Dr. Gerald Patterson for his permission to reprint this manual. The development of this revised manual was supported by Canada Council Grants S72-0461 and S70-1567, Eric J. Mash, principal investigator.

## I.  RULES, DEFINITIONS, AND PROCEDURES
## FOR INTERACTIONAL CODING

During any given period of observation time, one individual is selected as the subject of the observer's attention. During this time, the observer will record the subject's behavior alternately with other individuals' behavior. Occasionally during an observation period, the subject will not be interacting with other individuals (e.g., the subject is reading a book and his mother and father are reading a newspaper). The coding of these instances will be explained later in this part of the manual. The sequential coding process is accomplished by having the coder observe the subject's behavior, then observe the reactions to the subject's behavior by other individuals in the situation, code these behaviors, then repeat this procedure again and again. The subject of the observer's attention must always be coded first. Therefore, in the coding of any sequence, the subject's behavior must precede the behavior of another individual or individuals. The coding process continues until a designated time period has elapsed. The actual time period allotted for the observation of any particular subject is variable depending upon the requirements or focus of interest for a given study.

A sequence is arbitrarily defined as *two* units of behavior, one unit being the behavior of the subject, the other unit being the reactions, if any, to the subject's behavior by another individual or individuals in the situation. Each unit in a sequence is comprised of *two or more* bits of information (see Fig. 1).

**SEQUENCE**
**TWO UNITS**

| Unit I | Unit II |
|:------:|:-------:|
| 1 \| 2 \| ... \|N | 1 \| 2 \| ... \|N |
| Two or More Bits | Two or More Bits |

*FIGURE 1.*

There are two *types* of bits in each unit: the first type being a numeric code for identifying the individual or individuals whose behavior makes up the unit; the second type is a code for the behavior or behaviors that make up the unit.

The numeric code ranges from 0 to 9. Family members are given numbers from 1 to 8; 1 is for the referred child; 2 is for the father; 3 is for the mother; 4 is for the remaining youngest child; 5 is for the next remaining youngest child, etc.

The behavior code consists of two capital letters which are mnemonics for the behaviors being observed (Fig. 2).

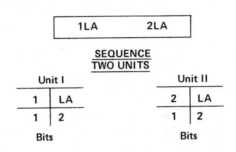

NOTE: *Each unit has two types of bits:*
    *(1)   "1" in the first unit, and "2" in the second unit are numeric codes.*
    *(2)   LA is the behavior code for both units.*

*FIGURE 2.*

Translated, the above code reads, the referred child laughed and then the father laughed.

In the coding of a unit, a numeric code must always precede a behavior code (e.g., 2LA is appropriate but LA2 is inappropriate). Also, each unit scored must have both a numeric *and* a behavior code (e.g., 2LA is appropriate but either 2 or LA alone is inappropriate). Sometimes it is necessary to code more than one behavior to describe a unit; this is acceptable up to two behaviors (e.g., 2LAAA is acceptable but 2LAAAPP is unacceptable). Also, sometimes it is necessary to code more than one individual to describe a unit. This is permissible up to two individuals (e.g., 2LA 3LA is permissible but 2LA 3LA 4LA is not permissible). Thus, the most information any unit can contain is two numeric codes with two behavior codes for each numeric code. Remembering the fact that the subject of an observation session must be recorded separately and his unit must precede the units containing the reactions of another individual or individuals, the most information any sequence can contain is three numeric codes and two behavior codes for each numeric code. This is a total of nine bits (Fig. 3).

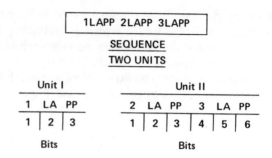

NOTE: *1, 2 and 3* = *Numeric Codes*
*LA and PP* = *Behavior Codes*

*FIGURE 3.*

In the above figure, 1 is the subject, therefore his unit precedes the other unit. Translated, the above code reads: the referred child laughed and showed physical positive behavior (e.g., a hug) and then the mother and father both laughed and demonstrated a physical response to the child (e.g., a kiss).

The numeric code 0 is reserved for the observer, in order to cover those instances when the subject directs his behavior to the observer. The observer in these instances must also score his reactions to the subject (Fig. 4).

```
                        ┌──────────────────────────┐
                        │  1QI              OIG     │
                        └──────────────────────────┘
                              SEQUENCE
                             TWO UNITS

                    Unit I                Unit II
                    ────────              ────────
                    1     QI              0    IG
                    ┌────┬────┐           ┌────┬────┐
                    │ 1  │ 2  │           │ 1  │ 2  │
                    └────┴────┘           └────┴────┘
                      Bits                  Bits
```

NOTE: *1 and 0*   = *Numeric Code*
*QI and IG* = *Behavior Code*

*FIGURE 4.*

Translated, the above code reads: the referred child asked an information question (e.g., What's that paper for?) and the observer ignored the question (e.g., he continued coding and did not respond to the child).

The number 9 is reserved to cover those instances where three or more individuals are reacting to the subject of the observer's attention. If more than two people are involved in a unit of a sequence and they are engaged in the *same* kind of behavior with respect to the subject, the proper numeric code is 9. Thus, 1LA 9AP would be coded if the referred child laughed and three or more other individuals all approved of the laughter. In those instances when three or more people are involved in a unit and they are exhibiting different behaviors with respect to the subject, the observer must subjectively choose the two most relevant behaviors. In scoring these instances, the observer codes a 9 as the first bit in the unit, and then scores it as a unit with more than one individual (Fig. 5).

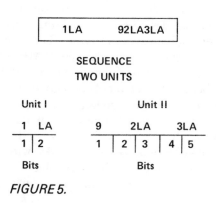

FIGURE 5.

Translated, the above code reads: the referred child laughed and then the mother laughed and the father laughed. Also, it denotes that the coder had to make a decision because three or more individuals were responding differently to the subject.

Sometimes while a subject's behavior is being coded, no other individuals will be interacting with him. In this instance, the proper code for these individuals is NR (No Response). This category is defined in Part V of the manual. NR is never to be scored for the subject of an observation period nor is it to be scored when one person is interacting with the subject and other individuals are not interacting with the subject. Individual or individuals interacting with the subject are given priority (e.g., 1LA 2LA 3NR is inappropriate; only when no one is interacting with the subject is NR an appropriate code).

From individual sequences, the observer will build up longer streams of behavior. The designated time period for which a subject is observed is arbitrarily divided up into thirty-second intervals. Each of these is represented by one line on the behavior-coding sheet (see page 000). The behavior-coding sheet contains seven blocks per line for the recording of behavioral sequences. Over time, the observer is expected to code, on the average, five sequences in each thirty-second interval. This information is presented here in order to facilitate understanding of Parts II and III of the manual. The behavior-coding sheet and observer requirements will be explained in more detail in Part IV of the manual. The important point to remember here is that for the purposes of coding, the time periods during which the subject is observed are divided into thirty-second intervals.

## II.  RULES AND PROCEDURES FOR SITUATIONAL CODING

During any given observational period, the observer will record the situational elements that describe the social and location aspects of the subject's and other individuals' behavior. The situational coding is accomplished by having the observer code, per thirty-second intervals, the modal situational elements that are representative of the subject's and the other individuals' behavior over this time period. By modal situational elements is meant the situational code that is most representative of a thirty-second interval (e.g., if the subject is in the kitchen doing his homework approximately 20 out of the 30 seconds in an interval, the proper situational code would be 1IWK). As with the interactional coding, the situational code describing the subject's behavior is scored first. The coding process continues until a designated time period has elapsed.

A situational code is comprised of one or more units. The units of a situational code are arbitrarily divided by location. Thus, since the subject is always scored first, the first unit in a situational code is always in reference to the location of the subject's behavior. Each unit is comprised of three or more bits (Fig. 6).

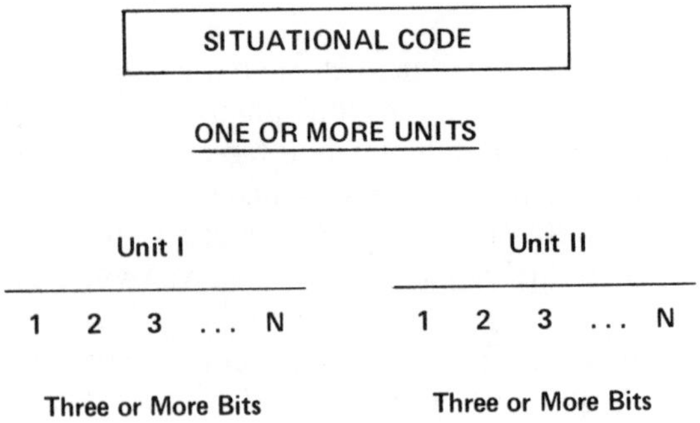

NOTE:  *Unit I is always in reference to the location of the subject's behavior.*

*FIGURE 6.*

There are three types of bits in each unit: the first type is a numeric code for identifying the individual whose behavior is being described; the second type is a code for describing the social situation; the third type indicates where the behavior is taking place.

The numeric code goes from 1 to 9. Family members are given numbers which are identical to their interaction numeric code (e.g., 1 is for the referred child, 2 is for the father, etc.). The social situation code consists of two capital letters which are mnemonics for the social situations. The location code consists of a capital letter which is a mnemonic for the location to be coded (definitions for these codes are presented in Part V of the manual).

In the scoring of any unit, the numeric code precedes the social situation code. The last bit of a unit is always the location code (Fig. 7).

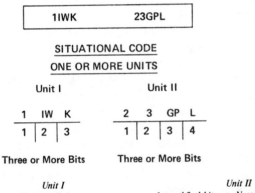

**FIGURE 7.**

Translated, the above units read: the referred child was engaged in independent work (e.g., doing his homework) in the kitchen, while mother and father were engaged in group play in the living room (playing cards).

In the coding of a unit, it is necessary that it contain all three types of bits, numeric code, social situation code, and location code (e.g., 1NO or NOK or 1K are inappropriate; 1NOK is an example of a properly scored unit).

In scoring a situational code, it is necessary to have a numeric code for every individual who is present at an observation session. However, in the scoring of any unit, it is not necessary that every numeric code have a *separate* social situation code. If a social situation code is representative of two or more individuals, their respective numeric codes followed by the appropriate social situation code is sufficient (Fig. 8).

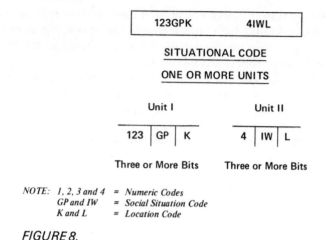

**NOTE:**  *1, 2, 3 and 4* = *Numeric Codes*
*GP and IW* = *Social Situation Code*
*K and L* = *Location Code*

*FIGURE 8.*

Translated, the above situation code reads: the referred child and his mother and father were engaged in group play (e.g., playing Monopoly) in the kitchen and the remaining youngest child was engaged in independent work (e.g., doing his homework in the living room).

In those instances when individuals are engaged in distinct group activities, it is necessary to separately score each group (e.g., if the whole family is in the living room and the mother and father are playing Scrabble while the referred child and his youngest brother are playing with a pet, the proper coding would be 14GP 23GPL).

If all the individuals of an observation session are in the *same* location as the subject, the situational code will contain only one unit.

If the same social situation code and location code are representative of *all* the individuals in the family, it is not necessary to score each numeric code separately. The numeric code X followed by the appropriate social situation and location code is all that is required (e.g., if the *whole* family is playing cards in the living room, the proper coding would be XGPL).

Finally, since the coding is on a modal basis, each numeric code can have only one social situation and location referent (e.g., 123GPKL or 1231WGPK would be inappropriate).

## III.  RULES AND PROCEDURES FOR PROXIMITY RECORDING

During any given period of observation, the observer will record the environmental variable of proximity (physical distance) between the persons interacting. Proximity coding[1] is accomplished by having the observer code, per thirty-second intervals, the modal physical distance between the individuals of a given observation session. In the last box of a line on the coding sheet, the observer is to indicate vertically the numeric code of individuals in the order of their proximity to the subject (e.g., $\frac{2}{3}_4$ would indicate that the father was closest to the subject, the mother was next, and the remaining youngest child was furthest away). Also, the observer is to indicate any individuals who are within six feet of the subject by putting a line under their numeric codes. Any individual who is within six feet of the subject is to be coded above the line (Fig. 9).

$$\frac{2}{\begin{array}{c}3\\4\end{array}}$$

> NOTE: *Individual 2 (father) is closest to the subject, then the mother, then the remaining youngest sibling. The father is the only individual within six feet of the subject. The rest are at a distance greater than six feet.*

**FIGURE 9.**

## IV.  RULES AND PROCEDURES FOR AN OBSERVATION SESSION

This section will cover the rules and procedures that are involved during an actual observation session. The necessity of spelling out rules in detail is to ensure that each observer follows the identical procedure, so that data from different observers are comparable. Another reason for the specification of rules is to facilitate data handling and analysis. If all observers are following the same rules and procedures the work of a key puncher is made much easier.

An example of the coding sheet is given on page 333. One observation sheet is designed for the coding of six minutes of behavior. For longer observation periods more than one sheet is used. From the observation sheet the data is transferred to cards for computer analysis. For this reason, the information on the coding sheet *must be accurate and complete.* At the top left-hand corner of the coding sheet are several blanks to be filled in with information concerning an observation session. In the space labeled ''family'' the observer is to write the last name of the

[1]The procedure for proximity coding follows the format described by Dr. S. Johnson, Department of Psychology, University of Oregon.

family being observed. Also, the observer is to write down the family number. This is a number given to each family on the basis of their time of entry into the project. The observer should then indicate the date and time at which the observation is taken. The "phase" blank should not be filled in by the observer. In the "location" blank, the observer should indicate where the observation is taking place (e.g., home, laboratory, school, etc.). "Session number" refers to which observation is presently underway *for a given location* (e.g., laboratory session 1 refers to the fact that it is the first observation session in the laboratory). "Calibrator" should be filled in with a "yes" or a "no." This refers to the situation where another observer (calibrator) is coding the same session. In the "standard situation" blank, the observer puts the initials of the standard situation (these are mnemonics for standard laboratory situations and are described elsewhere). In the "session length" blank, the observer should note how long a given observation period has lasted. In the "subject" blank, the observer should put down the name and appropriate numeric code of the person who is being coded as the subject. In the "absent" blank, the observer should note any family members who are not present during an observation session. The preceding information is then coded into a 21-digit number which is placed in the "ID" blank on the upper right side of the coding sheet. The ID number must always come out to 21 digits; so, if a space is available for two digits and only one digit is used, the remaining space to the left is filled in with a "0." The following is a list of the spaces and the information to be filled in with the appropriate numbers.

*Spaces:*   1, 2        Study number
            3, 4, 5      Family number
            6, 7, 8, 9, 10, 11        Date
            12, 13       Phase
            14, 15       Location
            16, 17       Session number
            18, 19       Standard situation
            20, 21       Number of pages

To the right of the descriptive information at the top of the coding sheet, the observer has the mnemonic devices for the behavioral codes. Then the main body of the sheet begins with a line which is divided into nine segments. Going from left to right, the first seven segments are reserved for the coding of behavioral sequences. The eighth segment is for situational coding, and the ninth segment is for proximity coding. *Each* of the first seven segments of a line are for coding one sequence of behavior. The number of segments used on a line depends on the rate at which the behavior is occurring. However, an observer should average five behavior sequences per data line (thirty-second interval). The observer keeps track of each thirty seconds with a timing device built into a clipboard which is used to hold the coding sheets. This timing device gives off an auditory signal through an ear plug and a visual cue (red light), every thirty seconds. At the end of every thirty-second interval, the observer should code the situation and proximity code in their respective segments (eight and nine). The observer must begin a new line at the end of a thirty-second interval; however, if the auditory signal occurs in the middle of a behavior sequence, the observer should complete that behavior sequence, code, situation, and location and then go to the next line.

During the observation period several events can occur that may result in breaks in the coding process; and because of these events, a series of symbols has been devised to record these breaks when they occur. If the observer is forced to take a break while coding a line, then the point at which the break occurred is indicated by the symbol "U." If the subject takes a break while he is being coded within a line, the observer writes "K" at the point where the break occurred (e.g., subject goes to bathroom, or goes upstairs to get a book). If the observer breaks at the end of a line, the letter "B" is used; if the subject breaks at the end of a line, the letter "A" is used. When a break has occurred in the middle of a line, the observer resumes coding on the next line. Next to the symbol indicating a break, the observer should note the length of the break.

To aid the observers in the coding process, behavior sequences, situational codes, or proximity codes that are *repeated* need not be coded with their standard code. Instead a dash is used (e.g., 1LA2AP ————).

Below the area that is used for coding, a space is provided marked "description." At the end of a given observation period, the observer should note in this space any unusual events that occurred during that observation period and write brief statements with respect to the situational coding (e.g., if a session is characterized by group play, a statement such as "playing Monopoly" would be appropriate). If an observer uses the "WC" category, he should define it in the space provided for comments. Also, any event that occurred that was difficult to code should be included so the observer can obtain clarification on how the event should be coded.

At the bottom of the coding sheet, the observer has the social situation and location codes listed alphabetically with their appropriate mnemonic.

There are also certain guidelines that an observer should follow. An observer should try and be as "unobtrusive" as possible. He should place himself in such a position that he can view and hear the interaction without much difficulty. Should any area of the situation be obscured from his vantage point, he must move if this is necessary to observe the subject.

## V.  DEFINITIONS OF BEHAVIOR CATEGORIES, SITUATIONS, AND LOCATIONS

AA *Approval-Activity.*   This category is used whenever a person gives clear "gestural" or "verbal" approval of the *behavior* of another person and *doesn't include a personal pronoun referring to that person.* This category is also used when a person expresses approval of another individual's attributes without the use of a personal pronoun referring to the person. Examples: head nods, clapping of hands, smiles, "That's right," "That's nice," "This is fun," "That's a nice shirt," "Thanks," "Good," "Perfect."

*Note:* AA is more than attention. The approver must indicate clear interest and involvement with the other individual. AA is to be scored for the verbal response "yes" if it occurs in the context of a right and wrong answer (e.g., the mother says, "What is this?" while pointing at a picture of a duck and the child says, "A duck." Then the mother says, "Yes." The "yes" is properly coded AA).

AP *Approval-Person.*   This category is used whenever a person gives approval of the behavior of another person with the use of a personal pronoun referring to the person. Examples: "I like you," "I love you," "You're a good boy," "Thank you," "You're nice," "You're sweet," "You're smart," "You're a big boy."

*Note:* This category is also used whenever a person explicitly states approval of another individual's attributes (e.g., clothes, hair, etc.) with the use of a personal pronoun referring to the person (e.g., mother says to her daughter, "I like your hair style" or "You have a nice smile").

AB *Approval of Both Person and Activity.*   This category is used whenever a person gives explicit approval of the behavior of another person and includes a personal pronoun referring to that person. The person must also indicate the behavior that is being approved. Examples: "You did that nicely," "Thank you for bringing me the paper," "You're a gentleman for not fighting with your sister," "You're doing a good job."

AT *Attention.*   This category is used whenever a person looks at another person or listens to another person.

*Note:* AT is more than a fleeting glance. It requires a sustained involvement or interest (e.g., mother is reading a story to her son and he is sustaining his gaze on his mother's face).

AV *Aversive Command.* This category is used whenever a direct request is made of another person, and unpleasant consequences are added to the request. Also, this category is used whenever the consequence for noncompliance is stated as being unpleasant. Examples: "Put it down or I'll smack you," "Give me some candy or I'll scream," "If you don't come here, you're going to get it," "If you don't stop that, you can't go outside," "You better shut the door."

*Note:* The important characteristic of this category is an element of *threat* which is either implicit or explicit in the statement.

CA *Command Attention.* This category is used whenever a direct request is made to another person to attend to some object or activity. Also, this category is used whenever a request is made to another person to attend to the person making the request. Examples: "See," "Watch," "Look," "Johnny," "Sis," "Mommy," "Daddy," "Over here," "Listen."

CM *Command.* This category is used when a direct, reasonable, and clearly stated request is made to another person and the behavior required by the person to whom the command is directed is made explicit in the command statement. In those instances where compliance will not follow directly, but is likely to occur before the observer is finished coding on the subject's observation sheet, the immediate response should be coded and when compliance or noncompliance occurs that should be coded (e.g., the mother tells the child to pick up her toys before coming to dinner, and the child says, "OK," and in a minute picks up her toys; while the child is picking up the toys, compliance would be the proper coding for this behavior). Examples: "Sit down," "Come here," "Take the cup into the kitchen," "Give me some candy," "I want to play," "Clean the kitchen," "Count to ten," "Be quiet."

PC *Command Positive.* This category is used whenever a direct request is made to another person and pleasant consequences are added to the request. Also, this category is used whenever the consequences for compliance are stated as being pleasant. Examples: "If you are good, you can watch T.V.," "Clean your plate and you can have some cake," "Let me play and I'll be good," "If you're good, you can play," "Come here and I'll give you a kiss."

*Note:* The important characteristic of this category is that the request either implicitly or explicitly contain an element of potential *future reward.*

CN *Command Negative.* This category is used whenever a direct request is made of another person for the cessation of any ongoing activity or imminent activity. It is also used when requests are made for a postponement or temporary halting of an activity or imminent activity. Examples: "Don't do that," "Cut that out," "Hold it a minute," "Later," "Stop it," "Quit shouting."

CP *Command Prime.* This category is used whenever a direct request is made to another person and the behavior required by the person to whom the command is directed is nebulous or unclear. Examples: "Be good," "Act nice," "Be a big boy," "Act grown up," "Be a lady."
   *Note:* In those instances where a request is made for a behavior that is not likely to occur before the observer is finished coding on the subject's observation sheet, the request should be scored as CP (e.g., child says, "Take me to the circus next week").

CO *Compliance.* This category is used whenever a person does what is requested of him by CM, AV, PC, CN, CA. These include all the command categories with the exclusion of CP. This category is also used whenever a person does what is requested of him by QO or DY. Remember, CO need not occur immediately as other behaviors may intervene. The length of time during which CO is to be scored is dependent upon the content of the command (CM, AV, etc.), DY, or QO request. If the request specifies a time element or if a period of time greater than one scoring interval is required before the task requested is completed, CO should be scored for the duration of the time element or until the task is completed. However, if the person who made the request shifts to an activity not related to the requested behavior, CO scoring is to be discontinued. Examples: "Pick up all the toys," "Do the dishes," "Sit down until we are finished eating dinner."
   *Note:* CO is also scored if a person asks permission for obtaining an object and the person he is asking gives him the object (e.g., child says, "Can I have some candy?" and the mother reaches in a dish and hands the child the candy).

CS *Consent.* This category is used whenever a person gives clear verbal or gestural permission for a person to engage in an activity or to obtain an object. This category is also used when a person agrees to do what is requested of him by another person. This would be in response to the command behaviors and also DY, QO. Examples: Mother says, "Bring me the chair," and the child says, "OK." Father says, "Can I help you?" and the child says, "Yes." Sister says, "Don't do that," and child says, "I won't." Child says, "Can I go outside?" and Father nods head up and down.
   *Note:* CS is not to be confused with compliance. CS does not indicate that the person actually *did* what was requested of him but rather that he

expressed intent to do so. CO or NC should always be scored when they occur in conjunction with CS (e.g., the mother says, "Bring me the cup," and child says, "I will," but does not bring the cup; the child's response would be scored 1CS NC).

CR *Cry.* This category is used whenever person sheds tears, sobs, etc. —no exceptions.

DM *Demonstrate.* This category is used whenever one person shows another person how to do something by providing an example of the behavior to be performed. Examples: Father shows son how to stack blocks. Mother shows daughter how to turn on the oven. Brother shows sister how to do new dance. Child shows family how to do new math.

*Note:* DM is reserved primarily for *physical* behaviors when one person is instructing another person in the performance of a behavior.

DA *Disapproval of an Activity.* This category is used whenever a person gives clear gestural or verbal disapproval of the behavior of another person and doesn't include a personal pronoun referring to the person. This category is also used when a person expresses disapproval of another person's attributes (e.g., clothes, hair) without the use of a personal pronoun referring to that person. Examples: shaking finger, shaking head from side to side, "tsk, tsk," "That's not nice," "Wrong," "That's not right," "I don't like that," "I hate that skirt."

*Note:* The verbal response "No" is to be coded as DA if it is in the context of a right or wrong answer or when one person is correcting another person (e.g., if a child puts the toys in the bookcase and the mother says "No," the mother's response is to be coded as DA).

DP *Disapproval of Person.* This category is used whenever a person gives verbal disapproval of the behavior of another person with the use of a personal pronoun referring to that person. Examples: "I hate you," "I can't stand you," "You're an idiot," "You're a baby," "You stink," "You're clumsy," "You're wrong."

*Note:* DP is also scored when a person makes explicit his disapproval of another individual's attributes (e.g., clothes, hair, ability, etc.) with the use of a personal pronoun referring to that person (e.g., Father says to his son, "I hate your hair," or "Your hair is *too* long").

DB *Disapproval of Both Person and Activity.* This category is used whenever a person gives explicit verbal disapproval of another person's behavior and includes the use of a personal pronoun referring to the person. The person must also indicate the behavior that is disapproved.

Examples: ''You did that sloppily,'' ''You're playing like a monkey,'' ''You did a crummy job,'' ''I don't like what you're doing,'' ''I hate when you do that,'' ''You did that wrong.''

DY *Dependency.* This category is used whenever a person requests assistance in doing a task that he is capable of doing himself. An everyday request should not be coded as DY unless it meets two criteria: that the person is capable of doing the task himself and that it is an imposition on the person doing the task. Examples: Child age ten, says to mother, ''Tie my shoes.'' Father in kitchen says to mother in living room, ''Come here and pour me some coffee.''

DS *Destructiveness.* This category is used whenever a person destroys, damages, or *attempts* to damage or destroy any object. The value of the object or the amount of damage done is of no consideration. Examples: Child throws his toy down, father kicks living room chair, sister lights a match to her comb, brother pulls the arm off a toy soldier.

*Note:* The damage need not actually occur but the potential for damage must have existed (e.g., if the child attempts to throw vase but is stopped in process by father, the child's response is coded DS).

HR *High Rate.* This category is applicable to any behavior, not covered by the other categories, that if carried on for a long period of time would be aversive. HR is reserved primarily for physical behaviors. Examples: running up and down the stairs, ''roughhousing,'' jumping up and down.

IA *Independent Activity.* This category is used whenever a person is engaged in *independent* play or work and no other code is applicable. The person is not interacting with another individual. Examples: child is doing homework, mother is cooking dinner, father is reading a newspaper, sister is combing her hair.

IG *Ignore.* This category is used whenever a person directs a behavior to another person and that person does not actively respond. Examples: Father is reading the newspaper and child says, ''What time is it?'' and father continues reading. Mother is doing the dishes and child says, ''Mommy,'' and mother doesn't look up but continues with the dishes.

IN *Indulgence.* This category is used whenever one person stops what he is doing in order to do some behavior for another person which that person is capable of doing himself. IN takes a special effort of the helping person to stop his ongoing activity to perform an unnecesssary act. Examples: father does his son's homework, mother cuts the meat for a 12-year-old boy, sister washes hands and face for her 14-year-old brother.

LA *Laugh.* This category is used whenever a person expresses mirth (vocal and facial).

LE *Leaves.* This category is used whenever the subject of the observer's attention leaves the coding area.

MM *Imitate.* This category is used when one person repeats the behavior that has been DM to him by another person. Examples: Mother shows daughter how to cut cookies and then daughter cuts cookies. Brother shows sister how to cut out dolls and then sister cuts out dolls.

> *Note:* MM is primarily reserved for physical behaviors but may also be used for verbal behaviors (e.g., father says, "Where's dinner?" and son immediately says, "Where's dinner?").

NE *Negativism.* This category is used whenever a person makes a statement in which the content of the statement may be neutral but the tone of voice by which it is delivered conveys an attitude of "don't bug me."

> *Note:* This category is not used if the content of the statement can be scored as disapproval.

NI *Nonverbal Interaction.* This category is used whenever a person is playing or working with another person and no other code is applicable. Examples: Child and his father are building a model airplane together. Father and mother are working on the weekly budget.

NC *Non-Compliance.* This category is used whenever a person does not do what is requested of him by CM, AV, CN, PC, or CA. These include all the command categories with the exclusion of CP. NC is also used whenever a person does not do what is requested of him by DY or QO. The length of time during which NC is to be scored is dependent upon the content of the command (CM, AV, etc.), DY or QO, request. If the request specifies a time element or if a period of time greater than one scoring interval is required before the task requested is completed, NC should be scored for the duration of the time element or until the person who made the request either sanctions the NC or shifts to an activity not related to the requested behavior. Examples: Mother says, "Do the dishes," and the child responds, "No," and doesn't move. Mother then says, "OK." There would be only one NC scored for this instance.

NR *No Response.* This category is used whenever there is no responding among individuals. This category is used when other individuals are not reacting to the subject with any other code.

**PN** *Physical Negative.* This category is used whenever a person physically assaults another *person*. This category is also used when one person "roughly" takes an object from another person or if one person physically restrains another person from engaging in an activity or from obtaining an object. Examples: biting, slapping, spanking, punching, kicking, spitting, father holds child and does not let him go outside, one child grabs a toy away from another child, mother removes child from a chair because he was attempting to get some cookies.

*Note:* The circumstances surrounding the act are not to concern the observer, only the fact that the act may be physically aversive to the recipient (e.g., if two children are "fooling" around and one slaps the other, the slap is scored as PN). Remember, PN is only scored for assaults on other persons. Assaults on objects are to be scored DS.

**PP** *Physical Positive.* This category is used whenever one person touches another person in a friendly or affectionate manner. Examples: hugs, kisses, pats on the back, holding hands, running hands through hair, arm around shoulders, arm around waist.

**QI** *Question Information.* This category is used whenever one person requests information from another person and the question cannot be coded as either QS or QO. Examples: "What time is it?" "What color is this?" "Where are my slippers?" "When are you leaving?" "Who were you talking to yesterday?" "Why?" "Are you hungry?" "Do you want to play?"

*Note:* The response made to a QI will, on most occasions, be coded as TA (e.g., if the mother says, "Are you hungry?" and then the child says, "Yes," this would be coded 3QI 1TA).

**QO** *Question Other-Activity.* This category is used whenever one person asks another person to perform some activity and the context in which the statement is given makes it a form of command-question. Examples: "Would you take out the garbage?" "Will you help me lift the table?" "Would you do your homework?" "Will you wash the car?"

*Note:* Tone of voice and facial expressions should be used as clues in scoring this category (i.e., the father says in a stern voice, "Will you do your homework?").

**QS** *Question Self-Activity.* This category is used whenever one person asks another person's permission to obtain some object or to engage in some activity. Examples: "Can I play?" "Can I watch T.V.?" "Can I have some candy?" "Can I stay out late?"

**RF** *Refusal.* This category is used whenever a person gives clear verbal or gestural refusal to engage in an activity or to receive an object. This category is also used when a person does not agree to do what is requested of him by another person. This would be in response to the command behaviors and DY, QO. Examples: Father says, ''Take out the garbage.'' Son shakes head from side to side. Mother says, 'Clean the dishes.'' Son says, ''I won't.''

*Note:* RF is not to be confused with NC. RF does not indicate that the person actually did not do what was requested. CO or NC should always be scored when they are in conjunction with RF. (Father says, ''Take out the garbage,'' and son says, ''No,'' while he is in the process of taking it out.)

SS *Self-Stimulation.* This category is used whenever a person engages in self-stimulation activity and it cannot be coded by any other activity. Examples: swinging a foot, scratching oneself, rocking, humming, looking around the room, nail biting, thumb sucking.

TA *Talk.* This category is used for any verbal communication that is not covered by any other code.

TE *Tease.* This category is used whenever one person teases another. The observer must subjectively decide what constitutes teasing behavior. Teasing may occur in either a positive or negative context. In either instance, tease may be coded. In most instances other behaviors are likely to be coded in conjunction with tease (PP, PN, LA, etc.). Examples: Child is trying to do his homework and sister is tickling him in the ribs, father is trying to do income tax returns and mother is blowing in his ear, sister is playfully tickling brother, mother mimicking child's whine.

WH *Whine.* This category is used whenever a vocal response occurs in a slurring, high-pitched, nasal, falsetto voice.

WC *Wild Card.* This category is reserved for unique or unusual behaviors that are not covered by other categories.

*Note:* If the observer uses WC, it is his obligation to define it.

YE *Yell.* This category is used whenever a person makes a vocal response of an intense nature to the extent that it may be aversive. Examples: screams, shouts, talking loudly.

## Social Situation Codes

CF *Conflict.* This code is to be used whenever two or more individuals are fighting (verbal or physical). This category is also used whenever two or more individuals are arguing. Examples: Mother and father are yelling at each other. Two children are arguing about which T.V. program to watch. Brother and sister are arguing over whose turn it is to do the dishes.

GP *Group Play.* This category is used whenever a person is playing with another person or persons. This category can be scored if it is an activity with clearly defined rules or if no rules are formalized but the activity is of game nature. Examples: Two people are playing Monopoly or Scrabble or leapfrog. Two children are playing with soldiers. The whole family is playing charades. Two children are playing with a pet. Playing cards.

IP *Independent Play.* This category is used whenever a person is playing by himself. This category is used whenever a person is engaged in an activity with a toy or the individual activity is of a game or leisure nature. Examples: building a tower with some blocks, reading a newspaper or a comic book, fooling around with a dog, playing solitaire.

IW *Independent Work.* This category is used whenever a person is working alone. Work can be either performing a household chore or when an individual is performing a task directly related to outside interests (e.g., school or job). This category is also used if an individual is performing a behavior that may lead to a skill relating to the above activities. Examples: doing dishes, doing homework, doing the income taxes, taking out the garbage, learning how to cook or clean, personal grooming.

GW *Group Work.* This category is used whenever two or more persons are working on the same task. The activity must fit the work category. Examples: Mother and daughter are doing the dishes. Father and son are cleaning the living room. Sister is combing younger sister's hair. Mother is teaching daughter how to set the table.

NO *Normative.* This category is used whenever none of the other situational codes are applicable. Examples: eating, conversation, when a person is not engaged in any activity—he is just sitting.

### Location Codes

L   Living Room.

K   Kitchen.

D   At desk.

P   Playground.

H   Hallway.

To illustrate the use of the behavior code, a sample interaction with its proper coding (see Fig. 10) is given below. The time element has been speeded up considerably in order to illustrate general rules and the use of a variety of behavior and situational codes.

The referred child is John, age ten; he is the present subject of the observer's attention. His sister, Patty, age four, is number 4. Mother is number 3, and father is number 2. The observation takes place at 4:30 p.m. on July 16, 1971. The location is the home, and it is the first observation session conducted there. The family was the first family accepted into the project. All the members of the family are present at this observation session. John is in the living room doing his homework alone. The rest of the family is in the living room discussing the day's events. The father is physically closest to John, followed by his mother and sister, in that order.

John is doing his homework.
Family is discussing day's events.

> (approximately 20 seconds)

John is doing his homework.
Father, without leaving his seat, says, ''John, what are you doing?''

John continues with his work.
Father says, ''What are you doing?''

John answers in a negative tone of voice, ''My homework.''
Father turns away from John and again joins family in discussion.

John leaves his homework and sits on couch next to father.
Father says to John, ''Did you finish your homework?''

John replies, ''Yes.''
Father says, ''That's a good boy.''

John listens to discussion.

> (approximately 10 seconds)

John says to mother, ''What's for dinner?''

Mother says, "Leftovers."

John says, "I want to eat right now."
Mother says, "OK, let's eat now."

The family moves into the kitchen and begins to eat dinner.

John is eating dinner.
Family is eating dinner.

                   (approximately 15 seconds)

John is eating dinner.
Patty says to John, "Pass me the butter."

John passes Patty the butter.
Patty says, "Thank you."

Family continues to eat dinner.

                   (approximately 10 seconds)

John is eating dinner.
Father says to John, "Did you wash your hands?"

John replies, "No."
Father says, "Would you go and wash your hands?"

John says, "Later."
Father says, "Wash your hands or you have to go to your room."

John gets up from table and goes over to the sink and washes his hands.
Family continues eating.

                   (approximately 10 seconds)

John returns to table and resumes eating.
Patty says to John, "You're a slob."

John says, "Shut up, or I'll belt you."
Patty resumes eating.

John continues eating.

Family continues eating.

|
    (approximately 10 seconds)
↓

John is eating.
Mother says to John, "Would you help me with the dishes?"

John replies, "No."
Mother says, "That's OK, I'll do them myself."

Family finishes eating.

John and his father and sister go into the living room while mother remains in the kitchen doing the dishes. John begins to read a comic book. His father and sister are fooling around on the floor.

John is reading comic book.
Father and sister fooling around on the floor.

|
    (approximately 25 seconds)
↓

John says, "Hey, shut up."
Father and sister continue at same pace.

John resumes reading.
Father and sister continue playing.

|
    (approximately 20 seconds)
↓

*Observer takes a break for approximately 30 seconds.*

John is reading.
Patty grabs away John's comic book.

John hits Patty.
Patty cries.

John grabs back the comic book.
Father says, "What's going on?"

John explains.
Father says, "OK."

John resumes reading.

Father is consoling sister.

*At this point John goes to his room for approximately two minutes.*

John returns to the living room.

John says, ''Can I play with you guys?''
Father and sister nod heads in agreement.

John is playing with his father and sister.

(approximately 15 seconds)

John is playing.
Patty says, ''Let's play with your soldiers.''

John says, ''OK,'' and proceeds to get the soldiers.
Father goes into kitchen and Patty is watching John get the soldiers.

John and Patty begin playing with soldiers.

(approximately 20 seconds)

While John and Patty are playing, Patty breaks one of the soldiers.

John says, ''You idiot,'' and hits Patty.
Patty hits John back and then runs into the kitchen.

John continues playing alone.

FAMILY __LAST NAME -01__
DATE __JULY 16, 1971__
TIME __4:30 P.M.__
OBSERVER __J.M.__
PHASE _____
LOCATION __Home__
SESSION NO. __1__
CALIBRATOR __No__
STAN. SITUATION _____
SESSION LENGTH __6 min.__
SUBJECT __John - 1__
ABSENT __None__

## CODING SHEET    ID _____ 38. ____

### BEHAVIOR CODES

| | | | |
|---|---|---|---|
| AA | CS | IN | QS |
| AB | CR | LA | QI |
| AP | DA | LE | RF |
| AT | DM | MM | SS |
| AV | DP | NE | TA |
| CA | DB | NI | TE |
| CM | DY | NC | WH |
| PC | DS | NR | WC |
| CN | HR | PN | YE |
| CP | IA | PP | |
| CO | IG | QO | |

| # | BEHAVIOR | | | | | | | Situation | Pr. |
|---|---|---|---|---|---|---|---|---|---|
| 1 | I IA 9NR | — | — | IIA 2CAQI | INCIG 2QI | INE 9NR | — | IIW 234 NOL | 2 3 4 |
| 2 | IIA 2QI | ITA 2AA | IAT 9NR | — | IQI 37A | | | XNOL | 2 3 4 |
| 3 | ICM 3CSCO | INI 9NI | — | — | INI 4CM | ICO 4AP | | X NOK | — |
| 4 | INI 9NI | — | INI 2QI | ITA 2QO | | | | — | — |
| 5 | INCCN 2NCAV | ICO 9NR | — | INI 4DP | IAV 4CO | | | — | — |
| 6 | INI 9NI | — | INI 3QO | IRENC 3AA | INI 9NI | | | — | — |
| 7 | IIA 2NR 4NR | — | — | — | ICACN 2NC 4NC | | | IIP 2AGPL 3IWK | 2 4 3 |
| 8 | IIA 2NR 4NR | — | — | "U"- | 30 seconds | | | — | — |
| 9 | IIA 4PN | IPN 4CR | IPN 2QI | ITA 2TA | ITA 2NR 4NR | "A"-2 minutes | | I4CF 2NOL 3IWK | — |
| 10 | IQS 2CS 4CS | INI 2NI 4ND | — | — | INI 4CM | | | I246 PL 3IWK | 2 4 3 |
| 11 | ICOCS 4AT | INI 4NI | — | — | INI 4DS | | | I4GPL 2ND 3IWK | 4 2 3 |
| 12 | IDPPN 4PN | IIA 9NR | — | — | — | | | IIPL 24NO 3IWK | 2 3 4 |

DESCRIPTION __3-6 Family eating dinner__ _____

_____

_____

Social Situation Codes
CF  GP  GW  IP  IW  NO

Location Codes
L   K

*FIGURE 10.   Completed coding sheet.*

# 21

---

## Manual of Instructions for the Behavior Ratings Used for the Observation of Interpersonal Behavior

*Peter M. Lewinsohn*

### INTRODUCTION

In order to achieve meaningful and reliable ratings of behavior, many conditions have to be met. Perhaps foremost among these are the motivation, alertness, and conscientiousness of the raters themselves. It is also generally recognized that reliable ratings of behavior can be achieved only to the extent that the rating categories are clearly defined, are behaviorally anchored, and involve a minimum of inferential behavior on the part of the raters.

### GENERAL PHILOSOPHY

Any rating scheme incorporates implicit and explicit assumptions and value judgments. This one is no exception. One value judgment involves the decision to restrict our observation to verbal behavior. We also assume that in coding interpersonal behavior, it is meaningful to

Reprinted by permission of author.
Members of the Depression Team — Ted Alper, Sandra Johannson, Julian Libet, Martin Shaffer, Carolyn Rosenberry, Chuck Sterin, Rita Stewart, and Malcolm Weinstein — have all made valuable contributions.

distinguish between "actions" and "reactions." The distinction depends in part upon temporal considerations, that is, actions always precede reactions. Actions are also conceptualized as being more "emitted" than reactions, that is, they are less obviously contingent upon some interpersonal cue for their occurrence.

*Example:* A. "Viet Nam is going from bad to worse" (action). B. "I would rather not talk about that" (reaction). We distinguish between actions and reactions made in order to focus upon the behavior of people as well as upon the social consequences of that behavior. It is recognized that in an ongoing, fast-moving, interpersonal situation it may often be difficult to distinguish between actions and reactions and that a behavior which starts out as a reaction eventually assumes the characteristics of an action. If in the previous example, B continues his statement with "Didn't I see you at the Union yesterday?" he has gone on to emit a behavior which should be coded as an action.

   *Decision rule:* If a "reaction" is continued into the next 30-second time interval, it is scored as an action from then on out.

Actions sometimes have an obvious *object.* Often from the content of a communication or from the fact that A looks at B while talking, we can infer that B is the *object* of A's action. Much of the time, however, especially in groups, actions seem to be addressed to more than one person.

   *Decision rule:* An individual is scored as being the object of an action only when there is no doubt in the mind of the rater that B is the object of A's action. When in doubt, do not score B as object.

Behavior emitted by a person (the reactor) following an action is coded as a reaction. It is possible to have more than one person reacting to a single action, but each individual reactor and his reaction should be specified (rather than lumping all reactors into a category such as "group," for example). These distinctions are schematically represented in Figure 1. Actions are scored as being one of a relatively small number of broad interactional categories. Distinction between positive and negative reactions is made.

FIGURE 1. Behavior rating schedule.

## "ACTION"

### "REACTION"

| Interactional Categories | | Positive | | | Negative | | |
|---|---|---|---|---|---|---|---|
| Psychol. Complaint (PC) | Psy C | Affection (AF) | Aff | Criticism (CF) | Crit |
| Somatic Complaint (SC) | Som C | Approval (AP) | App | Disapproval (CP) | Disapp |
| Criticism (CI, CO) | Crit-I, -O | Agree (AG) | Agr | Disagree (OG) | Disagree |
| Praise (PR) | Pr | Laughter (LP) | L+ | Ignore (IG) | Ign |
| Information Request (IM) | I- | Interest (IN) | Int | Change Topic (CG) | Ch T |
| Personal Problem (PP, PM) | PP +, -, + | Continues talking about (CT) topic | Con T | Interrupts (IR) | Inter |
| Instrument Problem (IL) | IP | Physical Affection (PA) | Phys Aff | Physical Punishment (PU) | Pun |
| Other People's Problems (OI, OE) | OP-I, -O | | | | |
| Talking about abstract, (TA) impersonal, general, etc. | Ta | | | | |

Content-Topics

| | |
|---|---|
| School | Sch |
| Self | X, Y, Z |
| Other People (group, family) | X, Y, Z |
| Treatment | Rx |
| Sex | Sx |
| Therapist | T |

Object

Source _____ Reactor

Action _____ Reaction

337

## CATEGORIES USED FOR CODING ACTIONS

Psy C *Psychological Complaint.* Any statement reporting past, present, or the anticipation of future, psychological, mental, cognitive, or emotional discomfort or pain. (This includes all pain which is non-physical.) Included are expressions of anxiety, depression, guilt, failure, as well as reports of being hurt, worthless, stupid, having been insulted, deserted, empty, etc. Also included are complaints of loss of sleep and having nightmares. The category is intended for statements referring to negative feeling states. It is to be differentiated from the category Personal Problem (PP), which is more specific and refers to an *action* that was or was not taken. The statement, ''I don't have the grades I should have,'' would be scored as Psy C. However, the statement, ''I didn't study for the exam,'' would be coded as PP. Crying is to be scored as Psy C if the source seems to be saying, ''I'm feeling bad.''

Som C *Somatic Complaint.* Any statement expressing a discomfort that is attributed by the subject, or by most people, to a physical cause. Included here are what are traditionally referred to as somatic, psychosomatic, hysterical, as well as certain psychotic symptoms such as hallucinations. The latter are scored Som C only when they do involve a correlated psychological pain.

Crit *Criticism.* Any verbal statement expressing anger, hostility, critical and destructive feelings toward an individual, a group of persons, or an organization, is scored Crit. If the object of the verbal statement is a member of the group under observation (the therapists, the family, the group members), it is scored CRIT-I. If it pertains to someone outside the group, it is scored CRIT-O. A separate category (Instrument Problem) is used for criticism directed toward inanimate objects.

Pr *Praise.* Verbalizations expressing positive attitudes about an individual, a group of individuals, or an organization including statements reflecting attitudes about the self.
  *Examples:* ''This gives me a chance to find out about myself.'' ''People here let me know what they think about me.'' ''I feel that I am a worthwhile person now.''

I− *Information Request.* This category includes all verbal behaviors that are clearly ''intended'' to elicit a verbal response from another person. They are distinguished from psychological and somatic complaints that do not directly demand a response, and they are also distinguished from statements indicative of personal problems, even though these two may *implicitly* call for a verbal response. Included are all direct requests for help.

*Examples:* requests for time, for personal and other factual information: "Please pass me the butter."

PP *Personal Problem.* A statement scored as a personal problem is one that indicates that the source has either committed a negative (as judged by him) act or has failed to commit some positive (as judged by him) act. The first "plus" or "minus" sign indicates whether or not the source committed an act, "plus" indicating that he did commit an act, and "minus" indicating that he did not. The second sign indicates the source's evaluation of the desirability of the action in question; "plus" means that he judges the action to be a positive one, and "minus" means he views the action as negative.

*Examples:* "I smoked dope yesterday (PP+−)." "I didn't study for the exam (PP−+)." *Examples of statements not scored as personal problems:* "I didn't know what to do (scored Psy C)." "I stopped taking dope (scored Ta)." "I feel much better about being able to meet people now than I used to (scored Pr)." In other words, statements reflecting that the person has solved a problem and statements indicating that he feels himself to be in conflict between alternate courses of action are not scored as personal problem. Personal problems must involve an *action* that was or was not taken. The statement, "I'm sorry," should be scored as PP+−.

IP *Instrument Problem.* Statements describing a state of deficiency or malfunctioning which involves an inanimate object or state.

*Examples:* "The air conditioning is not working." "This room is too small." "It's too hot here." "It's too noisy, too dark, etc."

OP *Other People's Problems.* Any statement referring to the problems faced by another person. If the other person is a member of the group under observation (the family, the group) it is scored OP-I. If it pertains to someone outside the group it is scored OP-O. Other people's problems have to be carefully distinguished from statements that need to be scored as criticism. A statement is scored as OP if it seems to involve an objective, somewhat sympathetic, nonhostile statement of another person's situation as seen by the speaker. The rater may at times have to exercise some judgment in distinguishing between an OP and a Crit statement, e.g., "My mother is crazy," may represent the speaker's objective and sympathetic (?) perception of his mother's difficulties or it may represent a strongly hostile and derogatory statement about her.

*Examples of statements that are not scored as other people's problems:* "We're not making any progress because the therapist is inadequate (Crit)." "A's problem is trivial (Crit)."

Ta *Talking About Things in General, Etc.* This is a catch-all category intended to be used to score verbalizations that do not fit into any of the other interactional categories.

## Content-Topic

In addition to being assigned one of the above-mentioned interactional categories, actions are also scored for content or topic. From previous experience, we have found that some content categories occur in almost all of the situations we are likely to observe. Each family or group has somewhat idiosyncratic topics. Therefore, the first one or two observation periods are used to generate content categories to be used with that situation. Figure 1 shows the content-topic categories likely to be useful in most situations.

# CATEGORIES USED FOR CODING REACTIONS

The major distinction we wish to make is between positive and negative reactions. A reaction is defined as a positive when, in the *judgment of the rater,* it has positive reinforcing value for the person toward whom it is directed. A negative reaction is defined as one that is assumed by the rater to possess negative reinforcing value for the person toward whom it is directed. There are additional relatively subtle distinctions, which we make within each of these categories. If, while making his observation, the rater has difficulty in deciding which one of these is appropriate, he should at least rate the behavior as being positive or negative.

## Positive Reactions

1. *Affection.* Statements expressing a liking for another person. Examples: "I think you are nice." "I like you."
2. *Approval.* Statements approving of the action(s) of another person. Examples: "I like the way you dress." "I like the way you are behaving." "You seem to have become more active."
3. *Agree.* Statements endorsing an *opinion* or an *idea* expressed by another person.
4. *Laughter.* Laughter and smiling that is either directed or clearly

related toward another person's action. Nervous and sarcastic and hostile kinds of laughter are not scored in this category.

5. *Interest.* Verbal statements expressing an interest for the topic of the previous action. This can be shown any number of ways. Example: "I think this is an important topic." "Tell me more about it." Any verbalization which clearly facilitates and encourages further discussion of the topic of the previous action.

The reactor does more than merely continue the topic. He shows his interest by asking questions, elaborating on the theme, providing more information about it, expressing enthusiasm for it, etc. In a group therapy situation, the therapist's reflections or "mmm's" will usually be scored in this category.

6. *Continues Talking about Topic.* This is the weakest possible positive reaction. The person continues to talk about the topic introduced by the source but he does so in a perfunctory, without being impolite, manner.

7. *Physical Affection.* Nonverbal interactions involving kissing, hugging, other signs of physical affection.

## Negative Reactions

1. *Criticism.* Verbal statements that are critical, hostile, derogatory of another person. Such a reaction must be scored relative to the action, and thus must be a criticism directed at the source of the action.

2. *Disapproval.* Verbal statements expressing criticism directed at some action or some other relatively specific aspect of another person. Whereas the category of Criticism refers to a more general criticism of a person, this category is more specific.

3. *Disagree.* Verbal statements expressing a disagreement with another person's ideas or opinions.

4. *Ignore.* An action is scored as having been ignored when it does not elicit a reaction within 10 seconds. An action is not scored as Ignore when the source continues on to another action without giving another person a chance to respond to his first action. In such an instance, there should be no reaction scored to the first action; the space for the reaction should be left blank.

5. *Change Topic.* This category is used to score reactions that introduce an unrelated topic and thus ignore the topic of the action. The rater judges whether the reaction is related or not related to the previous action. Examples: A: "It is hard to get acquainted with people at this university (Psy C)." B: "In my dorm, people hardly talk with each other (Continues talking about topic)." A: "It is awfully hot today (IP)." B: "I met a girl yesterday who was very nice (Change topic)."

This category is used only as a reaction to a specific action; it is not considered to be in this category if an action-reaction dyad has been completed.

6. *Interrupts.* Verbal behaviors that "take the floor away from" someone, or in some shape or form prevent him from completing his statement. "Interruptions" that are clearly indicative of great enthusiasm on the part of the reactor and that are clearly judged to be facilitative of the speaker's topic are not scored as interruptions.

7. *Physical Punishment.* Any physical act of spanking, hitting, throwing objects at another person are scored as physical punishment.

## GENERAL PROCEDURAL CONSIDERATIONS

Observations are recorded on data sheets similar to the one shown in Figure 2, in which succeeding lines always represent 10-second intervals.

The rater must always be sure to have written in the name of the family (or group), his own name, the date, time of day, and any other identifying information deemed to be important. Succeeding pages should be numbered, starting with Page 2, and at the end the rater should staple all the forms for a given session or period together. Observations are timed by means of an auditory click and a small light, both of which occur at 10-second intervals. If more than one rater is involved, their earphones should be plugged into the same timer pad. Raters commonly find it difficult to code interactions in beginning observations of a new group or family, and to facilitate recall, it helps to write in catch words and phrases. If a person is not shown as having done anything during a given interval, he is assumed not to have emitted any verbal behavior during this interval.

GROUP:                                          RATER:

DATE:

TIME:

---

1.
$$\frac{T}{I-_____} B \ ConT$$
$$R_x$$

    A: What are we supposed to do here?  Addressed to T.
    B responds:  I guess anybody knows.

---

2.
$$A:\underline{I-_____}\overset{B}{} B-Int$$
his work

    A: What did you do at the office today?
    B: Oh, you should have been there, etc.

---

3.    S:  Crit_____M Ch T
                "people"

    Sam: "People are so phony these days."
    Martha: "I was late for class today."

---

4.

---

5.

---

6.

---

7.

*FIGURE 2.    Observation data sheet.*

# 22

## A System for Recording Individualized Behavioral Data in a Token Program

*Jesse B. Milby, Jr.*   *Marion MacDonald*
*Herman C. Willcutt*   *Kathy Whitfield*
*Jesse W. Hawk, Jr.*

An integral part of all token economy programs is the observation, quantification, recording, and analyzing of patient behavioral data. As in any information system, this needs to be accomplished in a manner as efficient, accurate, and easily retrievable as possible. The data also should reflect, as precisely as possible, empirical behavioral phenomena and not represent statistical artifacts. A data matrix is described that embodies many of the characteristics described above.

### Program Description

This data collection system is used on a token economy program on a closed psychiatric ward at the Veterans Administration Hospital in Birmingham, Alabama. The program has been in operation since July 8, 1969. The facility is generally for short-term psychiatric admissions with the average stay being 34 hospital days. Some idea of the diagnostic breakdown within the patient population may be gained from the following data collected over a two-month period, from September

Reprinted from *Journal of Applied Behavior Analysis,* 1973, 6, 333-338. Copyright © 1973 by the Society for the Experimental Analysis of Behavior, Inc. Reprinted by permission.

Development of this system was supported by a grant from the Research Committee of the VA Hospital in Birmingham, Alabama.

through October 1969: functional psychosis—43%, personality disorders—38%, neurotic disorders—14%, and psychosis associated with organic brain syndrome—5%.

## Data Recording

As in most programs, this one involves certain behavioral contingencies expected of all patients. Examples are awakening on time, good grooming, and job performance. Since many of the patients are not severely regressed, but, rather, exhibit idiosyncratic maladaptive behavior, consideration is given to these ''special behaviors'' on an individualized basis. These behaviors are observed using the time sampling technique described by Milby (1970). They are quantified with the aid of operational definitions. Costs and earnings for common events requiring behaviors expected of all patients are recorded at the time of pay-off directly onto the data matrix. Costs and earnings for individual activities and special behaviors are recorded at the time of pay-off on an individual patient's card, which he carries with him at all times. Figure 1 shows the

**EARN**                                                    **COST**

| Event | Spec. Beh. | Time | Cost | Init. |
|-------|-----------|------|------|-------|
| Staff |           |      |      |       |
| PRN   |           |      |      |       |
| TV    |           |      |      |       |
| Coffee|           |      |      |       |
| Nap   |           |      |      |       |
| Pool  |           |      |      |       |
| Card Games |      |      |      |       |

NAME _____ DATE _____

| Event | Time | Pay | Init. |
|-------|------|-----|-------|
| Asmt. on time | | | |
| C.T. | | | |
| Reading | | | |
| Job | | | |
| Job Gigs | | | |
| Special Behaviors | | | |

VA Form 10-2a(521) Sept. 1969 (test)

*FIGURE 1.    Two sides of the 3 x 5 in. card on which individual earnings, spendings, and special behaviors are recorded for each patient at the time of their occurrence.*

patient card that each individual carries on his person. This card is carried in the shirt pocket of every patient and is used to record events only where tokens are exchanged. The staff member who collects or delivers tokens for the observed event records the time and the numbers of tokens exchanged and signs his initials.

A patient's token balance at any given moment may be obtained by considering the earnings and expenditures recorded on the card, in addition to those already recorded on the matrix. This balance results if the difference between earnings and expenditures is appropriately added to or subtracted from the entered balance for the previous day. This provides a useful source of feedback for both patients and staff.

## Special Features of the Data Matrix

The data matrix is a summary matrix that incorporates all information necessary for the daily functioning of the program. It incorporates data from four major sources: (1) common events, such as arising on time and breakfast; (2) individual activities, such as job performance and use of PRN medicine; (3) idiosyncratic maladaptive behaviors designated as special coded behavior, such as delusional speech and social interaction; and, (4) results of 12 to 15 time samples taken on as many as six patients daily and recorded by nursing personnel on time sample forms. Although a wide variety of ''special behaviors'' is possible on a ward, note that these are entered in a coded fashion in comparatively few columns. Such codes as D.S. for delusional speech and S.I. for social interaction are used.

Figure 2 shows the data matrix. The matrix includes data transferred from the individual 3 × 5 in. patient cards and from time sample forms. Common events for all patients, such as arising on time, meals, etc., are recorded directly onto the matrix, which is kept on a clipboard and may be carried from area to area. It is divided into five main sections. Reading from left to right, the first section (1) provides space for the patient's name and his job assignment. Typically, his duty hours for the job are also entered under job assignment. (2) The second section provides for recording all earnings for the day. Entries here are made from the individual patient cards and are added to those earnings, which are recorded directly onto the matrix. (3) The third section provides for recording all spendings for the day. Entries here are also made from individual cards and added to those recorded directly onto the matrix. (4) The fourth section provides for calculating the new balance for the next day. Here, space is provided for recording total earnings and spendings. The difference between these two entries is then added to or subtracted from the previous balance and the result is entered as the new balance. (5) The fifth section provides for recording time sample data for the day. These data are used in establishing baselines and assessing treatment procedures. Data entered here are the percent of time samples in which the target behavior was observed. If more than three target behaviors are being sampled in any patient, diagonal lines can be drawn across the box space for each of the three coded behavior boxes and percentages may then be entered in top left and bottom right of each box. This section also provides space for recording the number of time samples made on each patient and percentage reliability. Reliability is recorded as percentage agreement on frequency of target behavior by two observers taking simultaneous, but independent, samples of behavior.

The matrix allows for quick and easy data summary and retrieval at any time during a given 24-hour period. This is an advantage, especially in dealing with patients who may try to acquire tokens in devious ways or otherwise manipulate to avoid therapeutic contingencies. It also provides for easy computation of a "daily" or "weekly ward index" (Colman & Boren, 1970), which provides feedback to the staff about the overall functioning of the program.

The average time spent in daily preparation of the master matrix for 20 patients during a three-week period was 1 hour, 27 minutes. This job was done by the nursing assistant who works the midnight to 8:00 a.m. shift. He transfers data from individual cards onto the master and summarizes and balances it for that 24-hour period. Another part of his duties, not included in the average time recorded above, is to add new data points to the target behavior graphs of all patients being specially observed or time sampled. Thus, in 1 hour, 27 minutes, plus the time it takes to add data points to a few graphs, a complete record of the ward and of all individual patients on the ward is kept up to date for easy reference.

Use of both a Master Sheet and individual cards provides advantages not found in the Colman and Boren (1970) system. The individual cards provide feedback to patients many times per day regarding their behavior and its effect on the environment. Such feedback in and of itself has been shown to be effective in modifying behavior (Cooper, Thompson, & Baer, 1970; Leitenberg, Agras, Thompson, & Wright, 1968; O'Brien & Azrin, 1970; Panyon, Boozer, & Morris, 1970; Suchotliff, Greaves, Stecker, & Berke, 1970). Use of the individual cards on which staff members make notes and sign their initials also provides important discriminative stimuli for delivery of social reinforcement by staff members.

Because data are transferred from the individual cards to the Master Sheet there is a possibility that errors in transfer of data could interfere with the usefulness of the Master. To assess this possibility, the reliability of data transfer from cards to Master over 16 days was checked. Two staff members independently transferred data from the same patient cards to a Master Sheet. The number of disagreements on any entry were noted and expressed as a percentage of the total entries possible for that day.

## RECORDING SYSTEM FOR A TOKEN PROGRAM

| Date<br>NAME | JOB ASMT. | EARNINGS | | | | | | | | | | | | SPENDINGS | | | | | | | | | | | | | | | | Balances | | | | Obs. Behavior | | | | |
|---|---|---|---|---|---|---|---|---|---|---|---|---|---|---|---|---|---|---|---|---|---|---|---|---|---|---|---|---|---|---|---|---|---|---|---|---|---|---|
| | | Extra Duty | Rising | Bed Made | Grooming | Bed Area | Asmt. on Time | C.T./A.C. | Job/% Max. | Paper | 1) Special Behav. | 2) Special Behav. | Special Code | Breakfast | Privileges | Lunch | Supper | Bed | Semi-Private | Pass | Staff | PRN Medicine | TV | Nap | Pool | Coffee | Cards and Games | Special Behavior | Special Code | Total Earned | Total Spent | Previous Balance | New Balance | % Coded Behav. (1) | % Coded Behav. (2) | % Coded Behav. (3) | No. of Samples | % of Reliability |
| | | | | | | | | | | | | | | | | | | | | | | | | | | | | | | | | | | | | | | |
| | | | | | | | | | | | | | | | | | | | | | | | | | | | | | | | | | | | | | | |
| | | | | | | | | | | | | | | | | | | | | | | | | | | | | | | | | | | | | | | |
| | | | | | | | | | | | | | | | | | | | | | | | | | | | | | | | | | | | | | | |
| | | | | | | | | | | | | | | | | | | | | | | | | | | | | | | | | | | | | | | |
| | | | | | | | | | | | | | | | | | | | | | | | | | | | | | | | | | | | | | | |
| | | | | | | | | | | | | | | | | | | | | | | | | | | | | | | | | | | | | | | |
| | | | | | | | | | | | | | | | | | | | | | | | | | | | | | | | | | | | | | | |
| | | | | | | | | | | | | | | | | | | | | | | | | | | | | | | | | | | | | | | |
| | | | | | | | | | | | | | | | | | | | | | | | | | | | | | | | | | | | | | | |
| | | | | | | | | | | | | | | | | | | | | | | | | | | | | | | | | | | | | | | |
| | | | | | | | | | | | | | | | | | | | | | | | | | | | | | | | | | | | | | | |
| | | | | | | | | | | | | | | | | | | | | | | | | | | | | | | | | | | | | | | |
| | | | | | | | | | | | | | | | | | | | | | | | | | | | | | | | | | | | | | | |
| | | | | | | | | | | | | | | | | | | | | | | | | | | | | | | | | | | | | | | |
| | | | | | | | | | | | | | | | | | | | | | | | | | | | | | | | | | | | | | | |
| | | | | | | | | | | | | | | | | | | | | | | | | | | | | | | | | | | | | | | |
| | | | | | | | | | | | | | | | | | | | | | | | | | | | | | | | | | | | | | | |
| | | | | | | | | | | | | | | | | | | | | | | | | | | | | | | | | | | | | | | |
| | | | | | | | | | | | | | | | | | | | | | | | | | | | | | | | | | | | | | | |

*FIGURE 2. The master data matrix, which incorporates and summarizes all data gathered on the token economy program during a 24-hour period.*

Reliability over the 16-day period, expressed as percentage agreement, ranged from 91.3% to 100% with the mode being 100%.

To assess the reliability of behavioral measures, two nursing staff members simultaneously observed and independently recorded observations during prescheduled 30-second periods throughout the day. No effort was made to ensure that the same two staff members made reliability measures, so that most of the staff participated in the reliability assessment, and each had different co-observers at various times.

The timed 30-second observation period was indicated by one observer to the other via unobtrusive signal. At the end of the 30-second

TABLE 1. *Summary of Behavioral Observation Data and Two Kinds of Reliability Measures on All Patients Admitted to the Token Economy Program During a Two-Month Period.*

| Target behavior | No. patients observed | Total observations | Frequency detection | Frequency agreements | Reliability | Occurrence reliability |
|---|---|---|---|---|---|---|
| Social interaction | 16 | 348 | 126 | 341 | 98% | 94% |
| Pacing | 7 | 187 | 16 | 186 | 99% | 94% |
| Whining and complaining | 6 | 140 | 1 | 140 | 100% | 100% |
| Inappropriate lying down | 7 | 195 | 32 | 192 | 98% | 91% |
| Delusional speech | 6 | 99 | 1 | 99 | 100% | 100% |
| Inappropriate verbal behavior | 6 | 87 | 4 | 84 | 97% | 75% |
| Talking to self | 4 | 124 | 7 | 124 | 100% | 100% |
| Inappropriate motor behavior | 3 | 61 | 10 | 61 | 100% | 100% |
| Verbal aggressive behavior | 2 | 60 | 1 | 60 | 100% | 100% |
| Self-initiated social interaction | 2 | 92 | 2 | 92 | 100% | 100% |
| Sitting alone | 2 | 64 | 41 | 64 | 100% | 100% |
| Arising during sleep | 2 | 36 | — | 36 | 100% | — |
| Inappropriate laughing and giggling | 1 | 23 | 3 | 22 | 96% | 67% |
| Head on table | 1 | 31 | 15 | 31 | 100% | 100% |
| Self-derogatory verbal behavior | 1 | 57 | — | 57 | 100% | 100% |
| Assertive behavior | 2 | 69 | — | 69 | 97% | — |

period, each observer independently indicated whether each of the target behaviors for that patient did or did not occur during the 30 seconds. Fourteen to 23 such observations were made on two to three patients per day over a one- to three-day period. As many as eight target behaviors were observed for any one patient. Number of patients observed, total observations, frequency detections by one or both observers, frequency agreements between observers as to whether target behavior did or did not occur, and reliability and occurrence reliability are found in Table 1. Reliability is expressed as percent agreement between observers on occurrence-nonoccurrence of the behavior, i.e., agreements/total observations. Occurrence reliability is expressed as the percent agreements between observers when the behavior is detected, i.e., detection agreements/total detections. The table summarizes the reliability data gathered on all research patients admitted to the token economy program over the two-month period from March 21 to May 23, 1972. Operational definitions for the first three behaviors in the table are: (1) *Social Interaction*—"Talking to, working with, or playing with another person during the observation period." (2) *Pacing*—"Walking which involves at least one turn of approximately 180° during the observation period." (3) *Whining and Complaining*—"Talking about one's body or physical condition to anyone but a nurse or physician during the observation period." A list of complete operational definitions for each of the behaviors listed in Table 1 may be obtained by writing to the first author.

Inclusion of occurrence reliability in the table reflects a concern with reliability of behavioral observations where the behavior occurs infrequently. When a target behavior occurs once per day or less, standard reliability measures, usually expressed as total agreements on whether the behavior did or did not occur divided by total observations, can reflect high agreement but only on the nonoccurence of a behavior. Though it is important to have high reliability about the nonoccurrence of behavior, such high percent reliability can be deceptive and not represent reliability of agreement *when the target behavior occurs.* For this reason, we have regularly kept records of both kinds of reliability on new target behaviors, usually until operational definitions have been refined, several staff members exposed to the patient, and total reliability percentages in the 95 to 100% range produced. Although we are not happy with occurrence reliabilities around 67%, and strive for 90% or above, we find that agreement on two of three incidents of a behavior that occurs once or less a day is still valuable for treatment and often very difficult to improve upon. We usually find occurrence reliability varies according to how frequently the behavior occurs, tending to be lower when the behavior occurs less than once or twice per day. For example, the two lowest occurrence reliabilities in the table are for: (1) "Inappropriate laughing and giggling," 67%, three detections in 23 observations over two days and

(2) "Inappropriate verbal behavior," 75%, four detections in 87 observations of six different patients.

The investigators believe that this master data matrix and card system is an efficient and accurate way of recording individualized as well as standard behavioral measures. Even though individualizing contingencies opens up the possibility of bulky data, this system has circumvented many of the problems and involves a relatively small amount of time in summarizing and retrieving information.

## REFERENCES

Colman, A. D., & Boren, J. J. An information system for measuring patient behavior and its use by staff. *Journal of Applied Behavior Analysis,* 1969, *2,* 207-214.

Cooper, M. L., Thompson, C. L., & Baer, D. M. The experimental modification of teacher attending behavior. *Journal of Applied Behavior Analysis,* 1970, *3,* 153-157.

Leitenberg, H., Agras, W. S., Thompson, L., & Wright, D. Feedback in behavior modification: an experimental analysis in two phobic cases. *Journal of Applied Behavior Analysis,* 1968, *1,* 131-137.

Milby, J. B., Jr. Modification of extreme social isolation by contingent social reinforcement. *Journal of Applied Behavior Analysis,* 1970, *3,* 149-152.

O'Brien, F., & Azrin, N. H. Behavioral engineering: control of posture by informational feedback. *Journal of Applied Behavior Analysis,* 1970, *3,* 235-240.

Panyan, M., Boozer, H., & Morris, N. Feedback to attendants as a reinforcer for applying operant techniques. *Journal of Applied Behavior Analysis,* 1970, *3,* 1-4.

Suchotliff, L., Greaves, S., Stecker, H., & Berke, R. *Critical variables in the token economy.* Unpublished paper presented at the meeting of the American Psychological Association, Miami, September, 1970.

# REFERENCES TO EDITORS' COMMENTS

Alevizos, P. N., & Berck, P. L. An instructional aid for staff training in behavioral assessment. Unpublished manuscript, Camarillo Neuropsychiatric Institute Research Program, 1974. Described in a Communication, *Journal of Applied Behavior Analysis*, 1975, 7, 472 & 660.

Allport, G. *Personality: A psychological interpretation.* New York: Holt, 1937.

Anthony, R. N., & Duerfeldt, P. H. The effect of tension level and contingent reinforcement on fear reduction. *Behavior Therapy*, 1970, 1, 445-464.

Arkowitz, H., Lichtenstein, E., McGovern, K., & Heines, P. The behavioral assessment of social competence in males. *Behavior Therapy*, 1975, 6, 3-13.

Arrington, R. E. *Interrelations in the behavior of young children.* New York: Columbia University Press, 1932.

Baer, D. M., Wolf, M. M., & Risley, T. R. Some current dimensions of applied behavior analysis. *Journal of Applied Behavior Analysis*, 1968, 1, 91-97.

Bandura, A. *Principles of behavior modification.* New York: Holt, Rinehart & Winston, 1969.

Bandura, A. Behavior theory and the models of man. *American Psychologist*, 1974, 12, 859-869.

Bandura, A., Blanchard, E. B., & Ritter, R. The relative efficacy of desensitization and modeling approaches for inducing behavioral, affective, and attitudinal changes. *Journal of Personality and Social Psychology*, 1969, 13, 173-199.

Barocas, R., & Weiss, B. Behavioral assessment of lead intoxication in children. *Environmental Health Perspectives*, 1974, 47-52.

Barton, M. C., Witherspoon, A. D., & Jenkins, W. O. Maladaptive behavior record (MBR). In A. D. Witherspoon, E. K. deValera, W. O. Jenkins, and W. L. Sanford (Eds.), *Behavioral interview guide.* Montgomery, Ala.: Rehabilitation Research Foundation, 1973.

Battle, C. C., Imber, S. D., Hoehn-Saric, R., Stone, A. R., Nash, E. R., & Frank, J. D. Target complaints as criteria of improvement. *American Journal of Psychotherapy*, 1966, 20, 184-192.

Bean, K. L. Desensitization, behavior rehearsal, then reality: A preliminary report on a new procedure. *Behavior Therapy*, 1970, *1*, 542-545.

Bechtel, R. B. The study of man: Human movement and architecture. *Transaction*, 1967, *4*, 53-56.

Beck, A. T., Ward, B. H., Mendelsohn, M., Mock, J., & Erbaugh, J. An inventory for measuring depression. *Archives of General Psychiatry*, 1961, *4*, 561-571.

Beck, A. T., Weissman, A., Lester, D., & Trexler, L. The measurement of pessimism: The hopelessness scale. *Journal of Consulting and Clinical Psychology*, 1974, *42*, 861-865.

Becker, W. C., Madsen, C. H., Arnold, C. R., & Thomas, D. R. The contingent use of teacher attention and praise in reducing classroom behavior problems. *Journal of Special Education*, 1967, *1*, 287-307.

Bem, D. J., & Allen, A. On predicting some of the people some of the time: The search for cross-situational consistencies in behavior. *Psychological Review*, 1974, *81*, 506-520.

Bernal, M. E., Delfini, L., North, J., & Kreutzer, S. L. Comparison of boys' behavior in homes and classrooms. In E. J. Mash, L. A. Hamerlynck, and L. C. Handy (Eds.) *Behavior modification and families*. New York: Brunner/Mazel, 1976.

Bernal, M. E., Gibson, D. M., Williams, D. E., & Pesses, D. I. A device for automatic audio tape recording. *Journal of Applied Behavior Analysis*, 1971, *4*, 151-156.

Bernal, M. E., Kreutzer, S. L., North, J. A., & Pelc, R. E. Scoring system for home and school: Rationale, use, reliability, and validity. Paper presented at the meeting of the American Psychological Association, Montreal, Canada, 1973.

Bernal, M. E., & North, J. A. A system for scoring home and school behaviors. Revision 10. Unpublished manuscript, University of Denver, 1972.

Bernstein, D. A., & Nietzel, M. T. Behavioral avoidance tests: The effects of demand characteristics and repeated measures on two types of subjects. *Behavior Therapy*, 1974, *5*, 183-192.

Bersoff, D. N. "Current functioning" myth: An overlooked fallacy in psychological assessment. *Journal of Consulting and Clinical Psychology*, 1971, *37*, 391-393.

Bersoff, D. N. Silk purses into sow's ears: The decline of psychological testing and the suggestion for its redemption. *American Psychologist*, 1973, *28*, 892-899.

Bersoff, D. N. Behavioral approaches to assessment and observation in the school. In J. M. Magary (Ed.), *Handbook of school psychological services*. St. Louis: C. V. Mosby, 1974.

Bersoff, D. N., & Ericson, C. R. A precise and valid measure of behavior and behavior change in the classroom. *Journal of School Psychology*, 1972, *10*, 361-366.

Bersoff, D. N., & Grieger, R. M. An interview model for the psychosituational assessment of children's behavior. *American Journal of Orthopsychiatry*, 1971, *41*, 483-493.

Bersoff, D. N., & Moyer, D. Positive reinforcement observation schedule

(PROS): Development and use. Paper presented at the annual meeting of the American Psychological Association, Montreal, Canada, August 1973.

Bijou, S. W., & Peterson, R. F. The psychological assessment of children: A functional analysis. In P. McReynolds (Ed.), *Advances in psychological assessment.* Vol. 2. Palo Alto, Calif.: Science and Behavior Books, 1971. Pp. 63-78.

Boer, A. P. Application of a simple recording system to the analysis of free-play behavior in autistic children. *Journal of Applied Behavior Analysis,* 1968, *1,* 335-340.

Boren, J., & Jagodzinski, M. A family program: Analysis and difficulties in implementation. Paper presented at the meeting of the Association for the Advancement of Behavior Therapy, Miami Beach, Florida, 1973.

Borkovec, T. D., Stone, N. M., O'Brien, G. T., & Kaloupek, D. G. Evaluation of a clinically relevant target behavior for analog outcome research. *Behavior Therapy,* 1974, *5,* 503-513.

Bowers, K. S. Situationism in psychology: An analysis and a critique. *Psychological Review, 1973, 80,* 307-336.

Brady, J. P. Metronome-conditioned speech retraining for stuttering. *Behavior Therapy,* 1971, *2,* 129-150.

Briddell, D. W., & Nathan, P. E. Behavior assessment and modification with alcoholics: Current status and future trends. Unpublished manuscript, Rutgers University, 1975.

Budd, K., Rogers, A., & Schilmoeller, K. An observer training program for an applied setting. Paper presented at the annual meeting of the American Psychological Association, Honolulu, Hawaii, September 1972.

Carter, R. D., & Thomas, E. J. A case application of a signalling system (SAM) to the assessment and modification of selected problems of marital communication. *Behavior Therapy,* 1973, *4,* 629-645.

Cataldo, M. F., & Risley, T. R. Evaluation of living environments: The MANIFEST description of ward activities. In P. O. Davidson, F. W. Clark, and L. A. Hamerlynck (Eds.), *Evaluation of behavioral programs: In community, residential and school settings.* Champaign, Ill.: Research Press, 1974.

Cattell, R. B. *Handbook for the IPAT Anxiety Scale.* Champaign, Ill.: Institute for Personality and Ability Testing, 1957.

Cattell, R. B., & Rickels, K. Diagnostic power of IPAT objective anxiety neuroticism tests. *Archives of General Psychiatry,* 1965, *11,* 459-465.

Cautela, J. R. Behavior therapy and the need for behavioral assessment. *Psychotherapy: Theory, Research and Practice,* 1968, *5,* 175-179.

Cautela, J. R. Covert reinforcement. *Behavior Therapy,* 1970, *1,* 33-50.

Cautela, J. R. Reinforcement survey schedule: Evaluation and current applications. *Psychological Reports,* 1972, *30,* 683-690.

Cautela, J. R., & Kastenbaum, R. A reinforcement survey schedule for use in therapy, training and research. *Psychological Reports,* 1967, *20,* 115-130.

Cautela, J. R., Steffen, J., & Wish, P. Covert reinforcement: An experimental test. Paper presented to the American Psychological Association, Miami, Florida, 1970.

Cautela, J. R., & Upper, D. A behavioral coding system. Unpublished manuscript, Boston College, 1973.

Cautela, J. R., & Wisocki, P. A. The use of the Reinforcement Survey Schedule in behavior modification. In R. D. Rubin, A. A. Lazarus, H. Fensterheim, and C. M. Franks (Eds.), *Advances in behavior therapy: 1969.* New York: Academic Press, 1971. Pp. 29–36.

Clement, P. W., & Richard, R. C. Children's reinforcement survey. Unpublished manuscript, Fuller Theological Seminary, Pasadena, California, 1970.

Cobb, J. A. The relationship of discrete classroom behaviors to fourth-grade academic achievement. *Oregon Research Institute Research Bulletin,* 1970, *10,* 1–18.

Cobb, J. A., & Hops, H. Coding manual for subject/peer/teacher sequential interactions in academic survival skills settings. CORBEH Report No. 4, University of Oregon, Eugene, 1971.

Cobb, J. A., & Ray, R. S. Manual for coding discrete behaviors in the school setting. Unpublished manuscript, Oregon Research Institute, 1970.

Conger, J. C. The modification of interview behavior by client use of social reinforcement. *Behavior Therapy,* 1971, *2,* 52–61.

Cooper, J. O. *Measurement and analysis of behavioral techniques.* Columbus, Ohio: Charles E. Merrill, 1974.

Costello, C. G. Depression: Loss of reinforcers or loss of reinforcer effectiveness? *Behavior Therapy,* 1972, *3,* 240–247.

Cotler, S. B., Applegate, G., King, L. W., & Kristal, S. Establishing a token economy program in a state hospital classroom: A lesson in training student to teacher. *Behavior Therapy,* 1972, *3,* 209–222.

Cox, F. N. Some effects of test anxiety and presence or absence of other persons on boys' performance on a repetitive motor task. *Journal of Experimental Child Psychology,* 1966, *3,* 100–112.

Cox, F. N. Some relationships between test anxiety, presence or absence of male persons, and boys' performance on a repetitive motor task. *Journal of Experimental Child Psychology,* 1968, *6,* 1–12.

Craik, K. H. Environmental psychology. In P. H. Mussen and M. R. Rosenzweig (Eds.), *Annual review of psychology,* 1973, 403–422.

Daley, M. F. The "reinforcement menu": Finding effective reinforcers. In J. D. Krumbholtz and C. Thoresen (Eds.), *Counselling and behavior change.* New York: Holt, Rinehart and Winston, 1971.

Daly, D. A., & Frick, J. V. The effects of punishing stuttering expectations and stuttering utterances: A comparative study. *Behavior Therapy,* 1970, *1,* 228–239.

Danaher, B. G. Theoretical foundations and clinical applications of the Premack Principle: Review and critique. *Behavior Therapy,* 1974, *5,* 307–324.

Davison, G, C., & Taffel, S. J. Effects of behavior therapy. Paper presented at the annual convention of the American Psychological Association, Honolulu, Hawaii, 1972.

Delfini, L. F., Bernal, M. E., & Rosen, P. M. A comparison of normal and deviant boys in their homes. In E. J. Mash, L. A. Hamerlynck, and L. C. Handy (Eds.), *Behavior modification and families.* New York: Brunner/Mazel, 1976.

Dooley, D. Nonverbal and verbal analysis of help-intended behavior. Paper presented at the Western Psychological Association meeting, Sacramento, California, 1975.

Dubanoski, R. A., & Parton, D. A. Effect of presence of a human model on imitative behavior in children. *Developmental Psychology,* 1971, *4,* 463-468.

Eisler, R. M., Hersen, M., & Agras, W. S. Videotape: A method for the controlled observation of nonverbal interpersonal behavior. *Behavior Therapy,* 1973, *4,* 420-425.

Ellett, C. D., & Bersoff, D. N. New tricks for old dogs: A modern approach to psychological assessment. Paper presented at the meeting of the American Psychological Association, Montreal, Canada, 1973.

Endler, N. S., Hunt, J. McV., & Rosenstein, A. J. An S-R inventory of anxiousness. *Psychological Monographs,* 1962, 76 (17, Whole no. 536).

Evans, I. M., & Nelson, R. O. A curriculum for the teaching of behavior assessment. *American Psychologist,* 1974, *29,* 598-606.

Eyberg, S. M., & Johnson, S. M. Multiple assessment of behavior modification with families: Effects of contingency contracting and order of treated problems. *Journal of Consulting and Clinical Psychology,* 1974, *42,* 594-606.

Farley, F. H., & Mealiea, W. L. Jr. Dissimulation and social desirability in the assessment of fear. *Behavior Therapy,* 1971, *2,* 101-102.

Feldman, M. P., & MacCulloch, M. J. *Homosexual behavior: Therapy and assessment.* Oxford: Pergamon Press, 1971.

Feldman, M., MacCulloch, M. J., Mallor, V., & Pinschoff, J. The application of anticipatory avoidance learning to the treatment of homosexuality: III. The sexual orientation method. *Behavior Research and Therapy,* 1966, *4,* 289-299.

Ferber, H., Keeley, S. N., & Shemberg, K. M. Training parents in behavior modification: Outcome of and problems encountered in a program after Patterson's work. *Behavior Therapy,* 1974, *5,* 415-419.

Ferster, C. B., & DeMyer, M. K. A method for the experimental analysis of the behavior of autistic children. *American Journal of Orthopsychiatry,* 1962, *32,* 89-98.

Franks, C. M. (Ed.) *Behavior therapy: Appraisal and status.* New York: McGraw-Hill, 1969.

Franks, C. M., & Wilson, G. T. W. (Eds.) *Annual review of behavior therapy: Theory and practice.* Vol. 1. New York: Brunner/Mazel, 1973.

Franks, C. M., & Wilson, G. T. W. (Eds.) *Annual review of behavior therapy: Theory and practice.* Vol. 2. New York: Brunner/Mazel, 1974.

Franks, C. M., & Wilson, G. T. W. (Eds.) *Annual review of behavior therapy: Theory and practice.* Vol. 3. New York: Brunner/Mazel, 1975.

Gagne, R. M. Observations of school learning. Paper presented at the annual meeting of the American Psychological Association, Montreal, Canada, 1973.

Gaines, D. M. A comparison of two observation methods: Percent vs. frequency. Paper presented at the annual meeting of the American Psychological Association, Montreal, Canada, 1973.

Galassi, J. P., DeLo, J. S., Galassi, M. D., & Bastien, S. The college self-expression scale: A measure of assertiveness. *Behavior Therapy,* 1974, *5,* 165-171.

Gambrill, E. D. The use of behavioral methods in a short-term detention setting. Unpublished manuscript, University of California at Berkeley, 1975.

Geer, J. H. The development of a scale to measure fear. *Behavior Research and Therapy,* 1965, *3,* 45-53.

Glaser, R. *The nature of reinforcement.* New York: Academic Press, 1971.

Glasgow, R. E., & Arkowitz, H. The behavioral assessment of male and female social competence in dyadic heterosexual interactions. *Behavior Therapy,* 1975, *6,* 488-498.

Goldberg, L. R. Some recent trends in personality assessment. Invited lecture presented at the meeting of the American Psychological Association, Washington, D.C., 1971.

Goldfried, M. R., & D'Zurilla, T. J. A behavioral-analytic model for assessing competence. In C. D. Spielberger (Ed.), *Current topics in clinical and community psychology.* New York: Academic Press, 1969. Pp. 151-196.

Goldfried, M. R., & Kent, R. N. Traditional versus behavioral personality assessment: A comparison of methodological and theoretical assumptions. *Psychological Bulletin,* 1972, *77,* 409-420.

Goldfried, M. R., & Pomeranz, D. M. Role of assessment in behavior modification. *Psychological Reports,* 1968, *23,* 75-87.

Goldfried, M. R., & Sprafkin, J. *Behavioral personality assessment.* Morristown, N.J.: General Learning Press, 1974.

Goldiamond, I. Toward a constructional approach to social problems: Ethical and constitutional issues raised by applied behavior analysis. *Behaviorism,* 1974, *2,* 1-84.

Goodenough, F. L. *Mental testing.* New York: Holt, Rinehart & Winston, 1949.

Goodwin, D. L., & Coate, T. J. The teacher-pupil interaction scale: An empirical method for analyzing the interactive effects of teacher and pupil behavior. Unpublished manuscript, California State University, San Jose, 1971.

Gottman, J. M., & McFall, R. M. Self-monitoring effects in a program for potential high school dropouts: A time-series analysis. *Journal of Consulting and Clinical Psychology,* 1972, *39,* 273-281.

Grant, R. Toward a psychosocial data base in comprehensive health care. Paper presented at the Symposium on the Problem-Oriented System, Atlanta, Georgia, 1972.

Grant, R., & Maletzky, B. Application of the Weed system to psychiatric records. *Psychiatry in Medicine,* 1972, *3,* 119-129.

Grim, P. F. Anxiety change produced by self-induced muscle tension and by relaxation with respiration feedback. *Behavior Therapy,* 1971, *2,* 11-17.

Hagen, R. L., Craighead, W. E., & Paul, G. L. Staff reactivity to evaluative behavioral assessment. *Behavior Therapy,* 1975, *6,* 201-205.

Hamilton, M. A rating scale for depression. *Journal of Neurology, Neurosurgery and Psychiatry,* 1960, *23,* 56-62.

Hartmann, D. P. Assessing the quality of observational data. Paper presented in the symposium entitled ''The Quality of Observational Data'' at the annual convention of the Western Psychological Association, San Francisco,

California, 1974.

Hawn, J., Brown, G., & LeBlanc, J. M. A comparison of three observation procedures: Consecutive intervals on-the-spot; consecutive intervals from video tape; 10-sec-on, 10-sec-off from video tape. Paper presented at the annual meeting of the American Psychological Association, Montreal, Canada, 1973.

Hekmat, H. The role of imagination in systematic desensitization. *Behavior Therapy*, 1972, *3*, 223-231.

Henderson, J. D., & Scoles, P. E. Conditioning techniques in a community-based operant environment for psychotic men. *Behavior Therapy*, 1970, *1*, 245-251.

Herman, S. H., Barlow, D. H., & Agras, W. S. An experimental analysis of classical conditioning as a method of increasing heterosexual arousal in homosexuals. *Behavior Therapy*, 1974, *5*, 33-47.

Herr, W. S. The natural history of a behavior modification program. *Newsletter of the Association for the Advancement of Behavior Therapy*, 1969, *4*, 11-12.

Hersen, M., Eisler, R. M., & Miller, P. M. Development of assertive responses: Clinical measurement and research considerations. *Behavior Research and Therapy*, 1973, *11*, 505-521.

Heyns, R. W., & Lippitt, R. Systematic observational techniques. In *Handbook of social psychology*. Vol. 1. Cambridge: Addison-Wesley, 1954.

Holland, C. J. An interview guide for behavioral counseling with parents. *Behavior Therapy*, 1970, *1*, 70-79

Homme, L. E. Perspectives in psychology: XXIV. Control of coverants, the operants of the mind. *Psychological Record*, 1965, *15*, 501-511.

Homme, L. E. *How to use contingency contracting in the classroom*. Champaign, Ill.: Research Press, 1970.

Hops, H., Wills, T. A., Patterson, G. R., & Weiss, R. L. *Marital interaction coding system*. Technical report 8, prepared under ONR Contract N00014-67-A-0446-0003, NR Number 170-720. Inter-personal conflict and group theory, December 1971.

Hutt, S. J., & Hutt, C. *Direct observation and measurement of behavior*. Springfield, Ill.: Charles C Thomas, 1970.

Jenkins, W. O. Prolegomena to the measurement and assessment of human behavior. Unpublished manuscript, Experimental Manpower Laboratory for Corrections, Rehabilitation Research Foundation, Draper Correctional Center, Elmore, Alabama, 1971.

Jersild, A. T., & Meigs, M. F. Direct observation as a research method. *Review of Educational Research*, 1939, *9*, 472-482.

Johansson, S., Lewinsohn, P. M., & Flippo, J. R. An application of the Premack principle to the verbal behavior of depressed subjects. Paper presented at the meeting of the Association for Advancement of Behavior Therapy, 1969.

Johnson, D. T., & Spielberger, C. D. The effects of relaxation training and the passage of time on measures of state and trait anxiety. *Journal of Clinical Psychology*, 1968, *24*, 20-23.

Johnson, S. M., & Bolstad, O. D. Methodological issues in naturalistic observation: Some problems and solutions for field research. In L. A.

Hamerlynck, L. C. Handy, and E. J. Mash (Eds.), *Behavior change: Methodology, concepts and practice.* Champaign, Ill.: Research Press, 1973. Pp. 7-67.

Johnson, S. M., Bolstad, O. D., & Lobitz, G. K. Generalization and contrast phenomena in behavior modification with children. In E. J. Mash, L. A. Hamerlynck, and L. C. Handy (Eds.), *Behavior modification and families.* New York: Brunner/Mazel, 1976.

Johnson, S. M., & Brown, R. A. Producing behavior change in parents of disturbed children. *Journal of Child Psychology and Psychiatry,* 1969, *10,* 107-121.

Johnson, S. M., & Christensen, A. Multiple criteria follow-up of behavior modifcation with families. Unpublished manuscript, University of Oregon, Eugene, 1974.

Johnson, S. M., Christensen, A., & Bellamy, G. T. Evaluation of family intervention through unobtrusive audio recordings: Experiences in bugging children. Unpublished manuscript, University of Oregon, 1975.

Johnson, S. M., & Lobitz, G. K. Demand characteristics in naturalistic observation. Unpublished manuscript, University of Oregon, Eugene, 1972.

Johnson, S. M., & White, G. Self-observation as an agent of behavioral change. *Behavior Therapy,* 1971, *2,* 488-497.

Johnson, W., Darly, F. L., & Spriesterbach, D. C. *Diagnostic methods in speech pathology.* New York: Harper & Row, 1963.

Jones, R. R. Intraindividual stability of behavioral observations: Implications for evaluating behavior modification treatment programs. Paper presented at the meeting of the Western Psychological Association, Portland, Oregon, April 1972.

Jones, R. R. Behavioral observation frequency data: Problems in scoring. In L. A. Hamerlynck, L. C. Handy, and E. J. Mash (Eds.), *Behavior change: Methodology, concepts and practice.* Champaign, Ill.: Research Press, 1973.

Jones, R. R. "Observation" by telephone: An economical behavior sampling technique. *Oregon Research Institute Technical Report,* 1974, *14,* No. 1.

Jones, R. R., Reid, J. B., & Patterson, G. R. Naturalistic observation in clinical assessment. In P. McReynolds (Ed.), *Advances in psychological assessment.* Vol. 3. San Francisco: Jossey-Bass, 1974.

Kanfer, 'F. H. Assessment for behavior modification. *Journal of Personality Assessment,* 1972, *36,* 418-423.

Kanfer, F. H., & Grimm, L. G. Promising trends toward the future development of behavior modification: Ten related areas in need of exploration. In W. E. Craighead, A. E. Kazdin, and M. J. Mahoney (Eds.), *Behavior modification: Principles, issues and applications.* Boston: Houghton Mifflin, 1976.

Kanfer, F. H., & Phillips, J. S. *Learning foundations of behavior therapy.* New York: Wiley, 1970.

Kanfer, F. H., & Saslow, G. Behavioral analysis: An alternative to the diagnostic classification. *Archives of General Psychiatry,* 1965, *12,* 529-538.

Kanfer, F. H., & Saslow, G. Behavioral diagnosis. In C. M. Franks (Ed.), *Behavior therapy: Appraisal and status.* New York: McGraw-Hill, 1969. Pp. 417-444.

Kass, R. E., & O'Leary, K. D. The effects of observer bias in field-experimental settings. Paper presented at a symposium entitled "Behavior Analysis in Education," University of Kansas, Lawrence, April 1970.

Katz, R. C., Johnson, C. A., & Gelfand, S. Modifying the dispensing of reinforcers: Some implications for behavior modification with hopitalized patients. *Behavior Therapy,* 1972, *3,* 579-588.

Katz, R. C., & Woolley, F. R. Improving patients' records through problem orientation. *Behavior Therapy,* 1975, *6,* 119-124.

Kazdin, A. E. Methodological and assessment considerations in evaluating reinforcement programs in applied settings. *Journal of Applied Behavior Analysis,* 1973, *6,* 517-531.

Kazdin, A. E. Self-monitoring and behavior change. In M. J. Mahoney and C. E. Thoresen (Eds.), *Self-control: Power to the person.* Monterey, Calif.: Brooks/Cole, 1974.

Keehn, J. D., Bloomfield, F. F., & Hug, M. A. Uses of the Reinforcement Survey Schedule with alcoholics. *Quarterly Journal of Studies on Alcohol,* 1970, *31,* 602-615.

Kenny, F. T., Solyom, L., & Solyom, C. Faradic disruption of obsessive ideation in the treatment of obsessive neurosis. *Behavior Therapy,* 1973, *4,* 448-457.

Kent, R. N., O'Leary, K. D., Diament, C., & Dietz, A. Expectation biases in observational evaluation of therapeutic change. *Journal of Consulting and Clinical Psychology,* 1974, *42,* 774-780.

Kent, R. N., O'Leary, K. D., & Kanowitz, J. Observer reliability as a function of circumstances of assessment. Paper presented at the annual meeting of the Western Psychological Association, San Francisco, Calif., 1974.

Kent, R. N., Wilson, G. T., & Nelson, R. Effects of false heartrate feedback on avoidance behavior: An investigation of "cognitive desensitization." *Behavior Therapy,* 1972, *3,* 1-6.

Kleinknecht, R. A., McCormick, C. E., & Thorndike, R. M. Stability of stated reinforcers as measured by the reinforcement survey schedule. *Behavior Therapy,* 1973, *4,* 407-413.

Klorman, R., Weerts, T. C., Hastings, J. E., Melamed, B. G., & Lang, P. J. Psychometric description of some specific-fear questionnaires. *Behavior Therapy,* 1974, *5,* 401-409.

Krasner, L. Why classify behavior? Paper presented at the American Psychological Association symposium on the Classification of Behavior, Washington, D.C., September 1969.

Krop, H., Calhoon, B., & Verrier, R. Modification of the "self concept" of emotionally disturbed children by covert reinforcement. *Behavior Therapy,* 1971, *2,* 201-204.

Kubany, E. S., & Sloggett, B. B. Coding procedure for teachers. *Journal of Applied Behavior Analysis,* 1973, *6,* 339-344.

Kuypers, D. S., Becker, W. C., & O'Leary, K. D. How to make a token system fail. *Exceptional Children,* 1968, *35,* 101-109.

Lang, P. J., & Lazovik, A. D. Experimental desensitization of a phobia. *Journal of Abnormal and Social Psychology,* 1963, *66,* 519-525.

Lavigueur, H., Peterson, R. F., Sheese, J. G., & Peterson, L. W. Behavioral treatment in the home: Effects on an untreated sibling and long-term follow-up. *Behavior Therapy.* 1973, *4,* 431-441.

Lawrence, P. S. The assessment and modification of assertive behavior. Unpublished doctoral dissertation, Arizona State University, 1970.

Lazarus, A. A. *Behavior therapy and beyond.* New York: McGraw-Hill, 1971.

LeLaurin, K., & Risley, T. R. The organization of daycare environments: "Zone" *versus* "man-to-man" staff assignments. *Journal of Applied Behavior Analysis,* 1972, *5,* 225-232.

Lewinsohn, P. M. Manual of instructions for the behavior ratings used for the observation of interpersonal behavior. Unpublished manuscript, University of Oregon, 1968.

Lewinsohn, P. M. A behavioral approach to depression. In R. J. Friedman and M. M. Katz (Eds.), *The psychology of depression: Contemporary theory and research.* New York: Wiley, 1974.

Lewinsohn, P. M., & Shaffer, M. Use of home observations as an integral part of the treatment of depression: Preliminary report and case studies. *Journal of Consulting and Clinical Psychology,* 1971, *37,* 87-94.

Liberman, R. P., & Smith, V. A multiple baseline study of systematic desensitization in a patient with multiple phobias. *Behavior Therapy,* 1972, *3,* 597-603.

Libet, J. M., & Lewinsohn, P. M. Concept of social skill with special reference to the behavior of depressed persons. *Journal of Consulting and Clinical Psychology,* 1973, *40,* 304-312.

Lick, J. R., & Bootzin, R. R. Expectancy, demand characteristics, and contact desensitization in behavior change. *Behavior Therapy,* 1970, *1,* 176-183.

Lindsley, O. R. A reliable wrist counter for recording behavior rates. *Journal of Applied Behavior Analysis,* 1968, *1,* 77-78.

Lipinski, D., & Nelson, R. Problems in the use of naturalistic observation as a means of behavioral assessment. *Behavior Therapy,* 1974, *5,* 341-351.

Lomont, J. F., & Sherman, L. J. Group systematic desensitization and group insight therapies for test anxiety. *Behavior Therapy,* 1971, *2,* 511-518.

Long, B. H. The reliability of coding. Technical Report No. 7 to the Office of Naval Research, Center for Research on Social Behavior, University of Delaware, Newark, Delaware, 1962.

Lovaas, O. I., Koegel, R., Simmons, J. Q., & Long, J. S. Some generalization and follow-up measures on autistic children in behavior therapy. *Journal of Applied Behavior Analysis,* 1973, *6,* 131-166.

Lutker, E. R., Tasto, D. L., & Jorgensen, G. A brief note on multihierarchy desensitization. *Behavior Therapy,* 1972, *3,* 619-621.

Lytton, H. Observational studies of parent-child interaction: A methodological review. *Child Development,* 1971, *42,* 651-684.

Lytton, H. Three approaches to the study of parent-child interaction: Ethological, interview and experimental. *Journal of Child Psychology and Psychiatry,* 1973, *14,* 1-17.

MacCulloch, M. J., Birtles, C. J., & Feldman, M. P. Anticipatory avoidance learning for the treatment of homosexuality: Recent developments and an automatic aversion therapy system. *Behavior Therapy,* 1971, *2,* 151-169.

MacPhillamy, D. J., & Lewinsohn, P. M. Pleasant Events Schedule: Form III-S.

Unpublished manuscript, University of Oregon, 1971.

MacPhillamy, D. J., & Lewinsohn, P. M. A scale for the measurement of positive reinforcement. Mimeo, University of Oregon, 1973.

Madsen, C. H., & Madsen, C. K. *Teaching discipline: A positive approach for educational development.* Boston: Allyn and Bacon, 1974.

Mahoney, M. J. *Cognition and behavior modification.* Cambridge, Mass.: Ballinger Publishing Company, 1974.

Mahoney, M. J., Kazdin, A. E., & Lesswing, N. J. Behavior modification: Delusion or deliverance? In C. M. Franks and G. T. W. Wilson (Eds.), *Annual review of behavior therapy: Theory and practice.* Vol. 2. New York: Brunner/Mazel, 1974.

Mahoney, M. J., & Thoresen, C. E. *Self-control: Power to the person.* Monterey, Calif.: Wadsworth, 1974.

Marks, I. M. Patterns of meaning in psychiatric patients: Semantic differential responses on obsessives and psychopaths. Mosley Monograph No. 13, Oxford University Press, 1965.

Martin, M. F., Gelfand, D. M., & Hartmann, D. P. Effects of adult and peer observers on boys' and girls' responses to an aggressive model. *Child Development,* 1971, *42,* 1271-1275.

Martin, S., Dysart, R., & Gonzalez, J. A comparison of family interaction in clinic and in home settings. Unpublished manuscript, University of Houston, 1975.

Martin, S., & Gonzalez, J. A comparison of three mothods of recording the same behavior. Unpublished manuscript, University of Houston, 1975.

Martin, S., Johnson, S. M., Johansson, S., & Wahl, G. The comparability of behavioral data in laboratory and natural settings. In E. J. Mash, L. A. Hamerlynck, and L. C. Handy (Eds.), *Behavior modification and families.* New York: Brunner/Mazel, 1976.

Mash, E. J. Behavior modification and methodology: A developmental perspective. *Journal of Educational Thought,* 1976, in press.

Mash, E. J., Hamerlynck, L. A., & Handy, L. A. (Eds.). *Behavior modification and families.* New York: Brunner/Mazel, 1976.

Mash, E. J., Handy, L. C., & Hamerlynck, L. A. (Eds.). *Behavior modification approaches to parenting.* New York: Brunner/Mazel, 1976.

Mash, E. J., Hamerlynck, L. A., & Handy, L. C. (Eds.). *Behavior modification and families.* New York: Brunner/Mazel, 1976.

Mash, E. J., & Makohoniuk, G. The effects of prior information and behavioral predictability on observer accuracy. *Child Development,* 1975, *46,* 513-519.

Mash, E. J., & McElwee, J. D. Situational effects on observer accuracy: Behavioral predictability, prior experience and complexity of coding categories. *Child Development,* 1974, *45,* 367-377.

Mash, E. J., & Terdal, L. G. Behavior-therapy assessment: Diagnosis, design and evaluation. *Psychological Reports,* 1974, *35,* 587-601.

Mash, E. J., Terdal, L., & Anderson, K. The response-class matrix: A procedure for recording parent-child interactions. *Journal of Consulting and Clinical Psychology,* 1973, *40,* 163-164.

Matarazzo, J. D., Wiens, A. N., Matarazzo, R. G., & Saslow, G. Speech and silence behavior in clinical psychotherapy and its laboratory correlates. In J. M. Shlien (Ed.), *Research in psychotherapy.* Vol. III. Washington, D.C.: American Psychological Association, 1968. Pp. 179-210.

McCullough, J. P., & Montgomery, L. E. A technique for measuring subjective arousal in therapy clients. *Behavior Therapy,* 1972, *3,* 627-628.

McFall, R. M., & Lillesand, D. V. Behavior rehearsal with modeling and coaching in assertive training. *Journal of Abnormal Psychology,* 1971, 77, 313-323.

McFall, R. M., & Marston, A. R. An experimental investigation of behavior rehearsal in assertive training. *Journal of Abnormal Psychology,* 1970, 76, 295-303.

McLean, P. D. A revision of the Reinforcement Survey Schedule. Unpublished manuscript, University of Calgary, Calgary, Alberta, 1970.

McLean, P. D. Therapeutic decision-making in the behavioral treatment of depression. Paper presented at the Seventh Banff International Conference on Behavior Modification, Banff, Alberta, Canada, 1975.

McLean, P. D., & Craig, K. D. Evaluating treatment effectiveness by monitoring changes in problematic behaviors. *Journal of Consulting and Clinical Psychology,* 1975, *43,* 105.

McLean, P. D., & Miles, J. E. Evaluation and the problem-oriented record in psychiatry. *Archives of General Psychiatry,* 1974, *31,* 621-625.

McNamara, J. R. Teacher and students as sources for behavior modification in the classroom. *Behavior Therapy,* 1971, *2,* 205-213.

Meichenbaum, D. H. *Cognitive factors in behavior modification: Modifying what clients say to themselves.* Research Report No. 25. Waterloo: University of Waterloo, 1971.

Meichenbaum, D. *Clinical implications of modifying what clients say to themselves.* Research Report No. 42. Waterloo: University of Waterloo, December 1972.

Meichenbaum, D. *Cognitive behavior modification.* Morristown, N.J.: General Learning Press, 1974.

Mercatoris, M., & Craighead, W. E. The effects of nonparticipant observation on teacher-pupil classroom behavior. *Journal of Educational Psychology,* 1974, *66,* 512-519.

Milby, J. B., Willicut, H. C., Hawk, J. W., MacDonald, M., & Whitfield, K. A system for recording individualized behavioral data in a token program. *Journal of Applied Behavior Analysis,* 1973, *6,* 333-338.

Miller, H. R., & Nawas, M. Control of aversive stimulus termination in systematic desensitization. *Behavior Research and Therapy,* 1970, *8,* 57-62.

Miller, P. M. Behavioral assessment in alcoholism research and treatment: Current techniques. *The International Journal of the Addictions,* 1973, *8,* 831-837.

Mischel, W. *Personality and assessment.* New York: Wiley, 1968.

Mischel, W. Toward a cognitive social learning reconceptualization of personality. *Psychological Review,* 1973, *80,* 252-283.

Moos, R. H. Behavioral effects of being observed: Reactions to a wireless transmitter. *Journal of Consulting and Clinical Psychology,* 1968, *32,* 383-388.

Moos, R. H., & Clemes, S. R. Multivariate study of the patient-therapist system. *Journal of Consulting Psychology*, 1967, *31*, 119-130.

Nelson, C. M., & McReynolds, W. T. Self-recording and control of behavior: A reply to Simkins. *Behavior Therapy*, 1971, *2*, 594-597.

Nelson, R. O., Lipinski, D. P., & Black, J. L. Manipulation of the direction of reactive changes in self-recording. Unpublished manuscript, University of North Carolina at Greensboro, 1975.

O'Leary, K. D. Diagnosis of children's behavior problems. In H. C. Quay and J. S. Werry (Eds.), *Behavior disorders of children*. New York: Wiley, 1973. Pp. 234-272.

O'Leary, K. D., & Becker, W. C. Behavior modification of an adjustment class: A token reinforcement program. *Exceptional Children*, 1967, *33*, 637-642.

O'Leary, K. D., Becker, W. C., Evans, M., & Saudargas, R. Token reinforcement in a public school: A replication and systematic analysis. *Journal of Applied Behavior Analysis*, 1969, *2*, 3-14.

O'Leary, K. D., & Kent, R. Behavior modification for social action: Research tactics and problems. In L. A. Hamerlynck, L. C. Handy, and E. J. Mash (Eds.), *Behavior change: Methodology, concepts and practice*. Champaign, Ill.: Research Press, 1973.

O'Leary, K. D., & Wilson, G. T. *Behavior therapy: Application and outcome*. Englewood Cliffs, N. J.: Prentice-Hall, 1975.

Olson, D. H., & Ryder, R. G. Inventory of marital conflicts (IMC): An experimental interaction procedure. *Journal of Marriage and Family*, 1970, *32*, 443-448.

Patterson, G. R. Behavioral intervention procedures in the classroom and the home. In A. E. Bergin and S. L. Garfield (Eds.), *Handbook of psychotherapy and behavior change: An empirical analysis*. New York: Wiley, 1971.

Patterson, G. R. Changes in status of family members as controlling stimuli: A basis for describing treatment process. In L. A. Hamerlynck, L. C. Handy, and E. J. Mash (Eds.), *Behavior change: Methodology, concepts and practice*. Champaign, Ill.: Research Press, 1973. Pp. 169-191.

Patterson, G. R. Interventions for boys with conduct problems: Multiple settings, treatments, and criteria. *Journal of Consulting and Clinical Psychology*, 1974, *42*, 471-481.

Patterson, G. R. The aggressive child: Victim and architect of a coercive system. In E. J. Mash, L. A. Hamerlynck, and L. C. Handy (Eds.), *Behavior modification and families*. New York: Brunner/Mazel, 1976.

Patterson, G. R., & Fagot, B. I. Selective responsiveness to social reinforcers and deviant behavior in children. *The Psychological Record*, 1967, *17*, 369-378.

Patterson, G. R., & Harris, A. Some methodological considerations for observation procedures. Paper presented at the meeting of the American Psychological Association, San Francisco, Calif., 1968.

Patterson, G. R., Ray, R. S., Shaw, D. A., & Cobb, J. A. Manual for coding family interactions, sixth revision, 1969. Available from ASIS National Auxiliary Publications Service, Inc., 909 Third Avenue, New York, N.Y., 10022. Document No. 01234.

Peine, H. A. Parent recording as a possible therapeutic technique. Unpublished manuscript, Western Michigan University, 1972.

Pelc, R. E. A comparison of home and school behavior of five-year-old boys. Paper presented at the meeting of the Rocky Mountain Psychological Association, 1973.

Peterson, D. R. *The clinical study of social behavior.* New York: Appleton-Century-Crofts, 1968.

Pomeranz, D. M., & Goldfield, M. R. An intake report outline for behavior modification. *Psychological Reports,* 1970, *26,* 447-450.

Premack, D. Toward empirical behavioral laws: I. Positive reinforcement. *Psychological Review,* 1959, *66,* 219-233.

Premack, D. Reinforcement theory. In D. Levine (Ed.), *Nebraska symposium on motivation: 1965.* Lincoln: University of Nebraska Press, 1965.

Premack, D. Catching up with common sense or two sides of a generalization: Reinforcement and punishment. In R. Glaser (Ed.), *The nature of reinforcement.* New York: Academic Press, 1971.

Purcell, K., & Brady, K. Adaptation to the invasion of privacy: Monitoring behavior with a miniature radio transmitter. *Merrill-Palmer Quarterly,* 1966, *12,* 242-252.

Rapoport, J. L., & Benoit, M. The relation of direct home observations to the clinic evaluation of hyperactive school age boys. *Journal of Child Psychology and Psychiatry,* 1975, *16,* 141-147.

Rathus, S. A. A ·30-item schedule for assessing assertive behavior. *Behavior Therapy,* 1973, *4,* 398-406.

Rehm, L. P., & Marston, A. R. Reduction of social anxiety through modification of self-reinforcement: An instigation therapy. *Journal of Consulting and Clinical Psychology,* 1968, *32,* 565-574.

Reid, J. B. Reliability assessment of observation data: A possible methodological problem. *Child Development,* 1970, *41,* 1143-1150.

Reid, J. B., & DeMaster, B. The efficacy of the spot-check procedure in maintaining the reliability of data collected by observers in quasi-natural settings: Two pilot studies. *Oregon Research Institute Bulletin,* 1972, *12,* 1-11.

Repp, A. C., Deitz, D. D., Boles, S. M., Deitz, S. M., & Repp, C. F. Differences among common methds for calculating interobserver agreement in applied behavioral studies. Unpublished manuscript, Georgia State University, 1973.

Rimm, D. C., & Masters, J. C. *Behavior therapy: Techniques and empirical findings.* New York: Academic Press, 1974.

Roberts, R. R., & Renzaglia, G. A. The influence of tape recording on counseling. *Journal of Counseling Psychology,* 1965, *12,* 10-16.

Robinson, J. C., & Lewinsohn, P. M. Experimental analysis of a technique based on the Premack Principle changing verbal behavior of depressed individuals. *Psychological Reports,* 1973, *32,* 199-210.

Romanczyk, R. G. Self-monitoring in the treatment of obesity: Parameters of reactivity. *Behavior Therapy,* 1974, *5,* 531-540.

Romanczyk, R. G., Kent, R. N., Diament, C., & O'Leary, K. D. Measuring the reliability of observational data: A reactive process. *Journal of Applied Behavior Analysis,* 1973, *6,* 175-184.

Ross, A. O. Diagnostic testing in a behaviorally oriented clinical training program. *Clinical Psychologist Newsletter,* 1974.

Royer, F. L., Flynn, W. F., & Osadca, B. S. Case history: Aversion therapy for fire setting by a deteriorated schizophrenic. *Behavior Therapy,* 1971, *2,* 229-232.

Rubin, B. M., Katkin, E. S., Weiss, B. W., & Effran, J. S. Factor analysis of a fear survey schedule. *Behaviour Research and Therapy,* 1968, *6,* 65-75.

Rubin, S. E., Lawlis, G. F., Tasto, D. L., & Namenek, T. Factor analysis of the 122-item fear survey schedule. *Behaviour Research and Therapy,* 1969, *7,* 381-386.

Rubin, B. K., & Stolz, S. B. Generalization of self-referent speech established in a retarded adolescent by operant procedures. *Behavior Therapy,* 1974, *5,* 93-106.

Rutner, I. T., & Pear, J. J. An observational methodology for investigating phobic behavior: Preliminary report. *Behavior Therapy,* 1972, *3,* 437-440.

Sallows, G. O. Responsiveness of deviant and normal children to naturally occurring parental consequences. Paper presented at the meeting of the Midwestern Psychological Association, Chicago, Ill., May 1973.

Scherer, M. W., & Nakamura, C. Y. A fear survey schedule for children (FSS-FC): A factor analytic comparison with manifest anxiety (CMAS). *Behaviour Research and Therapy,* 1968, *6,* 173-182.

Simkins, L. The reliability of self-recorded behaviors. *Behavior Therapy,* 1971, *2,* 83-87. (a)

Simkins, L. A rejoinder to Nelson and McReynolds on the self-recording of behavior. *Behavior Therapy,* 1971, *2,* 598-601. (b)

Skindrud, K. An evaluation of observer bias in experimental-field studies of social interaction. Unpublished doctoral dissertation, University of Oregon, 1972.

Skindrud, K. Field evaluation of observer bias under overt and covert monitoring. In L. A. Hamerlynck, L. C. Handy, & E. J. Mash (Eds.), *Behavior change: Methodology, concepts and practice.* Champaign, Ill.: Research Press, 1973. Pp. 97-118.

Skinner, B. F. *Science and human behavior.* New York: Macmillan, 1953.

Skinner, B. F. *Beyond freedom and dignity.* New York: Alfred A. Knopf, 1972.

Soskin, W. F., & John, V. The study of spontaneous talk. In R. Barker (Ed.), *The stream of behavior.* New York: Appleton-Century-Crofts, 1963.

Storrow, H. A. *Introduction to scientific psychiatry: A behavioristic approach to diagnosis and treatment.* New York: Appleton-Century-Crofts, 1967.

Stuart, R. B., & Stuart, F. M. *Marriage precounseling inventory and guide.* Champaign, Ill.: Research Press, 1972.

Stuart, R. B., & Stuart, F. M. *Family counselling inventory and guide.* Champaign, Ill.: Research Press, 1975. (a)

Stuart, R. B., & Stuart, F. M. *Inventory for couples planning to marry and guide.* Champaign, Ill.: Research Press, 1975. (b)

Stuart, F. M., Stuart, R. B., Maurice, W. D., & Szasz, G. *Sexual adjustment inventory and guide.* Champaign, Ill.: Research Press, 1975.

Suinn, R. The STABS, a measure of test-anxiety for behavior therapy: Normative data. *Behaviour Research and Therapy,* 1969, *7,* 335-339. (a)

Suinn, R. M. Changes in non-treated subjects over time: Data on a fear survey schedule and the test anxiety scale. *Behaviour Research and Therapy,* 1969, *7,* 205-206. (b)

Suinn, R. M., & Richardson, F. Anxiety management training: A nonspecific behavior therapy program for anxiety control. *Behavior Therapy,* 1971, *2,* 498-510.

Sullivan, H. S. *The psychiatric interview.* New York: W. W. Norton, 1954.

Tanner, B. A., Parrino, J. J., & Daniels, A. C. A token economy with "automated" data collection. *Behavior Therapy,* 1975, *6,* 111-118.

Taplin, P. S., & Reid, J. B. Effects of instructional set and experimental influence on observer reliability. *Child Development,* 1973, *44,* 547-554.

Tasto, D. L., & Hickson, R. Standardization and scaling of the 122-item fear survey schedule. *Behavior Therapy,* 1970, *1,* 473-484.

Tasto, D. L., Hickson, R., & Rubin, S. E. Scaled profile analysis of fear survey schedule factors. *Behavior Therapy,* 1971, *2,* 543-549.

Tasto, D. L., & Suinn, R. M. Fear survey schedule changes on total and factor scores due to non-treatment effects. *Behavior Therapy,* 1972, *3,* 275-278.

Tavormina, J. B. Relative effectiveness of behavioral and reflective group counselling with parents of mentally retarded children. *Journal of Consulting and Clinical Psychology,* 1975, *43,* 22-31.

Taylor, J. A. A personality scale of manifest anxiety. *Journal of Abnormal and Social Psychology,* 1953, *48,* 285-290.

Terdal, L. G., Jackson, R. J., & Garner, A. M. Mother-child interactions: A comparison between normal and developmentally delayed groups. In E. J. Mash, L. A. Hamerlynck, and L. C. Handy (Eds.), *Behavior modification and families.* New York: Brunner/Mazel, 1976.

Tharp, R. G., & Wetzel, R. J. *Behavior modification in the natural environment.* New York: Academic Press, 1969.

Thomson, C., Holmberg, M., & Baer, D. A comparison of three intermittent time-sampling procedures to continuous time-sampling. Presented at the meeting of the American Psychological Association, Montreal, Canada, 1973.

Thoresen, C. E., & Mahoney, M. J. *Behavioral self-control.* New York: Holt, Rinehart & Winston, 1974.

Thorndike, R. M., & Kleinknecht, R. A. Reliability of homogeneous scales of reinforcers: A cluster analysis of the reinforcement survey schedule. *Behavior Therapy,* 1974, *5,* 58-63.

Truax, C. B., Wargo, D. G., Carkhuff, R. R., Kodman, F. Jr., & Noles, E. A. Changes in self-concept during group psychotherapy as a function of alternate sessions and vicarious therapy pre-training in institutionalized mental patients and juvenile delinquents. *Journal of Consulting Psychology,* 1966, *30,* 309-314.

Wahler, R. G., & Cormier, W. H. The ecological interview: A first step in outpatient child behavior therapy. *Journal of Behavior Therapy and Experimental Psychiatry,* 1970, *1,* 279-289.

Wahler, R. G., Winkel, G. H., Peterson, R. F., & Morrison, D. C. Mothers as behavior therapists for their own children. *Behaviour Research and Therapy,* 1965, *3,* 113-124.

Walk, R. D. Self-ratings of fear in a fear-invoking situation. *Journal of Abnormal and Social Psychology,* 1956, *52,* 171-178.

Wallace, J. An abilities conception of personality: Some implications for personality measurement. *American Psychologist,* 1966, *21,* 132-138.

Wallace, J. What units shall we employ? Allport's question revisited. *Journal of Consulting Psychology,* 1967, *31,* 56-64.

Watson, D., & Friend, R. Measurement of social-evaluative anxiety. *Journal of Consulting and Clinical Psychology,* 1969, *33,* 448-457.

Watson, D. L., & Tharp, R. G. *Self-directed behavior: Self-modification for personal adjustment.* Monterey, Calif.: Brooks/Cole, 1972.

Weed L. Medical records that guide and teach. *New England Journal of Medicine,* 1968, *278,* 593-600.

Weed, L. *Medical records, medical education, and patient care.* Cleveland: Case Western Reserve University Press, 1969.

Weick, K. E. Systematic observational methods. In G. Lindzey and E. Aronson (Eds.), *Handbook of social psychology.* Vol. 2. 2nd Ed. Reading, Mass.: Addison-Wesley, 1968. Pp. 357-451.

Weiss, R. L. Operant conditioning techniques in psychological assessment. In Paul W. McReynolds (Ed.), *Advances in psychological assessment.* Vol. 1. Palo Alto: Science and Behavior Books, 1969.

Weller, L., & Luchterhand, E. Comparing interviews and observations on family functioning. *Journal of Marriage and the Family,* 1969, *31,* 115-122.

White, G. D. The effects of observer presence on mother and child behavior. Paper presented at the annual meeting of the Western Psychological Association, Anaheim, California, 1973.

Wiggins, J. S. *Personality and prediction: Principles of personality assessment.* Reading, Mass.: Addison-Wesley, 1973.

Wildman, B. G., Erickson, M. T., & Kent, R. N. The effect of two training procedures on observer agreement and variability of behavior ratings. *Child Development,* 1975, *46,* 520-524.

Willems, E. P. Go ye into all the world and modify behavior: An ecologist's view. *Representative Research in Social Psychology,* 1973, *4,* 93-105.

Willems, E. P. Behavioral technology and behavioral ecology. *Journal of Applied Behavior Analysis,* 1974, *7,* 151-165.

Wills, T. A., Weiss, R. L., & Patterson, G. R. A Behavioral analysis of the determinants of marital satisfaction. *Journal of Consulting and Clinical Psychology,* 1974, *42,* 802-811.

Witherspoon, A. D., de Valera, E. K., Jenkins, W. O., & Sanford, W. L. *Behavioral interview guide.* Montgomery, Ala.: Rehabilitation Research Foundation, 1973.

Wodarski, J. S., Feldman, R. A., & Pedi, S. J. Effects of different observational systems and time sequences upon non-participant observers' behavioral ratings. Unpublished manuscript, Washington University, St Louis, 1974.

Wolff, W. T., & Merrens, M. R. Behavioral assessment: A review of clinical methods. *Journal of Personality Assessment,* 1974, *38,* 3-16.

Wollersheim, J. P. Effectiveness of group therapy based upon learning principles in the treatment of overweight women. *Journal of Abnormal Psychology,* 1970, *76,* 462-474.

Wolpe, J. Transcript of initial interview in a case of depression. *Journal of*

*Behavior Therapy and Experimental Psychiatry,* 1970, *1,* 71-78.

Wolpe, J. *The practice of behavior therapy.* New York: Pergamon Press, 1973.

Wolpe, J., & Lang, P. J. A fear survey schedule for use in behavior therapy. *Behaviour Research and Therapy,* 1964, *2,* 27-30.

Wolpe, J., & Lazarus, A. A. *Behavior therapy techniques: A guide to the treatment of neuroses.* New York: Pergamon Press, 1966.

Wright, H. F. Observational child study. In P. H. Mussen (Ed.), *Handbook of research methods in child development.* New York: Wiley, 1960.

Yarrow, M. R., Campbell, J. D., & Burton, R. V. *Child rearing: An inquiry into research and methods.* San Francisco, Calif.: Jossey-Bass, Inc., 1968.

Yates, A. J. *Behavior therapy.* New York: Wiley, 1970.

Zifferblatt, S. M. The effectiveness of modes and schedules of reinforcement on work and social behavior and occupational therapy. *Behavior Therapy,* 1972, *3,* 567-578.

Zukerman, M., & Lubin, B. *Manual for the Multiple Affect Adjective Checklist.* San Diego: Educational and Industrial Testing Service, 1965.

# Author Index

# Subject Index

Aggression
  behavior modification and, 227
  diagnosis of, 90
Alcoholism
  intake procedures for, 121-123
  reinforcing stimuli and, 206
Antecedent-consequent relationships, 277, 306
Anxiety
  and depression, 110
  fear and, 155, 179-180
  in interview situation, 83, 228
  intra-personal differences, 17-18
  measurement of, 35, 39, 41-42, 143-144, 167-182
  as moderator, 181
  and neurosis, 217
  prediction of, 44-45
  reciprocal inhibition of, 217
  self-report of, 145
  *See also* Fear
Assertiveness
  authority figures and, 40
  measurement of, 188-191
  training in, 185
Assessment
  action oriented, 149
  behavior modification and, 33-35
  central role of, 1
  cognitive variables and, 11-12
  defined, 19-20
  evaluation in, 13

functional emphasis of, 2
goals, 16-17
heterogeneity of, 1
interviewing in, 81-88
pathology and, 21
procedures in, 1, 20-24
  observational measures, 261-263
  self-report measures, 141-147
tools of, 17, 20
traditional approach of, 35-38, 43-48, 217
Authority
  anxiety and, 181
  assertiveness toward, 40
  behavioral diagnosis and, 96-97
Aversive conditioning
  apparatus for, 81-82
  assessment and, 197

Baseline
  of activity, 230
  in applied analysis, 57-60
  in drinking behavior, 122
  in experiment design, 66-70
  individualized data and, 347
Baserate, 27
Behavior modification
  clinical psychology and, 33
  conformity and, 54
  consulting role in, 85
  covert events in, 11
  diagnosis and, 22